The Writings of
Henry D. Thoreau

Journal

Volume 8: 1854

Textual Center

The Writings of Henry D. Thoreau

Northern Illinois University

HENRY D. THOREAU

Journal

VOLUME 8: 1854

EDITED BY
SANDRA HARBERT PETRULIONIS

PRINCETON, NEW JERSEY
PRINCETON UNIVERSITY PRESS
MMII

COMMITTEE ON
SCHOLARLY EDITIONS
AN APPROVED EDITION
MODERN LANGUAGE
ASSOCIATION OF AMERICA
®

The Committee's emblem indicates that this volume is based on an examination of all available relevant textual sources, that it is edited according to principles articulated in the volume, that the source texts and the edited text's deviations from them are fully described, that the editorial principles and the text and the apparatus have undergone a peer review, that a rigorous schedule of verification and proofreading was followed to insure a high degree of accuracy in the presentation of the edition, and that the text is accompanied by appropriate textual and other historical contextual information.

The editorial preparation of this volume, and costs associated with its publication, were supported by grants from the National Endowment for the Humanities, an independent federal agency.

Published by Princeton University Press, 41 William Street, Princeton, New Jersey 08540
In the United Kingdom: Princeton University Press, 3 Market Place, Woodstock, Oxfordshire OX20 1SY

Library of Congress Cataloging-in-Publication Data
(Revised for vol. 8)

Thoreau, Henry David, 1817-1862.
Journal.

(The writings of Henry D. Thoreau)
"The complete Journal as Thoreau originally wrote it." Vol. 8, edited by Sandra Harbert Petrulionis.
Includes index.
Contents v. 1. 1837-1844.–v. 2. 1842-1848.–[etc.]–v. 8. 1854.
1. Thoreau, Henry David, 1817-1862.–Diaries. 2. Authors, American–19th century–Diaries. I. Petrulionis, Sandra Harbert. II. Title. III. Series: Thoreau, Henry David, 1817-1862. Works. 1971.
PS3053.A2 1981   818'.303 [B]   78-70325
ISBN 0-691-06361-3 (v. 1: alk. paper)   ISBN 0-691-06541-1 (v. 8: alk. paper)

Printed on acid-free paper. ∞

www.pup.princeton.edu

Printed in the United States of America

10   9   8   7   6   5   4   3   2   1

Editorial Board

Editor-in-Chief, Elizabeth Hall Witherell
Executive Committee
  William L. Howarth
  Robert N. Hudspeth
  Joseph J. Moldenhauer, *Textual Editor*
  William Rossi
  Nancy Craig Simmons
  Heather Kirk Thomas

The Writings

Walden, J. Lyndon Shanley (1971)
The Maine Woods, Joseph J. Moldenhauer (1972)
Reform Papers, Wendell Glick (1973)
Early Essays and Miscellanies,
  Joseph J. Moldenhauer et al. (1975)
A Week on the Concord and Merrimack Rivers,
  Carl F. Hovde et al. (1980)
Journal 1: 1837-1844, Elizabeth Hall Witherell et al.
  (1981)
Journal 2: 1842-1848, Robert Sattelmeyer (1984)
Translations, K. P. Van Anglen (1986)
Cape Cod, Joseph J. Moldenhauer (1988)
Journal 3: 1848-1851, Robert Sattelmeyer, Mark R.
  Patterson, and William Rossi (1990)
Journal 4: 1851-1852, Leonard N. Neufeldt and Nancy
  Craig Simmons (1992)
Journal 5: 1852-1853, Patrick F. O'Connell (1997)
Journal 6: 1853, William Rossi and Heather Kirk Thomas
  (2000)
Journal 8: 1854, Sandra Harbert Petrulionis (2002)

Contents

XVII

FEBRUARY 13, 1854–SEPTEMBER 3, 1854

Monday Feb. 13th 54

7 Am to Walden–

A warm morning–overcast–   The ice does not ring when I strike it with an axe. Tried to drive a stake in 2 places outside a wood but found it frozen–   Failed also in 2 places within the wood, but succeeded in a third.

Pm. It snows again spoiling the skating–which has lasted only one day–   I do not remember the winter when the ice remained uncovered a week.

Feb 14th.

Pm Down RR.

A moist thawing cloudy afternoon preparing to rain. The telegraph resounds at every post. It is a harp with one string–The first strain from the American lyre. In Stows wood by the deep Cut hear the *gnah gnah* of the white-breasted black capped nuthatch–   I went up the bank & stood by the fence. A little family of titmice gathered about me searching for their food both on the ground & on the trees with great industry & intentness & now & then pursuing each other–   There were two nuthatches at least talking to each other. One hung with his head down on a large pitch pine pecking the bark for a long time–leaden blue above with a black cap–& white breast–   It uttered almost constantly a faint but sharp *quivet* or creak–difficult to trace home–which appeared to be answered by a baser & louder *gnah gnah* from the other–   A downy woodpecker also with the red–spot on his hind head & his cassock open behind–showing his white robe–kept up an incessant loud tapping on another pitch pine – All at once an active little brown creeper make its appearance a small rather slender bird with a long tail & sparrow colored back–& white beneath. It commences at the bottom of a tree & glides up very rapidly–then suddenly darts to the bottom of a new

tree–& repeats the same movement–not resting long in
one place or on one tree. These birds are all feeding &
flitting along together–but the chicadees are the most
numerous & the most confiding. I observe that 3 of the
4 thus associated viz the chicadee–nuthatch–&
woodpecker have black crowns at least, the first two
very conspicuous black caps. I cannot but think that
this sprightly association and readiness to burst into
song has to do with the prospect of spring–more light
& warmth & thawing weather–   The titmice keep up
an incessant faint tinkling tchip–now and then one
utters a lively day day day–and once or twice one
commenced a gurgling strain quite novel startling &
spring like–   Beside this I heard the distant crowing of
cocks & the divine humming of the telegraph–all
spring promising sounds–   The chicadee has quite a
variety of notes–the *phebe* one I did not hear today.

I perceive that some of those pools by the Walden
Road which on the 9th ult looked so green–have frozen
blue–

This greater liveliness of the birds methinks I have
noticed commonly on warm thawing days toward
Spring. F. Browne Who has been chasing a white
rabbit this afternoon with a dog–says that they do not
run off far–often play round within the same swamp
only if it is large & return to where they were started.
Spoke of it as something unusual that one ran off so
far that he could not hear the dogs–but he returned &
was shot near where he started. He does not see their
forms–nor marks where they have been feeding.

Feb 16th '54

By this time in the winter I do not look for those
clear sparkling mornings–& delicate leaf frosts–which
methinks occur earlier in the winter–as if the air
of winter were somewhat tarnished and debauched.
–had lost its virgin purity–

Every judgment and action of a man qualifies every other–i.e. corrects our estimate of every other–as, for instance a man's idea of immortality who is a member of a church–or his praise of you coupled with his praise of those whom you do not esteem. For in this sense a man is awefully consistent–above his own consciousness. All a mans strength & all his weakness go to make up the authority of any particular opinion which he may utter. He is strong or weak with all his strength & weakness combined. If he is your friend you may have to consider that he loves you but perchance he also loves gingerbread–

It must be The leaves of the chimaphila umbellata Spotted Wintergreen which Channing left here day before yesterday.

I have not seen F. Hiemalis since last fall–the Snow-buntings only during the great & severe snow storm–no Pine Gross-beaks nor F– Linarias this winter.

Snows again this morning– For the last month the weather has been remarkably changeable; hardly 3 days together alike.

That is an era–not yet arrived–when the earth being partially thawed, melts the slight snows which fall on it.

Pm, to Walden & Flints–return by Turnpike.

Saw 2 large hawks circling over the Woods by walden–hunting– The first I have seen since Dec. 15th – That Indian trail on the hill side about Walden was revealed with remarkable distinctness to me standing on the middle of the pond–by the slight snow which which had lodged on it forming a clear, white line unobscured by weeds & twigs (For snow is a great revealer not only of tracks made in itself–but even in the earth before it fell–) It was quite distinct in many places where you would not have noticed it before A light snow will often reveal a faint foot or cart track in a field which was hardly discernible before–for it reprints it as it were in clear white type.   alto relievo. Went to the locality of the chimaphila maculata by Goosepond–

Columella after saying that many authors had believed that the climate (qualitatem caeli statumque) was changed by lapse of time (longo aevi situ), refers to Hipparchus as having given out that the time would be when the poles of the earth would be moved from their place (tempus fore, quo cardines mundi loco moverentur)–and as confirmatory of this he C. goes on to say that the vine & olive flourish now in some places where formerly they failed.

He gives the names of about 50 authors who had treated *de rusticis rebus* before him.

Feb 17th

Pm to Gowings Swamp

On the hill at the Deep Cut on the New Road the ground is frozen about 1 foot deep & they carry off lumps = nearly to a cartload at a time. Moore's man is digging a ditch by the roadside in his swamp   I am surprised to see that the earth there–under some snow it is true–is frozen only about 4 inches–   It may be owing to warm springs beneath–   The hill was comparatively bare of snow (and of trees there) and was more exposed. The Irishman showed me small stump–larch methinks–which he dug & cut out *from the bottom* of the ditch–very old ones. At Gowing's swamp I see where some one hunted white rabbits yesterday & perhaps the day before–with a dog. The hunter has run round and round it on firm ground while the hare & dog have cut across & circled about amid the blueberry bushes–   The track of the white rabbit is gigantic compared with that of the grey one. Indeed few, if any (?) of *our* wild animals make a larger track with their feet alone. Where I now stand the

track of all the feet has an expanse of 7 to 15
inches–this at intervals of from 2 to 3 feet–and
the width at the 2 fore feet is 5 inches
There is a considerable but slighter
impression of the paw behind
each foot–

   The mice tracks are very amusing. It is surprising
how numerous they are–& yet I rarely ever see one
– They must be nocturnal in their habits. Any
tussucky ground is scored with them– I see too where
they have run over the ice on the swamp–(there is a
mere suggaring of snow on it).–ever trying to make an
entrance–to get beneath it. You see deep & distinct
channels in the snow in some places as if a whole
colony had long travelled to & fro in them–a
high-way–a well known trail–but suddenly they will
come to an end–& yet they have not dived beneath the
surface for you see where the single traveller who did
it all has nimbly hopped along as if suddenly
scared–making but a slight impression squirrel like on
the snow. The squirrel also though rarely–will make a
channel for a short distance. These mice tracks are of
various sizes.–& sometimes when they are large & they
have taken long & regular hops 9 or 10 inches apart–in
a straight line they look at a little distance like a fox
track– I suspect that the mice sometimes build their
nests in bushes from the foundation–for in the swamp
hole on the new road–where I found 2 mice nests last
fall–I find one begun with a very few twigs and some
moss–close by where the others were–at the same
height & also on prinos bushes–plainly the work of
mice wholly– In the open part of Gowing's swamp I
find the andromeda polifolia. Neither here nor in Beck
Stow's does it grow very near the shore, in places
accessible in wet weather. Some larch cones are
empty–others contain seeds. In these swamps then

you have 3 kinds of andromeda–   The main swamp
is crowded with–high blueberry–Panicled
andromeda–prinos–swamp-pink &c &c (I did not
examine them particularly) & then in the middle or
deepest part will be an open space–not yet yet quite
given up to water–where the Andromeda Caliculata &
a few A. polifolia reign almost alone–   These are
pleasing gardens.

In the early part of winter there was no walking on
the snow–but after January perhaps–when the snow
banks had settled & their surfaces many times thawed
& frozen–become indurated in fact–you could walk on
the snow crust pretty well.

Feb. 18th

Pm to Yellow Birch Swamp–

As I remember January we had one? great thaw
succeeded by severe cold–   It was harder getting
about–though there may have been no more snow
because it was light–& there was more continuous
cold & clear sparkling weather–   But the last part of
January & all February thus far has been alternate
thaw & freeze & snow. It has more thaws–even as the
running (root of ρεω) occurs 2ce in it & but once in
January. I do not know but the more light & warmth
plainly enough accounts for the difference

It does not take so much fuel to keep us warm of
late. I begin to think that my wood will last. We begin
to have days precursors of Spring.

I see on ice by the river side front of N. Barrett's very
slender insects ⅓ of an inch long with grayish folded
wings–reaching far behind & 2 antennae Somewhat in
general appearance like the long wasps. At the old
mill-site saw 2 Pigeon woodpeckers dart into and out
of a white oak–   Saw the yellow under sides of their
wings. It is barely possible I am mistaken–but since
Wilson makes them common in Pennsylvania in

winter–I feel pretty sure. Such sights make me think
there must be bare ground not far off south. It is a
little affecting to walk over the hills now looking at the
rein-deer lichens here & there amid the snow–&
remember that ere long we shall find violets also in
their midst. What an odds the season makes– The
birds know it. Whether a rose-tinted water-lily is
sailing amid the pads–or neighbor Hobson is getting
out his ice with a cross cut saw while his oxen are
eating their stalks. I noticed that the ice which
Garrison cut the other day contained the lily pads &
stems within it. How different their environment now
from when the queenly flower floating on the
trembling surface exhaled its perfume amid a cloud of
insects. Hubbards wooded hill–is now almost bare of
trees. Barberries still hang on the bushes but all
shrivelled– I found a birds nest of grass & mud in a
barberry bush–filled full with them. It must have been
done by some quadruped or bird. The curls
of the yellow-birch bark form more or less
parallel straight lines up and down on all
sides of the tree–like parted hair blown aside
by the wind–or as when a vest bursts & blows
open– Rabbit tracks numerous there–Some
times quite a highway of tracks.–over & along
the frozen & snow covered brook. How pleasant the
sound of water flowing with a hollow sound under ice
from which it has settled away–where great white air
bubbles or hollows seen through the ice and dark
water alternately succeed each other. The mitchella
repens berries look very bright amid the still fresh
green leaves– In the birch swamp west of this are
many red? squirrel nests high in the birches. They are
composed within of fibres of bark. I see where the
squirrels have eaten walnuts along the wall & left the
shells on the snow.

Channing has some microscopic reading these days. But he says in effect that these works are purely material. The idealist views things in the large.

I read some of the the speeches in Congress about the Nebraska bill–a thing the like of which I have not done for a year– What trifling upon a serious subject– –While honest men are sawing wood for them outside– Your Congress Halls have an ale-house odor–a place for stale jokes & vulgar wit. It compels me to think of my fellow creatures as apes & babboons.

What a contrast between the upper and underside of many leaves–The indurated & colored upper side–& the tender more or less colorless under side –Male & female–Even when they are almost equally exposed. The underside is commonly white however as turned away from the light toward the earth – Many in which the contrast is finest are narrow revolute leaves–like the delicate & beautiful Andromeda polifolia–the ledum–Kalmia glauca.

De Quincy says that "the ancients had no experimental knowledge of severe climates." Neither have the English at home as compared with us of New England–nor we compared with the Esquimaux.

This is a common form of the birch scale–black I think–not white at any rate

The handsome lanceolate leaves of the Andromeda polifolia dark but pure & uniform dull red above–strongly revolute & of a delicate bluish white beneath deserve to be copied on to works of art.

Feb 19

Many College text books which were a weariness & a stumbling block–when *studied* I have since read a little in with pleasure & profit.

For several weeks–the fall has seemed far behind –spring comparatively near– Yet I cannot say that

there is any positive sign of spring yet–only we feel
that we are sloping toward it. The sky has sometimes a
warmth in its colors more like summer– A few birds
have possibly strayed northward–further than they
have wintered–

Pm to Fair Haven by river, back by R.R. Though the
wind is cold, the earth feels the heat of the sun higher
in the heavens & melts in ploughed fields. The willow
twigs rise out of the ice beside the river the silvery
down of each Catkin just peeping from under each
scale in some places–the work probably of last falls
sun–like a mouse peeping from under its covert. I
incline to walk now in swamps & on the river & ponds
–where I cannot walk in summer– I am struck by the
greenness of the green briar at this season still
covering the alders &c 12 feet high & full of shining &
fresh berries– The greenness of the sassafras shoots
makes a similar impression.

The large moths ap. love the neighborhood of
water–& are wont to suspend their coccoons over the
edge of the meadow & river–places more or less
inaccessible to men at least. I saw a button bush with
what at first sight looked like the open pods of the
locust or of the water asclepias attached– They were
the light ash-colored coccoons of the A. Promethea 4
or 5–with the completely withered & faded leaves
wrapt around them–& so artfully and admirably
secured to the twigs by fine silk wound round the
leaf-stalk & the twig–which last add nothing to
its strength being deciduous, but aid its deception
– They are taken at a little distance for a few curled &
withered leaves left on. Though the particular twigs on
which you find some coccoons may never or very
rarely retain any leaves the maple for instance–there
are enough leaves left on other shrubs & trees to
warrant their adopting this disguise. Yet it is startling

to think that the inference has in this case been drawn by some mind that as most other plants retain some leaves the walker will suspect these also to.

Each and all such disguises & other resources remind us that not some poor worms instinct merely, as we call it, but the mind of the universe rather which we share has been intended upon each particular object– All the wit in the world was brought to bear on each case to secure its end– It was long ago in a full senate of all intellects determined how coccoons had best be suspended– –kindred mind with mine that admires & approves decided it so. The hips of the late rose though more or less shrivelled are still red & handsome– It outlasts other hips– The sweetbriar's have lost their color & begun to decay. The former are still very abundant & showy in perfect corymbs of a dozen or so amid the button bushes. It might be called the water-rose. The trees in the maple swamp squeak from time to time like the first fainter sounds made by the red squirrel. I have little doubt the red squirrel must lay up food since I see them so rarely abroad. On the cherry twigs you see the shining clasp of catterpillar's eggs– The snow not only reveals a track but sometimes hands it down–to the ice that succeeds it. The sled track which I saw in the slight snow over the ice here Feb. 2nd–though we have had many snows since–& now there is no snow at all–is still perfectly marked on the ice.

Much study a weariness of the flesh! Ah–? But did not they intend that we should read & ponder–who covered the whole earth with alphabets–primers or bibles coarse or fine print–the very debris of the cliffs–the stivers of the rocks are covered with geograpic lichens–no surface is permitted to be bare long–as by an inevitable decree we have come to times at last when our very waste paper is printed. Was not he who creates lichens the abetter of Cadmus when he invented letters, Types almost arrange themselves into words & sentences as dust arranges itself under the magnet. Print!–it is a close-hugging lichen that forms on a favorable surface–which paper offers–   The linen gets itself wrought into paper–that the song of the shirt may be printed on it–   Who placed us with eyes between a microscopic and a telescopic world?

There are so many rocks under grapevine cliff–that ap for this reason the chopper saws instead of cuts his trees into lengths. The woodfern dryopteris marginalis (?) still green there. And are they not small saxifrages so perfectly green & fresh as if just started? in the crevices? I wait till sundown on Fair Haven to hear it boom but am disappointed–though I hear much slight crackling–but as for the previous cracking–it is so disruptive & produces such a commotion that it extends itself through snow drifts six inches deep, and is even more distinct there than in bare ice even to the sharpest angle of its forking. Saw an otter track near Walden.

Feb 20th

Channing saw yesterday 3 little birds olive green above with yellowish white breasts–& he thinks bars on wings–

Pm   Skating to Fair Haven Pond

Made a fire on the south side of the pond. using –canoe birch bark & oak leaves for kindlings. It is best to lay down first some large damp wood on the ice for a foundation–   Since the success of a fire depends very much on the bed of coals it makes–& if these are nearly quenched in the basin of melted ice–there is danger that it will go out, How much dry wood ready for the hunter inviting flames–is to be found in every forests–dry bark fibres & small dead twigs of the wht pine and other trees held up high &

dry as if for this very purpose. The occasional loud snapping of the fire was exhilirating. I put on some hemlock boughs & the rich salt crackling of its leaves–was like mustard to the ears–the firing of uncountable regiments. Dead trees love the fire.

We skated home in the dark–with an odor of smoke in our clothes. It was pleasant to dash over the the ice –feeling the inequalities which we could not see–now rising over considerable hillocks for it had settled on the meadows–now descending into corresponding hollows.

We have had but one no more this winter (and that I think was the first) of those gentle moist snows which lodge perfectly on the trees–and make perhaps the most beautiful sight of any. Much more common is what we have now, i.e.

Feb 21st   Am

A fine driving snow storm.

Have seen no good samples of the blue in snow this winter. At noon clears up.

Pm to Goose pond by Tuttle Path–

A little snow lodged on the N side of the woods gives them a hoary aspect–a mere sugaring however–   The snow has just ceased falling about 2 inches deep in the woods upon the old & on bare ground–but there is scarcely a track of any animal yet to be seen–except here and there the surface of the snow has been raised & broken interruptedly where some mouse came near the surface in its travels–and in one wood I see very numerous tracks probably of red squirrels–leading to & from 3 or 4 holes in the earth close together –somewhat like those in an ant's nest–quite a broad beaten path to some stumps with *Wht* pine cones on them–& single tracks to the base of trees. It has now got to be such weather that after a cold morning, it is colder in the house–or we feel colder–than outdoors by noon & are surprised that it is no colder when we come out. You cannot walk too early in new fallen snow–to get the sense of purity novelty & unexploredness. The snow has lodged more or less in perpendicular lines on the northerly sides of trees so that I am able to tell the points of compass as well as by the sun. I guide myself accordingly– It always gladdens me to see a willow though–catkinless, as well as leafless rising above the new-fallen untrodden snow in some dry hollow in the woods, for then I feel nearer to spring– These are some peculiarly dry & late looking ones I see there, but it is enough that they are willows.

The locust pods are open or opening–little beans they hold– What delicate satin-like inside linings they have.

The difference between the white & black? birch scales–(v 7 ps back) is that the wings of the first are curved backward like a real birds ⳤ The seeds of this also are broadly winged like an insect with 2 little antennae   The ice in the fields by the Poor House road–frozen puddles–amid the snow looking westward now while the sun is about setting in cold weather–are green.

Montanus in his ac. of New Netherland Amsterdam 1671 speaking of the beaver says "the wind-hairs which rise glittering above the back, fall off in the summer, & grow again in the fall."

Feb 22nd

I measured the thickness of the frozen ground at the deep cut on the new Bedford Road–about halfway up the hill. They dig under the frozen surface & then crack it off with iron wedges with much labor in pieces from 3 to 6 feet square– It was 18 inches thick & more there–Thicker higher up not so thick lower down the hill.

Saw in Sleepy Hollow a small hickory stump about 6 inches in diameter & 6 inches high–so completely regularly & beautifully covered by that winkle like fungus in concentric circles & successive layers that the core was concealed and you would have taken it for some cabbage like plant. This was the way the wound was healed. The cut surface of the stump was completely & thickly covered. Our neighbor Wetherbee was J Moore's companion when he took that great weight of pickerel this winter– He says it was 56 lbs in Flints in one day–& that 4 of them weighed 18 lbs & 7 ounces. My alder catkins in the pitcher have shed their pollen for a day or 2 & the willow catkins have pushed out ½ an inch or more & show red & yellowish.

Feb. 23d.

Am   The snow drives horizontally from the north or N westerly–in long waving lines like the outline of a swell or billow ⁓⁓⁓ the flakes do not fall perceptibly for the width of a house.

Pm   Saw some of those architectural drifts forming. The fine snow came driving along over the field like steam curling from a roof– As the current rises to go over the wall it produces a lull in the angle made by the wall & ground & accordingly just enough snow is deposited there to fill the triangular calm ⁓⁓⁓ but the greater part passes over & is deposited   in the longer calm– A portion of the wind also apparently passes through the chinks of the wall–& curves upward against the main drift–appearing to carve it & perforate it in various fashions holding many snowy particles in suspension–in vertical eddies. I am not sure to what extent the drift is carved & perforated–& to what originally deposited in these forms.

Not that ornamental beauty is to be neglected, but at least let it first be inward & essential like the lining of a shell of which the inhabitant is unconscious & not a mere outside garnishing. This forenoon a driving storm very severe. This afternoon fair but high wind & drifting snow

Feb 24th.

Pm to Walden & Fair Haven

In Wheelers Wood by RR. Nuthatches are faintly answering each other–tit for tat, on different keys–(a faint creak.) Now & then one utters a loud distinct gnah. This bird more than any I know loves to stand with its head downward–

Meanwhile chicadees with their silver tinkling are flitting high above through the tops of the pines. Measured the ice of Walden in 3 places–1 about 10 rods from the shore–16⅞ inches thick
25 rods from shore   ″
In middle   17¼– Call it then 17 inches on an average. *On* Fair Haven in the only place tried, it was 21 inches thick. The portion of the ice in Walden above water was *about* 1¼ inches–in Fair Haven *about* 1¾. This part then = $\frac{1}{13}$+ & $\frac{1}{12}$ respectively.

Tried the frost in 5 different & very *distant* woods in my walk– Found that though the ground is frozen more than 18 inches from 18 to 2½ feet thick on the open hill side on the New Bedford Road –notwithstanding some snow on it–I can drive a stake without any trouble in the midst of ordinary level mixed pine & oak woods where the snow is a foot deep–in *very thick* pine & oak woods where the snow is only 1 inch thick or none at all–and the ground does not slope to the N & E, and prob. the NW and in sproutlands where it is 20 inches thick in some places–and in springy meadows– In Moore's Swamp

it is frozen about 4 inches deep in openland. I think
that in an average year the ice in such a pond as Fair
Haven attains a greater thickness than the snow on a
level. The other day I thought that I smelled a fox
very strongly–& went a little further & found that it
was a skunk– May not their odors differ in intensity
chiefly? Observed in one of the little pond holes
between Walden & Fair Haven where a partridge had
travelled around in the snow amid the bordering
bushes 25 rods–had pecked the green leaves of the
lambkill & left fragments on the snow–& had paused at
each high blueberry bush, fed on its red buds &
shaken down fragments of its bark on the snow
– These buds appeared its main object. I finally
scared the bird.

I see such mice or mole tracks as these
under snow   open channel

               distinct tracks

The frozen earth at the new road cut is hauled off 20
rods by chains hooked round it–and it lies like great
blocks of yellow sandstone for building–cracked out
exactly square by wedges.

The sexton tells me that he had to dig the last grave
through 2 feet of frozen ground– I measured a block
today 2 feet 5 inches thick after being dragged a dozen
rods.

Feb 26 '54

Kane ashore far up Baffin's Bay says "How strangely
this crust we wander over asserts its identity through
all the disguises of climate!"

Speaking of the effects of refraction on the water he
says "The single repetition was visible all around us;
the secondary or inverted image sometimes above &
sometimes below the primary. But it was not
uncommon to see, also, the uplifted iceberg, with

its accompanying or false horizon, joined at its
summit by its inverted image, and then above a 2nd
horizon, a third berg in its natural position." He refers
to Agassiz at Lake Superior as suggesting "That it may
be simply the reflection of the landscape inverted
upon the surface of the lake, and reproduced with the
actual landscape." though there then was but one
inversion.

He says that he saw sledge tracks of Franklin's party
in the neighborhood of Wellington Sound made on the
snow 6 years old–which had been covered by the after
snows of 5 winters. This reminds me of the sled tracks
I saw this winter.

Kane says that some mornings in that winter in the
ice–they heard "a peculiar crisping or crackling
sound"– – "This sound, as the 'noise accompanying
the aurora', has been attributed by Wrangell and
others, ourselves among the rest, to changes of
atmospheric temperature acting upon the crust of the
snow." Kane thinks it is rather owing "to the unequal
contraction & dilatation" of unequally presenting
surfaces, "not to a sudden change of atmospheric
temperature acting upon the snow." Is not this the
same crackling I heard at Fair Haven on the 19th
ult–and are not most of the arctic phenomena to be
witnessed in our latitude on a smaller scale? At Fair
Haven it seemed a slighter contraction of the ice–not
enough to make it thunder.

This morning it began with snowing turned to a fine
freezing rain producing a glaze–   The most of a glaze
thus far but in the afternoon changed to pure rain.

Pm to Martial Miles in rain. The weeds trees &c are
covered with a glaze–   The blue-curl cups are
overflowing with icy drops–   All trees present a new
appearance–their twigs being bent down by the
ice–birches apple-trees &c–but above all the pines

– Tall feathery white pines–look like cockerel's tail in
a shower–both these & white pines their branches
being inclined downward have sharpened tops–like fir
& spruce trees–   Thus an arctic effect is produced
– Very young white & pitch pines are most
changed–all their branches drooping in a compact
pyramid toward the   ground except a single
                                          plume in the centre   They
have a singularly crest-fallen look.
The rain is fast washing off all the glaze on which I
had counted–thinking of the effect of tomorrows sun
on it. The wind rises & the rain increases. Deep pools
of water have formed in the fields–which have an
agreeable green or blue tint, sometimes the one
sometimes the other. Yet the quantity of water which
is fallen is by no means remarkable–but the ground
being frozen it is not soaked up. There is more water
on the surface than before this winter.

Feb 27th

Morning. Rain over–water in great part run off–wind
rising–river risen & meadows flooded. The rain water
& melted snow have run swiftly over the frozen ground
into the river, & raised it with the ice on it & flooded
the meadows–covering the ice there which remains on
the bottom–So that you have on the male side a
narrow canal above the ice–then a floating ice
everywhere bridging the river–& then a broad
meadowy flood above ice again.

Those blocks of frozen earth at the New Road cut
are in fact a sandstone whose cement is frost. They are
dragged by chains about them–& no drag–without
losing any appreciable part–for 20 rods. And have
preserved their form–their right angled edges for a
month–left to thaw on the sides of the New Road
embankments.

I remarked yesterday the rapidity with which water flowing over the icy ground sought its level. All that rain would hardly have produced a puddle in midsummer but now it produces a freshet & will perhaps break up the river.

It looks as if Nature had a good deal of work on her hands between now & April–to break up & melt 21 inches of ice on the ponds–beside melting all the snow–& before planting time to thaw from 1 to 2½ or 3 feet of frozen ground.

They who live in the outskirts of the town do not like to have woods very near their houses–but cut them down– They are more of a bugbear than an ornament in their eyes– They who live on the village street take still more pains to rear a pine grove about their houses.

The ground being frozen I saw the rain yesterday dripping or streaming from the edge of the bank at the base of the wooded hill beyond Wm Wheeler's as from the eaves of a house–& today the bank is lined with icicles.

Pm. to Flint's Pond.

Savin Wood– Rufus Hosmer accounts for a wooden pin confining a tenon in its mortice gradually working out–as in a gate for instance–(& this was the case on both sides of R.W.Es gate to which he stepped for illustration–) by saying that when the whole gate was wet & swelled perhaps a 16th of an inch–it carried the pin along with it & shrinking left it there–then swelled again & carried it ⅟₁₆ of an inch further & left it there again & so finally perhaps dropt it out.

Among the savins I saw where rabbits had gnawed many barbbery bushes–showing the yellow–& had eaten off many twigs some ½ inch in diameter–also Young hickories & had gnawed off & eaten their twigs

too in many places–hard as they are– They looked as
if a moose had browsed them– *One* small pitch pine
had lost some twigs too– I also saw where one which
I scared had dropped some umbelled pyrola leaves or
it *may* have been another creature. And had eaten of
some green rose-briar shoots. This gray
rabbit's tail was very short & white
beneath & curved short over his back in
running.

Feb. 28th–a pleasant morning.

What is the cause of that half ice–half water–along
the edge of the river now–of the consistency of
molassess or soft solder. I can think of no peculiarity
in its formation unless that this water–the river rising
–has flowed out over the ice in the night faster than it
froze. Stirred with a stick it shows a mass of crystals.

Probably you can study the habits of rabbits
partridges &c more easily in the winter–their tracks
being revealed by the snow.

This is now another rise of the river. I see that the
ice in hollows in the fields breaks up (partially) in
the same manner with that on the river–viz. around
the shore it is covered with water
& rests on the bottom–while
the middle is raised with the
water–& hence a ridge is
heaved up where the 2
ices meet. I am not certain
how far this overflowing of the ice next the shore–or
on the meadows may be owing to the flood from the
hills in the first instance running over then under it &
keeping it down–as well as to its adhesion to the
bottom.

F Brown tells me that he found a quantity of
winter-green in the crop of a partridge. I suggested
that it *might* be lambkil.

March. 1st

Here is our first Spring morning–ac– to the
Almanack. It is remarkable that the spring of the
Almanack & of Nature should correspond so closely
– The morning of the 26th ult. was good winter–but
there came a plentiful rain in the afternoon–&
yesterday & to-day are quite spring-like. This
morning–the air is still–& though clear enough a
yellowish light is widely diffused throughout the east
now just after sunrise– The sun-light looks & feels
warm & a *fine* vapor fills the lower atmosphere. I hear
the phebe–or spring note of the chicadee–& the
scream of the jay–is perfectly repeated by the echo
from a neighboring wood. For some days past–the
surface of the earth–covered with water–or with ice
where the snow is washed off has shone in the sun as
it does only at the approach of spring methinks–and
are not the frosts in the morning more like the early
frosts in the fall–common white-frosts?

As for the birds of the past winter–I have seen but 3
hawks–one early in the winter & 2 lately–have heard
the hooting owl pretty often late in the afternoon
– Crows have not been numerous–but their cawing
was heard chiefly in pleasanter mornings– Blue jays
have blown the trumpets of winter as usual but they as
all birds are most lively in spring-like days– The
chicadees have been the *prevailing* bird– The
partridge common enough– One ditcher tells me that
he saw 2 robins in Moore's swamp a month ago– I
have not seen a quail though a few have been killed
in the thaws,– 4 or 5 downy woodpeckers– The
white-breasted nuthatch 4 or 5 times– Tree sparrows
one or more at a time oftener than any bird that comes
to us from the north– 2 pigeon woodpeckers I think
lately– One dead shrike & perhaps 1 or 2 live ones
– Have heard of 2 white owls–1 about Thanksgiving

time & 1 in mid-winter– –1 shorteared owl in December
– Several flocks of Snow buntings for a week in the
severest storm, & in Dec last part– One grebe in
Walden just before it froze–completely–and 2 brown
creepers once in mid– of February– Channing says he
saw a little olivaceous green bird lately– I have not
seen an F. linaria–nor a Pine Grossbeak–nor an
F hiemalis this winter–though the first was the
prevailing bird last winter.

In correcting my mss–which I do with sufficient
phlegm. I find that I invariably turn out much that is
good along with the bad, which it is then impossible
for me to distinguish– –so much for keeping bad
company–but after the lapse of time having purified
the main body & thus created a distinct standard
for comparison–I can review the rejected sentence
& easily detect those which deserve to be
readmitted.

Pm to Walden via R.W.E's

I am surprised to see how bare Minott's hillside is
already– It is already spring there & Minott is
puttering outside in the sun– How wise in his
Grandfather to select such a site for a house–the
summers he has lived have been so much longer.

How pleasant the calm season & the warmth–(The
sun is even like a burning glass on my back–) & the
sight & sound of melting snow running down the hill. I
look in among the withered grass blades for some
starting greenness– I listen to hear the first blue-bird
in the soft air. I hear the dry clucking of hens which
have come abroad.

The ice at Walden is softened–the skating is
gone–with a stick you can loosen it to the depth of an
inch of the first freezing & turn it up in cakes.
Yesterday you could skate here–now only *close* to the
south shore.

I notice the redness of the andromeda leaves–but not so much as once–   The sand foliage is now in its prime.

March 2nd

A Corner man tells me that Witherel has seen a blue-bird & Martial Miles thought that he heard one. I doubt it. It may have been given to Witherel to see the first blue bird–so much has been with-holden from him.

What produces the peculiar softness of the air yesterday & today–as if it were the air of the south suddenly pillowed amid our wintry hills–   We have suddenly a different sky–a dif– atmosphere. It is as if the subtlest possible soft vapor were diffused through the atmosphere   Warm Air has come to us from the S, but charged with moisture–which will yet distill in rain or congeal into snow & hail–

The sand foliage is vital in its form–reminding me what are called the vitals of the animal body–   I am not sure that its arteries are even hollow   They are rather meandering channels with remarkably distinct sharp edges–formed instantaneously as by magic –   How rapidly & perfectly it organizes itself–   The material must be sufficiently cohesive. I suspect that a certain portion of clay is necessary. Mixed Sand & clay being saturated with melted ice & snow–the most liquid portion flows downward through the mass forming for itself instantly a perfect canal–using the best materials the mass–affords for its banks–   It digs & builds it in a twinkling–   The less fluid portions clog the artery change its course and form thick stems & leaves–   The lobe principle–lobe of the ear (labor-lapsus?)

On the outside all the life of the earth is expressed in the animal or vegetable–but make a deep cut in it & you find it vital– –you find in the very sands an

anticipation of the vegetable leaf– No wonder then
that plants grow & spring in it– The atoms have
already learned the law– Let a vegetable sap convey it
upwards and you have a vegetable leaf– No wonder
that the earth expresses itself outwardly in
leaves–which labors with the idea thus inwardly– The
overhanging leaf sees here its prototype. The earth is
pregnant with law–

The various shades of this sand foliage are very
agreeable to the eye. including all the different colors
which iron assumes–brown–grey–yellowish reddish–&
clay-color. Perhaps it produces the greater effect by
arranged the sands of the same color–side by
side.–bringing them together.

March 4th

a dull cloudy day

Pm To Walden via Hubbards Wood & foot of Cliff
Hill.

The snow has melted very rapidly the past week
– There is much bare ground– The checkerberries
are revealed–*somewhat* shrivelled many of them. I
look along the ditches & brooks–for tortoises & frogs
but the ditches are still full of dirty ice & they are not
yet seen in the brooks– In hubbards maple swamp–I
see the evergreen leaves of the gold thread as well as
the mitchella & large pyrola– I begin to snuff the air &
smell the ground. In the meadow beyond I see some
still fresh & perfect pitcher plant leaves–& every where
the green & reddish radical leaves of the golden
senecio–whose fragrance when bruised carries me
back or forward to an incredible season. Who would
believe that under the snow & ice lies still–or in mid
winter some green leaves–which bruised yield the
same odor that they do when their yellow blossoms
spot the meadows in June. Nothing so realizes the
summer to me now– This past winter the sphagnum

(?) in swamps & meadows has been frost bitten & blackened, but last winter it was fresh & handsome.

I see now adays the ground being laid bare great cracks in the earth revealed ⅓ of an inch wide running with a crinkling line for 20 rods or more through the pastures & under the walls (frost cracks of the past winter–sometimes they are revealed through ice 4 or 5 inches thick over them   I observed today where a crack had divided a piece of bark lying over it with the same irregular & finely meandering line
some times forking. Yesterday I saw a wasp slowly stretching himself & I think a fly outside of Minots house–in the sun by his woodshed. In the dry pasture under the Cliff Hill–the radical leaves of the Johnswort are now revealed every where in pretty radiating wreathes flat on the ground with leaves recurved reddish above green beneath & covered with dewy drops. I can no longer get on to the river ice. I do not find any willow catkins started. A red maple which I cut bleeds somewhat–only the upper side the cut however–   Is not this the earliest distinct motion of the spring? This stood in water–   Other trees were dry. Found a geiropodium (?) its globe now transparent, with the vermillion colored remnants of others (?) lying in jelly about–   In dry pastures I see that fungus? is it–split into 10 or 12 rays like a star & curved backward around a white bag–or inner membrane? Were they not the seeds of rose-hips which I saw abundantly in some creatures dung? The various cladonias are now very plump & erect–Not only exposed to view the ground being bare, but flourishing on account of the abundant moisture. Some light some dark green–& various more dusky shades. In one or 2 places on the snow under the cliffs I noticed more than ½ pint of partridge droppings

within a diameter of 6 inches   Were these all dropt in
one night by one bird–or in the course of several
nights–or by many birds? I saw that they had eaten the
buds of the small blueberry *vacillans*. In their manure
was what looked like woody fibres–may have been
fibres of leaves

I am surprised to see how fresh and tender is the
winter green bud–almost pure white–was it so 2
months ago–? It looks as if it had started under the
snow. What is that grey beetle of which I found many
under the bark of a large dead white pine ⅝ of an inch
long within an elliptical sort of log-fort ⅞ of an inch or
more in diam. piled around of fibers of the sap wood
perhaps ⅛ or ¹⁄₁₀ of an inch high–with some red bark
chankings? Sometimes a curious chrysalis instead like
a very narrow & long band box with flat & parallel top
& bottom. but highest at one end like a coffin   Also
some white grubs stretch themselves & some ear wig
shaped creatures under the bark

I find that the ice of Walden has melted or softened
so much that I sink an inch or more at every step and
hardly any where can I cut out a small cake the water
collects so fast in hole. But at last in a harder &
dryer place I succeeded–   It was now 15½ inches
thick–having lost about 1½ inches   Though the upper
side was white & rotten & saturated with water for 4 or
5 inches the under surface was still perfectly smooth &
so far unchanged–yet ready to flake off & did so readily
in my hand in flakes ½ to 1 inch thick leaving the
irregular undulating surface with which I am familiar
–   But this side was comparitively unchanged &
hard–though for 2¾ inches measuring upwards it was
whitish–then for 2½ inches remarkably clear (free
from air bubbles) and hard. Then by successive layers
it grew more white & soft till you reached the upper
surface. I think *that* that slight white ice beneath the
clear & dark–may have been produced by the recent

warmth of the water–though this is doubtful–   At any
rate this year the ice has melted *much* more above
than beneath. Least of all between 2¾ & 5 inches from
the underside.

Sunday March 5th 54

Ch. talking with Minott the other day about his
health–said 'I suppose you'd like to die now"   "No"
said Minot–"I've tough'd it through the winter & I
want to stay & hear the blue-birds once more."

The patches of bare ground grow larger & larger–of
snow less & less–even after a night you see a
difference. It is a clear morning with some wind
beginning to rise & for the first time I see the water
looking blue on the meadows.

Has not the John'swort 2 lives in winter sending out
radical shoots which creep flat on the ground under
the snow–in the summer–shooting upward &
blossoming?

Pm to Upper Nut-meadow

The river is breaking up. The meadows are already
partly bare, for it has only been cold enough to form a
thin ice on them since this last freshet & the old ice
still lies concealed on the bottom. Great fields of thick
ice from the channel or between the channel &
meadows are driven by the wind against the thick ice
on the channel– –   Hence the meadow ice *appears* to
breakup first.   the waves dash against the edge of the
ice & eat into it fast.

As I go along on the snow under clam shell Hill I
hear it sing around me–being melted next the ground
–   This is a spring sound–   I cannot yet see the
Marchantia? in the ditches for they are yet filled with
ice or flooded–

I see no horse-tail (unless one) nor flags &c yet
started in Nutmeadow–nor any minnows out. This
brook has run clear of ice a long time. Near Jennie's its
sides are strewn with the wreck of angelica stems &

asters– I go along looking at its deep sometimes
yellow shelving bottom sprinkled with red pebbles   In
the upper meadow The sweet gale grows rankly along
its edges slanted over the water almost horizontally so
as frequently to meet & conceal it altogether–   It is
here   a dark & sluggish water
        –comparatively shallow with a muddy bottom.
This sweet gale is now full of fruit. This & the water
andromeda are wild plants as it were driven to the
water's edge by the white man. Saw a wood tortoise at
the bottom–A reptile out of the mud before any bird &,
probably, quadruped. Not yet a frog I think. The down
of some willow catkins by this brook *may have* started
forward this spring–though it is doubtful–   Those
which look most forward now will not be so a fortnight
hence. It grew colder before I left–   I saw some
crystals begining to shoot on the pools
between the tussocks–shaped like feathers
or fan-coral–the most delicate I ever
saw–   Thus even ice begins with
crystal leaves–& birds feathers & wings
are leaves–& trees & rivers with
intervening earth are vast leaves–

Saw a small blackish caterpillar on the snow–where
do they come from? & crows as I think migrating
N Easterly–   They came in loose straggling flocks
about 20 to each–commonly silent ¼ to ½ a mile apart
till 4 flocks had passed & perhaps there were more.
Methinks I see them going SW in the fall.

Mar 6th

A cool morning–the bare water here & there on the
meadow begins to look smooth–& I look to see it
rippled by a muskrat–   The earth has to some extent
frozen dry–for the drying of the earth goes on in the
cold night as well as the warm day. The alders &
hedgerows are still silent–emit no notes–

Pm to Goose pond

Ac. to G. Emerson maple sap sometimes begins to
flow in the middle of Feb. but usually in the 2nd week
of March–especially in a clear bright day with a
westerly wind after a frosty night.

The brooks–the swift ones & those in swamps open
before the river–indeed some of the first have been
open the better part of the winter. I saw trout glance in
the Mill brook this afternoon–though near its sources,
in Hubbards Close, it is still covered with dark icy
snow–& the river into which it empties has not broken
up– Can they have come up from the sea?– like a
film or shadow they glance–before the eye–& you see
where the mud is roiled by them. Saw children
checkerberrying in a meadow. I see the
Skunk-cabbage started about the spring at head of
Hubbard's close–amid the green grass–& what looks
like the first probing of the skunk. The snow is now all
off on meadow ground–in thick evergreen woods–and
on the S sides of hills–but it is still deep in sprout
lands–on the north sides of hills–& is generally in
deciduous woods– In sprout-lands it is melted
beneath but upheld by the bushes. What bare ground
we have now is due then not so much to the increased
heat of the sun–& warmth of the air–as to the little
frost there was in the ground in so many localities
– This remark applies with less force however to the
S sides of hills. The ponds are hard enough for skating
again. Heard and saw the first blackbird–flying East
over the Deep Cut–with a tchuck-tchuck–& finally a
split whistle.

Mar. 7th

Pm to Anursnack–

I did not mention the drifts yesterday– Most of the
snow left on bare dry level ground–consists of the
remains of drifts particularly along fences–most on the

S side. Also much that looks like snow is softened ice in the lower parts of fields. Looking from Anursnack there is no perceptible difference as to snow between the N & S prospects–though the N. one is not extensive–but the snowiest view is westward– Has this anything to do with there being most snow inland? All the sides of steep hills are likely to be bare–washed bare by rain. (?) I do not know why there should be so much snow in sproutlands & deciduous woods unless it is because the sun has had less chance to thaw the frosts which yet have been thick there.

It is remarkable how true each plant is to its season. Why should not the fringed gentian put forth early in the spring instead of holding in till the latter part of Septemmber? I do not perceive enough difference in the temperature– How short a time it is with us!

I see many little white, or dirty white puff-balls –yellowish inside–commonly less than 1 inch in diameter on bare cultivated fields–& in pastures some great chocolate-colored ones (within). Both yield their dust. Heard the first blue-bird something like pe-a-wor–& then other slight warblings as if farther off. Was surprised to see the bird within 7 or 8 rods on the top of an oak on the orchard's edges under the hill. But he appeared silent while I heard others faintly warbling & twittering far in the orchard– When he flew I heard no more–& then I suspected that he had been ventriloquizing.–as if he hardly dared open his mouth yet–while there was so much winter left. It is an overcast & moist but rather warm afternoon. He revisits the apple trees & appears to find some worms. Probably not till now was his food to be found abundantly. Saw some fuzzy gnats in the air. Saw where a partridge had been eating many prinos berries now black & shrivelled. I suspect that they devour a great bulk–which has but little nutriment. The radical

leaves of the pinweeds are like the johns-wort with
leaves reflexed–most of them closer & finer– They
appear unaffected by frost.

The rad. leaves of the crow-foot every where are the
commonest green–as soon as the snow goes off– You
can hardly tell when it begins to spring.

Saw *Mt* cranberry near Brook's pigeon-place very
flat on the pasture raying out from a centre 6 feet each
way more than ¾ of an inch thick in the middle– Did
not know it was so woody–this one of the *winter-reds*,
perfectly fresh & glossy. The river *channel* is nearly
open everywhere– Saw on the alders by the river side
front of Hildreths a song sparrow–quirking its tail. It
flew across the river to the willows–& soon I heard its
well-known dry tchip-tchip. Saw methinks what I
called ephemerae last spring–one on the water–¾ inch
long–narrow–grey winged–several sets curved on the
back–

On winter-rye field top of Anursnack–what looked
like a *very large* hard core of a button wood ball–same
color   broke it with a stone & found it full of dark
earth. Was it not my pigeon's egg fungus turned dark
& hardened?

Mar. 8

Steady rain on the roof in the night–suggesting
April-like warmth– This will help melt the snow & ice
& take the frost out of the ground.

What pretty wreathes the *mt* cranberry
makes–curving upward at the extremity. The leaves
are now a dark glossy red–& wreathe & all are of such a
shape as might fitly be copied in wood or stone–or
architectural foliages

I wrote a letter for an Irishman night
before last–sending for his wife in Ireland to come to

this country– One sentence which he dictated was
–"Don't mind the rocking of the vessel, but take care
of the children that they be not lost overboard."

Lightning this evening–after a day of successive
rains.

March 9th

Am clearing up– Water is fast taking place of ice on
the river & meadows–& morning & evening we begin
to have some smooth water prospects– Saw this
morning a muskrat sitting "in a round form on the
ice"–or rather motionless like the top of a stake or a
mass of muck on the edge of the ice. He then dove for
a clam whose shells he kept on the ice beside him.

Boiled a handful of Rock tripe–Umbilicaria
Muhlenbergii–(which Tuckerman says "was the
favorite Rock-Tripe in Franklin's Journey"–) for more
than an hour– It produced a *black* pulp–looking
somewhat like boiled tea leaves–and was insipid like
rice or starch. The dark water in which it was boiled
had a bitter tast & was slightly gelatinous. The pulp
was not positively disagreeable to the palate. The
account in the young voyageurs is correct.

Pm. to Great meadows.

Peter H. says that he saw gulls? an shelldrakes about
a month ago when the meadow was flooded. I detect
the trout minnows not an inch long–by their quick
motions or quirks–soon concealing themselves   The
river channel is open–but there is a very *thin* ice of
recent formation over the greatest part of the
meadows. It is a still moist louring day & the water is
smooth– Saw several flocks of large greyish & whitish
or speckled ducks– I suppose the same that P. calls
shell-drakes. They like ducks commonly incline to fly
in a line about an equal distance apart. I hear the
common sort of quacking from them. It is pleasant to
see them at a distance alight on the water with a

slanting flight–launch themselves & sail along so
stately   The pieces of ice large & small drifting along
help to conceal them   supply so many objects on the
water. There is this last night's ice on the surface–but
the old ice still at the bottom of the meadows–   In the
spaces of still open water I see the reflections of the
hills & woods–which for so long I have not seen–& it
gives expression to the face of nature   The face of
nature is lit up by these reflections in still water in the
spring. Sometimes you see only the top of a distant hill
reflected far within the meadow–where a dull grey
field of ice intervenes between the water & the shore.

Mar 10th

rain–rain–the 3d day of more or less rain.

Pm C. miles road via Clam shell Hill.
misty & mizzling. The rad. leaves of the shepherds
purse are common–& fresh–also that early thistle by
nut-meadow Brook–with much down webbed–holding
the mist in drops–   Each alder catkin has a clear drop
at the end–though the air is filled with mist merely
which from time to time is blown in my face & I put up
my umbrella–   The beomyces is very perfect &
handsome today. It occurs to me that heavy rains &
sudden meltings of the snow–such as we had a
fortnight ago (Feb. 26) before the ground is thawed–so
that all the water–instead of being soaked up by the
ground–flows rapidly into the streams & ponds–is
necessary to swell & break them up. If we waited for
the direct influence of the sun on the ice–& the
influence of such water as would reach the river under
other circumstances–the spring would be very much
delayed. In the violent freshet there is a mechanic
force–added to the chemic. The willow catkins on the
Miles–I should say had decidedly started since I was
here last–& are all peeping from under their scales
conspicuously. At present I should say that the

vegetable kingdom showed the influence of the spring
as much in the air, as in the water–that is in the
flowing of the sap–the skunk cab– buds–and the
swelling of the willow catkins. I have detected very
little if anything starting in brooks or ditches–for the
first have far overflowed their banks & full of rapid &
sandy water–and the latter are still frequently full of
ice– But probably that depends on the year–whether
open or not–

   Saw a skunk in the Corner road–which I followed 60
rods or more. Out now about 4 pm–partly because it is
a dark foul day–. . .· ·· ·· ---··...... . .:-----. --..:

   · . .:· - ·· ·...,   It is a slender black
(and white) animal with its back remarkably arched
–standing high behind–and carrying its head
low–runs–even when undisturbed–with a singular
teter or undulation–like the walking of a Chinese lady.
Very slow–I hardly have to run to keep up with it. It
has a long tail which it regularly erects when I come
too near & prepares to discharge its liquid. It is white
at the end of the tail–& the hind head–& a line on the
front of the face–the rest black–except the flesh
colored nose (and I think feet). The back is more
arched & the fore & hind feet nearer together than in
my sketch. It tried repeatedly to get into the wall–& did
not show much cunning. Finally it steered, apparently,
for an old skunk or woodchuck hole under a wall
4 rods off–& got into it–or under the wall at least–for it
was stopped up– And there I view at leisure close to.
It has a remarkably long narrow pointed head & snout
which enable it to make those deep narrow holes in
the earth by which it probes for insects– Its eyes have
an innocent child-like bluish black expression. It made
a singular loud patting sound repeatedly on the frozen
ground under the wall–undoubtedly with its fore

feet–(I saw only the upper part of the animal) which
reminded me of what I have heard about you stopping
& stamping in order to stop the skunk. Probably it has
to do with its getting its food–patting the earth to get
the insects or worms–   Though why it did so then I
know not.

   Its track was **?**   **.**   **°**   **✦** **·**   **●** **✦** **·** **●** **✦**
small round showing the nails a little less than an inch
in diam– alternate 5 or 6 inches X 2 or 2½ sometimes
2 feet together–   There is something pathetic in such a
sight–next to seeing one of the human aborigines of
the country. I respect the skunk as a human being in a
very humble sphere. I have no doubt they have begun
to probe already where the ground permits–or as far as
it does–but what have they eat all winter?

   The weather is almost april like. We always have
much of this rainy–drizzling misty weather in early
spring–after which we expect to hear geese

Mar. 11th

   Fair weather after 3 rainy days–air full of birds
blue-birds songsparrows–chicadee–(phebe notes) &
blackbirds. Song sparrows toward the water with at
least 2 kinds or variations of their strain hard to
imitate–   quick
ozit ozit ozit, psa te te te tete ter twe ter is one   the
other began chip chip che we &c &c   blue birds
warbling curls on elms.

   Shall the earth be regarded as a graveyard–a
necropolis merely–& not also as a granary filled with
the seeds of life? Is not its fertility increased by this
decay?   a fertile compost not exhausted sand.

   On Tuesday the 7th ult I heard the first song
sparrow chirp–& saw it flit silently from alder to alder.
This pleasant morning after 3 days rain & mist they
generally forth burst into sprayey song from the low
trees along the river. The developing of their song is

gradual but sure like the expanding of a flower– This
is the first *song* I have heard.

Pm to Cliffs–

River higher than any time in the winter I think–yet
there being some ice on the meadows & the tops of
reflected trees being seen along its edges–aunt
thought the river had gone down & that this was the
ground. Muskrats are driven out of their holes. Heard
one's loud plash behind Hubbards. It comes up
brown-striped with wet– I could detect its progress
beneath in shallow water by the bubbles which came
up. I believe I saw to-day & have for some time
seen–lizzards in water wiggling away more swiftly than
tadpoles or frogs. From the hill the river & meadow is
about equally water & ice–rich blue water blown from
this side or that & islands or continents of white ice no
longer ice in place–. The distant *mts* are all white with
snow while our landscape is nearly bare.

Another year I must observe the alder & willow sap
as early as the mid. of Feb. at least. Fair Haven covered
with ice. Saw a hawk. Godwin saw a ground-squirrel a
fortnight ago–& heard a robin this morning. He has
caught skunks in traps set for minks with a piece of
muskrat   says the fox & skunk eat huckleberries &c.
Nowadays where snow banks have partly melted
against the banks by the road side in low ground–I see
in the grass numerous galleries where the mice or
moles have worked in the winter.

Mar. 12

Am Up RR to woods. We have white frosts these
mornings. This is the blackbird morning–their sprayey
notes and conqueree sing with the song-sparrows
jingle all along the river– Thus gradually they acquire
confidence to sing. It is a beautiful spring morning. I
hear *my* first robin peep distinctly at a distance on
some higher trees, oaks or ? on a high key–no singing

yet– I hear from an apple tree a faint cricket like
chirp–& a sparrow darts away–flying far *dashing from
side* to *side*– I think it must be the white-in-tail or
grass finch

Saw either a large mouse or a ground squirrel on the
snow near the edge of the wood–prob. the former. I
hear a jay loudly screaming phe-phay phe-phay– –a
loud shrill–chicadee's phebe– Now I see & hear the
lark sitting with head erect–neck outstretched in the
middle of a pasture–and I hear another far off singing
– Sing when they first come. All these birds do their
warbling especially in the still sunny hour after
sun-rise–as rivers tinkle at their sources– Now is the
time to be abroad & hear them–as you detect the
slightest ripple in smooth water. As with tinkling
sounds the sources of streams burst their icy fetters
–so the rills of music begin to flow & swell the general
quire of spring. Memorable is the warm light of the
spring sun on russet fields in the morning.

A new feature is being added to the landscape–and
that is expanses & reaches of blue water.

C. says he saw a gull to-day

            Pm to Balls Hill along river.

My companion tempts me to certain licences of
speech–i.e, to reckless & sweeping expressions which I
am wont to regret that I have used– That is I find that
I have used more harsh–extravagant & cynical
expressions concerning mankind and individuals than
I intended. I find it difficult to make to him a
sufficiently moderate statement. I think it is because I
have not his sympathy in my sober and constant view.
He asks for a paradox–an eccentric statement & too
often I give it to him–

Saw some small ducks–black & white perhaps teal
or widgeons. This great expanse of deep blue water
–deeper than the sky–why does it not blue my soul as

of yore. It is hard to soften me now. I see no gulls
myself. The time was when this great blue scene would
have tinged my spirit more.

Now is the season to look for Indian relics–the sandy
fields being just bared– I stand on the high lichen
covered & colored (greenish) hill beyond Abner
Buttrick's– I go further east & look across the
meadows to Bedford–& see that peculiar scenery of
March–in which I have taken so many rambles–The
earth just bare & beginning to be dry–the snow lying
on the N sides of hills–the gray deciduous trees & the
green pines soughing in the March wind–they look
now as if deserted by a companion–(the snow)   When
you walk over bare lichen-clad hills–just beginning to
be dry–& look afar over the blue water on the
meadows–You are beginning to break up your winter
quarters–& plan adventures for the new year–   The
scenery is like–yet unlike November–   You have the
same barren russet–but now instead of a dry hard cold
wind–a peculiarly soft moist air or else a raw wind.
Now is the reign of water. I see many crows on the
meadow by the water's edge these days. It is
astonishing how soon the ice has gone out of the
river–but it still lies on the bottom of the meadow. Is it
peculiar to the song-sparrow to dodge behind & hide
in walls & the like? Toward night the water becomes
smooth & beautiful. Men are eager to launch their
boats & paddle over the meadows–

The spring birds have come a little earlier this year
than last methinks–& I suspect the spring may be
earlier in the air–yet there is more ice & snow & frozen
ground still because the winter has been so much
more severe.

I am surprised to find that water froze pretty thick in
my chamber the night of the 14th of Mar '53 after a fire
in the evening–& that they were at work on the ice at

Lorings on the 16th. This is very different weather. The
ice is all out of the *river proper*–& all spoiled even on
Walden–

Mar. 13th

To Boston–   C. says he saw skater insects
today   Harris tells me that those grey insects within
these little log forts under the bark of the dead Wht
pine–which I found about a week ago–are Rhagium
lineatum. Bought a telescope today for 8 dollars–Best
military spyglass with 6 slides which shuts up to about
same size 15 dols & very powerful   Saw the squares of
achromatic glass from Paris which Clark–(e?) uses–50
odd dols apiece the larger–   It takes 2 together–one
called the flint–   These French glasses all one quality
of glass. My glass tried by Clark & approved–only a
part of the object glass available. Bring the edge of
the diaphragm against middle of the light & your nail
on object glass in line with these shows what is cut
off–   Sometimes may enlarge the hole in diaphragm
–   But if you do so you may have to enlarge the hole in
diaphragm near small end–which must be exactly as
large as the pencil of light there. As the diameter of the
pencil is to the diam. of the available portion of the
object glass so is the power–so many times it
magnifies–   A good glass because the form of the
blurred object is the same on each side of the focus *i.e*
shoved in or drawn out. C. was making a glass for
Amherst Col.

Mar 14th

Am–   Threatening rain after clear morning. Great
concert of songsparrows in willows & alders along
Swamp B. brook by river–   Hardly hear a *distinct*
strain–couples chasing each other & some field
sparrows with them.

R. W. E saw a small bird in the woods yesterday
which reminded him of the particolored warbler.

Pm to Great Meadows–

Raw thickening mists as if preceeding rain.

Counted over 40 robins with my glass in the meadow north of Sleepy Hollow–on the grass & on the snow– A large company of fox-colored sparrows in Heywoods maple swamp close by. I heard their loud sweet canary-like whistle 30 or 40 rods off–sounding richer than anything yet–some on the bushes singing –twee twee-twa twa ter tweer tweer twa–this the scheme of it only–there being no dental grit to it. They were shy flitting before me–& I heard a slight susurrus where many were busily scratching amid the leaves in the swamp–without seeing them & also saw many indistinctly– Wilson never heard but one sing–their common note there being a cheep. Saw fresh tracks in what looked like a woodchucks hole. No ice visible as I look over the meadows from Peter's–though it lies at the bottom. Scared up 4 black ducks from the flooded meadow on the right of the roadway as you go to Peters. The water being rough on the meadows they had ap. sought this smooth & shallow place–shut in by the woods.

Alder scales are visibly loosened their lower edges (i.e as they hang) showing a line of yellowish or greenish. The pads in open warm ditches are now decidedly the greatest growth of this season–though I am not sure how much is due to last fall.

From within the house at 5½ Pm I hear the loud honking of Geese–throw up the window & see a large flock in disordered harrow flying more directly north or even NW–than usual. Raw thick misty weather.

March 15

Plasant morning unexpectedly– Hear on the alders by the river the lill lill lill till of the first F hiemalis –mingled with song sparrows & tree sparrows. The sound of Barrett's Saw mill in the still morning comes

over the water very loud. I hear that peculiar
interesting loud hollow tapping of a wood pecker from
over the water.

I am sorry to think that you do not get a man's most
effective criticism until you provoke him– Severe
truth is expressed with some bitterness.

J Farmer tells me his dog started up a lark last winter
completely buried in the snow.

Painted my boat–

Mar 16th

Am– Another fine morning.

Willows & alders along watercourses all alive these
mornings & ringing with the trills & jingles & warbles
of birds even as the waters have lately broken loose &
tinkle below–song-sparrows blackbirds–not to
mention robins &c &c

The song sparrows are very abundant peopling each
bush–willow or alder for ¼ of a mile & pursuing each
other as if now selecting their mates– It is their song
which especially fills the air–made an incessant &
undistinguishable trill & jingle by their numbers– I
see ducks afar saling on the meadow leaving a long
furrow in the water behind them– Watch them at
leisure without scaring them with my glass–observe
their free & undisturbed motions– Some dark brown
partly on water alternately dipping with their tails up
partly on land– These I think may be summer ducks.
Others with bright white breasts &c & black heads
about same size or larger which may be Golden Eyes
–i e Brass-eyed Whistlers   They dive & are gone some
time & come up a rod off– At first I saw but one–then
a minute after 3– The first phoebe near the water is
heard.

Saw & heard honey-bees about my boat in the yard
–attracted probably by the beeswax in the grafting wax
which which was put on it a year ago. It is warm
weather. A thunder storm in the evening.

Friday Mar. 17th

A remarkably warm day for the season; too warm
while surveying without my great coat–almost like
May heats–

4 Pm to Cliffs– The grass is *slightly* greened on
south banksides–on the S side of the house. It begins
to be windy. Saw a small gyrinus at the brook bridge
behind Hubbard's grove. The first tinge of greens
appears to be due to moisture more than to direct
heat– It is not on bare dry banks–but in hollows
where the snow melts last that it is most conspicuous.
Fair Haven is open for half a dozen rods about the
shores. If this weather holds it will be entirely open in
a day or two

Sat. Mar. 18

Very high wind–this forenoon–began by filling the
air with a cloud of dust.   never felt it shake the house
so much–filled the house with dust through the
cracks–books stove papers covered with it. Blew down
Mr. Frosts chimney again. Took up my boat a very
heavy one which was lying on its bottom in the yard &
carried it 2 rods. The white caps of the waves on the
flooded meadow–seen from the window are a rare &
exciting spectacle–Such an angry face as our Concord
meadows rarely exhibit. Walked down the street to
P.O.   few inhabitants out more than in a rain–elms
bending & twisting & thrashing the air as if they
would come down every moment– I was cautious
about passing under them. Yet scarcely a rotten limb
in the street. The highest winds occur neither in
summer when the trees are covered with leaves, nor in
winter when they may be covered with ice. Saw a
flattened toad on the side walk   could it have been
last years?

Pm   walked round by the W side of the river to
Conantum.

Wind less violent. C has already seen a
yellow-spotted tortoise in a ditch. (2 sizeable elms
by river in Merricks pasture blown down–roots being
rotted off on water-side.) The willow catkins this side
M. Miles' are ⅝ inch long & show some red. Poplar
catkins nearly as large–color somewhat like a gray
rabbit. Old barn blown down on Conantum–   It fell
regularly like a weak box pushed over
without moving its bottom–the roof falling upon it a
little to lea-ward–   The hay is left exposed but does
not blow away. The river was at its height last night.
Before this we saw many robins and sparrows under
Clam-shell hill for shelter. Birds seek warm &
sheltered places in such weather–   It is very cold &
freezing this wind–   The water has been blown quite
across the Hubbards bridge causeway in some places
& incrusted the road with ice. Before looking this way
we had seen the whitened shore from Lupine Hill. It is
blown & dashes against the willows and incrusts them
with ice sometimes to the height of 3 feet–with icicles
shaped like bulls-horns–especially observable
where many osiers stand together and from
the more horizontal osiers &c depend
icicles 5 or 6 inches long very regularly
looking exactly like coarse rakes–apparently not the
result of melting but of the spray & water blown or
dashed upon them.
Only more regular.
A very wintry sight.

The water is in many places blown a rod on to the
shore & frozen. Saw where a woodchuck (probably)
had dug out quite a pile of gravel in the side of a hill–

Sunday–19

Cold & windy–the meadow ice bears where shallow.
Wm Rice 2d (?) saw a woodchuck last Sunday. Met his
father in Walden woods who described a flock of

crows he had just seen which followed him "eyeing down–eyeing down"

Saw in Mill-brook behind Shannons 3 or 4 shiners (the first) poised over the sand with a distinct longitudinal light colored line midway along their sides & a darker line below it. This is a noteworthy & characteristic lineament–or cypher or hieroglyphic–or type of spring. You look into some clear sandy bottomed brook–where it spreads into a deeper bay–yet flowing cold from ice & snow not far off–& see indistinctly poised over the sand on invisible fins the outlines of a shiner–scarcely to be distinguished from the sands behind it as if it were transparent–or as the material of which it was builded had all been picked up from them chiefly distinguished by the lines I have mentioned–

Goodwin killed a pigeon yesterday. Flints pond almost entirely open–much more than Fair Haven–

Tuesday Mar 21st

At sunrise to Clam Shell Hill. River skimmed over at Willow Bay last night. Thought I should find ducks cornered up by the ice– They get behind this hill for shelter– Saw what looked like clods of plowed meadow rising above the ice– Looked with glass & found it to be more than 30 black ducks asleep with their heads in their backs–motionless & thin ice formed about them– Soon one or two were moveing about slowly– There was an open space 8 or 10 rods by 1 or 2– At first all within a space of ap. less than a rod diameter. It was 6½ Am & the sun shining on them.–but bitter cold– How tough they are. I crawled far on my stomach & got a near view of them 30 rods off– At length they detected me & quacked– Some got out upon the ice & when I rose up all took to flight–in a great straggling flock which at a distance looked like crows–in no order– Yet when you see 2 or

3 the parallelism produced by their necks & bodies
steering the same way–gives the idea of order–

Wednesday Mar 22nd

Pm launch boat & paddle to Fair Haven–still very
cold– The most splendid show of ice shandeliers
–casters–hour glasses (½) that I ever saw or imagined
about the piers of the bridges–surpassing any crystal
so large–Rather like   Great waiters
the bases of columns
–teraced pedestals
–that is it–the
prototypes of
the ornaments of the copings & capitals.–perfect &
regular sharp cone-shaped drops hang from the first
figure a few inches above the water. I should have
described it then   It would have filled many pages
– Scared up my flock of black ducks & counted 40.
together. See crows along the waters edge   what do
they eat. Saw a small black duck with glass a dipper
(?) Fair Haven still covered & frozen anew in part.
Shores of meadow strewn with cranberries. The now
silvery willow catkins (notwithstanding the severe
cold) shine along the shore–over the cold water. & C
thinks some willow osiers decidedly more yellow.

Thursday 23d–

Snows & rains a little. The birds in yard–active now
–hiemalis–tree sparrow–& song-sparrow. The hiemalis
jingle easily distinguished. Hear all together on apple
trees these days. Minott confesses to me today that he
has not been to Boston since the last war or 1815. Aunt
said that he had not been 10 miles from home since
that he had not been to Acton since Miss Bowers lived
there–but he declared that he had been there to
Cornwallis & musters   When I asked if he would liked
to go to Boston–he answered he was going to another
Boston.

24th

Fair again–the snow melting. Great flocks of
hiemalis drifting about with their jingling note. The
same ducks under Clam Shell Hill. The elm buds were
ap. expanded before this cold which began on the 18th
ult. Goose-pond half open–   Flints has perhaps 15 or
20 acres of ice yet about shores–can hardly tell when it
is open this year. The black ducks–the most common
that I see–are the only ones whose note I know or
hear–a hoarse croaking quack–   How shy they are.

Sat 25th

Cold & windy. Down river in boat to Great
Meadows–freezes on oars.   too cold & windy almost
for ducks–they are in the smoother open water–(free
from ice) under the lea of hills. Got a boatload of drift
wood–rails–bridge timber–planks &c. White maple
buds bursting–making trees look like some fruit trees
with blossom buds.

Is not the small duck or two I see one at a time &
flying pretty high a teal? Willow osiers near Mill brook
mouth I am almost certain have acquired a fresher
color–at least they surprise me at a distance by their
green passing through yellowish to red at top.

Mar 26th

River froze over at Lily Bay.

Mar 27–   Saw a hawk–prob–marsh Hawk by
meadow

Mar 28

Pm to Wht Pond

Coldest day for a month or more–Severe as almost
any in the winter–   Saw this Pm either a snipe or a
woodcock–   It appeared rather small for the last
–   Pond opening on the NE. A flock of hiemalis
drifting from a wood over a field incessantly for 4 or
5 minutes–thousands of them, notwithstanding the
cold–   The fox-col– sparrow sings sweetly also. Saw a

small slate colored hawk–with wings transversely
mottled beneath probably the sharp-shinned H.

Got 1st proof of Walden–

Wednesday Mar 29th

Pm to Fair Haven– Coldest night–pump froze so as
to require thawing.– Saw 2 marsh hawks (?) white on
rump. A gull of pure white a wave of foam in the
air How simple & wave-like its outline the outline of
the wings presenting two curves–between which the
tail is merely the point of junction.– all wing
like a birch-scale. Tail remarkably absorbed–

Saw 2 white throated black beaked divers fly off
swiftly low over the water–with black tips of wings
curved short downward . Afterward saw one
scoot along out from the shore upon the water & dive
–& that was the last I could see of him though I
watched 4 or 5 minutes. Fair Haven half open–channel
wholly open– See thin cakes of ice at a distance now
& then blown up on their edges & glistening in the
sun. Had the experience of Arctic voyagers amid the
flow ice on a small scale. Think I saw a hen hawk. 2
circling over Cliffs

Mar 30th 54

6 Am to Island. First still hour since the Pm of the
17th ult– March truly came in like a lamb & went out
like a lion this year–remarkably & continuously
pleasant weather from the very first day till the 18th
–apparently an early spring–buds & birds well
advanced–then suddenly very severe cold & high
winds, cold enough to skim the river over in broad
places at night & commencing with the greatest &
most destructive gale for many a year felt far & wide–&
it has never ceased to blow since till this morning.
Vegetation is ac. put back. The ground these last cold
(13) days has been about bare of snow–but frozen
– Some had peas & potatoes in before it. 1st half of

month very pleasant & mild spring weather–last half
severe winter cold & high winds. The water at its
highest–(not very high) this month on the 17th. Ducks
have been lurking in sheltered places not frozen.
Robins feed along the edge of the river.– At the Island
I see & hear the cackle of this morning a pigeon
woodpecker–at the hollow poplar–had heard him
tapping distinctly from my boats place ¼+ of mile.
Great flocks of tree sparrows & some F hiemalis on the
ground & trees on the Island Neck–making the air and
bushes ring with their jingling– The former–some of
them–say somewhat like this a che che–ter twee
twee-tweer tweer twa   it sounded like a new bird.

The black ducks seem always to rise with that loud
hoarse croaking quacking. The river early is partly
filled with thin floating hardly cemented ice
–occasionally turned on its edge by the wind &
sparkling in the sun– If the sun had kept out of the
way one day in the past fortnight I think the river
would have frozen to bear.

Read an interesting article on Etienne Geoffroy St.
Hilaire the friend & contemporary of Cuvier–though
opposed to him in his philosophy– He believed
species to be variable.

In looking for anatomical resemblances he found
that he could not safely be guided by function–form
–structure–size–color &c–but only by the relative
position & mutual dependance of organs. Hence his le
Principe des Connexions & his maxim "An organ is
sooner destroyed than transposed"   "Un organ est
plutôt altéré, atrophié, anéanti, que transposé." A
principal formula of his was "Unity of Plan, Unity of
Composition." In the Westminster Rev. Jan '54.

Mar 31st

Weather changes at last to drizzling

In criticizing your writing trust your finest instinct.
There are many things which we come very near

questioning, but do not question. When I have sent
off my MSS to the printer certain objectionable
sentences or expressions are sure to obtrude
themselves on my attention with force–though I had
not consciously suspected them before. My critical
instinct then at once breaks the ice & comes to the
surface.

Ap. 1st

The tree sparrows–hiemalis–& song spars are
particularly lively & musical in the yard this rainy &
truly April day. The air rings with them. The robin now
begins to sing sweet powerfully–

Pm up Assabet to Dodges Brook
–Thence to Farmers

April has begun like itself–   It is warm & showery
–while I sail away with a light SW wind toward the
Rock–   Sometimes the sun seems just ready to burst
out–yet I know it will not–   The meadow is becoming
bare   It resounds with the sprayey notes of blackbirds
–   The birds sing this warm showery day after a
fortnight's cold (yesterday was wet too) with a
universal burst & flood of melody. Great flocks of
hiemalis &c pass overhead like schools of fishes in the
water many abreast. The white maple stamens are
beginning to peep out from the wet & weather-beaten
buds. The earliest alders are just ready to bloom–to
show their yellow–on the first decidedly warm & sunny
day. The water is smooth at last & dark–ice no longer
forms on the oars. It is pleasant to paddle under the
dripping hemlocks this dark day–   They make more of
a wilderness impression than pines. The lines of saw
dust from Barrets Mill at different heights on the steep
wet bank under the hemlocks–rather enhances the
impression of freshness & wildness, as if it were a new
country. Saw a painted tortoise on the bottom–   The
bark of Poplar boughs which have been held in the ice
along the sides of the river the past winter are gnawed

probably by muskrats. Saw floating a good-sized
rooster with out a head the red stump sticking out
–probably killed by an owl. Heard a bird whose note
was very much like that of the purple finch–loud &
clear. First *smelled* the musk-rat.

Yesterday & today I hear the cackle of the flicker so
agreeable from association   It brings the year about.
From afar on some blasted tree it makes all the vale
wink its swelling flicker (?). Saw at farmer his
snow-grubs (the same I had seen v. back)   Haris in
this weeks NE Farmer thinks on comparing them with
Eng. plates that they are the larvae of one of the
species of Crane-fly Tipula. I saw some–still in F's
pasture. Did they not come out from the roots of the
grass prematurely in the winter & so become food for
birds? The ground in Farmer's garden was in some
places whitened with the droppings of the snow birds
after seeds of weeds–F hiemalis & others. The hiemalis
is in the largest flocks of any at this season–   You see
them come drifting over a rising ground just like snow
flakes before a north-east wind.

I was surprised to see how Farmers young pears 3 or
4 feet high on quince stocks had been broken down by
the snow drifts broken over & over
apparently the snow freezing over them
& then at last by its weight breaking them down.

I hear the jingle of the hiemalis from within the
house–sounding like a trill.

Ap 2nd

Pm. To Conantum via Nut Meadow Brook

Saw black ducks in water & on land–can see their
light throats a great way with my glass. They do not
dive but dip.

That liverwort in the J Hosmer ditch is now obvious
–   It has little green cups on its frond with a fringed
mouth–but I saw something similar but shorter &

more orbicular yesterday under the hemlock bank
with little black dots on it. The radical leaves of some
plants appear to have started–look brighter–The
shepherd's purse–& plainly the skunk-cabbage. In the
brook there is the least possible springing yet a little
yellow lily in the ditch & sweet flag *starting* in the
brook.

I was just sitting on the rail over the brook when I
heard some thing which reminded me of the song of
the robin in rainy days in past springs–   Why is it that
not the note itself–but something which reminds me
of it should affect me most? The ideal instead of the
actual.

At Lee's cliff the red stemmed moss. The slippery
elm is about as forward as the common with its rusty
buds. The saxifrage is the most spring-like plant
methinks yet.

The tree sparrows make the alders &c ring   they
have a metallic chirp & a short canary-like warble.
They keep company with the hiemalis.

Ap 3d

Saw from window with glass 7 ducks on
meadow-water–Only one or 2 conspicuously white
–These black heads–white throats & breasts & along
sides–the rest of the ducks brownish prob. young
males & females–   Prob. the Golden Eye–   Jardine
says it is rare to see more than one full-plumaged male
in a flock–

Pm to Cliffs by boat–

Did I see crow black birds with the red-wings & hear
its harsher chattering?

The water has gone down so much that I have to
steer carefully to avoid the thick hummocks left here &
there on the meadow by the ice–   I see the deep holes
they were taken out of. A muskrat has just built a small
cabin–of a bushel of mouthfuls on one. No clams up

yet. I see a very little snow ice still at a distance on the N sides of hills & walls. The wind is S Easterly. This is methinks the first hazy day–though not so warm as the 17 of March– The aspect of the woods reminds me of landscapes–& the sough of the wind in the pines sounds warmer whispering of summer. I think I may say that Flints broke up entirely on the first wet day after the cold spell–i.e. the 31st of Mar–though I have not been there lately– Fair Haven will last some days yet.

Ap 4th '54

All day surveying a woodlot in Acton for Abel Hosmer. He says that he has seen the small slate-colored hawk pursue & catch doves i.e. the sharp-shinned– Has found some trouble in driving off a large slate-colored hawk from a hen in his yard at which he pounced again close by him–undoubtedly a goshawk– Has also noticed the butcher bird catching other birds. calls him the "mock-bird." I observe that all the farmers have pretty much the same stories of this kind to tell. They will describe a large bold slate-colored hawk (the goshawk) about here some 2 years ago which caught some of their hens, & the like. The afternoon very pleasant.

Ap 5th

This morn. heard a familiar twittering over the house looked up & saw white bellied swallows. Mother saw them yesterday.

Surveying all day for Mr Hoar in Carlisle near Hitchinson's & near I. Green's

See many hawks about yesterday & today –marsh-hawks & perhaps henhawks–These being pleasant days– It proved very pleasant & warm & while surveying in the woods with my great coat off I heard a few stertorous sounds from the croaking frog. Also as we rode along to Green's we saw many of the

large butterfly dark with buffedged wings & also small
reddish ones in the dry sproutlands– The same warm
& pleasant weather brings them out to flutter along the
roadside in sproutlands–that does the hawks to sail
along the meadowside & over the wood– Saw the first
frog by the road side–I believe a speckled i.e. *palustris*
& at the Green Lot–heard the hyla.

These days when a soft W or SW wind blows & it is
truly warm & an outside coat is oppressive–these bring
out the butterflies & the frogs–& the marsh hawks
which prey on the last. Just so simple is every year.
Whatever year it may be– I am surveying perhaps in
the woods– I have taken off my outside coat perhaps
for the first time & hung it on a tree. The zephyr is
positively agreeable on my cheek– I am thinking what
an elysian day it is–and how I seem always to be
keeping the flocks of Admetus such days–that is my
luck–when I hear a single short well known stertorous
croak from some pool half filled with dry leaves. You
may see anything now–the buffedged butterfly & many
hawks–along the meadow–& hark–while I was writing
down that field note the shrill peep of the hylodes was
born to me from afar through the woods.

I road with my employer a dozen miles today
keeping a profound silence almost all the way–as the
most simple & natural course. I treated him simply as
if he had bronchitis & could not speak–just as I would
a sick man a crazy man or an idiot– The disease was
only an unconquerable stiffness in a well-meaning &
sensible man–

Begin to look off hills & see the landscape again
through a slight haze with warm wind on the cheek.

Ap. 6th
Pm Up Assabet.

A still warmer day than yesterday–a warm moist rain
smelling W. wind. I am surprised find so much of the

white maples already out. The light colored stamens
show to some rods   Probably they *began* as early as
day before yesterday. They resound with the hum of
honey bees–heard a dozen rods off–& you see
thousands of them about the flowers against the sky.
They know where to look for the white maple & when
– This susurrus carries me forward some months
toward summer– I was reminded *before* of those still
warm summer noons when the breams nests are left
dry & the fishes retreat from the shallows into the
cooler depths & the cows stand up to their bellies in
the river– The reminiscence came over me like a
summer's dream–

The alders, both kinds, just above the hemlocks
have just begun to shed their pollen. They are hardly
as forward as the wht maples–but these are not in so
warm a position as some– I am in doubt which (alder
or maple) may be earliest this year–Have not looked so
closely as last year. In clearing out the assabet Spring
–disturbed 2 small speckled (palustris) frogs just
beginning to move. Saw flying over what I at first
thought a gull–then a fishhawk?

Heard the snipe over the meadows this
evening   probably to be heard for a night or
2   sounds on different keys as if approaching or
receeding–over the meadows recently become bare

April 7th 54

6 Am Down RR to Cliffs.

The P. tremuloides in a day or two– The hazel
stigmas are well out & the catkins loose–but no pollen
shed yet. On the Cliff I find after long & careful search
one sedge above the rocks low amid the withered
blades of last year–out–its little yellow beard amid the
dry blades & few green ones–the first *herbaceous*
flowering I have detected. Fair Haven is completely

open– It must have been so first either on the 5th or
6th ult.
Sat. Ap. 8th
6 Am to Clam-shell Hill.

Am surprised to find the skunk cabbage out
–shedding pollen–(a few)   This was probably the case
in some places on the 5th & 6th. There has been very
little growth visible in its spathes for a month. Its
spring seems to be in the fall partly. This spring it has
suffered more than usual owing to the severe cold of
the last half of march. Did I see a grass-finch? Cheneys
elm begins to show stamens. That remarkably warm
1st half of March appears to have advanced the plants
very much–& as soon as the cold last half was past
they burst out almost together. Spearer's lights 2 or 3
nights past.
Pm
To Lee's Cliff via Clam-shell.

Methinks I do not see such great & lively flocks of
hiemalis & tree sparrows in the morning since the
warm days, the 4th 5th & 6th, Perchance after the
warmer days which bring out the frogs & butterflies
–the alders & maples–the greater part of them leave for
the north & give place to New comers.

At the Lyceum the other night I felt that the lecturer
had chosen a theme too foreign to himself & so failed
to interest me as much as formerly–   He described
things not in or near to his heart–but toward his
extremities and superficies. The poet deals with his
privatest experience. There was no *central* nor
centralizing thought in the lecture.

Some southward banks & hill sides are now
considerably tinged with green–not observed at a
distance–   I see the celandine & catnep (?) beginning
to look green along the graveyard fence. The stigmas

of the hazels (beyond Clam Shell) are a splendid
crimson star when brought between me & the light. I
cannot find any of their catkins shedding pollen yet,
but they may tomorrow. On the 5th saw a man sowing
rye. Heard a prolonged dream from frog? in the river
meadow–or was it a toad?

See black ducks–& hear their hoarse quacking. They
commonly rise 60 rods off   They feed as often on the
land as in the water–& look as clumsy there as the
tame do.

At Nut Meadow Brook saw or rather heard a
muskrat plunge into the brook before me–& saw him
endeavoring in vain to bury himself in the sandy
bottom–looking like an amphibious animal–   I
stooped & taking him by the tail which projected
–tossed him ashore–   He did not lose the points of
compass but turned directly to the brook again though
it was toward me– –& plunging in buried himself in the
mud & that was the last I saw of him–   I see many
yellow-spot tortoises today–some of them quite rusty
looking.

The alders are pretty generally–they are either
yellowish–greenish–or reddish. At Heart-leaf Pond the
croaking frogs are in full blast–   I saw many on the
surface–small ferruginous or darker brown–bodies
2 inches long–spread out on the surface–& from time
to time swimming about–& toward each other or
diving–   Most utter a short croak several times
–   Others use a peculiar squirming & nasal variation
hard to imitate some what like er-wăh (not broad war
or wor) er-wăh er-wăh er-wăh.   did I see their
spawn?   faster & faster–the nasal between the 2
syllables–something like what what what spoken
nasally. Then all will be silent. They have spells at it. A
turtle dove went off with a slight whistling note. The
willow near Miles tomorrow or next day *if fair*–   That

at the bridge equally early. The poplar catkins
(P. tremuloides) on Conantum are beginning to curve
downward with their red anthers not yet open within
the down–mulberry-like– Ap– will open tomorrow if
warm say the 10th. The polypody & marginal (?) shield
fern & the spleenwort are evergreens at Lees Cliff. The
slippery elm. Ap in 2 or 3 days   Am surprised to find 2
crowfoot blossoms withered. They undoubtedly
opened the 5 or 6th, say the last–   They must be
earlier here than at the Cliffs where I have observed
them the last 2 years. They are a *little earlier* than the
saxifrage around them here–of which last I find one
specimen at last in a favorable angle of the rock just
opening. I have not allowed enough for the difference
of localities. The columbine shows the most spring
growth of any plant. What is that plant with narrow
toothed leaves which has already shot up so strait 4 or
5 inches on the shelves of the rock?   arabis laevigata?
–   Saw a large bird sail along over the edge of
Wheelers Cranberry meadow just below Fair Haven
–which I at first thought a gull–but with my glass
found it was a hawk & had a perfectly white head & tail
& broad black or blackish wings. It sailed & circled
along over the low cliff & the crows dived at it in the
field of my glass–& I saw it well both above & beneath
as it turned–& then it passed off to hover over the
Cliffs at a greater height–   It was undoubtedly a
white-headed eagle–   It was to the eye but a large
hawk.

   Saw several yellow red poles–(sylvia petechia) on
the willows by the Hubbard bridge   Am not sure I
heard their note–   May have mistaken it formerly for
the Pine warbler–   Its chestnut crown would
distinguish it. Hazel the *very first* male open.

   I find that I can criticize my composition best when
I stand at a little distance from it–when I do not see it,

for instance–. I make a little chapter of contents which
enables me to recall it page by page to my mind–&
judge it more impartially when my MSS is out of the
way. The distraction of surveying enables me rapidly
to take new points of view. A day or two surveying is
equal to a journey.

Pickerel have darted in shallows for nearly a week.

Some poets mature early & die young. Their fruits
have a delicious flavor like strawberries–but do not
keep till fall or winter– Others are slower in coming to
their growth   Their fruits may be less delicious–but
are a more lasting food & are so hardened by the sun
of summer & the coolness of autumn that they keep
sound over winter– The first are June eatings–early
but soon withering–the last are russets which last till
June again.

Ap 9th

I have not noticed any fox col– sparrows for a week
– A large catkinned sallow (?) by the R.R. 10 rods this
side the jog on the W *just* bursting out with its pinkish
orange (before bursting) anthers– There is a little ice
snow still under the N side of hills. Saw several more
red-polls with their rich glowing yellow breasts by the
causeway sides– Saw a wren on the edge of Nathan
Stows wood & field–with some of the habits of a
creeper–lurking along a fallen pine & birch in and out
in a restless manner with tail up–a snuff-colored bird
with many white spots–& a fine chirping note. Can it
be the winter or the wood wren? Callitriche just
started from bottom–pollywogs 2 inches long.
Chrysosplenium out (a few–perhaps a day or 2 where
they rest just on the surface of the water. Cowslip in
Hubbards Close will open the first warm & sunny
hour–Perhaps already at 2nd Division. The skunk
cabbage leaves are unfolding at Bristers Hill edge. & a
grass-like groove leaved plant 3 or 4 inches high

–nosing of skunks now a days–and since frost out in spots– The beaked hazel stigmas out–put it just after the common.

Lycopodium lucidulum is as green as ever– I am surprised to find Walden completely open– When did it open? Ac. to all accounts it must have been between the 6th & 9th   Fair Haven must have opened entirely the 5th or 6th & Walden very nearly at the same time–this proves how steadily it has been melting notwithstanding the severe cold of the last half of March. i.e. it is less affected by transient heat or cold than most ponds. The flowers have blossomed very suddenly this year as soon as the long cold spell was over–and almost all together. As yet the landscape generally wears its november russet.

Ap. 10th 54

April rain. How sure a rain is to bring the tree-sparrows into the yard–to sing–sweetly canary-like.

I bought me a spy-glass some weeks since. I buy but few things–and those not till long after I began to want them–so that when I do get them I am prepared to make a perfect use of them and extract their whole sweet.

Saw a dead sucker yesterday–

Pm to Great meadows by boat & sail back– There are many snipes now feeding in the meadows–which you come close upon & then they go off with hoarse cr-rr-ack cr-r-r-ack– They dive down suddenly from a considerable height sometimes when they alight. A boy fired at a blue-winged teal a week ago. A great many red wings along the waters edge in the meadow –some of these blackbirds quite black–& some *ap. larger*–than the rest– Are they all red-wings? The crimson stigmas like the hazel of the white maple, generally by themselves–make handsome show.

Ap. 11th

Am– Heard the clear rather loud–and rich warble of
a purple-finch and saw him on an elm. Wilson says
they feed on the coverings of the blossoms. It is a
distinct & peculiar note not to be confounded with
anything before it.– I suspect that I heard one on the
1st of april q. v.

Pm   Surveying in Lincoln

Large anthills in the woods–but no ants–

Evening on river– Fine
full moon–river smooth–hear a slight snoring of frogs
on the bared meadows– Is it not the R. palustris? This
the first moon to walk by.

Wednesday Ap 12th.

Surveying for Parks in Lincoln. A white frost this
morning, after the clear moonlight. Parks says he saw
a buffedged butterfly a month ago i.e. before the 17th
March. The hazels are well out today It being a warm
(off-coat) day & their pollen yellows my clothes. When
I went to Mr P's house at noon He addressed me
–"Now, what will you have to drink?" & soon appeared
stirring a glass of gin for himself.

Waited at Lincoln Depot an hour & a half. Heard the
Telegraph harp. I perceived distinctly that man melts
at the sound of music, just like a rock exposed to a
furnace heat. They need not have fabled that Orpheus
moved the rocks & trees, for there is no thing more
insensible than man he sets the fashion to the
rocks–and it is as surprising to see him melted, as
when children see their lead begin to flow in a
crucible. I observe that it is when I have been intently,
and it may be laboriously, at work, and am somewhat
listless or abandoned after it, reposing, that the muse
visits me–& I see or hear beauty. It is from out the
shadow of my toil that I look into the light. The music
of the spheres is but another name for the vulcanic

force   May not such a record as this be kept on one
page of the Book of Life–"A man was melted to-day."

Ap. 13th

A clear & pleasant morning. Walked down as far as
Moores at 8 am & returned along the hill. Heard the
first chip bird sitting on an apple with its head up &
bill open jingling tche-tche-tche-tche-tche &c very
fast. Hear them in various parts of the town. On the
hill near moore's hear the F juncorum–phē-phē-phē
phē phē–phēr-phe-ē-ē-ē-ē-ē-ē-ē– How sweet it
sounds in a clear warm morning in a woodside
pasture–amid the old corn hills–or in sproutlands a
clear & distinct–"like a spoon in a cup" the last part
very fast & ringing. Hear the Pine-warbler also. & *think
I see* a female red-wing flying with some males. Did I
see a baywing? Heard a purple finch on an elm, like a
faint robin.

Pm   sail to Bittern Cliff.

The surface of the water–toward the sun–reflecting
the light with different degrees of brilliancy is very
exhilirating to look at. The red maple–in a day or two–I
begin to see the anthers in some buds–so much more
of the scales of the buds is now uncovered that the
tops of the swamps at a distance are reddened.

A couple of large ducks–which because they flew
low over the water & appeared *black* with a little
white–I thought not black ducks–possibly–velvet or a
merganser. The black ducks rise at once to a
considerable height & often circle about to
reconnoitre.

The golden brown tassels of the alder are very rich
now– The poplar tremuloides by Miles Swamp has
been out–*the earliest catkins* maybe 2 or 3 days. On the
eve–of the 5 ult the body of a man was found in the
river between Fair Haven Pond & Lees–much wasted
– How these events disturb our associations & tarnish

the landscape. It is a serious injury done to a stream.
One or two crowfoots on Lee's Cliff fully out–surprise
me like a flame bursting from the russet ground. The
saxfrage is pretty common–ahead of the crowfoot
now–& its peduncles have shot up. The slippery elm is
behind the common–(which is fully out beside it–) It
will open apparently in about 2 days of pleasant
weather 15 sheds pollen in chamber say 18– I can see
the anthers plainly in its great rusty fusty globular
buds– A small brown hawk with white on rump–I
think too small for a marsh hawk sailed low over the
meadow. Heard now at 5½ Pm that faint bull-frog like
note from the meadows–er-er-er

Many of the button bushes have been broken off
about 18 inches above the present level of the water
(which is rather low) ap. by the ice. Saw a piece of
meadow 12 feet in diameter which had been dropped
on the NW side of Willow Bay on a bare shore–thickly
set with button bushes 5 feet high–perfectly erect
which will no doubt flourish there this summer
– Thus the transplanting of fluviatile plants is carried
on on a very large & effective scale. Even in one year a
considerable plantation will thus be made on what
had been a bare shore–& its character changed. The
meadow cannot be kept smooth– The winter-rye
fields quite green contrasting with the russet

Saw an old log–stripped of bark–either poplar or
maple–4 feet long–its whole upper half covered with
that handsome winkle-like fungus– They are steel
colored & of a velvety appearance–somewhat
semicircular with concentric growths (?) of different
shades–passing from quite black within–through a
slaty blue to (at present) a buff edge   saw some the
16 (inst) wholly faded out to this color on an oak
stump.–Beneath cream color. There are many minute
ones ⅒ of an inch in diameter–the shell like leaf or

ear springing from one side– The full grown are
sometimes united into one leaf for 8 or 9 inches in one
level along the log–tier above tier– –with a scolloped
edge– They are handsomest when 2 or more are
opposed meeting at their bases & make a concentric
circle. They remind you of shells also of butterflies.
The great variety & regularity of the shading are very
interesting. They spring from a slight base rising by a
narrow neck. They grow on stumps & other dead wood
on land–even drift wood left high–just as some marine
shells their relatives grow on drift wood. They are a
sort of dimple. Does not the whole at last fade out to
the buff of the edge.

Friday Ap 14 '54

6 Am to Nawshawtuct– There is a general tinge of
green now discernible through the russet on the bared
meadows & the hills–the green blades just peeping
forth amid the withered ones– Can they be redwings
which I have seen for some time with the redwings
–without red or buff– They have a split-note–perhaps
no *gurgle-éé*. There are spider webs on the meadow
lately bared. It is difficult to find the snipe–though you
stand near where he alights. Saw yellow red-polls on
Cheney's elm–a clear metallic chip & jerks of the tail–

Ap 15th   morning

Snow & snowing–4 inches deep– Yesterday was
very cold– Now I trust it will come down–& out of the
air. Many birds must be hard put to it some tree
sparrows & song sparrows have got close up to the sill
of the house on the S side where there is a line of grass
visible–for shelter. When Father came down this
morning he found a sparrow squatting in a chair in the
kitchen– Does'nt know how it came there. I examined
it a long time but could not make it out. It was 5 or 6
inches long with a somewhat finch-like bill–(bluish
black above & light below) general aspect above pale

brown–mottled with buffish & whitish–bay–& a *little* black on the wings. The crown a faint bay divided by an ashy line with a broad ashy line over eye–& a distincter bay or chestnut line from the angle of the mouth backward. legs *pale clear flesh color–feet black*–claws slender–2 *faint* whitish bars on wings –(the tips of feathers) The breast ashy-white with many dark or black spots edged with bay in chains–*No yellow* about it. A rounded tail–long–& of a pretty uniform pale brown or bay ashy on the inner vanes–but *no white nor black* in it– A rather slender bird. It made me *think* of the bay wing–& of the savannah sparrow

Pm. This cold moist–snowy day–it is easier to see the birds & get near them. They are driven to the first bare ground that shows itself in the road–& the weather &c makes them more indifferent to your approach. The tree sparrows look much stouter & more chubby than usual–their feathers being puffed up & darker also–perhaps with wet   also the robins & bluebirds are puffed up– I see the white undersides of many Purple finches busily & silently feeding on the elm blossoms within a few feet of me–& now & then their bloody heads & breasts   they utter a faint clear chip– Their feathers are much ruffled. The yellow red-poll hops along the limbs within 4 or 5 feet of me.

Martins. the 13th first The arrival of the Purple finches appears to be coincident with the blossoming of the elm–on whose blossoms it feeds–

Johnson in his Wonder-working Providence speaks of "an army of caterpillars" in N E in 1649 so great "that the cart wheels in their passage were painted green with running over the great swarms of them."

Ap 16th '54

A cold disagreeable day–sun not fairly out–yet the snow of yesterday melts apace–you can almost see it

melt. Each time I look out I see more of russet or green
– At first the bare ground showed itself in the middle
of the road & rapidly widened giving the birds wider
pasture; then the grass in the fields began to peep
through & the landscape to acquire a russet hue
again– The green blades under the south side of
the houses & hills appear to have grown wonderfully
since the snow fell & to be several shades darker
green.

   Pm to Epigaea. Saw a fox-col. sparrow still & black
ducks. There are 4 or 5 cowslips open at the 2nd Div.
meadow–1st prob. about the 11th ult. The buds of the
shad bush are much expanded & show considerable
green or yellowish–more than native shrub or tree that
I think of. The may-flower under the snow will not
open for some days at least–maybe a week. The
winkle-fungi are arranged either on the upper half of a
prostrate log–or one above another around a dead
stump– Saw some today almost completely faded to a
dark cream color (or the buff of the edge of mine)
though though alternating with some faint
steel-colored lines.

   When I meet one of my neighbors these days who is
ridiculously stately being offended–I say in my mind
Farewell–. I will wait till you get your manners off
– Why make politeness of so much consequence
when you are ready to assassinate with a word. I do
not like any better to be assassinated with a rapier,
than to be knocked down with a bludgeon. You are so
grand that I cannot get within ten feet of you. Why will
men so try to impose on one another? Why not be
simple & pass for what they are worth only? O such
thin skins, such crockery, as I have to deal with! Do
they not know that I can laugh? Some who have so
much dignity that they cannot be contradicted.
Perhaps somebody will introduce me one day–& then

we may have some intercourse. I meet with several
who cannot afford to be simple & true men but
personate, so to speak, their own ideal of themselves,
try-ing to make the manners supply the place of the
man– They are puff-balls filled with dust and ashes.
Ap 17th 54   Snows again.
   It is remarkable how the American mind runs to
statistics. Consider the number of meteorological
observers & other annual phenomena. The
Smithsonian Institute is a truly national Institution.
Every Shopkeeper makes a record of the arrival of the
first martin or blue-bird to his box. Dod the broker
told me last spring that he knew when the first
blue-bird came to his boxes–he made a memorandum
of it. John Brown Merchant tells me this morning that
the martins first came to his box on the 13th ult–he
"made a minute of it." Beside so many entries in their
day books & ledgers–They record these things.
   Did not see a linaria the past winter though they
were the prevailing bird the winter before. There are
but few F. hiemalis about now   they appear to have
gone north mostly on the advent of warmer weather
about the 5th of April. I look up these snowy days &
see purple finches silently feeding on the elms where I
had heard no sound– They sing somewhat like a
robin–continuously–with a loud canary like twee twee
& che che che– The tree sparrow is still the prevailing
bird

                    Ap 18th
   For 3 or 4 days the lilack buds have looked
green   the most advanced that I have seen   The
earliest gooseberry still earlier in garden (though
smaller buds.
               Pm to stone-heaps by boat
   Scared up snipes on the meadows edge which go off
with their strange zigzag crazy flight & a distressed

sound–craik craik or cr-r-ack cr-r-rack. One booms
now at 3 Pm. They circle round & round & zigzag high
over the meadow & finally alight again descending
abruptly–from that height. Was surprised to see a
wagtail thrush The golden crowned at the Assabet
Spring which inquisitively followed me along the
shore over the snow hopping quite near. I should say
this was the G.C. Thrush without doubt though I saw
none of the gold–if this & several more which I saw
had not kept close to the water. May *possibly* be the
aquaticus. Have a jerk of the forked tail. The male
yellow red-polls breast & underparts are of a
peculiarly splendid and lively yellow–glowing. It is
remarkable that they too are found about willows &c
along the water. Saw another warbler–a–about the
same size in the same localities–*somewhat* creeper like
very restless–more *like* the Tennesee w. than any
methinks. Light slate or bluish slate head & shoulders
–yellowish backward–all white beneath–& a distinct
white spot on the wing–a harsh grating note (?) b
(?)   Saw 2 wood ducks probably–saw a white spot
behind eyes–they went off with a shriller craik than the
black ducks.

I now feel pretty sure that they were crow black
birds which I saw april third with the red wings–   They
are stout fellows with out any red epaulet–& go off
with a hoarser *chuck chuck* with rounded tail. They
make that split singing–& with the red wing feed along
the waters edge. Heard a red wing sing his bobylee in
new wise as if he tossed up a fourpence & it rattled on
some counter in the air as it went up. Saw today a
lesser blackbird–size of cow bird–*slaty black*–on
meadow edge–what was it?

The snow is sprinkled along the street with the large
scales of *buds* from the trees–thus revealing what kind
of *fall* is going on at this season.

Ap 19th

Hear the tree sparrows at Willow hedge-row this morning–ah ha ha yip yip yip yip or twitter twitter twe twe twe–or ah ha ha twitter twitter twe   Very Canary like yet clear as if of aspirated vowels alone –no *t* or *r*

Hear a pine warbler–its note like the jingle of the F. hiemalis on an elm in the street.

Yesterday as I was returning down the Assabet –paddling leisurely in the stern–the sun came out after 2 days of storm or louring weather and shone on the banks covered with snow–   The water which had been perfectly smooth all the afternoon looked smoother yet–and I think that I never beheld so pure and refulgent a white as the upright snowy banks presented. Snow never looks so white in winter.

I had chosen to come to the river that afternoon for there, the air being warm though the earth was covered with snow there was least change. The few sparrows & warblers along the water's edge & on the twigs over the water seemed to forget the wintry prospect. I was surprised to find the river so full of sawdust from the pail factory & Barrett's mill that I could not easily distinguish if the stone heaps had been repaired. There was not a square 3 inches clear. And I saw the saw dust deposited by an eddy in one place on the bottom like a sand-bank. a foot or more deep half a mile below the mill   That is a good stream to explore any summer weather–because the woods border it immediately & you can observe a greater variety of small birds. I can approach them more nearly in my boat than on foot. Melvin was inspecting his traps. From time to time masses of snow overhanging the water & floated saturated down the stream.

The calm bright hour after the sun came out was

very pleasant. I first saw the crescent of clear sky
widening rapidly in the NNW horizon–then the
cheerful sun light on hills & houses northward &
finally it shone out on the north bank & on myself &
on the S. shore–and one song-sparrow when he felt its
influence sang as if with a new influx of joy. How
longed for by the birds–   Farmer says that he saw a
man catch a blue-bird yesterday which was dying in
the snow. As I watched the sparrow sitting in the cold
shadow while the sun was already shining on the
northern bank I wondered that he did not at once fly
to it–ay that he had not kept pace with the sun or fair
weather from the first–   But thus nature rules it &
these winged creatures wait to be shined on or shaded
like ourselves. It was at this time looking down the
river that I saw the 2 woodducks sailing out from the
shore in the smooth water–at first suspecting that they
were tame. Birds are positively curious–e.g. the thrush
I saw that afternoon which hopped out to the end of
the overhanging alders within a few feet to reconoitre
me & my boat.

This is the 5th day that the ground has been covered
with snow–   There first fell about 4 inches on the
morning of the 15th   This had ⅔ melted on the eve of
the 16   Then as much more fell on the 17 with which
tonight (eve of 19th) the ground is still more than half
covered. There has been sleighing. I do not remember
the like   The water was slightly skimmed over along
the edge of the river this morning. A farmer *plowing in*
snow

Pm to Cliffs.

The P. grandid. will not open for a day or 2. There is
considerable growth in the water at the Boiling Spring.
The callitriche is most forward a foot or more long
with its delicate or pretty cup like whorls of leaves
resting on the surface. I see no signs of a blossom.

What is that narrow tooth-leafed & red
stemmed plant which has grown nearly as
much in the water? crosswise. Then there is
the cress next underway. Yet on the whole I think
the columbine in the most favorable places about even
with these. The latter have been less checked the last 4
or 5 days. I saw yesterday at the bottom of the water by
the sides of the river a *yellowish half unfolded* pad
here & there– The green tinge from new springing
grass in the wet meadow as I looked low from my boat
was much more obvious & spring like– I was struck
the same day with the very rigid & sharp triangular
points of a kind of sedge rising 4 or 5 inches above the
water–perhaps that kind that makes the wreck in the
fall. As if it were prepared to contend with the ice
which forms in the night after it has started. That
pretty little moss in beds on the rocks &c at the cliffs
–shows its little reddish cup-like blossoms
now-a-days.

A man was plowing in snow this morning. Saw a
bull-frog in Hayden's pond hole & a small green
grasshopper– A turtle dove flew away from the
birches & lit in his stubble field, and each time when it
flew I heard a note continuously uttered like a pig.
woodpecker or a robin at a distance.

S humilis? out–i.e. the S. in Stows field–prob.
before the 15th say 14th   The sweet-gale below
Emerson's *today*. just out. the male–with its amber
dust.

I thought yesterday that the sparrows must rejoice
to sit in the sun again & dry their feathers & feel its
warmth. I read today that a boy found 26 bluebirds
dead in a hollow tree on the 1st of april in Great
Barrington– That was just after that long cold spell.

It is remarkable how scarce & silent the birds are
even in a pleasant afternoon like this compared with

the morning. Within a few days the warblers have
begun to come. They are of every hue–   Nature made
them to show her colors with. There are as many as
there are colors and shades–   In certain lights nothing
as yesterday against the snow can be more splendid &
celestial than the color of the blue-bird–   On the
creeping juniper there appear to be buds but not
blossoms yet.

Do I ever see the Marsh-hawk   I think the early
large h was it.–   Is it not the sharp-shinned which I
have mistaken for it?

A man came to me yesterday to offer me as a
naturalist a 2 headed calf which his cow had brought
forth–but I felt nothing but disgust at the idea–&
began to ask myself what enormity I had committed to
have such an offer made to me.

I am not intrested in mere phenomena, though it
were the explosion of a planet– –only as it may have
lain in the experience of a human being.

Ap 20

Am to Nawshawtuct–   Heard on the 14th a singular
note on or near the hill like a Guinea-hen or other
fowl–or a squeaking pump-handle. Heard again this
morning & saw 2 large dark birds go off from a walnut
with a loud squeaking quack–   Is it a strange large
woodpecker–or possibly a teal?? Heard the same at
star light–Ker *chuck ker-chuck–ker-chuck*   I think it is
the red-wing only sings bobylee–   Saw one pursuing a
female (?)   I am not sure whether these or the crow
black birds are the earliest. Saw a small black-striped
warbler or fly-catcher?–c–on a willow. Hear the *long*
drawn scold of a flicker–sounding very loud over the
water.

Pm to Island & Hill

A willow coming out–fairly with honey-bees
humming on it in a warm nook–the most forward I

have noticed–for the cold weather has held them in
check–& now different kinds of bees & flies about
them. What a sunny sight & summer sound!

A striped snake on a warm sunny bank. The painted
tortoises are fairly out sunning today.

A very pleasant & warm afternoon–the earth seems
to be waking up–   Frogs croak in the clear pools on
the hill side where rocks have been taken out–& there
is frog-spawn there & little tad poles are very lively in
the sunny water.

I find some advantage in describing the experience
of a day on the day following. At this distance it is
more ideal like the landscape seen with the head
inverted or reflections in water.

4 Pm To Moore's Swamp–

[they are blossom buds] most forward–except the
spiraea–earliest gooseberry in garden thimbleberry &
the lilack–then the chokeberry blossom?–& then
maybe high blue berry blossom? of those I have
noticed.   red maple in a warm place shows anthers &
will open to-morrow if pleasant say 22nd. In the ditch
in the Brown Meadow several yellow lily buds pushed
up 4 or 5 inches. But *water* plants *on the whole* not
decidedly ahead of land or air plants. The pine warbler
on the oakes–running about somewhat creeper like &
now & then uttering a loud ringing vetter vetter vetter
vetter vetter vet faster & faster–with its bright yellow
throat & forked tail.

At starlight by river side–a few faint stertorous
sounds from the awakening meadow–and one or two
faint bulfrogish notes–er-er-er

The sound of the snipes winnowing the evening air
now at starlight invisible but for an instant high over
the meadows is heard far into the village hoo hoo hoo
hoo hoo hoo rising higher & higher or dying away as
they circle round–A ghostly sound–   Is that bittern like

squeak made by them? I do not mean the night-hawk
like squeak.

Ap. 21st

6 Am   Heard the bay-wing sparrow in the redeemed
meadows–none yesterday morning. At a distance hear
only the end of its strain like the ring of a small piece
of steel dropped on an anvil. A few F hiemalis still
about. Are not those little whorls of black pointed
scales the female blossom of the Thuja occidentalis?

Scarcely an April shower yet

How can a man be a wise man, if he does n't know
any better how to live than other men.?–if he is only
more cunning & intellectually subtle? Does Wisdom
work in a treadmill. Does wisdom fail? or does she
teach how to succeed by her example? Is she merely
the miller which grinds the finest logic? Did Plato get
his *living* in a better way or more successfully than his
contemporaries? Did he succumb to the difficulties of
life like other men. Did he merely prevail over them by
indifference or by assuming grand airs–or find it easier
to live because his aunt remembered him in her will?

Pm to Saw Mill Brook

As I was handling the arbor vitae today an odor like
strawberries came from–Is that terebinthine. The lilac
is *beginning to open* today. The snows go off and the
lustre of the winter-green is undiminished. The large
black ants are at work on their hills

The great–scolloped leaf betrays the P.
grandidentata–   How silent & deserted the woods are!
I do not fairly see a chicadee even. Snow with its tracks
would make it seem more inhabited. How we prize
any redness on the ground.–A red stain in a stone or
even a coxcomb lichen on a stump! The Hellebore at
the brook has shot up 6 or 8 inches with its compact
bundles & will soon catch the cabbage. It is *now* one
of the most forward plants.

That goose berry at the brook is the most forward
shrub or tree at present that I can find out of doors in
Concord. It shows more of a leaf than the lilac–or
Missouri currant–which may come next. As I go up the
hill beyond the brook–while the hylodes are heard
behind–I perceive the faintest possible flower-like
scent as from the earth–reminding me of anemonies &
houstonias. Can it be the budded mouse-ears under
my feet?   downy-swaddled–they lie along flat to the
earth like a child on its mother's bosom. I sit on a rock
awhile just below the old trough. These are those early
times when the rich golden brown tassels of the alder
tremble over the brooks–& not a leaf on their
twigs   We are far north with Sir John Franklin–   I see
the first of that bent lake grass on the smooth surface
of a flooded meadow with a dimple at its stem. It is a
warm sight. The fruit of the O. spectabilis? flowering
fern still perfect–   I see on the red cedar the male
blossom buds not yet quite open–& very minute
hollows with whitish scales at the ends of some of the
branchlets which I take to be the female flowers.

The song of the purple finch on the elms (he also
frequents firs & spruce) is rich & continuous–like but
fainter & more rapid than that of a robin–some of the
cherruwit in it & a little of the warble of the martin. A
martin was found dead the 18th after the snows. &
many blue-birds in Brookfield.

Ap 23d

A kingfisher with his crack. cr-r-r-rack.

rain yesterday & today–yet this morning the robin
sings & the blackbirds–& in the yard the tree sparrow,
hiemalis, & song-sparrow. A rain is sure to bring the
Tree spar. & hiemalis to the gardens. I suppose it must
be the seeds of weeds which they are so busily picking
from the bare ground–which their sharp eyes detect.

Geo. Minot says that he used to shoot the red
headed woodpecker–& found their nests on the
trees on his hill side. He used to steal up to the
pigeon-woodpeckers holes & clap his hand over them
& take out the old bird. Then let her go.

The first April showers are even fuller of promise & a
certain moist serenity than the sunny days. How
thickly the green blades are starting up amid the
russet. The tinge of green is gradually increasing in the
face of the russet earth.

Now that the very earliest shrubs are *beginning to
unfold*–Spiraea–gooseberry–honeysuckle
vine–lilac–Missouri currant– Manny herbaceous
plants not evergreen merely make quite a show–as
the skunk cabbage in favorable places Nuphar in the
most favorable places though muddy yellow &
dilapidated–callitriche & the narrow tooth leafed
water plant &c&c–cowslip–columbine–(cress &
chrysosplenium–are not both chiefly evergreen?)
celandine–catnep–saxifrage–dandelion–clover–golden
senecio–sweet flag hellebore (the most forward buds
begin to open🌱–) thistle–shepherd's purse–meadow
saxifrage–   🌱–elder probably

As for the birds I have this to remark– The crows
still frequent the meadows– The lark sings morn &
eve– The black birds red wing & crow–have since
their arrival kept up their bobylee & chattering & split
notes on the willows & maples by the river and along
the meadows edge– They appear to depend much (as
well as crows & robins) on the meadow just left bare
for their food– They are the noisist birds yet– –both
still fly in flocks–though the male red wings have
begun to chase the females– Robins still frequent the
meadows in flocks & sing in the rain– The song
sparrows not in such flocks nor singing so

tumultuously along the water courses in the morning
as in the last half of march– How wary they are–they
will dodge you for half an hour behind a wall or a
twig–& only a stone will make them start–looking
every which way in a minute– So the blackbirds, both
kinds–sidle till they bring a twig bet. me & them. The
flock of black ducks which stayed by so long is now
reduced to a quarter part their number– Before the
4th or 5th of April the F hiemalis was ap. the most
abundant bird of any in great drifting flocks with their
lively jingle–their light col bill against slate
breasts   then on the advent of warmer weather–the
greater part departed– Have the Fox-sparrows gone
also?– I have not seen them of late. As for hawks–after
the one or two larger (perhaps) henhawks in the
winter–& a smaller one in Dec (?)–the first were *large*
Marsh? hawks on trees on the meadow edge or
skimming along it–since which the eagle–the
sharp-shinned–& the smaller brown & white rumped
over meadows which may be the same–&c &c Have
seen the black duck–golden eye–merganser–blue?
winged teal–wood duck– The golden eye seems to
have gone Heard a nuthatch yesterday Ap 22d The
tree spars are the prevailing bird on ground and most
numerous of any for the past month except one white
the hiemalis. They are a chubby little bird with a clear
chestnut crown–a dark spot on the other wise clear
whitish breast–& two light bars on the wings– The
pigeon woodpecker now scolds long & loud morning &
evening. The snipes are still feeding on the
meadows The turtle dove darts solitary about as if
lost. or it had lost its mate– The yellow red poll with a
faint clear *chip* is the commonest *yellow* bird on hills
&c about water. The *chip* sparrow does not sing much
in morning yet. New kinds of warblers have begun to
come within a few days.

I saw yesterday the smoke of the 1st burning of brush which I have noticed, though the leaves cannot be very dry yet.

Pm to Lees Cliff on foot.

It has cleared up. At ivy bridge I see the honey-bees entering the crypts of the skunk-cabbage–whose tips have been bitten by the frost & cold. The first sweet gale which opened a day or 2 ago on the sunny sides of brooks where the sun reached it above the bank–was an interesting sight–full of amber dust. Those are blossom not leaf buds so forward on the shad bush. The Myrtle-bird Yellow-rump warble–was not this warbler C of the 20th? on the willows alders & the wall by Hubbards bridge Slate & white spotted with yellow. – Its note is a *fine* rapid somewhat hissing or whistling se se se se se ser riddler se *somewhat* like the common yellowbird's. The yel red polls are very common on the willows & alders and in the road near the bridge– They keep jerking their tails. I heard one male sing a jingle like che ve ve ve ve vē very fast & accenting the last syllable. They are quite tame. I sit a awhile on the lee side of Conants wood in the sun amid the dry oak leaves & hear from time to time the *fine* ringing note of a pine warbler which I do not see. It reminds me of former days and indescribable things.

Swarms of those little fuzzy gnats now make a faint huming about the railing of the bridge. The bay-wing has a light ring at some distance around the eye– It is also too dark for my prisoner of the 15th ult. Saw my white-headed eagle again 1st at the same place the outlet of Fair Haven Pond. It was a fine sight– He is mainly–i.e. his wings & body–so black against the sky–& they contrast so strongly with his white head & tail. He was first flying low over the water; then rose gradually & circled westward toward White Pond.

Lying on the ground with my glass I could watch him
very easily–& by turns he gave me all possible views
of himself. When I observed him edgewise I noticed
that the tips of his wings curved upward slightly
the more like a stereotyped
undulation   He rose very high at last–till I almost
lost him in the clouds–circling or rather *looping*
along westward   high over river & wood &

farm, effectually concealed in the sky. We who live this
plodding life here below never know how many eagles
fly over us–   They are concealed in the empyrean. I
think I have got the worth of my glass now that it has
revealed to me the white-headed eagle. Now I see him
edgewise like a black ripple in the air–his white-head
still as ever turned to earth–& now he turns his
underside to me–& I behold the full breadth of his
broad black wings somewhat ragged at the edges–   I
had first seen 2 white ducks far off just above the
outlet of the pond–mistaking them for the foaming
crest of a wave–   These flew soon perhaps scared by
the eagle–   I think they were a male & female red
breasted Merganser though I did see the red of the
breast, for I saw his *red bill*–& his head was not large
with a crest like the golden eye very white on breast &
sides–the female–browner–   As ducks often do, they
first flew directly & unhesitatingly up the stream, low
over the water, for half a mile–then turned & came
down–flying 30 or 40 feet above the water the male
leading till they were out of sight. This is the way with
them I notice–they first fly in one direction & then go
off to alight in another. When they came down the
river the male leading–they were a very good example
of the peculiar flight of ducks–   They appeared

perfectly in a line one behind the other–when they are
not they preserve perfect parallelism– This is because
of their long necks & feet–the wings appearing to be
attached mid-way–and moreover in this case of their
perfectly level flight–as if learned from skimming over
the water. Directly after rose 2 blue herons from the
meadow– I find but one red-maple fairly in blossom
on a few twigs over the water today. I think therefore
the 22nd will do for the very earliest.

Had a glimpse of a very small warbler–b'–on a pitch
pine & heard a pleasant & unusual whistle from
him.   was it b' of the 18th??–v ap 26   The Slippery elm
with its dull pinkish (?) blossoms now fully out. I think
on account of the snow it could not have opened
before the *18th*. The sedge was abundant long before
the Crowfoot or saxifrage was– It must be put earlier
than I have allowed. Crowfoot is not yet abundant
though it was earlier than saxifrage–which has now
gone ahead. A thimbleberry under this cliff is at least
as forward as any gooseberry. I find a new plant now 6
or 8 inches high & which will blossom in 2 or 3 days
the arabis laevigata? The columbine is well budded.
Some alders are still handsome–here is a *common*
one very handsome drooping clusters of 3 4 or 5
reddish-brown & greenish yellow catkins 2 to 3 inches
long–with the small reddish female blossoms
stretched over them– How the hazel catkins elongate
themselves at last!

Monday Ap 24th

Am up RR– The river slightly risen again owing to
rain of yesterday morn & day before– Its greatest
height this year was the 17 of march. This is the next
rise of any consequence. As I stand still listening on
the frosty sleepers at Woods crossing by the lupines–I
hear the loud & distinct pump-a-gor of a stake driver.

Thus he announces himself. I find the Shep. Purse
open in Cheney's garden at last. It has run up 8 or
10 inches in some places & *may* have been open a
week–but say just after the snow of the 19th. After a
very mild winter, like that of 52 & 53 it will be one of
the very earliest flowers–say 2d or next after the
chickweed–But last winter it was killed down by the
cold. Yet it is *hardier & more forward* now than the
chickweed–which is still dead & bleached.

Saw a black blackbird without red with a
purplish-green black neck–& somewhat less than a
red-wing in company with 2 smaller slaty black
females (?)   can they be rusty grackles?

Pm up Assabet–& thence to Cedar swamp
The larch will ap. blossom in 1 or 2 days at least both
its low & broad purple coned male flowers & its purple
tipped female cones–Its little leaf-bundles & beginning
to burst. Heard amid the white cedars the fine clear
singing warbler of yesterday–whose harsh note I *may*
have heard the 18th–twer er te te–twer er te te–twer er
te-te tèr but very clear & fast–   Go to new trees like
cedars & firs & you hear new birds–   They increase the
strangeness   Also other strange plants are found
there. I have also observed that the early birds are
about the early trees–like maples alders–willows
–elms &c–

The white cedar female blossoms are *open* & as the
brown male ones are loosened the next day in the
house–   I think the 25th may be called their first day. I
find a raspberry–(thickly clothed with bristles) in this
swamp–as early as the thimble berry. This then might
be put after the gooseberry among native plants
–because this is not so much indebted to a favorable
position–   The gooseberry not at all–growing in a
sheltered i.e. covered swamp. New plant flower

budded at Cedar swamp amid–the high blue-berry
–Pan. Andromeda–clethra &c &c. upright Dense
racemes of reddish flower buds on reddish terminal
shoots.

   Saw a large thin whitish fungus or spunk–14¾ inches
by 8½ from the tree & 2 or 3 thick with concentric
growths of various thickness–within a foot of the
ground on a maple stump– There was a grap-vine &
some other small plants grown directly through–which
it had ap. grown round– The first red maple
blossoms–so very red   over the water are
very interesting. Saw a very   *large* hawk slaty
above & white beneath low over river   was it not a
goshawk? The king fisher flies with a crack-erc'ràck &
a limping or flitting flight from tree to tree before us &
finally after ⅓ of a mile circles round to our rear. He
sits rather low over the water. Now that he has come I
suppose that the fishes on which he preys rise within
reach. Are not they barn swallows v 29th sailing so
thick over the river now at 5½ Pm.

Ap 25

   Am. I think I hear near Geo. Heywoods the tull-lull
yes? Heard & saw my warbler? b' v. n. page of the 23 &
4th on Mr Emersons pines. It is the smallest bird I
have seen this year. Sits still amid the pines not far
below the top–& sings very sweetly loud & clear &
seems farther off than it is–beginning first with very
fine wiry notes & then increasing in volume & melody
till it ends with tweeter tweeter tweeter ter twe. some
of it a martin-like warble– Has sometimes a harsh
scolding note. It is all light perhaps ashy white
beneath–has a little narrow forked tail–ashy (?) under
wings which are consid. shorter than tail–& light
above & below eye–perhaps a whitish bar on wings.
olivaceous (?) above– I think it may be the *golden*

crested wren–though I hardly saw the upper parts–or
possibly the small blue-gray flycatcher. I do not find
the *male* blossoms of the red cedar open yet.

Pm to Ind. Cedar Hill.

Quite warm & the frogs are snoring on the
meadow   I swelter under my great-coat. The
P. Grandidentata is fairly begun–say very first the 23d.
Many shad-flies in the air, and alighting on my
clothes. The summer approach by almost insensibly
increasing lieferungs of heat–each awakening some
new bird or quadruped or reptile. At first we were
compelled to take off our mittens–then to unbutton
our great coat–& *now* perhaps to take it off
occasionally. I have not left it at home yet and wear
thin boots. For some time we have done with little
fire–nowadays let it go out in the afternoon. (To day
(26th) I sat without any.)

Each creature awaits with confidence its proper
degree of heat. I think I saw a pigeon yesterday.
G. Minot says that he saw some a week ago. Saw a
Golden crested wren in the woods near Goose
Pond–(This must be my warblers a & b of Ap 18 b' of
ap 23 & 25)   It sounded far off–and like an imitation of
a robin–a long strain & often repeated–   I was quite
near it before I was aware of it it sounding still like a
faint imitation of a robin–& of a golden robin which
later I often mistook for him.

some chicadees & yellow red polls were first
apparent then my wren on the pitch-pines & young
oaks–   He appeared curious to observe me. A very
interesting & active little fellow darting about amid the
tree tops–& his song quite remarkable & rich & loud
for his size. Begins with a very fine note before its
pipes are filled–not audible at a little distance–then
woriter weter &c &c winding up with *teter teter* all clear
& round. His song is comical & reminds me of the

thrasher. This was at 4 Pm when most birds do not
sing. I saw it yesterday pluming itself & stretching its
little wings– Our smallest bird methinks except the
humming bird– The snuff-colored white spotted
wren I saw some time ago was considerably larger.
Just before this saw on the low bushes–shruboaks &c
by path a large sparrow with ferruginous brown &
white-barred wings–the white-throated sparrow
–uttered a faint ringing chirp. The first partridge
drums in one or two places–As if the earth's pulse now
beat audibly with the increased flow of life. It slightly
flutters all Nature & makes her heart palpitate– Also,
as I stand listening for the wren, & sweltering in my
great-coat–I hear the woods filled with the hum of
insects–as if my hearing were affected–& thus the
summer's quire begins– The silent spaces have
begun to be filled with notes of birds and insects & the
peep & croak & snore of frogs–even as living green
blades are everywhere pushing up amid the sere
ones. I heard that same snoring which I hear on the
river meadows on an inland meadow this Pm–where I
think no bullfrogs are–are they not then the palustris
or else the shad frog? There are now many new
insects in the air. Black ducks still on Flints. The fertile
fruit stems of the flowering (?) fern by the side of the
Flints Pond path more than a foot high are a rich
ornament to the ground–brown four or 5 inches long
& turned to one side contrasting with the lighter
rachis (?)

Saw my thrush of the 18 by the pond– It appears
dark olive ferruginous on rump & tail–with a dark
streak slanting from each cheek & flesh col– legs– The
red cedar has fairly begun today maybe the 1st
yesterday– Put the red yesterday & the white today
 – As I approach the red cedars now I perceive a
delicious straw-berry-like fragrance in the air–like that

from the arbor vitae. The creeping Juniper ap. open
but not yet open. Though I see some amber on the
sweet fern I am in doubt whether to say today or
tomorrow. The wild red cherry (if that is one near
Everetts) privet & buckthorn are *beginning* to leaf
out– The *abele* will prob. blossom to-morrow

Ap 26 '54

Heard at 8 Am the peculiar loud & distinct ring of
the first toad at a distance– April morning weather
–threatening showeriness.

2½ Pm to Lees Cliff on foot–

A still warm overcast day with a SW wind–(this is
what the Indians made so much of) & the finest
possible dew like rain in the air from time to time–now
more of the sun. It is now so warm that I go back to
leave my greatcoat for the first time & the cooler smell
of possible rain is refreshing.

The toads ring more or less

> When the toads begin to ring,
> Then thinner clothing bring
> or off your greatcoat fling

It is not time yet for thin clothes. Did I hear a tree toad
today? As I go over Hubbards land I see A Wheeler
burning brush–clearing up on Fair Haven   Great
volumes or clouds of white smoke are blown gently
north-eastward–while the bright scarlet flame is seen
here & there creeping along its edge. They begin to
burn on the lee side.

The farmers are now busily plowing–*some* setting
out roots & planting. I seem to perceive a slight
fragrance in the air. Found part of a birds head &
bill–I think that of the thrush I saw on the 18th &
yesterday. The bill with notch & what part of the head
is left are exactly like the hermit thrush in F Brown's
collection except that mine is yellow inside bill but his
has prob. faded. & I see that the latter's legs which W
calls dusky are light enough for my bird–& the colors

above olivacious (& foxy rump & tail are the same–but
the h't's spots on breast appear darker– I think I have
seen or heard of more dead birds than usual this
season–read of blue birds–heard of a martin (both
killed by cold)   also seen a dead robin or 2 & this
thrush. The woods are full of myrtle birds this
afternoon–more common & commonly heard than
any–especially along the edge of woods on oaks &c
–their note an oft repeated fine jingle–a ché che,
ché che, ché che or–a tweedle tweedle tweedle
tweedle-twe   as I heard the tull lull from the same
quarter from time to time I think it came from it
–perhaps it may be written–a tea le, tea le, tea le.
These small birds and all small birds seen against the
sky at a little distance look black– There is not
breadth enough to their colors to make any
impression–they are mere motes intercepting the
light–the substance of a shadow– Birds sing all day
when it is warm still & overcast as now–much more
than in clear weather–& the hyla too is heard–as at
evening– The hylodes commonly begins early in the
afternoon & its quire increases till evening– I hear
now snipes far over the medow incessantly at 3¼ pm.
The men bogging in the meadow do not hear them,
and much else–

    The swamp sparrow–very dark with chestnut &
black–& quirk of the tail, flits shyly under the alders
along the cause-way–hides or lurks behind the trunks
like song sparrow & hardly rests a moment in one
place

    The Lark on the top of an apple-tree sings–a tchea te
che then perhaps tche tchea–only a plaintive clear
round note. Hear the first chewink hopping & che
winking among the shrub oaks.

    To day the air is full of birds–they attend the
opening of the buds– The trees *begin* to leaf & the leaf
like wings of birds are in the air– The buds start then

the insects then the birds. Saw prob. a pigeon hawk
skim straight & low over field & wood & another the
next day ap– dark slate col. It is warm & still, almost
sultry, as if there might be a thunder shower before
night. Now look down on Fair Haven. How pleasant in
spring a still overcast warm day like this when the
water is smooth! The sweet gale in blossom forming
islets surrounded by water on the meadow–looks like
sere brown leaves left on. At the Cliff the Prob. T.
Stricta is *just* out today–the honeysuck will be say *the
very earliest* tomorrow v. May 1st– A barberry bush
quite forwardly leafing under the rock–& a young
apple   The early goose berry quite green

         9 Pm   Quite a heavy thunder shower–the
2nd lightning I think–   The vivid lightning, as I walk
the street–reveals the contrast between day & night.
The rising cloud in the west makes it very dark &
difficult to find my way–when there comes a flash
which lights up the street for a moment almost as
brightly as the day–far more so than moonlight–& I see
a person on the sidewalk before me 50 rods off–

             Ap 27 54

 7 Am to Cliffs–   Equisetum arvense on the RR–&
may have been 2 or 3 days–did not look.

 I am at length convinced of the increased freshness
(green or yellow,) of the willow bark in the spring.
Some a clear yellow others a delightful liquid green
– The bark peels well now–how long? The rain of last
night is helping to bring down the oak leaves. The
wood-thrush afar–so superior a strain to that of other
birds. I was doubting if it would affect me as of yore
but it did measurably–   I did not believe there could
be such differences. This is the gospel according to the
wood-thrush. He makes a sabbath out of a week day
– I could go to hear him–could buy a pew in his
church–   Did he ever practise pulpit eloquence? He is

right on the slavery question– The brown thrasher
too is along– I find a threadlike stamen now between
the nutlets of the callitriche prb. 3 or 4 days–some
creature appears to have eaten this plant.

The yellow red polls still numerous–sing chill-lill lill
lill lill lill– The meadow sweet & sweet fern are
beginning to leaf–& the currant in garden. Stood on
cliffs about 7 Am. Through a warm mistiness I see the
waters with their reflections in the morning sun–while
the woodthrush & huckle-berry bird &c are heard–an
unprofaned hour I *hear* the black & white creepers
note–seeser seeser seeser se   What a shy fellow my
hermit thrush! I hear the beat of a partridge & the
spring hoot of an owl now at 7 Am   Hear a faint sort of
oven birds (?) note

It is only the irresolute & idle who have no leisure
for their proper pursuit. Be preoccupied with this,
devoted to it, & no accident can befal you–no idle
engagements distract you. No man ever had the
opportunity to postpone a high calling to a
disagreeable *duty*. Misfortunes occur only when a man
is false to his Genius. You cannot hear music and
noise at the same time. We avoid all the calamities that
may occur in a lower sphere by abiding perpetually in
a higher. Most men are engaged in business the
greater part of their lives, because the soul abhors a
vaccuum–& they have not discovered any continueous
employment for man's nobler faculties. Accordingly
they do not pine–because they are not greatly
disappointed. A little relaxation in your exertion a little
idleness will let in sickness & death into your own
body or your family–& their attendant duties–&
distractions. Every human being is the artificer of his
own fate in these respects. The well have no time to be
sick. Events–circumstances &c have their origin in
ourselves. They spring from seeds which we have

sown. Though I may call it a European War, it is only a phase or trait in my biography that I wot of. The most foreign scrap of news which the journals report to me–from Turkey or Japan–is but a hue of my inmost thought.

Forbes says that the guides who crossed the alps with him lost the skin of their faces–(Ap from the reflection from the snow.)

It is remarkable that the rise & fall of Walden though unsteady & whether periodical or merely occasional are not completed but after many years. I have observed one rise & part of 2 falls. It attains its maximum slowly & surely though unsteadily. It is remarkable that this fluctuation, whether periodical or not, requires many years for its accomplishment–and I expect that a dozen or 15 years hence it will again be as low as I have ever known it.

The salix alba begins to leaf & the catkins are ¾ of an inch long. The balm of Gilead is in bloom about 1½ or 2 inches long & some hang down straight   Quite warm today– In the afternoon the wind changed to east & ap. the cool air from the sea condensed the vapor in our atmosphere making us think it would rain every moment; but it did not till midnight.

Ap. 28 '54

6 Am– Dug up 2 of half a dozen the only black spruce suitable to transplant that I know of hereabouts.

Rain all day making the grass look green–

Nawshawtuct now in the rain looks about as green as a Roxbury Russet. i.e. the russet is yielding to the green. Perhaps the greenness of the landscape may be said to begin fairly now. For the last half of this month indeed a tinge of green has been discernible on the sides of hills. Saw yesterday some cows turned out to pasture on such a hillside   thought they would soon eat up all the grass. This is coincident then with the leafing of the gooseberry or earliest native shrub.

1t you may say is the starting of a few radical leaves &c & grass blades in favorable localities & the blossoming of the earliest trees & herbs

2ndly during the last half of april the earth acquires a distinct tinge of green which finally prevails over the russet–

3d Then begins the leafing of the earliest shrubs & trees & the decided greenness & floweriness of the earth. in May.

4th Then the decided leafiness in June & the first great crop of the year–the leaf or grass crop.

Ap 29

The ideal of a market is a place where all things are bought and sold. At an agricultural meeting in New York the other day (one said that he had lately heard a man inquiring for Spurrey seed: he wanted it to sow on drifting sand.) His presumption had been that if he wanted it, i.e. if there was a demand; there was a supply to satisfy that demand. He went simply to the shop instead of going to the weed itself. But the supply does not anticipate the demand.

This is the 2nd day of rain & the river has risen about as high as any time this year–

Pm to Cliffs by boat in the misty rain.

The barn swallows are very numerous flying low over the water in the rain   I think that those which I saw on the 24 ult were barn and not bank swallows. What an entertainment this river affords! It is subject to so great overflows–owing to its broad intervals, that a day's rain produces a new landscape. Let it rain *heavily* one whole day–& the river will be increased from half a dozen rods in width to nearly a mile in some places–and where I walked dry shod yesterday a-Maying I sail with a smacking breeze to-day, & fancy

that I am a sailor on the ocean. It is an advantage
which all towns do not possess. Off the cliffs I met a
blue-heron flying slowly down stream– He flaps
slowly & heavily–his long level straight & sharp
bill projecting forward–then his keel-like neck
doubled up–& finally his legs thrust out straight
behind– His wings, as I looked
after him, presented this outline
He alighted on a rock & stood erect awhile.

I am surprised to find a few andromedas out just
behind the alders at the oak on Cardinal shore
– Possibly yesterday the very first though it
rained– – At last I find one houstonia just *out* there.

The mouse ear is now fairly in blossom in many
places. It never looks so pretty as now in an april rain,
covered with pearly drops– Its coryms of 5 heads with
one in the center (all tinged red) look like a breast pin
set with pearls.

J Farmer says that this rain will kill many caterpillars
just hatched

As nearly as I can remember & judge plants were
generally out at the following dates–

Wht maple	Ap	7th
Alders		8th
Skunk cab.		9th
Sedge		11
Earliest willows		12 fairly begun not common
		till ap. 20.
hazels		12
P. Tremuloides		14
Crowfoot		13
Saxifrage	Ap.	13
Slip. elm		22nd
com. elm		12th
Cowslip		24th

Sweet gale	23
S humilis	23
red maple	26
Larch	28 (?)
red cedar	26
White	27 (?)
P. Grandidentata	Ap. 26
Sweet Fern	29th
Field horse tail.	28th
Mouse-ear	29th

May 1st

A fine clear morning after 3 days of rain our principal rain storm this year–raising the river higher than it has been yet.

6 Am up RR.

everything looks bright & as if it were washed clean. The red maples–now fully in bloom–show red tops at a distance–   Is that a black cherry so forward in the cow-killer?

When I first found the saxifrage open–I observed that its leave had been eaten considerably.

9 Am to Cliffs & thence by boat to Fair Haven–

I see the scrolls of the ferns just pushed up–but yet wholly invested with wool. The sweet fern has not yet blossomed–its anthers are green & close–but its leaves just beginning to expand are covered with highscented amber-like dots–   Alder leaves beg. to expand in favorable places. The viburnum (lentago or nudum) leaves unexpectedly forward at the Cliff brook & about Miles swamp. I am not sure that I distinguish the nudum now–but suspect the other to be most forward –   Snakes are now common on warm banks. At Lee's Cliff find the early cinquefoil X   I think that the columbine cannot be said to have blossomed there before today. the very earliest. A choke cherry is very strongly flower budded & considerably leaved out there. The early rose is beginning to leaf out.

At Miles swamp–   Benzoin will ap. open tomorrow before any leaves begin. The creeping juniper appears to be now just in bloom–   I see only the female flower–   I sail back with a fair SW wind–   The water is strewn with myriads of wrecked shad-flies erect on the surface–with their wings up like so many schooners all headed one way
What an abundance of food they must afford to the fishes–   Now & then they try to fly & fall on the water again. They ap. reach from one end of the river to the other 1 to a square yard or 2. The scleranthus is out XX & a tuft of that brownish flowered kind of sedge

Pm Up Assabet by boat to Cedar Swamp.

The earliest shrubs & trees to leaf have been thus far–in this order   The earliest gooseberry–raspberries –thimble berry–(perhaps in favorable places only) wild red cherry (if that is one near Everetts v May 5th   It is.)   meadowsweet–red currant & 2d Gooseberry I think here   sweet fern (but is *very* slow to go forward)–S alba & also a small dark native willow Ap 27–Young Black-cherry (if that is one in the Cow catcher and others are as forward)   Choke cherry young shoots–vib (am not sure if lentago is earlier than nudum   as both are leafing put the lentago 1st & nudum next)   Diervilla (if that light stemmed plant on Island is it v May 5)   Barberry (perhaps in favorable places only) & some young apples in like places –Alders (in fav. places–early rose–   Saw 2 black ducks–   Have seen no F. hiemalis for 5 or 6 days. Hear a G. crested wren–at Cedar swamp–   I think that I may

have mistaken the note of the myrtle bird–for that of
the creeper the other morning– A Peet weet–&
methinks I have heard it a day or 2

I have seen Goodwin & Haynes all day hunting
muskrats & ducks–stealthily paddling along the
riverside or by the willows & buttonbushes now the
river is so high & shooting any rat that may expose
himself– In one instance a rat they had wounded
looked exactly like the end of an old rider stripped of
bark–as it lay just on the surface close to the shore
within a few feet of them– Haynes would not at first
believe it a muskrat only 6 or 8 feet off–& the dog
could not find it. How pitiful a man looks about this
sport– Haynes reminded me of the penobscots.

Early starlight by river-side the water smooth &
broad   I hear the loud and incessant cackling of prob.
a pig. woodpecker–what some time since I thought to
be a dif. kind–   Thousands of robins are filling the air
with their trills–mingling with the peeping of hylodes
& ringing of frogs & now the snipes have just begun
their winnowing sounds & squeaks–& I hear Barret's
saw mill beside–& whenever a gun fires–Wheelers
peacock screams.

The flowers of the larch which I examined on the
24th ult have enlarged some what & may now certainly
be considered in blossom–*though the pollen* is *not
quite distinct*– I am not certain whether the 26th was
not too early. The crimson scales of the female cones
are still more conspicuous.

May 2nd '54

The cracks in the ground made by the frost last
winter are still quite distinct.

It is the young black-cherry which is so forward now
May 3d.

Pm in rain to Nawshawtuct   The river rising still
–   What I have called the small pewee on the willow by

my boat–quite small, uttering a short tchevet from
time to time. Some common cherries are quite
forward in leafing say next after the black. The pyrus
arbutifolia of plants I observed would follow the
cherry in leafing   It just begins to show *minute* glossy
leaves. The meadow sweet begins to look fairly
green–with its little tender green leaves making thin
wreaths of green against the bare stems of other plants
this & the gooseberry.–   the next plant in this respect
to the earliest gooseberry in the garden which appears
to be the same with that in the swamp–   I see wood
turtles which appear to be full & hard with eggs.
Yesterday I counted half a dozen dead yel. spot turtles
about Beck Stow's. There is a small dark native willow
in the meadows as early to leaf as the S. alba–with
young catkins–

Anemone nemorosa near the ferns & the sassafras
–ap yesterday XX. The ferns invested with rusty
wool–(Cinamomea?) have pushed up 8 or ten inches &
show some of the green leaf–

May 5th 54

Pm To Boiling Spring–Laurel-glen & Hubbard's
Close–   I observe the following plants leafing in about
this order to be added to the list of May 1st

Elder   has made shoots 2 or 3 inches long–much more
than any other shrub or tree–but is not
common enough to show–   Possibly it should
rank with or next to the gooseberry–

Mt ash larger leaves now than any tree (& the 1st tree
to show green at a little dist.

Cultivated cherry

Pyrus arbutifolia

Horse chestnut

Hazel just passing from buds to leaves

Late gooseberry in garden–

Early apples

? Probably Pears
Wild red cherry in woods
Dwarf or sand-cherry
Hard-hack
Diervilla near laurel glen (comes on fast after
    this)   May 11 is *one* of the most forward of all
Low blackberry–
    Some Young red-maple buds beg. to expand
    Against the wall in front of young Farrar's house a
scroll shaped slender fern now 3 inches high–stem
invested with narrow shining brown scales ⅓ inch
long. The S. tristis now out (not out May 1st) ap the
3d   The same of the Sweet Fern   The red maple
keyes ⟍ are now about ¾ inch long (with stems–)   I
see no ⟋ leaves on black–red–or shrub oaks now
–their buds expanding & showing a green, or yellowish
point–but they still hang on the white oak. May 3d &
4th it rained again–especially hard the night of the 4th
& the river is now very high–far higher than in any
other freshet this year–will reach its height prob.
tomorrow–
    Heard what I should call the twitter & mew of a
goldfinch & saw the bird go over with ricochet flight.
The oak leaves ap. hang on till the buds fairly expand.
Thalictrum anemonoides by Bristers spring on
hillside–ap. X   Some skunk cab. leaves are now 8 or
9 inches wide near there   These & the hellebore make
far the greatest show of any herbs yet. The peculiarly
beautiful clean & tender green of the grass there!
Green herbs of all kinds–tansy–buttercups &c &c &c
now make more or less show–   Put this with the grassy
season's beginning. Have not observed a tree sparrow
for 4 or 5 days. The Emerson children found blue &
white violets May 1st at Hub's close–prob. v. ovata &
blanda but I have not been able to find any yet. S. alba
XX

May 6th 54

PM to Epigaea via Clam Shell Hill.

There is no such thing as pure *objective* observation– You observation–to be interesting i.e. to be significant must be *subjective* The sum of what the writer of whatever class has to report is simply some human experience–whether he be poet or philosopher or man of science– The man of most science is the man most alive–whose life is the greatest event–senses that take cognizance of outward things merely are of no avail. It matters not where or how far you travel –the farther commonly the worse–but how much alive you are. If it is possible to conceive of an event outside to humanity–it is not of the slightest significance –though it were the explosion of a planet– Every important worker will report what life there is in him– It makes no odds into what seeming deserts the poet is born. Though all his neighbors pronounce it a Sahara–it will be a paradise to him–for the desert which we see is the ressult of the barrenness of our experience. No mere wilful activity whatever–whether in writing verses or collecting statistics will produce true poetry or science– If you are really a sick man it is indeed to be regretted for you cannot accomplish so much as if you were well. All that a man has to say or do that can possibly concern mankind, is in some shape or other to tell the story of his love– And if he is fortunate an keeps alive he will be forever in love – This alone is to be alive to the extremities– It is a pity that this divine creature should ever suffer from cold feet–a still greater pity that the coldness so often reaches to his heart– I look over the report of the doings of a scientific association–and am surprised that there is so little life to be reported– I am put off with a parcel of dry technical terms– Any thing living is easily & naturally expressed in popular language. I

cannot help suspecting that the life of these learned
professers has been almost as inhuman & wooden as a
rain guage or self-registering magnetic machine. They
communicate no fact which rises to the temperature
of blood heat   It does'nt all amount to one rhyme.

The ducks appear to be gone–(though the water is
higher than any time since that greatest of all rises I
think–Reached its height yesterday–The arches are
quite concealed) swept by with the spring snow & ice
& wind–though today it has spit a little snow & is *very*
windy (NW) and cold enough for gloves– Is not that
the true spring when the F. hiemalis & tree sparrows
are with us singing in the bold mornings–with the
song spars–& ducks and gulls are about? The V. ovata
this end of Clamshell Hill–perhaps a day or two–let it
go then May 1st–also Dandelions perhaps the 1st
yesterday– This flower makes a great show–a sun
itself in the grass– How emphatic it is– You cannot
but observe it set in the liquid green grass even at a
distance– I am surprised that the sight of it does not
affect me more–but I look at it as unmoved as if but a
day had elapsed since I saw it in the fall. As I
remember–the most obvious & startling flowers as yet
have been the crowfoot cowslip–& dandelion–so much
of a high color against the russet or green– We do not
realize yet so high & brilliant a flower as the red lily or
arethusa– Horse mint is an inch or two high & it
refreshing to scent it again. The Equisetum Sylvaticum
XX has just bloomed against Hosmers gap.

It is the young shoots of the choke cherry which are
the more forward–those which are not blossom
budded–& this is the case with most trees & shrubs
– These are growing while the older are
blossoming. female flower of sweet gale   how
long   At ministerial swamp the anthers of the larch
appear now effoete. I am surprised to find a larch

whose female cones are pure white (not rose or
crimson)   The bundles of larch leaves are now fairly
separating. Meadow saxifrage just out at 2d Div. The
cowslip now makes *a show* there though not
elsewhere–& not there as much as it will. There is a
large & dense field of a small rush there already a foot
high whose old & dead tops look like blossoms at a
distance. The may flower is in perfection. It has prob.
been out more than a week.

   Returned over the hill back of J.P Brown's–   Was
surprised at the appearance of the flood–seen now
from the same side with the westering sun–it looks like
a *dark blue* liquid like indgo poured in amid the
hills–with great bays making up between them
–flooding the causeways & over the channel of each
tributary brook–another Musketaquid making for
inland. I see in the distant the light feathery willow
rows on the Causeway stretching across it–the trees
just blooming & coming into leaf–and islolated red
topped maples standing far in the midst of the flood.
This dark blue water is the more interesting because it
is not a permanent feature in the landscape. Those
white froth lines conform to the direction of the wind
& are from 4 to 7 or 8 feet apart.

   Rembering my voyage of May 1st–& Goodwin &
Haynes–hunting–you might have passed up & down
the river 3 or 4 miles & yet not have seen one
muskrat–yet they killed 6 at least–   One in stern
paddling slowly along while the other sat with his gun
ready cocked & the dog erect in the prow–all eyes
constanly scanning the surface amid the buttonbushes
& willows–for the rats are not easy to distinguish from
a bunch of dried grass or a stick–   Suddenly one is
seen resting on his perch & crack goes the gun and
over the dog instantly goes to fetch him. These men
represent a class which probably always exists even in

the most civilized community & allies it to the most
savage. Goodwin said in the morning–that he was
laying stone–but it was so muddy on account of the
rain that he told Haynes he would like to take a cruise
out–

May 7 54

I have noticed the steel-colored velvet-like lichen on
the stumps of maples especially–also on oaks &
hickories. Sometimes where a maple grove has been
cut down some years every stump will be densely
clothed with them.

Our principal rain this spring was Ap. 28-9-& 30 &
again May 3d & 4th ap. the settling storm of the
season. The great source of freshets far & wide– I
observed the swallows yesterday–barn-swallows &
some of those white bellied with grayish brown
backs–flying close to the surface of the water near the
edge of the flooded meadow. Probably they follow
their insect-prey.

Pm to Cliffs.

The causeways being flooded I have to think before
I set out on my walk how I shall get back across the
river.

The earliest flowers might be called May-day
flowers–if indeed the sedge is not too far gone for
one then. A white throated sparrow still (in
woods)   Viburnum lentago & nudum are both leafing
& I believe I can only put the former first because it
flowers first. Cress at the boiling spring one flower
XXX. As I ascend Cliff Hill the 2 leaves of the sol. seal
now spot the forest floor pushed up amid the dry
leaves. Vac. Pennsylvanicum leafing–   Flowers–e.g.
willow & hazel catkins are self registering indicators of
fair weather. I remember how I waited for the hazel
catkins to become relaxed & shed their pollen–but
they delayed–till at last there came a pleasanter &

warmer day & I took off my great coat while surveying
in the woods–& then when I went to dinner at noon
–hazel catkins in full flower were dangling from the
banks by the roadside & yellowed my clothes with
their pollen. If man is thankful for the serene & warm
day–much more are the flowers– From the Cliffs I
again admire the flood–the now green hills rising out
of it   It is dark blue–clay slate & light blue as you stand
with regard to the sun   With the sun high on one side
it is a dirty or clayey slate–directly in front covered
with silvery sparkles far to the right or north dark blue
farther to the SW light blue. My eyes are attracted to
the level line where the water meets the hills now in
time of flood. converting that place in to a virgin or
temporary shore. There is no strand–nothing worn;
but if it is calm we fancy the water slightly heaped
above this line as when it is poured gently into a
goblet. (How in the spring we value any smoothness
gentleness–warmth!) It does not beat but simply lave
the hills   already the peetweet futters & teters along it
aflight farther back–submerging the blossoming
flowers which I went to find– I see the sweet-gale
deeply buried & the V. blanda &c &c,. & the A.
calyculata and the cowslips–   I see their deluged faces
at the bottom and their wrecked petals afloat. I paddle
right over Mile's meadow where the bottom is covered
with cowslips in full bloom–their lustre dimmed they
look up with tearful faces. Little promontories at Lee's
Cliff clothed with young pines make into the water–yet
they are rarely submerged–as if Nature or the trees
remembered even the highest floods & kept out of
their way–avoiding the shore–leaving a certain neutral
ground. Early strawberry just out X   I found an
Amelanchier botryapium XX with its tender reddish
green leaves *already* fluttering in the wind & stipules
clothed with white silky hairs–& its blossom so far

advanced that I thought it would open tomorrow
– But a little farther there was another which did not
rise above the rock but caught all the reflected heat
which to my surprise was fully open– Yet a part
which did rise above the rock was not open– What
indicators of warmth. No thermometer could show it
better. The amelanchier botryapium leaves begin now
to expand. The Juniper branches are now tipped with
yellowish & expanding leaf-buds–put it just before the
larch. I begin to see cows turned out to pasture. I am
inclined to think some of these are coarse windy days
when I cannot hear any bird.

What are are those small ferns under the eaves of
the rocks at the cliffs–their little balls unrolling as they
ascend–now 3 or 4 inches high

How many plants have these crimson or red
stigmas–Maples–hazels–sweet gale–sweet-fern   High
blackberry leafing.

The leaves are now off the young oaks & shrub oaks
on the plain below the cliffs except the wht. oaks
which leaf later. I noticed it else where first May 5th
–when, or a day or two before perhaps, they suddenly
cast off their winter clothing–& the plain now appears
thinly covered with gray stems–but in a short month
they will have put on a new green coat. They wear
their leaves almost all the year. The partridge & rabbit
must do without their shelter now a little while

A ruby-crested wren by the Cliff brook–   This was
the same I have called golden crowned–& so described
by W–I should say except that I saw its ruby crest–a
chubby little bird–saw its ruby crest & heard its harsh
note–   I did nt see the crest of the G.C. & I did not
hear this R.C. sing like the former.   have I seen the
two? The birds I have described as such were the
same. Hellebore is the most noticeable herb now.
Alders–young maples of all kinds–& ostrya–are now

beginning to leaf. I observe the phenomena of the
sea-shore by our river side–now that there is quite a
sea on it & the meadow.–though the waves are but
8 inches or a foot high. As on the sea beach the waves
are not equally high & do not break with an equally
loud roar on the shore–there is an interval of 4 or 5 or
half a dozen waves before between the larger ones. In
the middle of the meadow where the waves run
highest only the middle & highest parts of the waves
are whitened with foam–where they are thinnest &
yield to the wind apparently while their broad bases
are detained by union with the water–but next the
shore where their bases are much more detained by
friction on the bottom   their tops for their whole
length curve over very regularly like a snow drift & the
water is evenly poured as over a dam & falls with foam
& a roar on the water & shore–   It is exhilirating to
stoop low & look over the rolling waves N.W. The black
rolling waves remind me of the backs of waves–   It is
remarkable how cleanly the water desposits its
wreck–now spotted with cranberries–   There is a bare
space of clean grass perfectly clean and about a foot
wide now left between the utmost edge of the breakers
& the steep & abrupt edge of the wreck. So much it has
gone down. Thus perfectly the water deposits what
floats on it on the land. The oak buds–black–shrub–&c
except wht oak–are now conspicuously swolen–   A
spreading red maple in bloom–seen against a
favorable background–as water looking down from a
hill side–is a very handsome object–presenting not a
dense mass of color–but an open graceful & etherial
top of light crimson or scarlet–not too obvious &
staring–slightly tinging the landscape as becomes the
season,–a veil of rich workmanship & high color
against the sky or water or other trees.

At sunset across the flooded meadow to
Nawshawtuct. The water becoming calm. The sun is
just disappearing as I reach the hill-top–& the
horizon's edge appears with beautiful distinctness. As
the twilight approaches or deepens the *mts* those
pillars which point the way to heaven assume a deeper
blue. As yet the aspect of the forest at a distance is not
changed from its winter appearance, except where the
maple tops in blossom in low lands tinges it red. & the
elm tops are in fruit in the streets–and is there not
general but slight reddish tinge from expanding buds?
Scared up ducks of some kind.

May 8th

Am to Nawshawtuct–   A female red-wing I have not
seen any before. Hear a yellow bird in the direction of
the willows–its note coarsely represented by
che-che-che-char-char char–   No *great* flocks of
black-birds on tree tops now–nor so many of robins.

Saw a small hawk flying low about size of a robin
–tail with black bars–prob a sparrow hawk–prob the
same I have seen before. (Saw one at Boston next day
–mine was the Pig. hawk–slaty above–the male–&
coarsely barred with black on tail–   I saw these distinct
bars at a distance as mine flew. It appeared hardly
larger than a robin. Prob. this the only hawk of this
size that I have seen this season. The sparrow-hawk is
a rather reddish brown & *finely* & thickly barred above
with black. Missouri currant XXX. I hear the voices of
farmers driving their cows past to their up country
pastures now–   The first of any consequence go by
now–

Pm by boat to Fair Haven–

The water has fallen a foot or more but I cannot get
under the stone bridge–so haul over the road. There is
a fair & strong wind with which to sail up stream &

then I can leave my boat depending on the wind
changing to SW soon. It is long since I have sailed on
so broad a tide.

How dead would the globe seem–especially at this
season, if it were not for these water surfaces. We are
slow to realize water–the beauty & magic of it. It is
interestingly strange to us forever–   Immortal water
–alive even in the superficies–restlessly heaving now &
tossing me & my boat & sparkling with life. I look
round with a thrill on this bright fluctuating surface on
which no man can walk–whereon is–no trace of foot
step–unstained as glass. When I got off this end of the
Hollowell Place I found myself in quite a sea with a
smacking wind directly aft. I felt no little exhiliration
yet at the same time a slight awe, as I drove before this
strong wind over the great black backed waves–I
judged to be at least 20 inches or 2 feet high–cutting
through them. and heard their surging & felt them toss
me. I was even obliged to head across them & not get
into their troughs–for then I could hardly keep my
legs. They were crested with a dirty-white foam & were
10 or 12 feet from crest to crest. They were so black–as
no sea I have seen–large & powerful & made such a
roaring around me–that I could not but regard–them
as gambolling monsters. of the deep.

They were melainai–what is the Greek for waves?
This is our black sea. You see a *perfectly black* mass
about 2 feet high & perhaps 4 or 5 feet thick & of
indefinite length–round backed or perhaps forming a
sharp ridge with a dirty white crest–tumbling like a
whale unceasingly before you. Only one of the epithets
which the poets have applied to the color of the sea
will apply to this water–mlaine μελαινα (?) θαλασσα. I
was delighted to find that our usually peaceful river
could toss me so–   How much more exciting–than to
be planting potatoes with those men in the field–what

a dif world! The waves increased in height till reached
the bridge–the impulse of wind & waves increasing
with the breadth of the sea. It is remarkabable that it
requires a very wide expanse to produce so great an
undulate– The length of this meadow lake in the
direction of the wind is about a mile–its breadth
varying from a mile to a quarter of a mile–& the great
commotion is toward the southerly end– Yet after
passing the bridge I was surprised to find an almost
smooth expanse as far as I could see–though the
waves were small about 3 inches high at 50 rods
distance. I lay awhile in that smooth water & though I
heard the waves lashing the other side of the cause
way I could hardly realize what a sea I just sailed
through. It sounded like the breakers on the sea shore
heard from terra-firma.

   Lee's Cliff is now a perfect natural rockery for
flowers– These gray cliffs & scattered rocks with
upright faces below reflect the heat like a hot-house
– The ground is whitened with the little white cymes
of the saxifrage now shot up to 6 or 8 inches, and more
flower-like dangling scarlet columbines are seen
against the grey rocks–& here & there the earth is
spotted with yellow crowfoots–and a *few* early
cinque-foils–(not to mention houstonias the now
mostly effoete sedge–the few v. ovatas whose deep
violet is another kind of *flame* as the crowfoot is
yellow–hanging their heads low in the sod. & the as yet
inconspicuous veronica) While the early amelanchier
botryapium overhangs the rock & grows on the
shelves–with its loose open flowered racemes curving
downward waving and rather delicate or graceful
racemes of narrow petalled white flowers red on the
back–& innocently cherry-scented. as if it had drunk
cherry-bounce & you smelled its breath. To which is to
be added the scent of bruised catnep–& the greenness

produced by many other forward herbs–& all
resounding with the hum of insects–and all this while
flowers are rare elsewhere. It is as if you had taken a
step suddenly a month forward–or had entered a
green-house.

The rummy scent of the different cherries is
remarkable. The veronica serpyllifolia out say
yesterday X   Not observed unless looking for it–like
an infants hood–its pretty little blue-veined face.
Cerastium viscosum ap. today X first.

As I returned I saw in the Miles meadow on the
bottom 2 painted tortoises fighting. Their sternums
were not particularly depressed–   The smaller had got
firmly hold of the loose skin of the larger's neck with
his jaws & most of the time his head was held within
the others shell–but though he thus had the "upper
hands" he had the least command of himself & was on
his edge–   They were very moderate–for the most part
quite still as if weary & were not to be scared by me
– Then they struggled a little & their flippers merely
paddling the water–& I could here the edges of their
shells strike together–   I took them out into the boat
holding by the smaller which did not let go of the
larger & so raising both together–   Nor did he let go
when they were laid in the boat. But When I put them
into the water again they instantly separated &
concealed themselves.

The hornbeam has lost its leaves–in this respect put
it before the wht oak–and for present after the other
oaks–judging from buds. Feverbush well out now.

Tuesday May 9th   To Boston & Cambridge.

Currant in garden X, but ours may be a late kind.
Purple finch still here–   Looking at the birds at the Nat
Hist Rooms–I find that I have not seen the crow
blackbird at all yet–this season–   Perhaps I have seen
the rusty blackbird–though I am not sure what those

slaty black ones are as large as the redwings–nor those pure-black fellows–unless rusty-black birds. I think that my blackbirds of the morning of the *24* may have been cow-birds.

Sat on end of long wharf– Was surprised to observe that so many of the men on board the shipping were pure countrymen in dress & habits–& the sea-port is no more than a country town to which they come atrading– I found about the wharves steering the coasters & unloading the ships men in farmer's dress As I watched the various craft successively unfurling their sails & getting to sea–I felt more than for many years inclined to let the wind blow me also to other climes.

Harris showed me a list of plants (in Hovey's Magazine–(I think for 42 or 3) not in Big's Botany–17 or 18 of them–among the rest a pine I have not seen–&c &c q.v. That early narrow curved winged insect on ice & river which I thought an ephemera he says is a *Sialis*–or may be rather a *Perla*– Thinks it the Donatia palmata–I gave him– Says the Shad flys (with streamers & erect wings–are ephemerae– he spoke of podura nivalis–I think meaning ours.

Planted melons.

May 10th

Now in the mornings I hear the chip-bird under my windows at & before sunrise. Warbling vireo on the elms– The chimney swallow A peach X? out in yard where it had been covered by the snow– The cultivated cherry in bloom X

8 Am to Talls Island–taking boat at Cliffs–

Had some rain about day-light which I think makes the weather uncertain for the day–a damp april-like mistiness in the air– I take an umbrella with me – The S. alba (& also 1 or 2 small native ones by river

of similar habits) their catkins together with their
leaves make the greatest show now of any trees (which
are indigenous or have fairly established themselves)
though a *very few* scattered *young* trembles suddenly
streak the hillsides with their tender green in some
places–& perhaps *young* balm of gileads show in
someplaces–not important here–rather with birches
but with the willows it is general–and from their size &
being massed together they are seen afar–   The
S. alba–*partly* indeed from its commonness & growing
together–is the first of *field* trees whose growth makes
an impression on the careless & distant observer–A
tender yellowish green–   (The mt ash–Horsechestnut
& perhaps some other cultivated trees–indeed if we
regard them separately & their leaves alone which are
much larger–are now ahead of the willows)   The
birches of all kinds with catkins begin to show a light
green   The inquisitive yorrick of the wilson's thrush,
though I hear no veery note–this at entrance of
deep-cut–   The oven bird & note loud &
unmistakeable making the hollow woods sing–   This is
decidedly smaller than what I have taken to be the
hermit thrush. The black and white creeper
unmistakable from its creeping habit. It holds up its
head to sing sharp & fine te che, te che, te che, te che,
te che te che te chē. The oven birds note is much
louder broader & more swinging. The latter sits on a
low twig quite within the wood. Yesterday was a quite
warm day & these new birds I hear directly after it–

   Vac. Pennsylvanicum X 1st just out & I see a
Humblebee about some others which are not
open–knocking at their doors–which if open would
be too small for him to enter. V pedata already
numerous–say yesterday without doubt–X at Lupine
Knoll–paler than the ovata–their pale faces–   The field
sparrow resembles a more slender tree sparrow

without the spot on breast with a light colored bill &
legs & feet–ashy white breast & beneath eye a
drab–callow look–note *phe phe phe phe phe phe,–phe
phe-e-e-e-e*   holds up its head the while   Thorns are
leafing   V. blanda by corner road at brook–& below
Cliff Hill spring. Canoe birch & White do leafing

There is a dew or rather rain drop in the centre of
the sundial (lupine) leaf–where its 7 or 8 leafets
meet–over the sand. Cornel sericea leafing along river.
I hear the fine wiry mew of the songsparrow–   A
Catbird mewing.

Saw coupled on a hillock by the water 2 what I
should have called black snakes–a uniform very dark
brown–the male much the smallest–   The undside
–what little I noticed of the rear of the latter was a
bluish slate–but when they ran into *the water*–I
observed dull–yellowish transverse bars on the back of
the female–(did not observe the other there) and when
I turned over the male had a glimpse of a reddish or
orange belly.–   Were they water adders or black
snakes–   The largest was perhaps between 3 & 4 feet
–   If that is the leaf of the arrow-wood which looks so
much like a cornel it will rank next to the Viburnum
nudum v plant by bridge. In Boston yesterday an
ornithologist said significantly–"if you held the bird in
your hand"–but I would rather hold it in my affections
–   The wind is SW & I have to row or paddle up. The
shad-bush in blossom–is the first to show like a fruit
tree–like a pale peach–on the hill sides–seen afar amid
gray twigs amid leafless shruboaks &c before even its
own leaves are much expanded–   I dragged & pushed
my boat over the road at Dea Farrar's Brook–carrying
a roller with me–   It is warm rowing with a thick coat
–   Heard the first regular bullfrog trump–not *very* loud
however–at the swamp   Wht-oaks SW of Pantry.
Heard the night warbler   Saw 3 ducks on Sudbury

meadows still one partly white the others all dusky
prob. black ducks. As to the first with a large dark head
& white breast & sides I am not sure whether it was a
golden eye or whistler. Dined at Talls Island. The
tupelo terminates abruptly as if mutilated at top–and
the slender straggling branches decline thence
downward–often longer than the tree is high. The
shores of these meadows do not invite me to land on
them–they are too low– A lake requires some high
land close to it– Meeting House hill is the most
accessible hereabouts. Anemones common
now– They love to grow under brush or tree tops
which the choppers have left– Shad leaves develop
fast P. pines started for 2 or 3 days in some places the
largest shoots now 4 inches– Returning stopped at
Rices– He was feeding his chickens with Ind meal &
water– While talking with him heard bobolinks. I had
seen what looked like a great stake just sticking out
above the surface of the water on the meadows &
again covered as if it were fastened at one end– It
finally disappeared and probably was a large mud
turtle. Rice told me that he had hunted them– You go
a little later in this month–a calm forenoon when the
water is smooth–& "the wind must be south"–& see
them on the surface– Dea Farrars meadow in time of
flood (I had come through this) was a good place. It
began to sprinkle–& Rice said he had got "to bush that
field"–of grain before it rained–& I made haste back
with a fair wind & umbrella with sail. Were those
cowbirds in Mile's meadow about or near the cows?
Alders generally have fairly begun to leaf I came on
rapidly in a sprinkling rain–which ceased when I
reached Bittern Cliff & the water smoothed somewhat
– I saw many red maple blossoms on the
surface. Their keys now droop gracefully about
the stems– A fresh growing scent comes from

the moistened earth & vegetation–& I perceive the
sweetness of the willows on the causeway.

–Above the RR bridge I saw a kingfisher twice
sustain himself in one place about 40 feet above the
meadow by a rapid motion of his wings–somewhat like
a devils needle–not progressing an inch–ap. over a
fish. Heard a tree-toad.

May 11th

6 Am to Laurel Hillside by Walden–

Earliest gooseberry in Garden open. X   Heard a
maryland yel. throat about alders at Trillium
woods–where I first heard one last year–but it finds
the alders cut down in the winter   Yellow birch ap.
open. its leaf as forward as the *blossom* (*comparitively*
–with other birches)   Many small swallows hovering
over Deep Cut–prob– bank swallows (?)   Hear the
golden-robin.

It is wonderful how surely these distinguished
travellers arrive when the season has sufficiently
revolved. Prunus Americana Canada Plum yesterday at
least at Mr Brooks' X (a Common Plum today X

To sum up leafing of trees &c since May 5th add
these

creeping Juniper

Larch–   bundles fairly separated on some trees

May 6   open slowly

Early blueberry

Amelanchier botryapium   It came forward fast

High blackberry

young Rock Maple

    "   Red   "

    "   White?

Alders generally

Ostrya

Some young trembles suddenly leafed

2 Balm of Gileads

Some Thorns
Yel birch
Canoe birch
White   ″
pitch pine   some shoots now 4 inches long
Cornus sericea.

                    Pm to Saw Mill Brook
    White Pines have started   put them with Pitch
– Nepeta just out X   I am in a little doubt about the
wrens (I do not refer to that snuff colored one)
whether I have seen more than one–all that makes me
doubt is that I saw or ruby perhaps it might be called
fiery crest on the last–not golden–

    Amelanchier oblongifolia say yesterday X   It does
not leaf till it flowers   prob. the one whose fruit I
gathered last year–   Sweet gale has just begun to leaf

    The willows on the turnpike now resound with the
hum of bees & I hear the yellowbird & maryland
yellow throat amid them. These *yellow* birds are
concealed by the yellow of the willows. The cornels
generally have fairly started excepting the C. Florida
(have not noticed the bunch berry & round leaved)
and for aught I have seen yet may be placed in the
order of their flowering–alternate–pannicled–sericea
–putting all on the day of the sericea i.e. yesterday.
Wild red cherry in road near Everetts open XXX

    The most forward oak *leafets* are I think in one place
a red say just started–but I see shrub oak & swamp
white catkins in a few places an inch long–   Some
shrub-oak flower buds are yellowish some reddish.

    The thalictrum anemonoides is a perfect & regular
white star–but methinks lacks the interesting red tinge
of the other. Some young chestnuts have begun–The
lower branches and are earlier than any oaks. White
birches are *suddenly* leafing in some places so as to

make an open veil or gauze of green against the other
trees– Young horn-beams–just before cornels–the old
ones just begun to leaf Various slender ferns without
wool springing up at Saw Mill Brook–some quite dark
also brake a foot high. The arrow-wood has just
begun. The *young* black birch leafing with
others While at the Falls I felt the air cooled & hear
the muttering of dist. thunder in the N.W. & see a dark
cloud in that direction indistinctly through the wood.
That distant thundershower very much cools our
atmosphere. And I make haste through the woods
homeward via Hubbards Close. Hear the evergreen
forest note. The true poet will ever live aloof from
society wild to it–as the finest singer is the
wood-thrush a forest bird. The shower is apparently
going by on the north. There is a low dark blue black
arch–crescentlike in the horizon sweeping the distant
earth there with a dusky rainy brush–and all men like
the earth seem to wear an aspect of expectation
– There is an uncommon stillness here disturbed only
by a rush of the wind from time to time– In the village
I meet men making haste to their homes for though
the heavy cloud has gone quite by the shower will
probably strike us with its tail.

Rock maple keys &c now 2 inches long prob. been
out some days. Those by the path on common not out
at all. Now I have got home there is at last a still cooler
wind with a rush–& at last a smart shower–slanting to
the ground, without thunder–

My errand this afternoon was chiefly to look at the
gooseberry at Saw Mill Brook– We have 2 kinds in
garden–the earliest of same date to leaf with that in the
swamp–but very thorny–& one later just open
XXX The last is ap. the same with that by Everett's
also just open XX & with that this side of E. woods I

also know one other i.e. the one at Saw Mill Brook
plainly distant with long petioled & glossy leaves–but
as yet I find no flowers– I will call this for the present
the swamp gooseberry– Stellaria media–ap. not long.
Butternut beginning to leaf–

On meadows in boat at Sunset.   to Island &c
The rain is over– There is a bow in the east   The
earth is refreshed–the grass is wet–the air is warm
again & still– The rain has smoothed the water to a
glassy smoothness. It is very beautiful on the water
now–the breadth of the flood not yet essentially
diminished.

The ostrya will ap. shed its pollen tomorrow   High
blueberry is just leafing– I see the kingbird

It is remarkable that the rad. leaves of golden rod
should be already so obvious. e.g. the broad leaved at
Saw Mill Brook   What need of this haste? Now at last I
see crow black birds without doubt–they have prob.
been here before for they are put down under april in
the bird book (for 37)   They fly as if carrying or
dragging their precious long tails (broad at the end
through the air. Their note is like a great rusty spring &
also a hoarse chuck. On the whole I think they must
have been rusty grackles which I mistook for this bird.
& I think I saw their silvery irides–look like red wings
without the red spot. Ground ivy *just* begins to leaf–

I am surprised to find the great poplar at the island
conspicuously in leaf–leaves more than an inch
broad–from top to bottom of the tree & are already
fluttering in the wind.–& others near it–Conspicuously
before any other native tree–as tenderly green wet &
glossy as if this shower & opened them. The full grown
wht maples are as forward in leafing now as the young
red & sugar ones are now–only its leaves are smaller
than the last– Put the young at a venture after the low

blackberry–the old just before the other maples. The balm of gilead is rapidly expanding & I scent it in the twilight 20 rods off.

The earliest of our indigenous trees then to leaf *conspicuously* is the early tremble (the one or more willows which when they leaf flower like the S alba–with their small leaves are *shrubs* hardly trees) Next to it–close upon it–*some* white birches –and ap. close upon this the balm of gilead & *wht* maple–2 days however *may* include them all. The wild red cherry & black cherry though earlier to begin are not now *conspicuous*–but I am not sure that some of the other birches where young in favorable places may not be as forward as the white. probably not to any extent But the S. Alba &c precedes them all V pm of 17th inst

It is surprising what an electrifying effect this shower appears to have had– It is like the christening of the summer–& I suspect that summer weather may be always ushered in in a similar manner–thunder shower rainbow–smooth water & warmer night–a rainbow on the brow of summer– Nature has placed this gem on the brow of her daughter Not only the wet grass looks many shades greener in the twilight but the old pine needles also. The toads are heard to ring more generally & louder than before–& the bull frogs trump regularly though not very loudly –reminding us that they are at hand and not drowned out by the freshet– All creatures are more awake than ever. Now sometime after sunset the robins scold & sing–(but their great singing time is earlier in the season) & the maryland yellow throat is heard amid the alders & willows by the water side–& the peetweet –& blackbirds–& sometimes a kingbird–& the tree toad somewhat. Sweetbriar just begun to leaf–generally–?

May 12

5½ Am to Nawshawtuct–   *Quite* a fog risen up from
the river– I cannot see over it from the hill at 6 Am.
The first I have seen. The grass is now high enough to
be wet. I see many perfectly geometrical cobwebs on
the trees with from 26 to 30 odd rays 6 inches to 18 in
diameter but no spiders– I suspect they were spun
this last warm night very generally–no insects in them
yet. They are the more conspicuous for being thickly
strung with minute drops of the mist or dew like a
chain of beads– Are they not meteorologists? A robins
nest in an apple tree with 3 eggs, first nest I have
seen–also a redwings nest–bird about it did not look
in–before the river is low enough for them to build on
its brink   V. cucullata ap. today first X near the
sassafrasses– A small white birch XXX catkin. Fir
balsam just begins fairly to loosen bundles– Were
they blue winged teal flew by–for there was a large
white spot on the sides aft– I think I scared up the
same last night.

Is not this the first day of summer when first I sit
with the window open & forget fire? & hear the golden
robin & king bird &c &c? not to mention the bobolink
–vireo–yellow-bird &c & the trump of bull frogs heard
last evening.

Pm to Climbing fern.

I have seen a little blue moth a long time   My thick
sack is too much yesterday & today   The golden robin
makes me think of a thinner coat. I see that the great
thrush–brown thrasher–from its markings is still of the
same family with the wood thrush &c– These genera
are very curious. A shrub or bear oak beginning to
leaf– Am struck with the fact that the Assabet has
relieved itself of its extra waters to a much greater
extent than the main branch. Wooly aphides on
alder– Large black birches not quite leafing nor in

bloom. In one bunch of v. ovatas in Ministerial Swamp path–counted 11 an unusual number. What are those handsome conical crimson red buds not burst on the White spruce–? The leaves of the larch begin to make a show   Mosquito. The climbing fern is evergreen only the flowery top dies & spreads by horizontal roots   I perceive no growth yet. The Amelanchier Oblongifolia–has denser & smaller racemes more erect (?) broader petalled & not tinged with red on the back. Its downy leaves are now less conspicuous & interesting than the other's–   On the whole it is not so interesting a variety.

The bear berry is well out, perhaps a quarter part of them–   May 6th I thought it would open in a day or 2–say then the 8th X

At last I hear the veery strain–   Why not as soon as the yorrick? Heard again the evergreen forest note. It is a slender bird about size of white-eyed vireo with a black throat & I think some yellow above with dark & (light beneath, in the tops of pines & oaks–   The only warblers at all like it are Black throated Green–Black throated Blue–Black-poll–& Golden winged–& maybe orange crowned.

May 13th

The portion of the peach trees in bloom in our garden shows the height of the snow drifts in the winter–   4 Pm to V. Muhlenbergii Brook–   The bass suddenly expanding its little round leaves–prob began about the 11th   Uvularias–amid the dry tree tops near the azaleas ap. yesterday–   Saw the crow blackbird fly over turning his tail in the wind into a vertical position to serve for a rudder, then sailing with it horizontal. The great red maples begin to leaf–& the young leafets of the red? oaks up the assabet on Hosmer's land & one at rock–now begin to be conspicuous.

Waxwork begins to leaf. The sand cherry judging from what I saw yesterday will begin to flower today.

As for the birds I have not for some time noticed crows in flocks– The voices of the early spring birds are silenced or drowned in multitude of sounds– The black ducks are probably all gone. Are the rusty grackles still here? Birds generally are now building & sitting– Methinks I heard one snipe night before last? I have not noticed the pine warbler–nor the myrtle birds for a fortnight. The chip-sparrow is lively in the morning– I suspect the purple finches are all gone within a few days– The black & white creeper is musical nowadays–and thrushes & the catbird &c &c   Goldfinch heard pretty often–

Insects have just *begun* to be troublesome.

May 14th

Pm to Hill by boat– a st Domingo Cuckoo –blackbilled with red round eye–a silent long slender graceful bird dark cinnamon (?) above pure white beneath– It is in a leisurely manner picking the young caterpillars out of a nest (now about ⅓ of an inch long) with its long curved bill. Not timid. Black willows have begun to leaf–if they are such in front of Monroe's.

Wht ash & common elm *began* to leaf yesterday if I have not named the elm before. The former will ap. open tomorrow XX. The black ash i.e. that by the river may have been open a day or two. Apple in bloom X   Swamp white oak perhaps will open tomorrow.   no.   no. Celtis has begun to leaf. I think I may say that the white-oak leaves have now fallen–saw but one or two small trees with them day before yesterday

Sumach began to leaf say yesterday– Pear opened say the 12th   The leafing goes on now rapidly these warm & moist showery days.

May 15

Judging from those in garden the witch-hazel began to leaf–yesterday–black alder and red azalea today.

Pm up Assabet–

The golden willow catkins are suddenly falling & cover my boat. High blueberry has flowered–say yesterday XX   Swamp-pink leafing say yesterday. The amelanchier botryapium Some of them have lost blossoms & show *minute* fruit. This I suspect the first *sign* of all edible fruit. unless is gooseberry? or currant? C. Florida began to leaf say yesterday. The round leafed cornel (at Island) is as early as any of the cornels to leaf–put it for the present with the alternifolia   Gaylusccia begins to leaf to day & is sticky   Polygonatum pubescens will ap. blossom tomorrow XXX   Hickories make a show suddenly–their buds are so large say yesterday–   Young white oaks also yesterday   Old ones hardly today–but their catkins quite prominent. Young wht-oak (& black oak) leafets now very handsome red on underside. Black oaks appear to have begun to leaf about the 13 immediately after the red   The large P. Grandid. by river not leafing yet.

Looked off from hill top   Trees generally are now bursting into leaf. The aspect of oak and other woods at a distance is somewhat like that of a very thick & reddish or yellowish mist about the evergreens–   In other directions the light graceful–& more distinct yellowish green forms of birches are seen–& in swamps the reddish or reddish brown crescents of the red maple tops–now covered with keys–   Oak leaves are as big as a mouse ear & the farmers are busily planting. It is suddenly very warm & looks as if there might be a thunder-shower coming up from the west. The C. black bird is distinguished by that harsh spring-like note– For the rest there is a sort of split whistle like a poor imitation of the red wing.

A yellow butterfly–

Have just been looking at Nuttall's N.A. Sylva –Much–research–fine plates–& print & paper–& unobjectionable periods– –but no turpentine or balsam–or quercitron–or salicine–or birch wine–or the aroma of the balm of gilead–no gallic or ulmic or even malic acid &c &c   The plates are greener & higher colored than the words   It is sapless if not leafless.

May 16 Tuesday

Saw an arum almost open the 11th say 16 (?) Though not shed pollen 16th at Conantum. Sug. maples large–beg. to leaf say 14 also   Mulberry in the How garden today–   Locust the 14–   White-spruce the earliest today. Button wood the 14th (*leafing* all)

Pm to Conantum by Boat with S.

V. peregrina in Channing's garden–   Purslane speedwell–*some* flowers withered. Some days at least–   Observed all the oaks I know except the chestnut & dwarf chestnut–& scarlet (?)   I see anthers perhaps to all but not yet any pollen–   Apparently the most forward in respect to blossoming will be the shrub oak–which possibly is now in bloom in some places–then ap. swamp white–then red & black–then white–white oak ap leafs with swamp white or say next day.   red & black oaks leaf about together–before swamp white & white   Earliest sassafras opened yesterday XXX–leafs today. Butternut will blossom tomorrow XX. The Great fern–by sassafras begins to bloom XXX prob. Osmunda Claytoniana 2 feet high now–   Interrupted Fern its very dark heads–soon surmounted with green. Lambkill beginning to leaf–   Green briar leaf yesterday   The rich crimson leaf buds of the grape yesterday globular (& some today)–are rapidly unfolding–scattered along the

vine   The various leaves unfolding are flower-like &
taken together are more interesting than any flower
–   Is that a hop–prob. clematis–one of the earlier
plants then by the path at landing on hill–with shoots
now 5 or 6 inches long?

Pads begin to appear & spread themselves out on
the surface here & there as the water goes down
–though it is still over the meadows
–with often a scolloped edge like those tin
platters on which country people sometimes bake
turn-overs. Golden robin building her nest   Their
round green buds here & there look like the heads of
tortoises–& I saw in the course of the afternoon 3 or 4
just begun to blossom XX   It is easy to see now that
the highest part of the meadow is next the river
–   There is generally a difference of a foot at least–

Saw around a hard hack stem on the meadow where
the water was about 2 feet deep a light brown globular
mass 2 inches or more in diameter which looked like a
thistle head full of some kind of seeds some of which
were separated from it by the agitation made by the
boat–but returned to it again–   I then saw that they
were living creatures–   It was a mass of gelatinous
spawn filled with little light colored pollywogs (?) or
possibly fishes (?) all head & tail–a long broad light
colored & thin tail which was vertical appended to a
head with 2 eyes. These were about ¼ of an inch long
& when washed off in the water wiggled back to the
mass again.   quite warm–cows already stand in water
in the shade of the bridge   I stopped to get some water
at the springy bank just above the RR. I dug a little
hollow with my hands so that I could dip some up
with a skunk cabbage leaf–and while waiting for it to
settle I thought by a squirming & wriggling movement
on the bottom that the sand was all alive with some
kind of worms or insects–   There were in fact some

worm-skins? on it. Looking closer, however, I found
that this motion & appearance was produced by the
bursting up of the water–which not only trickled down
from the bank above–but burst up from beneath
–   The sandy bottom was speckled with hundreds of
small regularly formed orifices like those in a pepper
box–about which the particles of sand kept in
motion–had made me mistake it for squirming
worms–   There was considerable loam or soil mixed
with the sand. These orifices separated by slight
intervals like those in the nose of a water-pot–gave to
the spring an unexpectedly regular appearance–   It is
surprising how quickly one of these springs will run
clear–   Also drank at what I will call alder spring at
Clam-shell Hill. Looked in to several red-wings black
birds nests which are now being built–but no eggs yet.
They are generally hung between 2 twigs–say of button
bush. I noticed at one nest what looked like a tow
string securely tied about a twig at each end about
6 inches apart left loose in the middle. It was not a
string but I think a strip of milkweed pod &c water
asclepias probably–may be a foot long & very strong
–   How remarkable that this bird should have found
out the strength of this which I was so slow to find
out!

The leaf buds at last suddenly burst–   It is now very
difficult to compare one with another or keep the sum
of them–   The bursting in to leaf of the greater
number *including the latest* is accomplished within a
week–say from the 13th of may this year to prob. the
20th   That is within these dates they acquire minute
leafets. This same is the principal planting week
methinks–   The Clethra well leafed–say with the bass
(?) andromeda calyculata leaf tomorrow

The red or crimsoned young leaves of the black &
red (?) oaks–the former like red damask & the

marroon? red inclining to flesh color salmon-red (?) of
the white oak–all arranged now like little parasols
in white oak 5 leafets are as interesting &
beautiful as flowers. downy & velvet-like.
Sorrel well out in some warm places   R. bulbosus will
flower tomorrow under Clam shell. Yesterday when
the blossoms of the Golden Willow began to fall–the
blossoms of the apple began to open. Landed at
Conantum by the red-cherry grove above arrowhead
field   the red cherries 6 inches in diameter & 25 or 30
high in full bloom–with a reddish smooth bark. It is a
splendid day–so clear & bright & fresh–the warmth of
the air & the bright tender verdure putting forth on
all sides make an impression of luxuriance &
genialness–so perfectly fresh & uncankered. A sweet
scent fills the air from the expanding leafets or some
other source–   The earth is all fragrant as one flower.
& bobolinks tinkle in the air   Nature now is perfectly
genial to man–

I noticed the dark shadow of Conantum Cliff from
the water–   Why do I notice it at this season
particularly? Is it because a shadow is more grateful to
the sight now that warm weather has come? Or is there
anything in the contrast between the rich green of the
grass & the cool dark shade? As we walked along to
the C. Cliff–I saw *many* Potentilla Canadensis var
Pumila X now spotting the ground. V. vacillans just
out XX   Arenaria serpyllifolia XXX tomorrow
– Myosotis stricta in several places–how long?
Trillium out X possibly yesterday. Maiden hair ferns
some up some starting–unclenching their little red
fists   Fever bush say leafed about the 12   Returning
the water is smoother than common–quite glassy in
some places–   It is getting to be difficult to cross the
meadows or float close under the edge of the wood.
But the wind changes to east & blows agreeably fresh.

How fair & Elysian these rounded & now green Indian hills with their cool dark shadows on the E side! There are great summer clouds in the sky blocked rhomboidal masses tier above tier–white glowing above–darker beneath

On Hubbards meadow–saw a motion in the water as if a pickerel had darted away–approached & saw a mid sized snapping turtle on the bottom–managed at last after stripping off my coat & rolling up my shirt sleeve–by thrusting in my arm to the should to get him by the tail & lift him aboard– He tried to get under the boat. He snapped at my shoe & got the toe in his mouth. His back was covered with green moss (?) or the like mostly concealing the scales–in this were small leaches– Great rough but not hard scales on his legs– He made a pretty loud hissing like a cross dog by his breathing. It was wonderful how suddenly this sluggish creature would snap at anything As he lay under the seat I scratched his back–& filling himself with air & rage his head would suddenly fly upward his shell striking the seat–just as a steel trap goes off–& though I was prepared for it it never failed to startle me it was so swift & sudden– He slowly inflated himself & then suddenly went off like a percussion lock snapping the air– – Thus undoubtedly he catches fishes as a toad catches flies– His carinated tail & great triangular points in the rear edge of his shell. Nature does not forget beauty of outline even in a mud turtle's shell

Rhodora well out prob 2 days–leaf as long or yesterday. The stink pots have climbed 2 or 3 feet up the willows & hang there– I suspect that they appear first about the same time with the snapping turtles–

Far and near I see painted turtles sunning or tumbling off the little hummocks laid bare by the descending water–their shells shining in the sun.

May 17th

5½ Am to Island

The water is now tepid in the morning–to the hands–(may have been a day or 2–) as I slip my hands down the paddle.

Hear the wood pewee–the warm weather sound.

As I was returning over the meadow this side of the island–I saw the snout of a mud turtle above the surface–little more than an inch of the point–& paddled toward it– Then as he moved slowly on the surfaced different parts of his shell & head just appearing looked just like the scolloped edges of some pads which had just reached the surface. I pushed up & found a large snapping turtle on the bottom. He appeared of a dirty-brown there very nearly the color of the bottom at present–with his great head as big as an infants–and his vigilant eyes as he paddled about on the bottom in his attempts to escape–he looked not merely repulsive–but to some extent terrible even as a crocodile–. At length after thrusting my arm in up to the shoulder 2 or 3 times I succeeded in getting him in to the boat where I secured him with a lever under a seat– I could get him from the landing to the house only by turning him over & drawing him by the tail –the hard crests of which afforded a good hold. For he was so heavy that I could not hold him off so far as to prevent his snapping at my legs   He weighed 30 & a half pounds.

extreme length of shell	15½ inches	
Length of shell in middle	15	
Greatest width of shell	12½	this was toward the rear
Tail (beyond shell)	11½	

His head & neck is was not easy to measure–but judging from the proportions of one described by Storer they must have been 10 inches long at least–which makes the whole length 37 inches. Width of head 4½ inches; with the skin of the neck more than 5. His sternum which was slightly depressed was 10½ X 5½. Depth from back to sternum about 7 inches. There were 6 great scollops or rather triangular points on the hind edge of his shell–3 on each side–the middle one of each three the longest–about ¾ of an inch– He had surprisingly stout hooked jaws of a grey color or bluish grey–the upper shutting over the under– ～ –a more or less sharp triangular beak corresponding to one below & his flippers were armed with very stout claws 1¼ inches long– He had a very ugly & spiteful face (with a vigilant grey eye–which was never shut in any position of the head) surrounded by the thick & ample folds of the skin about his neck– His shell was comparatively smooth & free from moss a dirty black – He was a *dirty* or speckled white beneath. He made the most remarkable & awkward appearance when walking. The edge of his shell was lifted about 8 inches from the ground–tilting now to this side then to that –his great scaly legs or flippers hanging with flesh & loose skin–slowly & gravely (?) hissing the while. His walking was perfectly elephantine. Thus he stalked along a low conical mountain–dragging his tail with his head turned upwards with the ugliest & most venomous look– –on his flippers half-leg half fin. But he didnt proceed far before he sank down to rest– If he could support a world on his back when lying down he certainly could not stand up under it.

All said that he walked like an elephant   When ly-ing on his back–showing his *dirty* white & warty underside–with his tail curved round–he reminded you forcibly of pictures of the dragon. He could not easily turn himself back– Tried many times in vain

resting between-whiles   Would inflate himself &
convulsively spring with head & all upward–so as to
lift his shell from the ground–& he would strike his
head on the ground lift up his shell & catch at the
earth with his claws.

His back was of two great blunt ridges with a hollow
between down the middle of which was a slight but
distinct ridge also–   There was also a ridge of spines
more or less hard on each side of his crested tail. Some
of these spines on the crest of the tail were nearly half
an inch high–   Storer says that they have 5 *Claws* on
the forelegs but only 4 on the hind ones–   In this there
was a *perfectly* distinct 5th *toe* (?) on the hind legs
though it did not pierce the skin–and on the fore legs it
did not much more. S. does not say how many toes he
has.

These claws must be powerful to dig with. This then
is the season for hunting them–now that the water
is warmer before the pads are common & the water is
getting shallow on the meadows–   E. Wood, Senior
speaks of 2 seen fighting for a long time in the river in
front of his house last year. I have heard of one being
found in the meadow in the winter surrounded by
frozen mud.

Is not this the heaviest animal found wild in this
township–? Certainly none but the otter approaches it.
Farrar says that when he was eleven one which he
could not lift into the boat towed him across the
river–weighed 29

Lilack is out X & Horse chestnut XXX   The female
flowers–crimson cones of the white spruce but not yet
the staminate.

The turtle was very sluggish though capable of
putting forth great strength   He would just squeeze
into a flour barrel–& would not quite lie flat in it when

his head & tail were drawn in– There was triangular place on the bottom of his mouth–& an orifice within it through which apparently he breathed. the orifice opening & shutting. I hear of a man who injured his back seriously for many years by carrying one some distance at arms length to prevent his biting him. They are frequently seen fighting & their shells heard striking together.

Pm to Cedar Swamp via Assabet

The Tupelo began to leaf ap. yesterday.

The large green keys of the white maples are now conspicuous looking like the wings of insects. Azalea nudiflora in woods begins to leaf *now*. later than the white kind. V. Muhlenbergii out–say yesterday XXX. It is a pale violet. Judging from the aspect of the lentago yesterday I should put its leafing decidedly before the v. nudum. Also ap. the late rose soon after the one observed and the moss about same time with first. The swamp white & white oak are slow to leaf– Large maples too are not rapid but the birches aspens & balm of gileads burst out suddenly into leaf & make a great show– Also the *young* sugar maples in the street now and for some days have made a show of of broad luxuriant leaves–early & rapidly   In the case of the early aspen you could almost see the leaves expand & acquire a darker green–under the influence of the sun & genial atmosphere–   Now they are only as big as a nine pence–tomorrow or sooner they are as big as a pistareen & the next day they are as big as a dollar. – So too the green veils or screens of the birches rapidly thickened. This from its far greater prevalence than the aspens–balm of gilead–white maples &c is the first to give the woodlands anywhere generally a (fresh) green aspect–   It is the first to clothe large tracts of deciduous woodlands with green–& perchance it marks an epoch in the season. the *transition* decidedly and generally from bare twigs to leaves. When the birches have put on their green sacks then a new season has come.– The light reflected from their tender yellowish green is like sunlight.

The turtle's snapping impressed me as something mechanical like a spring–as if there was no volition about– Its very suddenness seemed too great for a conscious movement– Perhaps in these cold blooded & sluggish animals there is a near approach to the purely material & mechanical. Their very tenacity of life seems to be owing to their insensitivity or small amount of life–indeed to be an irritation of the muscles. One man tells me of a turtle's head which the day after it was cut off snapped at a dogs tail & made him him run off yelping. and I have witnessed something similar myself– I can think of nothing but a merely animated jaw as it were a piece of mechanism. There is in this creature a tremendous development of the jaw–and long after the head is cut off this snaps vigorously when irritated, like a piece of mechanism. A naturalist tells me that he dissected one & laid its heart aside, and he found it beating or palpitating the next morning. They are some times baited with eels & caught with a hook– Apparently the best time to hunt them is in the morning when the water is smooth.

There is a surprising change since I last passed up the assabet–the fields are now clothed with so dark & rich a green–and the wooded shore is all lit up with the tender bright green of birches fluttering in the wind & shining in the light–& red-maple keys are seen at a distance against the tender green of birches & other trees–tinging them–

The wind is easterly–having changed–& produces an agreeable raw mistiness–*just* visible–between a dew & a fog for density– I sail up the stream but the wind is

hardly powerful enough to overcome the current &
sometimes I am almost at a standstill where the
stream is most contracted & swiftest–& there I sit
carelessly waiting for the struggle between wind &
current to decide itself– Then comes a stronger puff
& I see by the shore that I am advancing. to where the
stream is broader & runs less swiftly–where lighter
breezes can draw me. In contracted & swift running
places the wind & current are almost evenly matched
– It is a pleasing delay, to be referred to the
elements.   & meanwhile I survey the shrubs on shore.
The white cedar shows the least possible life in its
extremities now. Put it with the arbor vitae or after it.
Poison dogwood beg. to leaf say yesterday.
Nemopanthes out XX leafed several days ago– And
the clustered Andromeda leaf ap. a day or more before
it. Gold thread out X V. palmata X I cannot well
examine the stoneheaps the water is so deep
– Muskrats are now sometimes very bold lie on the
surface & come swimming directly toward the boat as
if to reconnoiter– This in 2 cases within a few days.
Pretty sure to see a crescent of light under their tails
when they dive. The splendid rhodora now sets the
swamps on fire with its masses of rich color– It is *one
of the first* flowers to catch the eye at a distance in
masses–so naked–unconcealed by its own leaves.

   Observed a rill emptying in above the stone-heaps
& afterward saw where it ran out of June-Berry
Meadow–& I considered how surely it would have
conducted me to the meadow–if I had traced it up. I
was impressed as it were by the intelligence of the
brook–which for ages in the wildest regions before
science is born knows so well the level of the
ground–& through whatever woods or other obstacles
finds its way. Who shall distinguish between the *law*
by which a brook finds its river–the *instinct*–a bird

performs its migrations–& the *knowledge* by which a
man steers his ship round the globe? The globe is the
richer for the variety of its inhabitants– Saw a large
grey-squirrel near the split rock in the assabet. He
went skipping up the limb of one tree & down the limb
of another–his great great grey rudder undulating
through the air–& occasionally hid himself behind the
main stem. The S nigra will open tomorrow XX

May 18th to Pedricks Meadow
V. lanceolata 2 days at least. Celandine yesterday XX
The V. pedatas beg. to be abundant   Chinquapin was
prob a little later to leaf & will be to flower than the
shrub oak. Its catkins light green remind me of those
of the swamp wht oak. Buttonwood balls ⅓ inch in
diam. have been blown off & *some* have a dull purplish
fuzzy surface–(most are solid green–) ap. just beg. to
blossom– Red cedar shows the least possible sign of
starting. The Pyrus prob. black fruited–in bloom as
much as 2 days   Huckleberry XXX. Now for the tassels
of the shrub oak–I can find no pollen yet about them
but as the oak catkins in my pitcher plucked yesterday
shed pollen today–I think I may say that the bear
shrub oak red & black oaks open tomorrow– I see the
pincushion or crimson tinged galls now on shrub-oaks
–around the bases of the young shoots Some green
shell ones on oak leaves like large peas–& small now
greenish white fungus like ones on swamp pink
– Thus early before the leaves are a quarter
expanded, the gall begins. I see potentillas already
ascending 5 or 6 inches but no flower on them–in the
midst of low ones in flower. Smilacina trifolia will ap
open to morrow in Pedrick's meadow–

A large clay brown & blotched snake–is it the
chicken snake–or water adder? Beach plum in full
bloom by red house–ap. 2 or 3 days   It is one of the
very latest plants to leaf only a few buds just begin to

show any green– One man has been a fishing–but
said the water & the wind were too high   caught a
few.

High winds all day wracking the young trees &
blowing off blossoms.

May 19

5½ Am to Nawshawtuct & Island

R purshii will ap open today XXX. Its little green
buds some what like a small yel. lily. The water has
now fallen so much that the grass is rapidly springing
up through it on the meadows. Redwings nest with 2
eggs   A geranium ap. yesterday XXX   Celtis for several
days   Button bush *beg.* to leaf say the 17. i.e. some of
its buds began to burst. Choke cherry out. X   Aralia
nudicaulis ap yesterday XXX   The red eye.

The early thorn looks as if it would open today

I hear the *sprayey* note frog now at sunset   Now for
4 or 5 days though they are now for the most part
large–or since the 15th came in the young & tender oak
leaves disposed umbrella-wise about the extremities of
last year's twigs have been very attractive from their
different tints of red–those of the black & white oaks
are methinks especially handsome–the former already
showing their minute & tender bristles–& all
handsomely lobed–some of the black oak leaves are
like a rich dark red velvet–the white oak have a paler &
more delicate tint somewhat flesh-colored–though
others are more like the black–what S calls a marroon
red. S of the bear scrub oak–the swamp white &
Chinquapin & more of a downy or silvery white. The
white pine shoots are now 2 or 3 inches long
generally–upright light marks on the body of dark
green– Those of the P. pine are less conspicuous.
Hemlock does not show yet– The light shoots an inch
or so long of the fir-balsam spots the trees– The larch

is a mass of fresh airy & cool green– Arbor vitae red
cedar & white show no life except on the closest
inspection. They are some of the latest trees– The
Juniper is about with the Fir balsam– I have already
described the oaks sufficiently. The hazel is now a
pretty green bush– Butternuts like hickories make a
show suddenly with their large buds. I have not
examined the birches except the white this year. The
alders are slow to expand their leaves but now *begin* to
show a mass of green along the river & with the
willows afford concealment to the birds' nests– The
birds appear to be waiting for this screen– The robins
nest and eggs is the earliest I see.

Saw one in the midst of a green briar over the water
the other day–before the briar had put out at all–which
shows some fore sight–for it will be perfectly invisible
if not inaccessible soon.

The great poplar is quite late to leaf especially those
that blossom–not yet do they show much–a silvery leaf

The golden willow is the only tree used about here
at the same time for a fence & for shade– It also
prevents the causeways from being washed away. The
black-willow is the largest as well as the handsomest
of our native willows. Young elms are leafing pretty
fast   old ones are late & slow– The samarae of the
elms first make a thick top leaf like before the leaves
come out. Ash-trees are like hickories in respect to the
size of the young leaves– The young leafets of the
wild holly (Nemopanthes) on the 17 were peculiarly
thin and pellucid yellow-green. I know of none others
like them. Those of the black alder are not only late
but dark– The button-bush is not only very late–but
the buds are slow to expand–& methinks are very far
apart so that they do not soon make a show–for the
most part at a little distance there is no appearance of

life in them even yet– The sweet viburnum & also the naked are early to make a show with their substantial leaves.

The anddromedas are all late, if I remember the clustered (?) the earliest. The common swamp pink is earlier to leaf but later to blossom than the nudiflora The Rhodora is late & is *naked* flowering. The mt laurel is one of the latest plants The resinous dotted leaves of the huckleberry are interesting. The high blueberries are are early (to bloom) & resound with the hum of bees. All The cornels beg. to leaf ap. *about* the same time   the C. Florida is rather late–though I do not know but the round-leaved is the earliest. I have not observed the dwarf– The witch-hazel is rather late & can afford to be. One kind of thorn is well leafed–the other not. The mt ash is the first tree which grows here either naturally or otherwise–to show green at a little distance– Is it not true that *trees* which belong peculiarly to a colder latitude are among our earliest–& those which prefer a warmer among our latest? The chokeberry's shining leaf is interesting. With what unobserved secure despatch nature advances– The amelanchiers have bloomed & already both kinds have shed their blossoms & show minute green fruit. There is not an instant's pause– The beach plum–such as I have observed–is the latest to begin to expand of all deciduous shrubs or trees–for aught I know– The sight of it suggests that we are near the sea-coast–that even our sands are in some sense littoral–or beaches.

The cherries are all early to leaf–but only one perhaps the wild red–& that in one place is in mass enough to make much show– The woodbine is well advanced–shoots 2 or 3 inches long– It must have beg. to leaf more than a week ago.

The linden leafs suddenly & rapidly–a round thin &
transparent looking (?) leaf–

A washing day–a strong rippling wind–& all things
bright.

May 20th

Woodbine shoots (Brick house) already 2 or 3 inches
long   Put it say with the red oak. Potentilla argentea
XXX   White spruce male flowers X   White ash–ap *a
day or 2.* Mr Pritchards–   The eng. hawthorne opens at
same time with our earlier thorn.

very low thunder clouds & showers far in the north
at sunset–saw the lightning but could not hear the
thunder the wind of which though not very strong, has
cooled the air. I saw in the northwest first rise in the
rose-tinted horizon sky–a dark narrow craggy cloud
narrow & projecting as no cloud on earth–seen against
the rose-tinged sky–the crest of a thunder storm
–beautiful & grand–   The steadily increasing sound of
toads & frogs along the river with each successive
warmer night is one of the most important
peculiarities of the season–   Their prevalence and
loudness is in proportion to the increased temperature
of the day–   It is the first earth song–beginning with
the crokers–(the crickets' not yet) as if the very meads
at last burst into a meadowy song. I hear a few
bulfrogs. & but few hylodes. Methinks we always have
at this time those washing winds as now–when the
chokeberry is in bloom–bright & breezy days blowing
off some apple blossoms–

Sunday May 21st

Quince XXX   a slight fog in morning.   some
bulfrogs in morning. & I see a yellow swelling throat.
They these throats come with the yellow lily
–   Cob-webs on grass the first I have noticed–this is
one of the *late* phenomena of Spring–   These little

dewy nets or gauze–a faery's washing–spread out in
the night are associated with the finest days of the
year– Days long enough & fair enough for the
worthiest deeds. When these begin to be seen then is
not summer come?

I notice the fir balsam sterile flowers already effete
                              Pm. to Deep Cut

A shower–heralded only by thunder & lightining–has
kept me in till late in the afternoon– The sterile
Equisetum arvense now well up green the bank–bluets
begin to whiten the fields– A tanager–the surprising
red bird–against the darkening green leaves– I see a
little growth in the mitchella. The larger P.
Grandidentatas *here* are pretty well leaved out & may
be put with the young ones. Trientalis perhaps
yesterday– Smilacina bifolia ap. tomorrow

Hear the squeak of a night hawk. The deciduous
trees now begin to balance the evergreens   Red oaks
are quite green. Young hemlocks have grown ¼ of an
inch old–just started. But by tomorrow they will show
their growth–by contrast more than the button bush
– Lycopodiums just started–light or yellowish green
tips. C. canadensis XX   The sing. berry Prinos leafs say
with the other. Was surprised to find a Nemopanthes
on the upland– Stows clearing– Dangleberry–leafs
say–next after the common huckleberry– Young
–chequerberry reddish shoots just begin to show
themselves–

                    Twilight on river–

The reddish white-lily pads here & there–& the
heart-leaves begin to be seen. a few pontederias like
long handled spoons   The water going rapidly down,
that often purplish bent grass is seen lying flat along it
a foot or more in parallel–blades like matting. It is
surprising how the grass shoots up now through the
shallow water on the meadows–so fresh & tender–you

can almost see it grow–for the fall of the water adds to
its apparent growth–& the river weeds too–flags
polygonums & potamogetons &c &c are rapidly
pushing up–   Sassafras is slow to leaf–   A
Whippoorwill.

May 22

5½ am. Up Assabet–

Now begins the slightly sultryish morning air into
which you awake early to hear the faint buzz of a fly or
hum of other insect. The teeming air–deep &
hollow–filled with some spiritus–pregnant–as not in
winter or spring–with room for imps–good angels &
bad–many chambers in it–infinite sounds. I partially
awake–the first time for a month at least.–   As if the
cope of the sky lifted–the heat stretched and swelled it
as a bladder–& it remained permanently higher &
more infinite for the summer–Suggesting that the
night has not been with its incidents.   naked fl Azalea
XXX–in garden & wood. The dew now wets me
completely each morning. Swamp white oak beg. to
blossom ap. yesterday–the anthers completely shed
their pollen at once–and an effete–only a small part as
yet however–   The red oak–i.e. at point of Island as I
did not observe it out on the 19–say 20th   The white
oak will ap. begin today XXX   NB–some not open on
the 26th.

The hemlock may have begun to bloom the 20   C
Florida XXX   Galls puff-like on naked azalea &
huckleberries. The late thorn is not much if any later
to leaf than the other ap.

Saw a small diving duck of some kind–suddenly
dash out from the side of the river above the
hemlocks–like my red-breasted merganser–plowing
the water with a great noise & flapping & dive in the
middle of the stream.–searching carefully   I after
saw its head out amid the alders on the opposite

side– When I returned–it again dived in the middle of
the stream. Why should it attract my attention first by
this rush. Shoots along half risen from the water
–striking it with its wings. I saw one of the same family
run thus a long way on the Penobscot– Ranunculus
Recurvatus out at V. Muhlenbergii brook–since the
17th say 19th

                                    10 Am to Fair Haven by boat.
   I see many young & tender dragon-flies both large
and small hanging to the grass tops & weeds & twigs
which rise above the water still going down– They are
weak & sluggish & tender looking & appear to have
lately crawled up these stems from the bottom where
they were hatched & to be waiting till they are
hardened in the sun–& air–(A *few* however are flying
vigorously as usual over the water–) Where the grass
& rushes are thick over the shallow water I see their
large gauze-like wings vibrating in the breeze and
shining in the sun. It is remarkable that such tender
organizations survive so many accidents. The black
oak–ap. beg. to blossom yesterday. X The bear shrub
oaks ap. began to bloom with the red–though they are
various– Put the Chinquapin with them immediately
after. Louse-wort fairly out in front of Geum on Hill.
Examined the button-bush hummock. It is about 18
feet by 10 at the widest part & from 1 to 1½ feet thick
– It consists chiefly of buttonbushes 4 or 5 feet high
& now as flourishing as any a high-blueberry–(killed)
& some water-silk weeds (springing up (5 or 6 inches)
at the foot of the dry stalks–together with the grass &
soil they grew in. Though these have been completely
covered by the freshet for some weeks since it was
deposited here–and exposed to high winds & waves
–It has not sensibly washed away– These masses
draw so much water that they ground commonly on
the edge of the river–proper–& so all things combine

to make this a border bush or edging–(They they are
sometimes when the water is high dropped in the
middle of the meadow–& make islands there)   They
thus help to define the limits of the river–& defend the
edge of the meadow–and the water being still high I
see at Fair Haven the sweeping lines formed by their
broad tops, mixed with willows in the midst of the
flood which mark the mid summer boundary of the
pond   They not only bear but require a good deal of
water for their roots. Apparently these will not feel
their removal at all. Every rod or two there is a great
hummock of meadow sward & soil without bushes.
The muskrats have already taken advantage of this
one to squat on & burrow under–and by raising the
shore it will afford them a refuge which they had not
before here–. Senecio XXX prob. earlier still at
Boiling Spring   Rhus radicans ap. leafs with the
Toxicodendron   The apple bloom is chiefly passed.
Rubus sempervirence put for leaf soon after R.
Canadensis   Is that the O. cinnamomea? at the dwarf
sumachs (which ap flowers with the Hill one) its
fertil fronds without leaves & its curved white
roots or bases regularly feather marked? The
Dwarf sumach is just starting, some of them,
decidedly later than the button bush!

   At Clam shell–the small oblong yellow heads of yel.
clover–some days. Tall butter-cup a day or 2
– Dandelions for some time gone to seed   Water
saxifrage now well out. As I started away from Clam
shell–It was quite warm–the seats–& the water glassy
smooth–but a little wind rose afterward. Muskrats are
frequently seen to dive a dozen rods from shore–& not
discovered again. A song sparrows callow young in
nest–   A sum. yellowbird close by sounded–*we we we
tchea tchea te che wiss wiss wiss.* I perceive some of
that peculiar fragrance from the marsh at the Hub.

causeway–though the marsh is mostly covered–is it a particular compound of odors? It is more remarkable & memorable than the scent of any particular plant–the fragrance as it were of the earth itself. The loud cawing of a crow heard echoing through a deep pine wood–how wild! Unconverted by all our preaching. Now and then the dumping sound of frogs– Large pin weed six inches high. Lupines have been out under Fair Haven Hill several days. V. pedatas blue the field there.

I rest in the orchard–doubtful whether to sit in shade or sun. Now the springing foliage is like a sun light on the woods   I was first attracted & surprised when I looked round & off to Conantum–at the smooth lawn-like green fields–& pasturing cows bucolical. reminding me of new butter. The air so clear–as not in summer–makes all things shine–as if all surfaces had been washed by the rains of spring & were not yet soiled or begrimmed or dulled. You see even to the *Mts* clearly–the grass so short & fresh–the tender yellowish green & silvery foliage of the deciduous trees lighting up the landscape–the birds now most musical–the sorrel *beginning* to redden the fields with ruddy health.– all these things make earth now a paradise.

How many times I have been surprised thus on turning about on this very spot at the fairness of the earth! The alders groves begin to look like great mosses so compact & curveing to the ground at their edges–as one system–

Pairs of yellow butterflies are seen coquetting Through the air higher & higher. Comandra ap yesterday XX   I am surprised as I go along the edge of the cliffs as the oppressive warmth of the air from the dry leaves in the woods on the rocks. Compared with the oaks & hickories the birches are now a dark green.

The order of lightness is ap–black oak silvery (and
prob large white)–red oaks & hickories *apparently*
more advanced & green.–White birches–& then pines.
young wht oaks on plain are reddish   (A pitch pine
sheds pollen on Cliffs. XXX   The pines are more
conspicuous now than ever–miles off–& the leaves are
not yet large enough to conceal them much.

It is noon–& I hear the cattle crashing their way
down the Cliff seeking the shade of the woods. They
climb–like goats. Others seek the water & the shade of
bridges.

Erigeron a day or 2. It loves moist hill-sides   Landed
next at the Miles Swamp–the dense cylindrical
racemes of the choke-cherry–some blasted into a puff
– Caterpillars prey on this too. I do not find any
arums open yet. There are many little gnats dead
within them. A rubus just opening near the arums   Is
it my triflorus? It is not Canadensis–Is not thorny nor
bristly–but hairy–(glandular hairy on peduncles) with
very narrow petals. & ap annual about 8 inches high
from ground in meadow. Bayberry at Lee's Cliff 2??
days elsewhere just beginning. Some Krigias out of
bloom   Galium aparine (?) a day or 2–but with 6?
leaves. Those scars where the woods were cut down
last winter now show–for they are comparatively
slow to be covered with green–only have dead
leaves–reddish brown spots. First observe the creak of
crickets   It is quite general amid these rocks–   The
song of only one is more interesting to me. It suggests
lateness–but only as we come to a knowledge of
eternity after some acquaintance with time–   It is only
late for all trivial & hurried pursuits–   It suggests a
wisdom mature, never late–being above all temporal
considerations–which possess the coolness & maturity
of autumn amidst the aspirations of Spring & the heats
of summer–   To the birds they say–ah–you speak like

children from impulse–nature speaks through you–but
with us it is ripe knowledge–the seasons do not revolve
for us; we sing their lullaby. So they chant–eternal at at
the roots of the grass. It is heaven where they are &
their dwelling need not be *heaved* up. Forever the
same–in May & in November (?) Serenely wise– Their
song has the security of prose– They have drunk no
wine but the dew– It is no transient love-strain
–hushed when the incubating season is past–but a
gloryfying of God & enjoying of him forever. They sit
aside from the revolution of the seasons– Their strain
is unvaried as Truth– Only in their saner moments do
men hear the crickets– It is balm to the philosopher.
It tempers his thoughts. They dwell forever in a
temperate latitude. By listening to whom–all voices are
tuned. In their song they ignore our accidents. They
are not concerned about the news– A quire has
begun which pauses not for any news–for it knows
only the eternal. I hear also Pe-a-wee pe-a-wee–& then
occasionally–Pee-yu the 1st syllable in a different &
higher kee emphasized–all very sweet & naive &
innocent.

Rubus canadensis out on the rocks XXX.

A hummingbird dashes by like a loud bumble-bee.

Tuesday May 23d

Pm to Cedar Swamp by Assabet.

The cobwebs–ap those I saw on the bushes the
morning of the 12th are now covered with insects &c
(small gnats &c) & are much dilapidated where birds
have flown through them. As I paddle up the Assabet
off the Hill I hear a loud rustling of the leaves–& see a
large scared tortioise sliding & tumbling down the
high steep bank a rod or more into the water– It has
probably been out to lay its eggs– The old coal-pit
heap is a favorite place for them. The wood-pewee

sings now in the woods behind the spring–in the
heat of the day (2 Pm) sitting on a low limb near me
–Pe-a-wee–pe-a-wee–&c 5 or 6 times at short & regular
intervals–looking about all the while–& then naively
Pee-a-oo emphasizing the 1st syllable–& begins again.
The last is in emphasis like the scream of a hen-hawk.
It flies off occasionally a few feet & catches an insect &
returns to its perch between the bars–not allowing this
to interrupt their order–   Scare up a splendid wood?
duck alternate blue & chestnut (?) forward–which flew
into & lit in the woods–or was it a teal. Afterward 2 of
them. & my diver of yesterday.

The bent grass now lies on the water–(commonly
light colored) for 2 feet–   When I first saw this on a
pool this spring–with the deep dimple where the blade
emerges from the surface–I suspected that the water
had risen gently in calm weather and was heaped
about the dry stems as against any surface before it is
wetted   But now the water is rapidly falling–& there is
considerable wind.–   Moreover when my boat has
passed over these blades I am surprised on looking
back to see the dimple still as perfect as before–   I lift
a blade so as to bring a part which was under water to
the surface & still there is a perfect dimple about it–the
water is plainly repelled from it. I pull one up from the
bottom & passing it over my lips am surprised to find
that the front side is perfectly dry from the root
upward & cannot be wet–but the back side is wet–   It
has sprung & grown in the water and yet one of its
surfaces has never been wet–   What an invaluable
composition it must be coated with. The same was the
case with the other erect grasses which I noticed
growing in the water–& with those which I plucked on
the bank & thrust into it. But the flags were wet both
sides. The one surface repels moisture perfectly. The

barbarea has been open several days. The first yellow
dawbug struggling in the river.

The white cedar has now grown quite *perceptibly* &
is in advance of any red cedar which I have seen. Saw
a humming bird on a white oak in the swamp   It is
strange to see this minute creature fit inhabitant of a
parterre. on an oak in the great wild cedar swamp
– The clustered andromeda appears just ready to
open–say rather the 25 XX.

The smilacina is abundant & well out here now   A
new warbler (?)

We soon get through with Nature. She excites an
expectation which she cannot satisfy. The merest child
which has rambled into a copse wood dreams of a
wilderness so wild and strange–& inexhaustible as
Nature can never show him. The red-bird which I saw
on my companion's string on election days–I thought
but the outmost sentinal–of the wild immortal
camp–of the wild & dazzling infantrie of the
wilderness–that the deeper woods abounded with
redder birds still–but now that I have threaded all our
woods & waded the swamps I have never yet met with
his compeer–still less his wilder kindred. The red-bird
which is the last of Nature is but the first of God–   The
Wht mts likewise were smooth mole-hills to my
expectation. We *condescend* to climb the crags of
earth–   It is our weary legs alone that praise them
– That forest on whose skirts the red-bird flits is
not of earth. I expected a fauna more infinite &
various–birds of more dazzling colors & more celestial
song–   How many springs shall I continue to see the
common sucker–*Catostomus Bostoniensis* floating
dead on our river. Will not Nature select her types
from a new fount? The vignette of the year. This earth
which is spread out like a map around me–is but the
lining of my inmost soul exposed–   In me is the sucker

that I see– No wholly extraneous object can compel
me to recognize it. I am guilty of suckers.

I go about to look at flowers & listen to the birds.
There was a time when the beauty & the music were
all within–& I sat & listened to my thoughts & there
was a song in them. I sat for hours on rocks and
wrestled with the melody which possessed me. I sat
and listend by the hour to a positive though faint &
distant music–not sung by any bird–nor vibrating
any earthly harp. When you walked with a joy which
knew not its own origin. When you were an organ of
which the world was but one poor broken pipe– I lay
long on the rocks foundered like a harp on the
sea-shore–that knows not how it is dealt with. You sat
on the earth as on a raft–listening to music that was
not of the earth–but which ruled & arranged it. Man
should be the harp articulate. When your cords were
tense.

Think of going abroad out of one self to hear
music–to Europe or Africa! Instead of so living as to be
the lyre–which the breath of the morning causes to
vibrate with that melody which creates worlds–to sit
up late & hear Jane Lind!

You may say that the oaks (all but the Chestnut oak I
have seen) were in bloom yesterday–i e shed pollen
more or less– Their blooming is soon over
– Water-bugs & skaters coupled.

Saw in Dakins land near the road at the bend of the
river–59 bank-swallows holes in a small upright
bank–within a space of 20 X 1½ feet (in the middle)
part above & part below the sand-line. This would give
over 100 birds to this bank– They continually circling
about over the meadow & river in front–often in pairs
one pursuing the other & filling the air with their
twittering.

Mulberry out today X

May 24th

4½ Am to Cliffs.

A considerable fog–but already rising & retreating to the river. There are dewy cobwebs on the grass.   the morning came in & awakened me early–for I slept with a window open–and the chip-bird was heard also. As I go along the causeway The sun rises red–with a great red halo through the fog. When I reach the hill–the fog over the river already has its erectile feathers up–   I am a little too late–   But the level expanse of it far in the east–now lit by the sun–with countless tree tops like oases seen in it–reminds of vast tracts of sand & of the sea shore–   It is like a greater dewy cobweb spread over the earth–   It gives a wholly new aspect to the world especially in that direction. The sun is eating up the fog. As I return down the hill my eyes are cast toward the very dark–*mts* in the N.W. horizon–the remnants of a hard blue scolloped rim to our saucer as if a more celestial ware had formerly been united there to our earthern. Old China are they worth keeping still on our sideboards though fragmentary.

The early cinquefoil now generally yellows the banks–   Put the sage willow with the black for the present–   The black spruce ap. blossomed with the white–but its leaf buds have not yet fairly started.

Pm to Pedrick's meadow

The side-fl– sandwort wel out in Moores Swamp   The pyrus has now for some days taken the place of the amelanchier–though it makes less show –   How sweet & peculiar the fragrance of the dif. kinds of Cedar! It is imparted to your hands. Ladies slipper since the 18th say 22nd   Waded into Beck Stow's. The water was so cold at first that I thought It would not be prudent to stand long in it–but when I got further from the bank it was comparatively warm–   True it was not then shaded nor quite so deep–but I suppose there were some springs in the bank. Surprised to find the Andromeda polifolia in bloom & ap past its prime–at least a week or more– The calyculata almost completely done & the high blueberry getting thin. It is in water a foot & a half deep & rises but little above it– The water must have been several inches higher when it began to bloom– A timid botanist would never pluck it– Its flowers are more interesting than any of its family almost globular–crystalline white even the calyx except its tips tinged with red or rose –Properly called water andromeda– You must wade into water a foot or 2 deep to get it–the leaves are not so conspicuously handsome as in the winter– Also the buck bean–ap. as old say a week–in the same depth of water. Potentilla Canadensis var. simplex perhaps 2 days. I find a male Juniper–with effete blossoms quite large yet so fresh that I suspect that I may have antedated it–Between Beck Stows & Pedrick's meadow.

The red cedar–has grown considerably after all – My Rubus Triflorus (only Big. & Gray place it on hill sides–) is nearly out of bloom– It is the same I found at the Miles swamp–has already some green fruit as big as the *smallest* peas. Must be more than a week old. It is the only annual rubus described. May it not be a new kind??

This evening I hear the hum of daw-bugs a few–but listen long in vain to hear a hylodes.

There being prob. no shrub or tree which has not begun to leaf now–I sum up the order of their leafing thus–(Wild & a few tame) Their buds begin to burst into leaf–

      The earliest Gooseberry in garden & swamp
        Ap 20
  ? –Elder longest shoots of any *in some* places
        (May 5)

Raspberry in swamps

Thimble berry (perhaps in favorable places
only–)

Wild red cherry in some places

Meadow sweet

? Red currant–but slow to advance–observed
only ours which is late?

? 2nd Gooseberry

Salix alba Ap. 27

?? Black currant not seen

Small dark native willow blossoming (?) & leafing

?? Early Willow 2 Colored? not seen

?? Muhlenbergs (?)   ″

Young Black Cherry

Choke cherry shoots

Viburnum lentago ⎫ not carefully

?   ″   Nudum ⎭ distinguished between–

Diervilla–advances fast

Barberry in favorable places

Some young apples ″   ″

Young Alders–slow to advance–both kinds–

Early Rose

?– –Moss Rose not seen

Sweet fern–slow to advance

Mt ash May 5 larger leaves than any tree & 1st to
show green at a distance

Cultivated cherry

Pyrus arbutifolia

? –Late pyrus not seen

Horse chestnut

Hazel May 5

? Beaked hazel–not distinguished

Early–large apples

Late goose berry in garden

? Pears not seen

Wild red cherry generally–or let it go with the
earliest.

?   Dwarf or Sand Cherry
     Hard-hack
??   –Clematis– – –shoots 5 or 6 inches long May 16
     Low blackberry
??   R. Triflorus 8 inches high May 22nd
?   Quince
??   May flower not seen
     Young red maples
??   Fever root–4 or 5 inches high May 12
     Creeping juniper comes forward like fir balsam
     Larch–open slowly   makes a show May 12
     V. Pennsylvanicum
     Amelanchier botryapium–fast
     High blackberry
?   Semper virens– –not seen
     Young rock-maple
?   Large White   "
     Alders generally
??   Linnaea–not seen
     Ostrya
     Amlelanchier oblongifolia
     Early trembles suddenly
??   Dwarf Cassandra–
     Balm of Gilead
     Early thorns
?   –Late   " not seen
     Yel. birch–
?   –Cockspur–thorn not seen
     Canoe-birch–shoots–
     White   –shoots
?   Black young (large not on 12)
?   Canada Plum
     Pitch pine
??   Bear berry not seen
?   Norway pine "   "
     White pine
     Young hornbeam

Cornus alternifolia
?   –Round leaved seen late
    Panicled– –Cornel
    Silky   "
    Sweetgale May 11
    Red oak
??   Scarlet (?)   "
    Bass–sudden
    Young chestnuts & lower limbs–full leafing of
      large not seen
??   Clethra seen late
    Old hornbeam
??   –Maple-leaved arrowwood not seen till late
    Arrow-wood
    Butter-nut
    High blueberry
    Rhus toxicodendron
?   var. radicans seen late
    Sweetbriar generally–earliest not seen
?   Swamp rose seen late
??   Beech not seen–
    White ash May 12
    Fir balsam
?   Fever-bush seen rather late
??   Wood-bine not seen
    Black-shrub oak
    Elm–young–
?   Slippery not seen
    Great red maples May 13
    clustered Andromeda 13
    young P. grandidentatas (large 3 or 4 days later?)
    Black oak
    Black willow
??   Sage   "   seen late
?   Chinquapin oak
??   Chestnut   "   not seen

Celtis
??   Cranberry
Locust 14th
Nemopanthes
?   Witch hazel in our garden
Swamp White oak–slow
?   Large Sugar Maples not well observed.
White swamp pink
Button wood
C. Florida
Panicled andromeda (not generally, several days
      later.
?   waxwork–seen but lost place
Pignut hickory–make a show suddenly
?   Mockernut ″
??   Black walnut
Young whit oak (old 15 slow
Prinos verticillatus 15
?   Single berry P. seen late
Huckleberries black
?   – – &c
NB   –Trees generally!!
??   Pinweeds seen late 6 or more inches high the
      large May 22nd
??   Cistus as early at least
Mulberry May 16
??   Carrion flower 4 or 5 feet long the 31st of May
White Spruce–slow
Sassafras–slow
Lambkill
??   –Mt Laurel–not seen early
??   Andromeda polifolia seen late
?   Rhodora   ″
Tupelo
Poison dogwood
???   Jersey tea

Azalea nudiflora 17

Button bush–but does not show being few buds.

Beach Plum 19   *scarcely* makes any show the
   24th no more than the button bush

? Red cedar ⎫
  White " ⎬ growth not obvious–& difference in
  arbor vitae ⎭ trees–not sure of date

Young hemlocks 20   old 21

checkerberry 20 shoots just visible

?) *Mt* sumach 22 (The 31st May it is much more
   forward than the button bush at Cliffs–

? Black spruce 24 hardly yet at Potters.

Of *common* deciduous shrubs or trees the button
bush is the latest to leaf–& from the fewness of its
buds–i.e. the great intervals between them they appear
later than other plants which leaf nearly at the same
time. Their being subject to overflows at this season
may have to do with this habit–as hard hacks &c under
these circumstances are equally late–

Of *all* deciduous shrubs & trees the *Mt* sumach at
Hubbards field is the latest to leaf. I have not observed
those under Fair Haven–v May 31

The beech plum at a little distance does not make so
much show of green even as the button bush– Do the
young shoots show more?

Tree toads heard oftener–& at evening I hear a daw
bug hum past– The mouse ear down begins to blow
in fields

25th

5½ Am to Hill.

Smilax XX– Heard & saw by the sassafras shore–the
rose-breasted grosbeak–a handsome bird with a loud
& very rich song–in character between that of a robin
& a red-eye. It sang steadily like a robin. Rose breast
–white beneath black head & above–white white on

shoulder & wings. The probably onoclea *just begin* to
light up the meadow with their yellowish green.

Friday May 26th

5½ Am to Climbing ivy

Pipe grass equisetum XXX   Butter cups now densely
spot the church yard.– now for the fragrance of firs–&
spruce–

Pm to Walden

Horse radish several days–rye 4 feet high   The
luxuriant & rapid growth of this hardy & valuable grass
is always surprising–   How genial must nature be to it!
It makes the revolution of the seasons seem a rapid
whirl. How quickly & densely it clothes the earth! Thus
early it suggests the harvest & fall. At sight of this deep
& dense field all vibrating with motion & light–looking
into the mass of its pale (?) green culms winter recedes
many degrees in my memory. This the early queen of
grasses with us (?)

Indian corn the 2nd–or later–   It always impresses
us at this season with a sense of genialness &
bountifulness–   Grasses universally shoot up like
grain now–in many places deceiving with the promise
of a luxuriant crop where in a few weeks they will be
dry & wiry–   Pastures look as if they were mowing
land. The season of grass–now everywhere green &
luxuriant.

The leaves have now grown so much that it difficult
to see the small birds in the tree tops–& it is too late
now to survey in woods conveniently. Saw Mr
Holbrook trying an experiment on an elm this
morning which he endeavored in vain to make
perpendicular last year with a brace–   It was about
6 inches in diameter–& he had sawed it a little more
than half through at about 6 feet from the ground &
then driven in an ashen wedge about ¾ of an inch

thick on the outside. This made it perpendicular–& he was about filling it with clay & protecting it. In Nathan Stow's Sprout-land every black cherry is completely stripped of leaves by the catterpillars and they look *as if* dead–only their great triangular white nests being left in their forks. I see where a frost killed the young Wht oak leaves & some hickories in deep-sproutland hollows ap about a week ago– –when the shoots were about an inch long & the leaves about the same– Ev. forest note still–the 1st syllable 3 times repeated er-er-er–&c–flitting amid the tops of the pines. Some young red or scarlet? oaks have already grown 18 inches *i.e.* within a fortnight–before their leaves have ⅔ expanded– In this instance perhaps they have accomplished more than half their years growth–as if being held back by winter their vegetative force had accumulated & now burst forth like a stream which has been dammed– They are properly called *shoots*. Gathered some small pincushion galls on a white oak–they are smaller & handsome more colored than those I first saw on shrub oaks about a week ago. They are shaped somewhat like little base-drum sticks with large pads– –on the end of last years twigs. It is a globular mass composed of fine crystalline rays–somewhat like stigmas–the ground white ones–thickly sprinkled with bright scarlet (rather than crimson) dimples. This is one of the most faery like productions of the woods. These young wht oak leaves–& young leaves generally are downy –downy-swaddled as if for protection against frosts &c– Are not the more tender the most downy? Why is the downy P. grandidentata so much later than the other? The lint now *begins* to come off the young leaves

The annular eclipse of the sun this afternoon is invisible on account of the clouds– Yet it seems to have created a strong wind by lowering the temperature? Yel– Bethlehem Star a day or more near the broom-rape–

May 27th '54
Pm to Saw Mill Brook

Geum rivale a day or 2 at Hubbard's Close   also the R triflorus abundant there along the brook next the maple swamp & still in bloom

Wild pinks (silene) ap *a day or 2*   The red-eye is an indefatigable singer, a succession of short bars with hardly an interval long continued–now at 3 Pm.

The Pin cushion galls on young wht oaks–& on shrub oaks are now in their prime–   It is a kind of crystalline wool–   Those which I have noticed on the shrub oaks are the largest and are crimson-spotted –while those on the young white oaks are scarlet spotted and for the most part about the size of a cranberry–   They are either at the extremity of last year's twig or saddled on it mid-way. No fruit perhaps catches my eye more–   It is remarkable that galls are apparently as early to form as the leaves to start–and that some of them are among the most beautiful products of the wood. Within small hard kernels in the midst of these I find minute white grubs. I see & hear the yellow-throated vireo–   It is *somewhat* similar (its strain) to that of the red eye *pre lia pre-li-ay* with longer intervals & occasionally a whistle like *tlea tlow* or *chowy chow* or tully ho (??) on a higher key. It flits about in the tops of the trees–   I find the pensile nest of a red-eye between a fork a shrub-chestnut near the path–   It is made–thus far–of bark–& different wooly & silky materials. The arums–some of them have bloomed prob. as early as the last I saw at the Miles swamp–   Viola pubescens must be about out of bloom?? Actaea alba fully out the whole raceme–say 2 days.

I see young goose-berries as big as *small* green peas.
Is that low 2 or 3 leaved plant without stem about Saw Mill brook a wood-lettuce? That tall swamp fern by Eb. Hub's Close with fertile fronds separate & now cinnamon colored–perhaps a little later than the Interrupted–appears to be the cinnamomea. Is that very wide loose-spread fern 3 or 4 feet high now beginning to fruit terminally–the spectabilis–a large specimen?

Sunday May 28th

The F hiemalis–fox col– sparrow–rusty grackles–tree sparrows (crow black birds have all gone by   it is here May 29th–all but the last long ago   NB   also the purple finch   The snipe has ceased (?) to boom–   I have not heard the phoebe of late & methinks the blue-bird & the Robin are not heard so often–(the former certainly not)   Those tumultuous morning concerts of sparrows tree & song–hiemalis–& grackles like leaves on the trees are past–& the woodland quire will rather be diminished than increased henceforth – But on the other hand toads & frogs & insects especially at night all through June betray by the sounds they make their sensitiveness to the increasing temperature–and their's especially is the music which ushers in the summer. Each warmer night like this–the toads & frogs ring with increased energy & already fill the air with sound–Though the bull-frogs have not yet begun to trump in earnest–   To this add the hum & creak of insects. These still herald or expect the summer. The birds do not foretel that.

12 Pm by boat to Lee's Cliff.

Larch cones are now conspicuous and handsome –dark crimson about ½ inch long   Pitch pine cones too are now handsome–   The larch has a little of the sweetness of the fir &c   Pontederias–flags–polygonum hydropiperoides (just showing itself)–that coarse utricularia often floating–potamogetons &c &c now begin to make a conspicuous border to the river–& its summer limits begin to be defined–   Pads began to be eaten by insects as soon as they appeared   Though it is still so low that I am obliged to lower my mast at the bridges. Even this spring the arches of the stone bridge were completely concealed by the flood–& yet at midsummer I can sail under them with out lowering my mast which is   feet high from the bottom of the boat. Critchicrotches have been edible some time in some places. It must be a kind of water milfoil whose leaves I now see variously divided under water & some nearly 2 feet long. At the *old* bridge at the hill–the water being quite smooth I saw a water bug cross straight from the S to the N. side–about 6 rods furrowing the water in a waving line

_____ there being no other insects near him on the surface. It took but about a minute. It was an interesting sight–proving that this little insect whose eyes are hardly raised above the plane of the water sees, or is cognizant of, the opposite shore. I have no doubt that they cross with ease & rapidity lakes a mile wide. It looked like an adventurous voyage for it   Probably he is in danger from fishy monsters–though it must be difficult for a fish to catch one. I see the exuviae or cases of some insects on the stems of water plants above the surface. The large devils needles are revealed by the reflection in the water–when I cannot see them in the air–and at first mistake them for swallows. Broom-rape perhaps yesterday XXX   Thimble berry out–(at Lee's Cliff day before yesterday at least XX)   Distinguished by the downy undersides of its leaves. I see those large thin

transparent radical heart? leaves floating on the
surface–as if bitten off by some creature. I see breams'
nests which have been freshly cleared out. & are
occupied   The *red* choke-berry is fully out–& I do not
know but it is as early as the black. Red clover at
Clam-shell a day or 2 X   Saw that common snake
–Coluber Eximius of Dekay Chequered Adder &c &c
–41 inches long. A Rather light brown above with large
dark brown irregularly quadrangular blotches
margined with black, and similar small ones on the
sides; abdomen light salmon white–whitest toward the
head–chequered with quadrangular blotches, very
light bluish slate in some lights and dark slate or black
in others. Abdominal plates 201 caudal scales 45. I
should think from Storer's description that his
specimen had lost its proper colors in spirits. He
describes not the colors of a living snake–but those
which alcohol might impart to it? It is as if you were to
describe the white man as very red in the face–having
seen a drunkard only.

   The huckle berries–excepting the late–are now
generally in blossom–their rich clear red contrasting
with the light green leaves–frequented by honey
bees–full of promise for the summer. One of the great
crops of the year–   The blossom of the V. vacillans is
larger & paler but higher colored on one side–and
more transparent (?) less concealed by leaves. These
are the blossoms of the Vacinieae or Whortleberry
Family–which affords so large a proportion of our
berries–   The crop of oranges lemons–nuts &
raisins–& figs quinces &c &c not to mention tobacco &
the like.–is of no importance to us compared with
these–   The berry-promising flower of the vaccinieae.
This crop grows wild all over the country–wholesome
–bountiful & free–a real ambrosia–(One is called

V. Vitis Idaea–Vine of Mt Ida) & yet men–the foolish
demons that they are–(devote themselves to culture of
tobacco–inventing slavery and a thousand other
curses–as the means–) With infinite pains &
inhumanity go raise tobacco all their lives. Tobacco
is the staple instead of huckleberries. Wreathes of
tobacco smoke go up from this land–the incense of a
million sensualists. With what authority can such
distinguish between Christians & Mahometans?
Finding the low blackberry nearly open I look long &
at last where the vine ran over a rock on the S hill-side
the reflected heat had caused it open fully its large
white blossoms–in such places ap. yesterday XX. The
high blackberry in similar places at least today XX. At
these rocks I hear a sharp peep–methinks of a peet
weet dashing away.   4 pale green? eggs finely
sprinkled with brown in a brown thrashers nest–on
the ground!! under a barberry bush. The night warbler
after his strain drops down almost perpendicularly
into a tree top and is lost. The crickets–though it is
every where an oppressively warm day Yesterday I had
a fire!! & I am compelled to take off my thinnish coat
–are heard particularly amid the rocks at Lee's Cliff
–They must love warmth. As if it were already autumn
there. White clover X under the rocks. I see the ebony
spleenwort full grown. The p. pines are *rather* past
bloom here–the cobwebs they contain yellowed with
their dust–probably generally in bloom elsewhere.
Turritis stricta ap out of bloom   Young Wild cherry
under rocks fully out 2 or 3 days; generally or
elsewhere not quite out–prob will *begin* tomorrow
   –It would be worth the while to ask ourselves
weekly–Is our life innocent enough? Do we live
inhumanely–toward man or beast–in thought or act?
To be serene & successful we must be at one with the

universe. The least conscious & needless injury
inflicted on any creature–is to its extent a suicide.
What peace–or life–can a murderer have?

Fair Haven Cliffs

The lint has begun to come off the young leaves
– The birches are still the darkest green to be seen in
large masses except evergreens– The last begin to be
less conspicuous–beginning to be lost in the sea of
verdure. The shrub-oak plain is now fairly greened
again–only slightly tinged with redness here & there
where are the youngest *wht* oak leaves.

As I sail down toward the clam shell hill about an
hour before sunset–the water is smoothed like
glass–though the breeze is as strong as before–. How
is this? Yet I have not seen much smooth water this
spring. I think the fall must be the time. The rounded
green hills are very fair & elysian. The low Clumps of
bushes on their sides just clothed with tender
verdure–look like islets half sunk & floating in a cool
sea of grass– They do not stand but float on the cool
glaucous swells. Though the grass is really short &
thin there. Whole schools of fishes leap out of water
at once with a loud plashing even many rods
distant–scared by my sail.

Cracks in the earth are still visible–& hips of the
late-rose still hold on under water in some places.

The inhumanity of science concerns me as when I
am tempted to kill a rare snake that I may ascertain its
species– I feel that this is not the means of acquiring
true knowledge.

Monday 29th May '54

Pm to Cedar Swamp by Assabet.

The white maple keys have begun to fall & float
down the stream like the wings of great insects.
Dandelion & mouse-ear down have been blowing for
some time & are seen on water– These are interesting

as methinks the first of the class of downy seeds which
are more common in the fall. There are myriads of
shad flies fluttering over the dark & still water under
the hill one every yard or 2 continually descending
almost falling to the surface of the water as if to drink
& then with perhaps a little difficulty rising again
–again to fall upon it and so on–   I see the same one
fall & rise 5 or 6 feet thus 4 or 5 times–others rise *much*
higher   And now comes along a large dragonfly &
snatches one. This 2 or 3 times   Other smaller insects
light colored are fluttering low close to the water–& in
some places are swarms of small black moths.

Viburnum lentago X in a warm place   The choke
cherry is leaving off to bloom now that the black
cherry is beginning–   The clustered andromeda is not
yet fully i.e. abundantly out.

The tall huckleberry in swamps is well out–   In the
longitudinal crevices of the white cedar bark there is
much clear yellow resin.

Raspberry XX prob. yesterday side of RR above
red-house–   See a purple finch & hear him–robin like
& rich warbling. S. Barret thinks that many chubs are
killed at mills and hence are seen floating. I see no
stone-heaps distinctly formed yet.

Saw what I thought my night-warbler sparrowlike
with chestnut (?) stripes on breast white or whitish
below & about eyes–& perhaps chestnut (??) head–

Stellaria Longifolia–ap. apetalous! 10 or 12 inches
high will soon open on the bank near the Ranunculus
abortivus.

These days it is left to one Mr Loring to say whether
a citizen of Massachusetts is a slave or not. Does any
one think that Justice or God awaits Mr Loring's
decision? Such a mans existence in this capacity under
these circumstances is as impertinent as the gnat that
settles on my paper. We do not ask him to make up his

mind, but to make up his packs. Why the U.S.
Government never performed an act of justice in its
life. And this unoffending citizen is held a prisoner by
the united states soldier–of whom the best you can say
is that he is a fool in a painted coat. Of what use a
governor or a legislature?   they are nothing but
politicians. I have listened of late to hear the voice of a
governor–Commander in chief of the forces of
Massachusetts– –   I heard only the creaking of the
crickets & the hum of the insects which now fills
the summer air. The governor's exploit is to review
the troops on muster days–   I have seen him on
horseback with his hat off listening to a chaplain's
prayer–that is all I have ever seen of a governor. I think
that I could manage to get along without one. When
freedom is most endangered–he dwells in the deepest
obscurity. A distinguished clergyman once told me
that he chose the profession of a clergyman because it
afforded the most leisure for literary pursuits–   I
would recommend to him the profession of a
governor–

   I see the papers full of soft speeches of the mayor &
the governor–& brother editors–   I see the the court
house full of armed men holding prisoner & trying a
Man to find out if he is not really a *Slave*. It is a
question about which there is great doubt.

   It is really the trial of Massachusetts–every moment
that she hesitates to set this man free–she is convicted.
The commissioner on her case is God. Perhaps the
most saddening aspect of the matter is the tone of
almost all the Boston papers–connected with the fact
that they are & have been of course sustained by a
majority of their readers–   They are feeble indeed–but
only as sin compared with rihghteousness & truth.
They are eminently time-serving. I have seen only the
Traveler–Journal–& Post. I never look at them except

at such a time as this. Their life is abject even as that
of the marines. Men in any office of government are
everywhere & forever politicians. Will mankind never
learn that policy is not morality–that it never secures
any moral right but always considers merely what is
"expedient"–chooses the available candidate–who is
always the Devil.

What is the position of Massachusetts? She leaves it
to a Mr Loring to decide whether one of her citizens is
a freeman or a slave. What is the value of such a *She's
Protection* to me? Perhaps I shall so conduct that she
will offer the *Freedom of Massachetts* in a Gold casket,
made in the form of a Court-House–perchance I spurn
with contempt any bribe which she or her truckling
men can offer. I do not vote at the polls– I wish to
record my vote here. Men are surprised because the
devil does not behave like an angel of light. The men
of the North–& of the South & east & west–are not men
of principle–

If they vote–they do not send men to Congress on
errands of humanity–but while their brothers & sisters
are being scourged and hung for loving liberty–while
(–insert here all the inhumanities that pandemonium
can conceive of–it is the mismanagement of wood iron
& stone & gold which concerns them. Do what you will
O Government with my mother & brother my father &
sister– I will obey your command to the letter– It
will indeed grieve me if you hurt them–if you deliver
them to overseers to be hunted by hounds–& to be
whipped to death–but never the less I will peaceably
pursue my chosen calling on this fair earth until
perhaps one day I shall have persuaded you to relent.
Such is the attitude, such are the words of
Massachusetts.

Rather than thus consent to establish Hell upon
earth–to be a party to this establishment–I would

touch a match to blow up earth & hell together. As I
love my life I would side with the Light & let the Dark
Earth roll from under me–calling my mother & my
brother to follow me.

Tuesday May 30th '54

White-weed X. Spergularia rubra ap a day or 2 side
of RR above red house. Yarrow XX

Pm to Clintonia Swamp & Pond

Saw a black snake dead 4 feet 3 inches long
slate-colored beneath. Saw what was called a
California Cat which a colored man brought home
from California. An animal at least a third smaller
than a cat & shaped more like a pole-cat or weasel.
brown-grey with a catlike tail of alternate black-&-
white rings–very large ears & eyes which were
prominent, long body like a weasel & sleeps with its
head between its fore paws–curling itself about–a rank
smell to it–   It was lost several days in our woods &
was caught again in a tree about a crow's nest.

Ranunculus repens–perhaps a day or 2   Channelled
peduncle & spreading calyx & conspicuously spotted
leaves. The leaves of the tall butter cup are much
larger & finely cut–&, as it were, peltate. Pickerel are
not easily detected–such is their color–as if they were
transparent. Vetch XXX. I see now green high
blueberries–& gooseberries in Hubbards close as well
as shadbush berries & strawberries. In this dark
cellar-like maple swamp are scattered at pretty regular

intervals tufts of green ferns O.
Cinnamomea above the dead brown
leaves broad tapering fronds curving over
on every side–from a compact center–now
3 or 4 feet high

Wood frogs skipping over the dead leaves whose
color they resemble–   Clintonia XX   Medeola X   The

last may be earlier– I am surprised to find arethusa abundantly out in Hubbards Close May be 2 or 3 days though not yet at Arethusa meadow prob on account of the recent freshet– It is so leafless that it shoots up unexpectedly It is all color a little hook of purple flame projecting from the meadow into the air. Some are comparatively pale. This high colored plant shoots up suddenly all flower in meadows where it is wet walking

A superb flower– Cotton grass here also prob 2 or 3 days for the same reason Eriophorum Polystachon –var Latifolium having rough peduncles.

The twigs of the dwarf-willow now gone to seed–are thickly invested with cotton–containing little green seed-vessels–like excrement of caterpillars & the shrubs look at a little distance like sand cherries in full bloom These are among the downy seeds that fly.

Found a ground robins nest under a tuft of dry sedge which the winter had bent down in sproutlands on the side of Heywood Peak–perfectly concealed –with 2 whitish eggs very thickly sprinkled with brown. Made of coarse grass & weed stems & lined with a *few* hairs & *stems* of the mahogany moss

The pink is certainly one of the finest of our flowers–& deserves the place it holds in my memory – It is now in its prime on the S side of the Heywood Peak–where it grows luxuriantly in dense rounded tufts or hemispheres raying out on every side & presenting an even & regular surface of expanded flowers– I count in one such tuft of an oval form 12 inches x 8 some 300 fully open & about 3 times as many buds–more than a thousand in all. Some tufts consist wholly of white ones with a very faint tinge of pink. This flower is as elegant in form as in color. though it is not fragrant. It is associated in my mind with the first heats of summer–or which announce its near approach. Few plants are so worthy of cultivation. The shrub oak pincushion? galls are larger whiter & less compact than those of the white-oak. I find the Linnaea & budded in Stow's wood by Deep Cut.

Sweet flag X.   waxwork June 1st X   I see my umbrella toad stool on the hill side has already pierced the ground.

May 31st

Old Election–cold weather   many go a-fishing today in earnest & one gets 40 pouts in river–

Locust XXX   Pm. to Miles Meadow by boat. A cold S E wind. Blue-eyed grass X ap in pretty good season   Saw a Greater Tell-tale–& this is the only one I have seen probably–distinguished by its size–   It is very watchful but not timid–allowing me to come quite near–while it stands on the look-out at the waters edge   It keeps nodding its head with an awkward jerk–& wades in the water to the middle of its yellow-legs–   It acts the part of the tell-tale though there are no birds here as if were with a flock   goes off with a loud & sharp phe phe phe phe or something like that. Remarkable as a sentinel for other birds

I think I see a few clams come up.

The *Mt* sumach at the cliffs is much more forward than at Hubbards–& perhaps is earlier to leaf than the button-bush. Alternate cornel ap yesterday XX Cock-spur thorn is well out how long?

Maiden hair fern how handsome–

June 1st   4½ Am to Hill   Fever-root X
The Umbrella toad-stool yesterday & now decaying a smaller one

It was so cold last night & still that I surely expected a frost & covered all our melons.– But either the wind changed or clouds came over in the night–& there was

no frost here. Here is another cool day– I sit with
window shut–& walk with a thick coat.–as yesterday
– Do we not always have these changes about the first
of June?

Pm to Bare Hill via Walden road
& Goose Pond–

Below the Alms house–I see a small sparrow–not
larger than the field sp. with a white line down the
middle of the head–a tawny throat & breast–a yellow
spot over the eye & another on the forward part of the
wings–flesh-colored legs upper mandible dusky–&
wings dark with faint lines of white undoubtedly the
Fringilla passerina– There were two– Its note was
that of my seringo, but very faint & short–sitting on the
wall or fence-post.

I see caterpillars now full grown clustered upon
their great nests on stripped cherry trees in the woods.
Hear my evergreen forest note–sounding rather
raspingly as usual where there are large oaks & pines
mingled–*er-er te, te ter twee* / or *er te, te ter twe*. It is
very difficult to discover–now that the leaves are
grown–as it frequents the tops of the trees. But I get a
glimpse of its black throat & I think yellow head– This
& the red-eye & wood pewee are singing now at
mid-day.

The pincushion galls of the shrub-oaks have but
little color compared compared with those of the
white-oak–and are now turning brown. The shrub oak
ones are larger–but plainer–less spotted & less
distinctly spotted than the others.

Galls are a surprising production of nature
–suggesting a union or connivance of 2 kingdoms the
animal & vegetable to produce– Many like the
ordinary black oak balls I see some fully grown–seem
as natural to the tree as its proper fruit–& plainly
anticipated by its whole economy. We hesitate to

pronounce them abortions. Their grub is a foster child
of the oak. I see equally if not more remarkable &
regular ones on a black shrub-oak of this form
attached to a leaf–green–a core like this
　　　being filled with air they burst with
　　　a puff when pressed.
　I see marks of a frost last night in sproutland
hollow–young white oaks & hickories & some other
oaks even have been touched & though not yet black,
their leaves are crisped & come off.

　In wood paths & elsewhere I now see countless
dragonflies which have lately taken wing–some of
those pretty little blue ones–and various colors. One of
those biting flies–stabs my finger severely
–wings half black with a green front–　Within
little more than a fortnight the woods from bare
twigs have become a Sea of verdure–& young *shoots*
have contended with one another in the race. The
leaves have unfurled all over the country like an
umbralla–shade is produced–& the birds are
concealed–& their economies go forward
uninterruptedly–and a covert is afforded to the
animals generally–　But thousands of worms & insects
are preying on the leaves while they are young &
tender–　Myriads of little parasols are suddenly spread
all the country over to shield the earth & the roots of
the trees from parching heat–& they begin to flutter &
rustle in the breeze. Chequerberry shoots in forward
places are now just fit to eat–they are so young &
tender　In a long walk I have found these somewhat
refreshing–

　From bare-hill there is a bluish mist on the
landscape–giving it a glaucous appearance

　Now I see gentle men and ladies sitting at anchor in
boats on the lakes in the calm afternoons–under

parasols–making use of nature–Not always
accumulating money. The farmer hoeing is wont to
look with scorn & pride on a man sitting in a
motionless boat a whole half day–but he does not
realize that the object of his own labor is perhaps
merely to add another dollar to his heap–nor through
what coarseness & inhumanity to his family & servants
he often accomplishes this. He has an Irish man or a
Canadian working for him by the month–& what
probably is the lesson that he is teaching him by
precept & example–? Will it make that laborer more of
a man?–this earth more like heaven–? The veiny leaved
hawkweed tomorrow XXX   I see the sand-cherry in
puffs like the Canada plum in some places.

Friday June 2nd

Pm up Assabet to Castilleja & Anursnack

While waiting for Mother & Sophia I look now from
the yard to the waving & slightly glaucous tinged June
meadows–edged by the cool shade–(gelid) of shrubs &
trees–a waving shore of shady bays & promontories
–Yet different from the August shades–   It is beautiful
& elysian. The air has now begun to be filled with a
bluish haze–   These virgin shades of the year–when
everything is tender fresh & green– –how full of
promise–promising bowers of shade in which heroes
may repose themselves–   I would fain be present at
the birth of shadow– –   It takes place with the first
expansion of the leaves. I find sanicle just out on the
Island XXX. The Black willows are already beautiful–&
the hemlocks with their bead work of new green–   Are
these not king-bird days when in clearer first June
days full of light–this aerial twittering bird flutters
from willow to willow & swings on the twigs–showing
his white edged tail–   The A. nudiflora has about done
or there was ap. little of it. I see some breams nests

near my old bathing place–above the stone-heaps
with sharp yellow-sandy edges like a milk pan from
within–showing considerably art (?) as well as labor.
⌢ Also there are 3
or 4 small stone heaps formed. We went near to the
Stone-bridge & crossed direct via the House-leek–of
which I brought home a bunch.

No S. longifolia–nor R. abortivus to be found yet in
bloom–though probably some of the 1st apetalous
have opened now. Lambkill XX   The painted cup
meadow is all lit up with ferns–on its springy slopes
– The handsome flowering fern–now rapidly
expanding & fruiting at the same time–colors these
moist slopes afar with its now commonly reddish
fronds–and then there are the Interrupted–& the
cinnamon ferns in very handsome & regular tufts–&
the brakes standing singly–& more backward. The
rhue just budded smells remarkably like a skunk and
also like a rank dog– –Strange affinity! Took tea at *Mrs.*
Barrett's. When we returned to our boat at 7 Pm–I
noticed first to my surprise that the river was all alive
with leaping fish–their heads seen continually darted
above water–& they were large fish too–   Looking up I
found that the whole atmosphere over the river was
full of shad flies. It was a *Great flight of Ephemerae*   It
was not so when I landed an hour & a half before.
They extended as high as I could see   It was like a
dense snow storm, and all (with very few exceptions)
flying as with one consent up the stream. Many
coupled in the air & many more with their bodies
curved   . They reach a mile or more from
the stone heaps to the mouth of the
assabet–but were densest where there were woods on
both sides–whether they came out of them–or they
made the air more still for them–   Those I examined

had 3 very long streamers behind the 2 outside about 1¼ inches– The fishes I saw rise for such as were struggling on the water close to the boat–were I am pretty sure suckers. This is like What the French fishermen call "Manna"– There were also swarms of small black millers close above the surface–and other small ones– Several dead suckers were floating. It seemed as if the suckers were now ascending the river In the air there was one or more at least to every foot. Apparently this phenomenon reached on this stream as far as it was wooded.

Caraway naturalized & out ap 2 or 3 days in S. Barrett's front yard.

Sat June *3d*   9 Am to Fair Haven with Blake & Brown

A very warm day–without a breeze– A king bird's nest in a fork of a black willow– Going up Fair Haven Hill the blossoms of the huckleberries & blue berries imparted a sweet scent to the whole hill-side. The cistus is well out on the cliffs–may be several days. At Lee's Cliff–where we dined the oxalis pretty early X (?) Hear the first but a faint locust. On the pond played a long with the bubbles which we made with our paddles on the smooth–perhaps unctuous surface–in which little hemispherical cases we saw our selves & boat small black & distinct–with a fainter reflection on the opposite side of the bubble (head to head) These lasted sometimes a minute before they burst. They reminded me more of Italy than of New England.

Crossed to Baker Farm & Mt Misery. To day having to seek a shady & the most airy place. At length we were glad when the east wind arose ruffled the water & cooled the air & wafted us homeward. Reflected how many times other similar bubbles which had now

burst–had reflected here the Indians his canoe &
paddle–with the same faithfullness that they now
image me & my boat.

June 4th

   8 Am. up Assabet to Barbarea shore with Blake &
Brown– Brown speaks of a great brown moth–prob
emperor moth which came out in Worcester a few
days ago. I see under the window half dead a large
sphinx-*like* moth which ap flew last night. The surface
of the still water nowadays with a kind of lint looking
like dust at a little distance– Is it the down of the
leaves blown off? In many places it reaches quite
across the river. It is interesting to distinguish the
different surfaces–Here broken in to waves & sparkling
with light–there where covered with this linty dust or
film merely undulating with-out breaking–& there
quite smooth & stagnant. I see in one place–a sharp &
distinct line as if there were a cobweb on the water
between the clear but ruffled water & the stagnant
filmy part–as if it were a slightly raised seam–&
particles of lint (?) are continually gliding in from the
clear space & arranging themselves along the edge of
the scum or film

   These warm & dry days which put Spring far
behind–the sound of the cricket at noon has a new
value & significance–so serene & cool. It is the
iced-cream of song– It is modulated shade. I see
now here & there deep furrows in the sandy bottom 2
or 3 inches wide leading from the middle of the river
toward the side and a clam on its edge at the end of
each. These are distinct whiter lines. Plainly then
about these times the clams are coming up to the
shore & I have caught them in the act. I now notice
froth on the pitch & white pines. The lower &
horizontal parts of the shaggy button bushes now left
bare are covered thickly with dry brown paper

confervae for the most part bleached almost white. It is very abundant & covers these stems more thickly than clothes on a line.

Pm to Walden

Now is the time observe the leaves–so fair in color & so perfect in form– I stood over a sprig of choke cherry with fair & perfect fair glossy green obovate & serrate leaves in the woods this pm–as if it were a rare flower.

Now the various forms of oak leaves in sproutlands –wet glossy–as if newly painted green & varnished–attract me   The chinquapin & black shruboak–are such leaves as I fancy crowns were made of– And in the washing breeze the lighter under sides begin to show–& a new light is flashed upon the year–lighting up & enlivening the landscape. Perhaps on the whole as most of the undersides are of a glaucous hue–they add to the glaucous mistiness of the atmosphere which now has begun to prevail– The *mts* are hidden. Methinks the first dry spell or drought may be beginning. The dust is powdery in the street & we do not always have dew in the night

The cracks in the ground made by the frost in the winter are still quite distinct.

In some cases fame is perpetually false and unjust. Or rather I should say that she *never* recognize the simple heroism of an action, but only as connected with its apparent consequence. It praises the interested energy of the Boston tea party, but will be comparatively silent about the more bloody & disinterestedly heroic attack on the Boston Court House–simply because the latter was unsuccessful. Fame is not just. It never finely or discriminatingly praises, but coarsely hurrahs. The truest Acts of heroism never reach her ear–are never published by her trumpet.

June 5th   6 Pm to Cliffs

Large yel. butterflies with black spots–since the 3d
–carrion flower X may be a day   Dangle berry–prob
June 3d X at Trillium Woods–   Now just before
sundown a Night-hawk is circling imp-like with
undulating irregular flight over the sproutland on the
Cliff-Hill–with an occasional squeak & showing the
spots on his wings–   He does not circle away from this
place–& I associate him with 2 grey eggs somewhere
on the ground beneath–& a mate there sitting.

This squeak & occasional booming is heard in the
evening air–while the stillness on the side of the village
makes more distinct the increased hum of insects. I
see at a distance a king bird or blackbird pursuing a
crow–lower down the hill–like a satellite revolving
about a black planet. I have come to this hill to see the
sun go down–to recover sanity & put myself again in
relation with Nature. I would fain drink a draught of
Nature's serenity–   Let deep answer to deep. Already I
see reddening clouds reflected in the smooth mirror of
the river–a delicate tint far off & elysian–unlike
anything in the sky as yet. The evergreens now look
even black by contrast with the sea of fresh & light
green foliage which surrounds them

Children have been to the Cliffs & woven wreathes
or chaplets of oak leaves–which they have left.–for
they were unconsciously attracted by the beauty of the
leaves now–   The sun goes down red & shorn of his
beams a sign of hot weather. as if the western horizon
or the lower stratum of the air were filled with the hot
dust of the day. The dust of his chariot eclipses his
beams. I love to sit here and look off in to the broad
deep vale in which the shades of night are beginning
to prevail. When the Sun has set the river becomes
more white & distinct in the landscape. The
pincushion galls have mostly turned brown–especially

the shruboak ones. Perhaps the sorrel was most
noticeable last week.

The caterpillars are & have been very numerous this
year– I see large trees (wild cherry & apple–)
completely stripped of leaves– Some of the latter 20
or 30 feet high are full of blossoms without a single
leaf. I return by moon-light–

Tuesday June 6th 54

I perceive the sweetness of the locust blossoms 15 or
20 rods off as I go down the street–

Pm. to Assabet bathing Place & return by Stone
Bridge.

I see now great boggy light green puffs on the
panicled andromeda–some with a reddish side–2 or
3 inches through. The Stellaria longifolia has been out
ap a day or 2. A slender rush flowered at the top at
bathing place some time

The painted tortoises are nowadays laying their
eggs– I see where they have just been digging in the
sand or gravel in a *hundred* places on the Southerly
sides of hills & banks near the river–but they have laid
their eggs in *very* few– I find none whole. Here is one
which has made its hole with the hind part of its shell
& its tail apparently & the ground is wet under it
– They make a great deal of water at these times–ap.
to soften the earth or to give it consistency–or both.
They are remarkably circumspect–& it is difficult to
see one working. They stop instantly & draw in their
heads & do not move till you are out of sight–& then
probably try a new place   They have dabbled in the
sand & left the marks of their tails all around. The
Black oaks birches &c &c are covered with ephemerae
of various sizes & colors–with one 2 3 or no
streamers–ready to take wing at evening–i.e. about 7.
I am covered with them & much incommoded. There
is garlic by the wall–not–yet out. The air over the river

meadows is saturated with sweetness–but I look round
in vain on the yellowish sensitive fern & the reddish
Eupatorium springing up. From time to time at mid
afternoon is heard the trump of a bull-frog–like a
Triton's horn.

I am struck now–by the large–light-purple–viola
palmatas rising above the grass near the river

There are the small–firm–few lobed wholsome dark
green shruboak leaf–light beneath

The more or less deeply cut, and more or less dark
green or sometimes reddish black oak–not light
beneath. These 2 bristle pointed

The very wet glossy obovatish–sinuate edged
swamp-white-oak–light beneath–

The small–narrower–sinuated–& still more
chestnut-like chinquapin–a little lighter beneath.

All these more or less glossy especially the
swamp-white & shrub.

Then the dull green–*sometimes* reddish more or less
deeply cut or fingered–unarmed round-lobed–wht
oak–not light beneath.

The last three without bristles.

I remember best the sort of rosettes made by the
wet glossy leaves at the ends of some swamp-white
oak leaves–also the wholesome & firm dark green
shrub oak leaves & some glossy & finely cut light green
black? or red? or scarlet?

I see some devils needles a brilliant green with
White & black–or open work & black wings–some with
clear black wings–some white bodies & black wings
&c.

White pine X

6½ Am Up Assabet

Rhus Toxicodendron yesterday XXX on
Rock   Smilacina racemosa prob June 4th XXX

Beautiful the hemlock-fans now broad at the ends of

the lower branches which slant down–seen in the shade against the dark hill-side–   Such is the contrast of the very light green just put forth on their edges with the old very dark–   I feast my eyes on it. Pignut. XXX   A crow-blackbird's nest in a wht maple–this side the leaning hemlocks–in a crotch 7 or 8 feet from ground–somewhat like a robin's but larger–made of coarse weed stems mikania & cranberry vines without leaves fish lines &c without & of mud lined with finer fibers or roots within–4 large but blind young covered with dark down. Sphinx moths about the flowers honeysuckles–at evening–a night or 2

Wednesday 7th

   6 Am up RR–   Vib dentatum XXX   Grape yesterday XXX   Vib. nudum June 5 XXX

   A thick fog this morning–through which at last rain falls–The first after a considerable & first dry spell. As yet nothing has suffered from dryness–the grass is very green & rank owing to the cold spring. the June grass converting hill-side pastures into mowing land. & the seeds or chaff (?) of many grass begin to fall on my shoes.

   Pm To Dugan Desert via Linnaea hills. Curled dock ap X Linnae abundantly out–some days–say 3d or 4th   It has not rained since morning–but continues cloudy & is warm & muggy–the sun almost coming out. The birds sing now more than ever as in the morning–and mosquitoes are very troublesome in the woods. The locusts so full of pendulous white racemes 5 inches long–filling the air with their sweetness–& resounding with the hum of humble & honey bees–are very interesting–   These racemes are strewn along the path by children–   Is that the C. Crus Galli–roadside bet. Joe Hosmer's & Tarbells? Again I am struck by the rank dog-like scent of the rhue budded to blossom. Along the wood paths & in wood-side pastures I see

the golden basins of the cistus. I am surprised at the
size of green berries–shad-bush low blueberries
–choke-cherries &c &c   It is but a step from flowers to
fruit. As I expected I find the desert scored by the
tracks of turtles made evidently last night though the
rain of this morning has obliterated the marks of their
tails   The tracks are about ⅞ of an inch in diameter–½
inch deep–2 inches apart (from center to center) in
each row–& the rows 4 or 5 inches apart–& they have
dabbled in the sand in many places & made some
small holes. Yesterday was hot & dusty–& this morning
it rained–did they choose such a time? Yesterday I saw
the painted & the wood tortoise out–now I see a
snapping turtle its shell about a foot long out here on
the damp sand with its head out–disturbed by me–   It
had just been excavating and its shell especially the
fore part & sides–& especially its snout–were deeply
covered with earth. It appears to use its shell as a kind
of spade whose handle is within tilting it now this way,
now that–& perhaps using its head & claws as a pick. It
was in a little cloud of mosquitoes which were
continually settling on its head & flippers–but which it
did not mind. Its sternum was slightly depressed–   It
seems that they are very frequently found fighting in
the water–& sometimes dead in the spring–maybe
killed by the ice. Some think that the suckers I see
floating are killed by the ice–   The linaria canadensis
well out near Heartleaf Pond. How long? Oenothera
pumila in low ground ap X   Angelica at Nut meadow
Brook XXX

    The low blackberry leaves on Dennis's Lupine hill
are now covered beneath with that orange rust   Were
those premature scarlet leaves which I saw at the Rock
on the 4th the shad-bush?   yes it was dying
– Common Iris some days–*one withered*   Saw again
what I have pronounced the Yellow-winged sparrow.

F. Passerina with white line down head–& yellow over
eyes–& my seringo note–but this time yellow of wings
not apparent–ochreous throat & breast. quite diff.
from the Bay winged & smaller–   NB   Does the
Baywing make the seringo note? Now the river is
reduced to summer width–   It is in the spring that we
observe those dark blue lakes on our meadows. Now
weeds are beginning to fill the stream–

This muggy evening I see fire-flies the first I have
seen or heard of at least–   This louring day has been a
regular fisherman's day–& I have seen many on the
river a general turn out.

Thursday 8th

Am   gentle–steady rain storm. The rosa nitida bud
which I plucked yesterday has blossomed today–so
that notwithstanding the rain I will put it down to
today XX–   Pm–on river–   Side saddle ap. tomorrow?
earliest & common Potamogeton X   Erigeron
strigosum slowly opening perhaps tomorrow. Meadow
rhue X with its rank dog-like scent   Ribwort plantain is
abundantly in bloom 15 or 16 inches high–how long?

Utricularia vulgaris ap X   young robins in nest

Herndon in his Exploration of the Amazon–says that
"There is wanting an industrious and active
population, who know what the comforts of life are,
and who have artificial wants to draw out the great
resources of the country".

But what are the "artifical wants" to be encouraged,
and the "great resources" of a country–surely not the
love of luxuries like the tobacco & slaves of his native
(?) Virginia–or that fertility of soil which produces
these–   The chief want is ever a life of deep
experiences–that is character–which alone draws out
"the great resources" of Nature–   When our wants
cease to be chiefly superficial & trivial–which is
commonly meant by artificial & begin to be wants

of character–then the great resources of a country
are taxed and drawn out–& the result the
staple-production is poetry.

Have the "great resources" of Virginia been drawn
out by such "artificial wants" as there exist. Was that
country really designed by its maker to produce slaves
& tobacco–or some thing more than freemen & food
for freemen? Wants of character–aspirations–this is
what is wanted–but what is called civilization does not
always substitute this for the barren simplicity of the
savage.

Friday June 9th 54

Pm to Well Meadow

The summer aspect of the river begins perhaps
when the Utricularia vulgaris is first seen on the
surface–as yesterday– As I go along the RR
causeway–I see in the cultivated grounds a lark
flashing his white tail & showing his handsome yellow
breast–with its black crescent like an Indian locket.
For a day or two I have heard the fine seringo-note of
the cherry-birds & seen them flying past–The only?
birds methinks that I see in small flocks now–except
swallows. The willow down & seeds are blowing over
the causeway. Veronica scutellata–ap several days. A
strawberry half-turned on the sand of the causeway
side–The first fruit or berry of the year that I have
tasted.

Ladies slippers are going to seed– I see some wht
oak pincushions nearly 2 inches through.

Is that galium out ap some days in the woods by
deep cut–near Linnaea–Triflorum   Call it the 1st for it
has less prickles or angles has smaller & less prickly
fruit–rath 3 separate than 3 couples & is more
spreading & reclining & is later? V. Maps. Compare
that at Lees–

I should like to know the birds of the woods better.
What birds inhabit our woods. I hear their various
notes ringing through them. What musicians compose
our woodland quire. They must be forever strange &
interesting to me. How prominent a place the vireo's
hold! It is probably the yellow-throated vireo I hear
now–a more interrupted red-eye with its prelia
–prelioit or tully-ho–invisible in the tops of the trees
– I see the thick flower-like huckle-berry apples.
Haynes (?) Goodwins comrade tells me that he used to
catch mud turtles in the ponds behind Provincetown
with a toad on a mackerel hook thrown into the pond
& the line tied to a stump or stake on shore. Invariably
the turtle when hooked crawled up following the line
to the stake–& was there found waiting–   Godwin baits
minks with muskrats. Find the great fringed orchis out
ap 2 or 3 days.   2 are almost fully out–2 or 3 only
budded–   A large spike of peculiarly delicate pale
purple flowers growing in the luxuriant & shady
swamp–amid–hellebores–ferns golden senecios &c &c.
It is remarkable that this one of the fairest of all our
flowers–should also be one of the rarest–For the most
part not seen at all–   I think that no other but myself
in Concord annually finds it–that so queenly a flower
should annually bloom so rarely & in such withdrawn
& secret places as to be rarely seen by man–   The
village belle–never sees this more delicate belle of the
swamp–   How little relation between our life & its!
Most of us never see it or hear of it. The seasons go by
to us as if it were not–A beauty reared in the shade–of
a convent–who has never strayed beyond the convent
bell. Only the skunk or owl or other inhabitant of the
swamp beholds it. In the damp twilight of the swamp
–where it is wet to the feet–How little anxious to
display its attractions. It does not pine because man

does not admire it. How independent on our race! It
lifts its delicate spike amid the hellebore & ferns in the
deep shade of the swamp–   I am inclined to think of it
as a relic of the past as much as the arrowhead–or the
tomahawk I found on the 7th ult. Ferns are 4 or 5 feet
high there.

7 Pm Up Assabet

The tupelo's stamens are loose–& will perhaps shed
pollen tomorrow or next day. It is twilight & the river is
covered with that dusty lint–as was the water next the
shore at Walden this pm–   Chimney & bank swallows
& still hovering over the river–& cherry birds fly past
–   The veery sings–& the tree toad–   The air is now
pretty full of shad flies–& there is an incessant sound
made by the fishes leaping for such as are struggling
on the surface–it sounds like the *lapsing* of a swift
stream–sucking amid rocks. The fishes make a
business of thus getting their evening meal–dimpling
the river like large drops as far as I can see
–Sometimes making a loud plashing. Meanwhile the
king fishers are on the look out for the fishes as they
rise & I saw one dive in the twilight & go off uttering
his cr-r-ack–cr-r- -rack

The mosquitoes encircle my head–& torment me–&
I see a great moth go fluttering over the tree tops & the
water–black against the sky–like a bat. The fishes
continue to leap by moonlight–a full moon–

Covered with disgrace–this state has sat down coolly
to try for their lives the men who attempted to do its
duty for it. And this is called justice! They who have
shown that they can behave particularly well–they
alone are put under bonds "for their good behavior"!
Such a judge & court are an impertinence.

Only they are guiltless who commit the crime of
contempt of such a court. It behooves every man to

see that his influence is on the side of justice–& let the
courts make their own characters. What is any
political organization worth–when it is in the
service of the Devil? I see that the Authorities the
Governor–Mayor–Commissioner–Marshall &c–are
either weak or unprincipled men–i.e. well disposed
but not equal to the occasion, or else of dull moral
perception–with the unprincipled & servile in their
pay. All sound moral sentiment is opposed to them. I
had thought that the governor was in some sense the
executive officer of the state–that it was his business to
see that the laws of the state were executed–but when
there is any special use for him he is useless–permits
the laws to go unexecuted–& is not heard from. While
the whole military force of the state if need be is at the
service of a slaveholder–to enable him to carry back a
slave–not a soldier is offered to save a citizen of
Massachusetts from being kidnapped–   Is this what all
these arms–all this "training" has been for these 78
years past. What is wanted is men of principle–who
recognize a higher law than the decision of the
majority. The marines & the militia whose bodies were
used lately–were not men of sense nor of principle–in
a high moral sense they were not *men* at all.

Justice is sweet & musical to hear–but injustice is
harsh & discordant–   The judge sits still grinding at
his organ–but it yields no music–& we hear only the
sound of the handle.

Sat June 10th 54

Pm to Conantum on foot–

The bay wing-sparrow apparently is not my seringo
after all–   What is the seringo? I see some with clear
dirty yellow breasts–but others as today with white
breasts dark streaked   Both have the yellow over
eye–& the white line on crown & agree in size–but I

have seen only one with distinct yellow on wings
– Both the last i.e. except only the bay-wing utter
the seringo note– Are they both yellow winged
sparrows–? or is the white breasted with streaks the
savannah sp?

The meadows now beg. to be yellow with senecio.
Side saddle generally out–petals hang down ap a day
or 2. It is a conspicuous flower. The fragrance of the
arethusa is like that of the ladies slipper or pleasanter–

I see many dead painted tortoises–the bugs now
devouring them–in the fields.

The lentago is just out of bloom now that the v.
nudum is fairly begun.

Saw probably a crows nest high in a white pine–2
crows with ragged wings circling high over it & me–not
noisy

Sunday June 11th 54

8½ Am to Framingham with Mrs Brown– All day
cloudy & cool without rain.

At 12 walked up the Sudbury river above Frank's to
Ashland–at first through the meadows–then over the
high hills in the vicinity. The stream narrows suddenly
in the middle of Framingham probably about the
outlet from Farm Pond & also Stony Brook. It is
merely a large brook from a rod to a rod and a half
wide–pursuing a serpentine course through
meadows–still deep & dark and sluggish for the most
part–and bordered with pads–thus preserving its
character below. Diervalla abundant on bank of river
at Frank's–out possibly yesterday XX. I see that red
sugar incrustation on red maple leaves.

Young song-sparrows have flown some days at
Frank's. Prunella well out–perhaps 2 or 3 days

From a high hill on the west of the river about a mile
from Franks–got a good view of Farm Pond eastward

–which empties into the river–with S Framingham–on
the SE side of it. I did not instantly detect it–the dark
hills & trees being reflected in it. How agreeable is a
still cloudy day–when large masses of clouds equally
dispersed float across the sky–not threatening
rain–but preserving a temperate air–to see a sheet of
water thus revealed by its reflections–a smooth glassy
mirror reflecting the light sky–& the dark & shady
woods. It is very much like a mirage. I went to a pretty
high hill east of & near to Ashland–where I found an
abundance of ripe–strawberries–earlier I am sure than
with us. A young man picking strawberries pointed
toward Hopkinton S westerly & said that it was 4 miles
thither straight–& 6 to White-hall Pond–(The source of
the river) but a great deal farther by the river–that
boats were used here at Ashland–& pouts & pickerel
caught. Grape out X   Saw in and near some woods 4 or
5 cow-blackbirds–with their light brown heads–their
strain an imperfect milky gurgling conqueree–an
unsuccessful effort. It made me think–for some
reason–of streams of milk bursting out a sort of music
between the staves of a keg. I saw a yellow spotted
tortoise come out undoubtedly to lay its eggs–which
had climbed to the top of a hill as much as 130 feet
above any water. A wood-tortoise had just made its
hole in the damp soil of Frank's garden–   Maple
viburnum well out–   It must come very soon after the
nudum–   The note of the Cuckoo is an agreeable
sound in the middle of these days. I think I saw wild
radish raphanus out as I rode along. These days
observe & admire the–forms of elms.

June 12

Pm to Walden–   Clover now reddens the fields
–grass in its prime–   Comfrey in front of Stows well
out some days ap. With the roses now fairly begun I

associate summer heats– Galium trifidum var latifolium? X Smooth angled–Some with linear leaves–? Is it tinctorium? Hear the evergreen forest note & see the bird on the top of a white pine somewhat creeper like along the boughs a golden head except a black streack from eyes–black throat–slate colored back–forked tail–white beneath er te, ter ter te, another bird with a *yellow* throat near by may have been the other sex– Is it the Golden Winged Warbler?

Pyrola chlorantha ap. X R lucida prob yesterday the 11th Judging from what I saw saturday i.e. the 10 A bud in pitcher the 13th The R nitida is the most common now The round leaved Cornel is well out at Heywood Peak–prob. 2 or 3 days. Perhaps this & the map. leaved Vib. are as early as the V. nudum & v. dentatum only more rare. Scared a king fisher on a bough over Walden–as he flew off he *hovered* 2 or 3 times 30 or 40 feet above the pond & at last dove & apparently caught a fish with which he flew off low over the water to a tree.

Mt Laurel at the pond X A narrow-leaved potamogeton well out at the bathing place–leaves 2 to 3 inches long. 4 leaved Loose strife XX

Silene Antirrhina–how long? Do I not see two birds with the seringo note–the Savannah? sparrow larger with not so bright a yellow over eyes–none on wing–& white breast & beneath former streaked with dark & perhaps a dark spot–& The smaller yellow-winged with spot on wing also–and ochreous breast & throat The first sings che che rar, che ra-a-a-a a-aru

Sundown to Clam Shell Hill

Night shade a day or 2– The cracks made by cold in pastures in the winter are still quite distinct. Phleum or herds grass ap X I sit on the Clam Shell Hill at sunset while several kinds of swallows are playing low over it chasing each other, and occasionally alighting

on the bare hill-side. The level rays of the sun shine
into & light up the trunk & limbs of a swamp white-oak
on Hubbard's meadow.

Tuesday June 13th '54.

I hear a quail this morning–

2 Pm by boat to Bittern Cliff & so to Lee's Cliff.

I hear the muttering of thunder and see a dark cloud
in the W.S.W. horizon–am uncertain how far up
stream I shall get. The nuphar lutea–var kalmiana ap 2
or 3 days in *some* places–generally not yet– Its leaf ap.
to be the prevailing pad   it is outside in the deepest
water, and is smaller an narrower in proportion to its
breadth than the other–with a small leaf stem–the
lobes overlapping. Now in shallow places near the
bends the large & conspicuous spikes of the broad
leaved potamogeton rise thickly above the water
– Though the plants are slanted downward by the
stream the spikes at their ends rise perpendicularly 2
or 3 inches–   My boat passes over these beds of
potamogetons pressing their spikes under water–   I
see the yellow water ranunculus in dense fields now in
some places on the side of the stream 2 or 3 inches
above water–& many gone to seed. See a white lily
bud.

The clams now lie up thickly at the Hubbard
bathing place–all on their edges–   The small iris is
budded near by. The clouds are rising up in the SW
irregular & ragged black pillars–in the form of men
and bears–the northern most with a glowing side. If it
rains hard I will run my boat ashore turn it over & get
under it–   I will not turn back–my afternoon shall not
be interrupted by a thunder shower. It is so warm that
I stop to drink where ever there is a spring–   The
flowering fern is reddish & yellowish green on the
meadows–   There are bare places on the meadow
from which the surface was carried off last winter. An

opposite cloud is rising fast in the E.N.E. & now the
lightning crinkles down it & I hear the heavy thunder
– It appears to be rising to meet the cloud in the
west–& I shall surely get wet– The comarum palustre
well out ap. 3 or 4 days–with its small dark & dull
purple petals on a dark purplish calyx ground. I
paddle slowly by farmers in small parties busily
hoeing corn & potatoes– The boy rides the horse
dragging the cultivator. They have a jug of sweetened
water in the grass at the end of the row– The
kingbirds eggs are not yet hatched. How often I see
Garfield–Uncle Daniel–the stout broad shouldered
farmer taking his way through the fields toward night
toward the river with his fish pole & basket over his
shoulder– He had on a live shiner 6 or 7 inches long
the other day & a cork above– He wanted to see if
he "couldn't catch a big pickerel." At Bittern Cliff
spring–a handsomely cut petalled geranium
–the whole rather elliptical in outline
forget the number of petals.

   The panicled cornel by Conants orchard wall will
open in a day or 2 prob. 14 well out the 16 elsewhere.
The small veronica with minute blue flowers at Lee's
cliff–how long. V. arvensis   Pennyroyal is 4 or 5 inches
high there.
   Galium circaezans–well out some days at Cliff–the
broad 3 nerved 4 leaves– The Thunder cloud in the
east has disappeared southward & that in the west has
changed to a vast black sheaf falling over on all sides
at top–but not rise fast. The little globular drooping
reddish buds of the Chimaphila umbellata
–(pipsissewa) are now very pretty. It is remarkable
how much the pads are eaten already– Some water
target leaves at Walden yesterday were scored as by
some litoral character. I see also the leaves of a
Columbine–with light markings being half eaten

through–and as there are eggs beneath–it may have
been done to let the light through to them. The krigia
seeds & down begin to fly– The common polypody &
ebony spleen wort show green fruit dots. It is
remarkable how many birds nests are broken out– At
least half that I examine again–have been disturbed
–only the broken shells left. viz–a chewink's & a brown
thrashers– The last was on the ground under a
barberry bush–was 6 or 7 inches in diameter without
of dead leaves & hay–then of small twigs–then of dark
root fibres within. no more lining. How beautiful the
solid cylinders of the lambkill now just before sunset
small ten sided rosy-crimson basins–about 2 inches
above the recurved drooping dry capsules of last
year–& sometimes those of the year before are 2
inches lower. The first rose-bug on one of these
flowers– Stopped to pick strawberries on Fair Haven.
When I have staid out thus till late many miles from
home–& have heard a cricket beginning to chirp
louder near me in the grass–I have felt that I was not
far from home after all–Began to be weaned from my
village home. There is froth on alders which comes off
onto my clothes. I see over the bream nests little
schools of countless minute minnows   can they be
the young breams? The breams being still in their
nests. It is surprising how thickly strewn our soil is
with arrow heads– I never see the surface broken in
sandy places but I think of them– I find them on all
sides–not only in corn & grain & potatoe & bean
fields–but in pastures and woods–by woodchucks
holes–& pigeon beds–and as to night–in a pasture
where a restless cow had pawed the ground. I float
home-ward over water almost perfectly smooth–yet
not methinks as in the fall–my sail so idle that I count
10 devils needles resting along it at once.
    Carpetweed ap X–& purslane X & Sweetbriar XXX.

Is not the rose pink–R. lucida paler than the
R nitida?

June 14th

Pm to Lime kiln with Mr Bacon of Natic

Sisymbrium amphibium (?) of Big. some days at foot
of Loring's land–   Common Mallows well out how
long? What is that sisymbrium or Mustard-like plant at
foot of Loring's? Erigeron strigosum?? out earliest say
yesterday XXX   Observed a ribwort near Simon
Brown's barn by road with elongated spikes & only
pistillate flowers–   Hedge mustard how long? Pepper
grass how long–sometime–   Scirpus lacustris maybe
some days. I see a black caterpillar on the black
willows nowadays with red spots. Mr Bacon thinks
that cherry birds are abundant where canker worms
are–says that only female mosquitoes sting (not his
observation alone)   That there is one or two arbor
vitae's native in Natic–   He has found the lygodium
palmatum there–   There is one pure-blooded Indian
woman there–Pearl I think he called her. He thought
those the exuviae of mosquitoes on the river weeds
under water–   Makes his own microscopes & uses
garnets–   He called the huckleberry apple a parasitic
plant–pterospora which grows on & changed the
nature of the huckleberry.–   Observed a diseased
andromed paniculata twig prematurely in blossom
–   Caught a locust properly Harvest-fly–(cicada)
drumming on a birch–which Bacon & Hill (of
Waltham) think like the septendecim except that ours
has not red eyes, but black ones. Harris's other kind
the Dog day Cicada (canicularis) or harvest fly–He says
it begins to be heard invariably at the beginning of
Dog days–he Harris heard it for many years in
succession with few exceptions on the 25th of July.
Bacon says he has seen pitch pine pollen in a cloud
going over a hill a mile off is pretty sure–

June 15th

5½ Am to Island & Hill–

A young painted tortoise on the surface of the
water–a big as a quarter of a dollar–with a reddish or
orange sternum. I suppose that my skater insect is the
hydrometer. Found a nest of tortoise eggs ap buried
last night–which I brought home 10 in all–one lying
wholly on the surface & buried in the garden. NB   The
soil *above* a dark virgin mould about a stump was
unexpectedly hard.

Pm up assabet to garlic wall–   That tall grass
op– the Merrick-swimming place is getting up pretty
well & blossoming with a broad & regular spike–for
some time–

This is the 3d afternoon that we have had a
rumbling thunder cloud arise in the east–not to
mention the west–but all signs have failed hitherto–& I
resolve to proceed on my voyage knowing that I have a
tight in my boat turned up–   The privet andromeda
XXX The froth on the alders andromeda &c not to
speak of the aphides–dirties & ap spots my clothes so
that–it is a serious objection to walking amid these
bushes these days–   I am covered with this spittle-like
froth–   At the assabet spring I must have been near a
black-& white creeper's nest–   It kept up a const
chipping–   Saw there also probably a chestnut-sided
warbler   A yellow crown chestnut stripe on sides
–white beneath & 2 yellowish bars on wings. A red oak
oak there has many large twigs drooping withered–ap.
weakened by some insect. May it not be the locust of
yesterday? Black willow is now gone to seed & its down
covers the water white amid the weeds. The swamp
pink ap 2 or even 3 days in one place–   Saw a wood
tortoise about 2 inches & a half with a black sternum
& the skin which becomes orange now ochreous
merely–or brown. The little painted tortoise of the

morning was red beneath. Both these young tortoises
have a distinct dorsal ridge. The garlic not in flower
yet– I observed no N. lutea–var Kalmianas on the
Assabet–

7 Pm to Cliff by RR

Cranberry. ap XX   Prinos laevigata ap 2
days   Methinks the birds sing a little feebler now a
days. The note of the bobolink begins to sound
somewhat rare–   The sun has set or is at least
concealed in a low mist   As I go up Fair Haven Hill I
feel the leaves in the sproutland oak–hickory &c cold &
wet to my hand with the heavy dew that is falling
–   They look dry–but when I rub them with my hand
they show moist or wet at once–   Probably I thus
spread minute drops of dew or mist on their surface
–   It cannot be the warmth of my hand–for when I
breath on them it has no effect. I see one or 2 early
blueberries prematurely turning. The Amelanchier
botryapium berries are already readened ⅔ over–& are
somewhat palatable & soft some of them–not fairly
ripe.

June 16

5 Am Up RR–

As the sun went down last night round & red in a
damp misty atmosphere–so now it rises in the same
manner–Though there is no dense fog. Poison
dog-wood yesterday–or say day before i.e. 14th & then
XXX   Rubus hispidus perhaps yesterday in the earliest
place over the sand then XXX   Mullein perhaps
yesterday XXX

Observed yesterday the erigeron with a purple
tinge   I cannot tell whether this which seems in other
respects the same with the white is the strigosum or
annuum–   The Calla which I plucked yesterday sheds
pollen today–say today then XX   A hypericum
perforatum seen last night will prob open today. XXX

I see on the Scirpus lacustris & pontederia leaves black patches for some days as if painted–of minute closely placed ova–above water–NB   I suspect that what I took for mil-foil is a sium. NB   Is not that new mustard-like plant behind Lorings & so on down the river–Nasturtium hispidum or hairy cress? Prob the 1st the 19th XXX   Heartleaf–XXX   Nymphaea odorata XXX. Again I scent the white water-lily & a season I had waited for is arrived. How indispensable all these experiences to make up the summer–   It is the emblem of purity & its scent suggests it–growing in stagnant & muddy–it bursts up so pure & fair to the eye & so sweet to the scent–as if to show us what purity & sweetness reside in & can be extracted from the slime & muck of earth–   I think I have plucked the first one that has opened for a mile at least–   What confirmation of our hopes is in the fragrance of the water lily. I shall not so soon despair of the world for it notwithstanding slavery–& the cowardice & want of principle of the North–   It suggests that the time may come when man's deeds will smell as sweet–   Such then is the odor our planet emits   Who can doubt then that nature is young & sound? If Nature can compound this fragrance still annually–I shall believe her still full of vigor–& that there is virtue in man too who perceives & loves it. It is as if all the pure & sweet & virtuous was extracted from the slime & decay of earth & presented thus in a flower–The resurrection of virtue! It reminds me that Nature has been partner to no Missouri compromise–   I scent no compromise in the fragrance of the white-water lily–   In it the sweet & pure & innocent are wholly sundered from the obscene & baleful. I do not scent in this the time serving irresolution of a Mass. Governor–nor of a Boston Mayor. All good actions have contributed to this fragrance. So behave that the odor of your actions may enhance the general sweetness of the atmosphere–That when I behold or scent a flower I may not be reminded how inconsistent are your actions with it. For all odor is but one form of advertisement of a moral quality– If fair actions had not been performed the lily would not smell sweet. The foul slime stands for the sloth & vice of man–The fragrant flower that springs from it–for the purity & courage which springs from its midst. It is these sights & sounds & fragrances put together that convince us of our immortality. No man believes against all evidence. Our external senses consent with our internal. This fragrance assures me that though all other men fall one shall stand fast–though a pestilence sweep over the earth, it shall at least spare one man. The Genius of nature is unimpaired– Her flowers are as fair & as fragrant as ever–

Three days in succession–the 13–14–& 15 ult. Thunder clouds with thunder & lightning have risen high in the east–threatening instant rain–& yet each time it has failed to reach us– –& thus it is almost invariably methinks with thunder clouds which rise in the east–they do not reach us. Perhaps they are generated along & confined to the Sea Coast.

The warmer–or at least *drier* weather has now prevailed about a fortnight– Once or twice the sun has gone down red shorn of his beams– There have been showers all around us but nothing to mention here yet– Yet it is not particularly dry– I hear nowadays the anxious notes of some birds–whose young have just flown–crow-black birds &c &c.

As for birds I think that their quire begins now to be decidedly less full & loud. I hear the phebe note of the chicadee occasionally– I see only a stray–prob summer duck very rarely on the river– The blue bird is lost & somewhat rare looking– The quail begins to

be *heard*– Very few if any hawks are commonly
noticed– The cow troopials have seen in small flocks
flitting about within a week–along low roads–the
song sparrows–Baywings–savannah (?) & yellow
winged (?) i.e. ochreous throated quite commonly
sing– woodpeckers not noticeable as in spring
– Rush-sparrow at sundown–
   Methought I heard a pine warbler today.
   Many chipbirds have flown– The blue herons
appear not to remain here this summer–& wood
thrushes are not so numerous within my range as
formerly. King fishers quite common–perhaps
especially at Walden where the water is clear–& on the
Assabet. The black & white creeper sings much– The
pine warbler as usual & the evergreen forest note
(golden winged (?) warbler.) Thrasher & catbird sing
still. Summer-yel bird–& Maryland yel– throat sing
still–& oven bird–& veery– The bobolink full strains
but further between. The red eye incessant at midday.
Gold finches twitter over as usual. The wood pewee
prominent–The night-hawk in full blast. Cherry birds
numerous the bold combattive looking fellows–&c &c
   Since Spring–say for a month or so we have had no
tumultuous water–waves running with white caps.
   Caterpillars have some time been grown on apple &
cherry trees & now the trees are leafing again– Other
caterpillars on oaks–black willows &c
   Dragon flies of various sizes & colors are now
extremely abundant hovering just over the surface of
the river & coupling there a blue & brown or a blue &
green one united–alighting on the least surface of a
weed– One kind of Cicada at least *began* a fortnight
ago–a sort of black eyed septendecim– Shad flies are
probably disappearing *Great* moths now abroad
– Rosebugs have just come–various plants are
frothy– –of all kinds as I have seen but odoratus

Tortoises are laying their eggs for some time– I find their eggs dropt–ap. young breams over nests– –frog spawn ap. in river–stringy ash color–

The effect of a good government is to make life more valuable–of a bad government to make it less valuable – We can afford that RR–and all merely material stock should depreciate–for that only compels us to live more simply & economically–but suppose the value of life itself should be depreciated.

Every man in New England capable of the sentiment of patriotism–must have lived the last three weeks with the sense of having suffered a vast indefinite loss. For my part my old & worthiest pursuits have lost I cannot say how much of their attraction. and I feel that my investment in life here is worth many percent less since Massachusetts–since Massachusetts last deliberately & forcibly restored an innocent man anthony Burns to slavery.

I dwelt before in the illusion that my life passed somewhere only *between* heaven & hell–but now I cannot persuade myself–that I do not dwell wholly within hell– The site of that political organization called *Mass*. is to me morally covered with scoriae & volcanic cinders such as Milton imagined–

If there is any hell more unprincipled than our rulers & our people–I feel curious to visit it. Life itself being worthless all things with it–that feed it are worth less– Suppose you have a small library with pictures to adorn the walls–a garden laid out around–& contemplate scientific & literary pursuits &c &c & discover suddenly that your villa with all its contents is located in hell–and that the justice of the peace is one of the devil's angels has a cloven foot & a forked tail–do not these things suddenly lose their value in your eyes. I feel that to some extent the state has

fatally interfered with my just & proper business– It
has not merely interrupted me in my passage through
court-street on errands of trade–but it has to some
extent interrupted me & and every man on his onward
& upward path in which he had trusted soon to leave
Court street far behind– I have found that hollow
which I had relied on for solid. I am surprised to see
men going about their business as if nothing had
happened–& say to my self unfortunates! they have
not heard the news–that the man whom I just met on
horseback should be so earnest to overtake his
newly-bought cows running away– –since all property
is insecure–& if they do not run away again–they may
be taken away from him when he gets them. Fool! does
he not know that his seed corn is worth less this
year– –that all beneficent harvests fail as he
approaches the empire of hell.

No prudent man will build a stone house under
these circumstances–or engage in any peaceful
enterprise which it requires a long time to accomplish.
Art is as long as ever–but life is more interrupted–&
less available for a man's proper pursuits– It is time
we had done referring to our ancestors– We have
used up all our inherited freedom–like the young bird
the albumen in the egg– If we would save our lives we
must fight for them. The discovery is what manner of
men your countrymen are. They steadily worship
Mammon–and on the 7th day curse God with a
tintimmarre from one end of the *Union* to the other. I
heard the other day of a meek & sleek devil of a bishop
somebody–who commended the law & order with
which Burns was given up– I would like before I sit
down to a table to inquire if there is one in the
company who styles himself or is styled bishop–& he
or I should go out of it–

Why will men be such fools as trust to lawyers for a *moral* reform– I do not believe that there is a judge in this country prepared to decide by the principle that a law is immoral & therefore of no force. They put themselves or rather are by character exactly on a level with the marine who discharges his musket in any direction in which he is ordered. They are just as much tools, and as little men.

Pm to Baker ditch–via almshouse Aut. Dandelion some time in Emerson's meadow pasture– Potentilla norvegica a day or 2 in low ground–very abundant at baker ditch with other weeds on a cleared & ditched swamp– Veiny leaved hawkweed of Heywood Peak–appears shut up at midday. (also the Aut. Dandelion) A veiny leaved hawkweed without veins –Is not this my–Gronovii– Pan. cornel well out on Heywood Peak

There is a cool east wind–(& has been afternoons for several days)–which has produced a very thick haze or a fog. I find a tortoise egg on this peak at least 60 feet above the pond. There is a fine ripple & sparkle on the pond seen through the mist– But what signifies the beauty of nature when men are base? We walk to lakes to see our serenity reflected in them– When we are not serene we go not to them. Who can be serene in a country where both rulers & ruled are without principle? The remembrance of the baseness of politicians spoils my walks–my thoughts are murder to the state– I endeavor in vain to observe Nature–my thoughts involuntarily go plotting against the state– I trust that all just men will conspire.

Dogs bane ap. tomorrow. I observed yesterday that the vib. dentatum was very conspicuous & prevalent along the river–as if few other flowers were in bloom–

An abundance of galium trifidum in low grounds

some smooth–some rough–with 4 leaves or 5 or 6–I
do not distinguish the varieties.– Am in doubt
whether the Polygonum which I find just opening at
the ditch (say tomorrow) is–sagittatum a rank
one–(or *arifolium*–the lobes of the leaves do not
spread thus / ⎰ but are ⎰ ⎱ 3 or 4 styles & 4 or
5 angled ⌣ ⌣
pods– Epilobium prob.   ⋃ coloratum–yet
rather downy–to-morrow– It is worth the while to see
the rank weeds which grow here on this cleared &
ditched swamp–   P. norvegica–touchmenot
– Polygonum sagittatum (?) night shade–&c &c– The
R. nitida grows along the edge of the ditches–the half
open flowers showing the deepest rosy tints–So
glowing that they make an evening or twilight of the
surrounding after noon–seeming to stand in the shade
or twilight– Already the bright petals of yesterday's
flowers are thickly strown along on the black mud at
the bottom of the ditch
   The R. nitida the earlier (?) with its narrow shiny
leaves & prickly stem–& its moderate sized rose-pink
petals

═══

   The R. lucida with its broader & duller leaves–but
larger & perhaps deeper colored & more purple
petals–perhaps yet higher scented. & its great yellow
center of stamens

═══

   The smaller lighter but perhaps more delicately
tinted, R. rubiginosa
   One and all drop their petals the 2nd day. I bring
home the buds of the three ready to expand at night–&
they next day they perfume my chamber.   add to
these the White lily–just begun–also the swamp pink
& prob morning glory & the great orchis & mt

Laurel–now in prime–and perhaps we must say that the fairest flowers are now to be found. Or say a few days later– (The arethusa is disappearing.)

It is 8 days since I plucked the great Orchis–one is perfectly fresh still in my pitcher. It may be plucked when the spike is only half opened & will open completely & keep perfectly fresh in a pitcher more than a week. Do I not live in a garden–in paradise–? I can go out each morning before breakfast–& do & gather these flowers, with which to perfume my chamber where I read & write–all day– The note of the cherry bird is fine & singing but peculiar & very noticeable. With its crest it is a resolute & combattive looking bird. The *mt* laurel is remarkable for its great dense & naked [for it runs to flower now] corymbs of large & handsome flowers– And this is a prevailing underwood on many of our *mt* sides–! Perhaps it is more appreciated in this neighborhood where it is comparatively rare–rare as poetry. Whitest in the shade.   mead. sweet tomorrow

Sat 17th June 1854

5 Am to Hill– A cold fog– These mornings those who walk in grass are thoroughly wetted above mid-leg. All the earth is dripping wet– I am surprised to feel how warm the water is–by contrast with the cold foggy air. The frogs seem glad to bury themselves in it. The dewy cobwebs are very thick this morning. little napkins of the fairies spread on the grass. Whorled utricularias ap. XXX. A potamogeton off Dodds with fine grassy threadlike leaves & stem (somewhat flattish) & small globular spikes–may be sometime? Ranunculus reptans maybe a day or more. A duck–prob. wood duck which is breeding here. From the hill–I am reminded of more youthful mornings–seeing the dark forms of the trees eastward in the lowgrounds–partly within & against the shining

white fog–the sun just risen over it–The mist fast
rolling away eastward from them.–their tops at last
streaking the mist & dividing it into vales–All beyond
them a submerged & unknown country as if they grew
on the sea shore– Why does the fog go off always
toward the sun–is seen in the E when it has
disappeared in the W? The waves of the foggy ocean
divide & flow back for us Israelites of a day to march
through– I hear the half-suppressed guttural sounds
of a red squirrel on a tree–at length he breaks out into
a sharp bark.

Slavery has produced no sweet scented flower like
the water-lily–for its flower must smell like itself. It will
be a carrion-flower.

Saw the sun reflected up from the Assabet to the hill
top–*thro'* the dispersing fog–giving to the water a
peculiarly pale golden hue–"gilding pale streams with
heavenly alchemy."

The judges & lawyers & all men of expediency
–consider not whether the Fugitive Slave law is right
but whether it is what they call constitutional– They
try the merits of the case by a very low & incompetent
standard. Pray, is virtue constitutional–or vice–is
equity constitutional or inequity. It is as impertinent
in important moral & vital questions like this to ask
whether a law is constitutional or not as to ask
–whether it is profitable or not– They persist in being
the servants of man & the worst of men rather than the
servants of God– Sir the question is not whether you
or your grandfather 70 years ago entered into an
agreement to serve the devil–and that service is not
accordingly now due–but whether you will not now for
once & at last serve God–in spite of your own past
recreancy or that of your ancestors–and obey that
eternal & only just Constitution which he & not any
Jefferson or Adams has written in your being. Is the

Constitution a thing to live by? or to die by? No as long
as we are alive we forget it & when we die we have
done with it. At most it is only to swear by. While they
are hurrying off christ to the cross–the ruler decides
that he cannot *constitutionally* interfere to save
him– The christians now & always are they who obey
the higher law.

This was meaner than to crucify Christ–for he could
take care of himself.

Pm To Walden–& Cliffs via almshouse
Rumex obtusifolius (?) may be some days. The
ever-green-forest bird at old place on Wht Pine & oak
tops–top of Brister's Hill on right–I think it has black
wings with white bars. Is it not the black-throated
green warbler? The unmistakable tanager sits on the
oaks at mid day & sings with a *hoarse* red eye note
pruit-prewee-prewa-prear-preā–(often more notes)
some of the latter notes clearer without the r. It does
not sing so continuously as the red eye but at short
intervals repeats its half-dozen notes. Iris virginica
well out–at Peltandra meadow–prob a day or
two–though not yet at arum meadow. The sorrel fields
are now turning brown– Another remarkably hazy
day–our view is confined–the horizon near–no *mts*–as
you look off only 4 or 5 miles you see a succession of
dark wooded ridges & vales filled with mist. It is dry
hazy June weather. We are more of the earth–farther
from heaven these days– We live in a grosser
element.–Are getting deeper into the mists of earth
–even the birds sing with less vigor & vivacity. The
season of hope & promise is past–already the season
of small fruits has arrived– The Indian marked the
mid-summer as the season when berries were ripe. We
are a little saddened because we begin to see the
interval between our hopes & their fulfillment. The
prospect of the heavens is taken away and we are

presented only with a few small berries– Before sundown I reached Fair Haven Hill & gathered strawberries– I find beds of large & lusty strawberry plants in sprout lands–but they appear to run to leaves & bear very little fruit–having spent themselves in leaves–by the time the dry weather arrives– It is those still earlier & more stinted plants which grow on dry uplands that bear the *early* fruit–formed before the droughts. But the meadows produce both leaves & fruit. I begin to see the flowering fern at a distance in the river meadows–

Butter & eggs some days perhaps–one or 2 well out while the rest show no forwardness. Tephrosia well out ap some days– Lupines are going to seed.

Morning glory ap yesterday– Well named Morning glory–Its broad bell–& trumpet shaped flowers faintly tinged with red are like the dawn itself. The new pitcher plant leaf is formed in some places–now free from insects. Pogonia *perhaps* a day or 2.

The sun goes down red again–like a high-colored flower of summer– As the white & yellow flowers of spring are giving place to the rose–and will soon to the red lily &c–so the yellow sun of spring–has become a red sun of June drought–round & red like a midsummer flower–production of torrid-heats.

Massachusetts sits waiting his decision as if the crime were not already committed. The crime consists first of all & chiefly in her permitting an innocent man to be tried for more than his life–for his liberty. They who talk about Mr Loring's decision–& not about their own & the State's consenting that he shall be the umpire in such a case–waste time in words & are weak in the head, if not in the heart alone.

June 9th continued– The amount of it–is if the majority vote the Devil to be God–the minority will live & behave accordingly–& obey the successful candidate–trusting that some time or other by some speaker's casting vote they may reinstate God again.

Some men act as if they believed that they could safely slide down hill a little way–or a good way–and would surely come to a place by & by whence they could slide up again. This is *expediency* or choosing that course which offers the fewest obstacles to the feet (of the slider–) But there is no–such thing as accomplishing a moral reform by the use of expediency or policy– There is no such thing as sliding up hill– In morals the only sliders are back-sliders.

Let the judge & the jury & the sheriff & the jailor cease to act under a corrupt-government–cease to be tools & become men.

Certainly Slavery–and all vice & iniquity have not had power enough to create any flower thus annually to charm the senses of men– It has no life– It is only a constant decaying & a death–offensive to all healthy nostrils– The unchangeable laws of the universe –by partial obedience to which even sin in a measure succeeds–are all on the side of the just & fair– It is his few good qualities mis-allied–which alone make the slave holder at all to be feared–it is because he is in some respects a better man than we–

Why who are the real opponents of slavery–? Are they the governors–the judges–the lawyers the politicians–? Or are they Garrison–Philips Parker & Co?

And at this very time I heard the sound of a drum in our streets– There were men or boys training–and for what? With an effort I could pardon the cocks for crowing still–for they had not been beaten that morning–but I could not excuse this rub a dub of the trainers.

Sunday June 18

Pm to Climbing Fern

The tephrosia is interesting for the contrast of
yellowish or cream color with red–. On every dry or
sandy bank I see the curled egg shells of tortoises
which the skunks have sucked. The R Lucida is pale
and low on dry sunny banks like that by Hosmer's
Pines. The leaves of what I call Rumex obtusifolius are
now lighter green & broader–& less curled & I think
shorter petioled than those of the curled D. & the root
is not yellow but white at core–   The Great Water?
Dock with its broad but pointed leaves is just
beginning to be obvious.

The flowering fern seed ripe–prob good while in
some places. There are many strawberries this
season–in meadows now–just fairly begun there–   The
meadows like this Nut Meadow are now full of the
taller grasses just beginning to flower–& the graceful
columns of the rhue–(thalictrum) not yet generally in
flower–and the large tree or shrublike archAngelica
with its great umbels now fairly in bloom along the
edge of the brook–

What we want is not mainly to colonize Nebrasca
with free men–but to colonize Massachusetts with free
men to be free ourselves–   As the enterprise of a few
individuals that is brave & practical–but as the
enterprise of a state it is cowardice & imbecility. What
odds where we squat or how much ground we cover–!
It is not the soil that we would make free–but men–

As for asking the south to grant us the trial by jury in
the case of run away slaves–It is as if–seeing a
righteous man sent to Hell we should run together &
petition the Devil first to grant him a trial by jury
–forgetting that there is another power to be
petinned–there there is another law and other
precedents.

Am surprised to find the cirsium horridulum or great yellow thistle out some already withering turned a dark purple–possibly a week old. I discover that I. Dugan found the eggs of my snapping turtle of June 7th ap– the same day. It did not go to a new place then after all– I opened the nest today– It is perhaps 5 or 6 rods from the brook–in the sand near its edge. The surface had been disturbed over a foot & a half in diameter–& was *slightly* concave. The nest commenced 5 inches beneath & at its neck was 2½ inches across & from this nearly 4 inches deep–& swelled out below to 4 inches in width.–Shaped like a short rounded bottle with a broad mouth–& the surrounding sand was quite firm. I took out 42 eggs closely packed–an Dugan says he had previously broken one which made 43   Daniel Foster says he found 42 this summer in a nest in his field in Princeton. They are a dirty white & spherical a little more than 1 & ¹⁄₁₆ of an inch in diameter–soft shelld so that my finger left a permanent dimple in them. It was now 10 days since they had been laid and a little more than one half of each was darker colored (prob. the lower half) & the other white & dry looking. I opened one but could detect no organization with the unarmed eye. The halves of the shell *immediately* as soon as emptied curled up   as we as we see them where the skunks   have sucked them. They must all have been laid at one time. If it were not for the skunks & prob. other animals–we should be over-run with them. Who can tell how many tortoise eggs are buried thus in this small desert.

Observed in 2 places golden crown thrushes near whose nests I must have been–hopping on the lower branches and in the underwood–a somewhat sparrow-like bird–with its golden brown crest & white circle about eye carrying the tail somewhat like a wren & inclined to run along the branches– Each had a worm in its bill–no doubt intended for its young. That is the chief employment of the birds now gathering food for their young. I think I heard the anxious peep of a robin whose young have just left the nest.

Examined as well as I could with the glass what I will call the *tweezer* bird– / Tra-wee, shreea-shre / –raspingly   I have heard perhaps as long as the Evergreen forest   It is a slender–somewhat small vireo like bird–yellow & yellowish all beneath–except a chestnutish (?) cresent 🔖 on breast–with ap. a white spot on the wing–and certainly a yellow or greenish yellow back between wings. Keeping rather high in the trees–   I could not see the general color of the upper-parts but thought it was dark olivaceous or maybe slaty. Can it be the blue-yellow-back warbler?

small grasshoppers very abundant in some dry grass. I find the Lygodium a late fern–now from a foot to 18 inches high & not yet flower budded or the leaves fully expanded–   Platanthera flava at the Harrington bathing place–possibly yesterday–an unimportant yellowish green spike of flowers. A large fresh stone heap 8 or 10 inches above water just below there. quite sharp like Teneriffe. Aralia hispida ap X. Typha latifolia may have shed pollen 2 or 3 days. I am surprised at the abundanc of its sulphur like pollen–on the least jar covering my hands & clothes–green at least–it does not burn. The female part of the spike green & solid & ap– *immature*. Epilobium angustifolium XXX up RR. this end of high wood.

Another round red sun of dry & dusty weather tonight–a red or red-purple helianthus–   every year men talk about the dry weather which has now begun as if it were something new & not to be expected.

Often certain words or syllables which have suggested themselves remind me better of a birds strain–than the most elaborate & closest imitation. Heard young partridges

It is not any such free soil party as I have seen–but a free man party–i.e. a party of free men–that is wanted– It is not any politicians even the truest & soundest–but strange as it may sound even godly men as Cromwell discovered–who are wanted to fight this battle–men not of policy but of probity. Politicians! I have looked into the eyes of two or three of them–but I saw nothing there to satisfy me– They will will vote for my man tomorrow if I will vote for theirs today – They will whirl round & round not only hoziontally like weather cocks–but vertically also–

My advice to the state is simply this–to dissolve her union with the slave holder instantly. She can find no respectable law or precedent which sanctions its continuance–and to each inhabitant of Mass. to dissolve his union with the state as long as she hesitates to do her duty.

Monday June 19th

Pm up Assabet– A Thunder shower in the north–will it strike us? How impressive this artillery of the heavens! It rises higher & higher– At length the thunder seems to roll quite across the sky and all round the horizon even where there are no clouds–& I row homeward in haste. How by magic the skirts of the cloud are gathered about us–& it shoots forward over our head–and the rain comes at a time & place which baffles all our calculations– Just before it the swamp white oak in Merricks pasture was a very beautiful sight with its rich shade of green–its top as it were incrusted with light Suddenly comes the gust & the big drops slanting from the north–& the birds fly as if rudderless–& the trees bow & are wrenched– It comes against the windows like hail & is blown over

the roofs like steam or smoke– It runs down the large
elm at Holbrooks & shatters the house near by. It soon
shines in silver puddles in the streets. This the first
rain of consequence for at least 3 weeks.

Amelanchier berries now generally reddening.

Methinks the botryapium has broader more ovate
often rounded & pointed leaves–the calyx-lobes
recurved on the fruit–While the oblongifolia is inclined
to obovate & narrower leaves–& erect calyx lobes.
Flowering Raspberry perhaps yesterday XXX

Men may talk about measures till all is blue & smells
of brimstone–& then go home & sit down & expect
their measures to do their duty for them– The only
measure is integrity & manhood.

Tuesday June 20th

Motherwort tomorrow XX. Elder XXX. A cloud of
minute black pollywogs in a muddy pool.

I see where the crickets are eating the wild
strawberries.

Pm. to Shadbush meadow. Heard a *new* bird
chut-cheeter-varrer-chutter-wit–on the low bushes
–about the size of Wilson's thrush–ap. Ap. Olivaceous?
above–most so on head–yellow front–dark bill–dark
wings with 2 white bars–all yellow or yellowish breast
& beneath– Perhaps never heard it before.
Cow-wheat ap. 2 or 3 days. A–3 leaved Lysimachia
Stricta ap. with reddish flower buds–not open.
Shadberries almost–but scarce There seems to be
much variety in the Rosa lucida some to have stouter
hooked prickles than the R. Carolina. Upland haying
begun. or *beginning*– Common nettle X

Wednesday June 21

We have had thick fog & rain fell through it this
morning– Pm. To Walden &c

Mitchella in Deep Cut woods–prob. a day or 2. Its
scent is agreeable & refreshing–between the
may-flower & rumcherry bark–or like peach-stone

meats. Pyrola secunda at Laurel Glen a day or 2 (?) ⅓
the spike now out. Most hieraciums venosum–are shut
by day some open this cloudy afternoon– When I see
the dense shady masses of weeds about water–already
an unexplorable maze–I am struck with the contrast
between this and the spring I wandered about in
search of the first faint greenness along the borders of
the brooks– Then an inch or two of green was
something remarkable & obvious afar–now there is a
dense mass of weeds along the water-side–where the
muskrats lurk & over head a canopy of leaves conceals
the birds & shuts out the sun. It is hard to realize that
the seeds of all this growth were buried in that bare
frozen earth.

   The glyceria is budded & drooping at the pond, but
hardly in flower. In the little meadow pool or bay in
Hubbard's shore I see 2 old pouts tending their
countless young close to the shore The former are
slate colored The latter are about ½ an inch long–&
very black–forming a dark mass from 8 to 12 inches in
diameter– The old one constantly circling around
them–over & under & *through*–as if anxiously
endeavoring to keep them together–from time to time
moving off 5 or 6 feet to reconnoitre. The whole mass
of the young–and there must be a thousand of them at
least–is incessantly moving, pushing forward &
stretching out. are often in the form of a great pout
–apparently keeping together by their own instinct
chiefly now on the bottom–now rising to the top,
alone they might be mistaken for pollywogs– The
old, at any rate, do not appear to be very successful in
their ap. efforts to communicate with & direct them.
At length they break into 4 parts. The old are evidently
very careful parents One has some wounds ap. In
the 2nd part of the story of Tanner–it is said
–"*Ah-wa-sis-sie*–Little catfish. The Indians say this fish

hatches its young in a hole in the mud, and that they accompany her for some time afterwards." Yet in Ware's Smellie it is said that fishes take no care of their young. I think also that I see the young breams in schools hovering over their nests while the old are still protecting them. I see 2 vars of Galium trifidum ap equally early–one smooth–the other rough–sometimes it grows in very dense tufts.

Peltandra well out ap. yesterday–quite abundant & pretty raised 2 or 3 inches above the water.

Prinos verticillata, possibly yesterday. Hypericum ellipticum XX– Eriocaulon XXX Partridges drum still. The effect of the pond on its shore while standing at a great height is remarkable– Though considerably lower than it was it appears much high–in some places–where it has worn away a barrier between itself and a meadow & so made the water deeper there.

Rambled up the grassy hollows in the sproutlands N (?) of Goose pond. I felt as if in a strange country–a pleasing sense of strangeness & distance Here in the midst of extensive sproutlands–are numerous open hollows more or less connected–where for some reason the wood does not spring up & I am glad of it–filled with a fine wiry grass–with the panicled andromeda, which loves dry places now in blossom around the edges–& small black cherries & sand cherries straggling down into them. The woodchuck loves such places–& now wobbles off with a peculiar loud squeak–like the sharp bark of a red squirrel–then stands erect at the entrance of his hole–ready to dive into it as soon as you approach. As wild & strange a place as you might find in the unexplored west or east. The quarter of a mile of sproutland which separates it from the highway–seems as complete a barrier as a thousand miles of earth. Your horizon is there all your own.

Indigo ap. a day in *some* places. Calopogon a day or
2 at least–in Hubbards Close–this handsomest of its
family after the arethusa.

Again I am attracted by the deep scarlet of the wild
moss rose half open in the grass–all glowing with rosy
light.

Friday June 23d

There has been a fogg haze dog-day like for perhaps
10 days more or less– To day it is so cold that we sit
by a fire– A little skunk ¼ or ⅓ grown at the edge of
the N river under hill. Birds do not sing this Pm
though cloudy as they did a month ago. I think they
are most lively about the end of May.

Pm Walden & Cliffs.

I see by the RR causeway–young barn-swallows on
the fences learning to fly. Lactuca maybe a day or
2–but the heads not upright yet. White weed now for
3 weeks has frosted the fields like snow–getting old.
Polyg. convolvulus XX   Wool grass tops–

Pyrola rotundifolia in cut woods tomorrow

A black snake in Abel Brooks now–on a warm dry
side of it his head concealed in a stump–rapidly
vibrating his tail which struck upon the leaves.   5 feet
one inch long. Uniform coal black above, with
greenish coaly reflections, bluish or slaty beneath,
white beneath head–about 189 abdominal plates. Tail
more than 1 foot long & slender–   When the head was
dead exerted great power with its body–could hardly
hold it.

Early blue berries have begun XXX on the Brown
sproutland Fair Haven. This the 3d summer since the
woods were cut. & the first for any quantity of berries I
think–so of Heywoods lot on Walden which I think was
cut also in 51-2.

Lysimachia stricta perhaps yesterday XXX at Lincoln

bound walden   After one or 2 cold & rainy days the air
is now clearer at last–   From the Cliffs the air is
beautifully clear showing the glossy & light-reflecting
greenness of the woods. It is a great relief to look into
the horizon–   There is more room under the heavens
– Specularia handsome dark purple–on Cliffs–how
long?

Disturbed 3 dif. broods of partridges in my walk this
pm. in dif. places–1 in deep cut woods–big as chickens
10 days old went flying in various directions a rod or 2
into the hill side–   Another–by Heywood meadow the
young 2½ inches long only not long hatched–making a
fine peep–   Held one in my hand where it squatted
without winking–   A 3d near Well meadow field. We
are now then in the very midst of them. Now leading
forth their young broods. The old bird will return
mewing and walk past within 10 feet

June 25th

Pm to Assabet Bathing place & Derby Bridge.

May weed say 27 XX   At Ludwigia poke-logan
–a cinder-like spawn in a white frothy jelly   A
green bittern ap. awkwardly alighting on the
trees & uttering its hoarse *zarry* note
zskeow-xskeow-xskeow   shadberry ripe. Garlic
open XX 18 inches high or more

The calla fruit is curving down–   I observe many
king fishers at Walden & on the assabet–very few–on
the dark and muddy south branch. Asclepias the
mucronate pointed what? yesterday XX   A raspberry
on sand by RR ripe XXXX

Through June the song of the birds is gradually
growing fainter. Epilobium coloratum XXX RR above
red house unless the one observed some time ago was
a downy coloratum–with *lanceolate* leaves   Trifolium
arvense X

Monday June 26

Pm up river to Purp. utricularia-shore

C. sericea yesterday at least– Small front-rank
polygonum XXX–a smut-like blast in the flower
– Small form of arrowhead in Hub aster meadow–ap
several days.

I am struck as I look toward the Dennis shore from
the bathing place–with the peculiar agreeable dark
shade of June a clear air–and bluish light on the grass
& bright silvery light reflected from fresh green leaves.
Sparganium ap ramosum–2 or 3 days– The largest ap.
the same but very rarely in blossom–found one
however–with a branched scape–but not concave
leaves except below– Gratiola XXX   Cicuta maculata
ap. tomorrow XXX

June 27

Pm Cliffs–via Hubbard meadow–

Smooth sumach at Texas house 2 days. Hellebore in
full bloom how long? For the most part does not
bloom. P. sagittatum prob also some time at Baker
Swamp. Oenothera biennis 2 or more days. Scutellaria
galericulata tomorrow. Polyg. persicaria
XXX   Marchantia Polymorpha ap X   Hydrocotyle a
day or 2 in Potter's field near Corner road by apple
tree– Blueberries pretty numerously ripe in Fair
Haven. P. Hutchinson Says that he can remember
when Haymakers from Sudbury 30 or 40 years ago
used to come down the river in numbers & unite with
Concord to clear the weeds out of the river in shallow
places & the larger streams emptying in. The 3 lecheas
show reddish & flower like at top– The 2d of Gray ap.
a little the most forward.

June 28

Am to Island– Tall anemone XXX   Pontederia
tomorrow XX

A thunder shower in the afternoon

June 29

Another clear morning after last evening's rain.

Pm to Lime kiln. Spurrey a good while. Cichorium at Simon Browns 3 or 4 days (early.)   also Catnep about 2 days. Canada Thistle yesterday XX   Earliest cultivated cherries a week ago.

Hazel-nut burrs now make a show. V. serpyllifolia still. The cherrybird's note is like the fine peep of young partridges or woodcocks. All the large black birches on Hubbard's Hill have just been cut down half a dozen or more, The two largest measure 2 feet $\frac{7}{12}$ in diam. on the stump at a foot from the ground –The others 5 or 6 inches less. The inner bark there about $\frac{5}{8}$ of an inch.

June 30th

Pm Walden & Hubbard's Close

Jersey tea XXX. Young oak shoots have grown from 1½ to 3 or 4 feet but now in some cases appear to be checked–& a large bud to have formed. Poke a day or 2 XXX   Small crypta Elatine–ap some days at least–at Callitriche pool.

R triflorus berries sometime–the earliest fruit of a rubus. The berries are very scarce light (wine?) red semitransparant showing the seed–a few 6 to 10 large shining grains–& rather acid. Lobelia spicata tomorrow XXX.

Sat. July 1st   Pm. to Cliffs

Hieracium Gronovii? ap. X ap allied to Venosum but stouter stemmed & pedicelled–with 4 or 5 leaves on the stem–hairy below & downy above. involucres & pedicels glandular bristly. Near springs.

From the hill I perceive that the air is beautifully clear after the rain of yesterday and not hot   fine grained. The landscape is fine as behind a glass–the horizon edge distinct–The distant vales toward the NW *mts* lie up open & clear & elysian like so many

Tempes. The shadows of trees are dark & distinct. On the river I see the 2 broad borders of pads reflecting the light–The dividing line between them & the water –their irregular edge perfectly distinct.

The clouds are separate glowing masses or blocks floating in the sky not threatening rain. I see from this hill their great shadows pass slowly here & there over the top of the green forest– Later a breeze rises & there is a sparkle on the river somewhat as in fall & Spring.

The wood thrush & tanager sing at 4 Pm–at Cliffs. The anychia almost in steep path beyond springs

Some boys brought me tonight a singular kind of spawn found attached to a pole floating in Fair Haven Pond. Some of it 6 feet below the surface–some at top–the uppermost as big as a water pail–a very *firm* & clear jelly–the surface covered with small rayed or star shaped spawn (?) A great quantity of it.

Sunday July 2nd

4 Am to Hill. Hear the chip-bird & robin very lively at dawn. From the hill–the sunrising I see a fine river fog wreathing the trees elms & maples by the shore– I mark the outlines of the elms & S. Purshiana–now so *still* & distinct looking east– It is clear summer now. The cocks crow hoarsely ushering in the long drawn thirsty summer day–A day for cows. The morning the spring of the day– A few bull frogs trump.

Pm to Flints Pond & Smith's Hill with C.

Thimbleberries XXX. Parsnip at Tuttles ap X Tobaccopipe well up. Spatulate or long leaved sundew some days. Hypericum Canadense some days   Pyrola elliptica ap. some days or directly after Rotundifolia on E. side of Smith's Hill. Asclepias Phytolaccoides–a

new plant–ap 2 or 3 days on Smith's Hill. A blue
high-blueberry X ripe. An abundance of red lilies in
the upland dry meadow–near Smith's spring trough
low from 1 to 2 feet high–up-right flowered–more or
less dark shade of red-freckled & sometimes wrinkle
edged petals–must have been some days. This has
come with the intense summer heats–a torrid July heat
like a red sunset threatening torrid heat. (Do we not
always have a dry time just before the huckleberries
turn?–)   I think this meadow was burnt over about a
year ago. Did that make the red lily grow? The spring
now seems far behind–yet I do not remember the
interval. I feel as if some broad invisible lethean gulf
lay behind between this & spring. Geum strictum also
N of near Assabett Bath Place out of bloom July 8.–a
new plant ap. a week or 10 days–some of the heads
alread ⅝ of an inch in diameter. Roadside at Gourgas
sproutland aspect of a buttercup–& P. Norvegica with
burrs.

I see some lysimachia stricta (?) with ends of petals
coppery reddish.

Monday July 3d

I hear the purple finch these days about the houses
–*à twitter witter weeter wee, à witter witter wee.*

Pm to Hubbard bridge by boat. On the great
hummock dropped on Dennis' meadow last winter–I
see now flourishing of small plants water-milkweed
–lysimachia stricta–hedge hog (?) grass–horse mint
–arrowhead–onoclea–viola lanceolata–gratiola–& the
small flowered hypericum. as well as meadow grass.

The river–& shores with their pads & weeds are now
in their midsummer–& hot weather condition–now
when the Pontederias have just begun to bloom. The
seething river is confined within two burnished
borders of pads–gleaming in the sun for a mile–& a

sharp snap is heard from them from time to time–next stands the upright phalanx of dark green pontederias–

When I have left the boat a short time the seats become intolerably hot. What a luxury to bathe now. It is gloriously hot–the first of this weather–   I cannot get wet enough   I must let the water soak into me. When you come out it is rapidly dried on you or absorbed into your body, & you want to go in again. I begin to inhabit the planet and see how I may be naturalized at last.

The clams are so thick on the bottom at Hub. bathing place–that standing up to my neck in water –I brought my feet together & lifted up between them so as to take off in my hand without dipping my head, 3 clams the first time, though many more dropped off.

When you consider the difficulty of carrying 2 melons under one arm–& that this was in the water–you may infer the number of the clams.

A cone flower–(new plant) Rudbeckia hirta (except that I call its disk not dull brown but dull or dark purple or marroon) in Arethusa meadow–   However Wood calls it dark purple   saw one (plucked June 25) –blossomed prob. about that time–   Many yesterday in meadows beyond alms house. Prob. introduced lately from west. Pycnanthemum muticum XXX at H. Corymbosum ditch. Proserpinacca at Skull cap pool ap 5 or 6 days XXX   *Touch me not* good while–10 days at least–some seeds now spring–

As I return down the river–the sun westering–I admire the silvery light on the tops & extremities of the now densely leaved golden willows–& swamp *wht* oaks & maples–from the under sides of the leaves. The leaves have so multiplied that you cannot see through the trees–these are solid depths of shade–on the surface of which the light is variously reflected–   Saw a fresh cherry stone–(must be cultivated cherry–wild not ripe) in the spring under Clam-shell Hill nearly half a mile from a cherry tree–   Must have been dropped by a bird.–

Mulberries some time.

July 4th   A sultry night the last–bear no covering–all windows open–

8 Am to Framingham. Great orange yel lily some days   wild yel.-lily drooping well out. Asclepias obtusifolia also day or 2–   Some Chestnut trees show at distance as if blossoming. Buckwheat how long? I prob. saw Asclepias purpurascens?? over the walls. A very hot day.

July 5th   Another very hot night & scarcely any dew this morning. Lysim. lanceolata var hybrida a day or 2–at Merrick bathing place   Bass at Island XXX

Pm to White pond–109 swallows on telegraph wire at bridge–within 8 rods & others flying about.   stachys aspera XX Clamshell ditch. The blue curls & fragrant everlasting with with their refreshing aroma show themselves now pushing up in dry fields–Bracing to the thought. Horsemint under Clam Shell ap yesterday XXX   On Lupine knoll picked up a dark colored spear head 3½ inches long lying on the bare sand–so hot that I could not long hold it tight in my hand. Now the earth begins to be parched–the corn curls & the 4 leaved loose strife &c &c wilts & withers. Seriocarpus XXX   Small circaea at Corner Spring some days. R carolina–ap a day or 2 corner Causeway–dull leaves with fine serrations 25 to 30+ on a side–& *narrow closed* stipules. Asclepias incarnata var pulchra. XXX

July 6th to Beck Stow's Pm.

Euphorbia maculata good while. Polyg. aviculare a day or 2 XXX–   Now a great show of elder blossoms.

Polygala sanguinea ap a day or more   Galium
asprellum in shade XXX prob earlier in sun. Partridges
⅓ grown

Veery still sings & toad rings.

On the hot sand of the new road at Beck stows
headed toward the water a rod or more off   had *some*
green conferva? on its shell and body–what is prob.
Cistuda Blandingii–Length of upper shell 6½ inches
breadth behind 4⅝–Tail beyond shell 2¼. Did not see
it shut its box; kept running out its long neck 4 inches
or more–could bend it directly back to the posterior
margin of the 3rd dorsal plate– Ran out its head
further & oftener than usual. The spots pale yellow or
buff. Upper half of head & neck blackish the former
quite smooth for 1⅝ inches & finely sprinkled with
yellowish spots, the latter warty. The snout lighter with
fine perpendicular black marks– Eyes large? irides
dull green golden. Under *jaw & throat clear chrome
yellow*. Under parts of neck & roots of fore legs duller
yellow–inner parts behind duller yellow still. Fore
legs with black scales more or less yellow spotted
above; at root & beneath pale yellow & yellowish
– Hind legs uniformly black above & but little lighter
beneath.

Tail black all round. No red or orange about the

animal– No hook or notch to
jaw   Plantain some days
& gnaphalium ap 2 or 3 days.

July 7th '54

Pm to Lygodium

Verbena urticifolia XX   Ilysanthes 3 or 4 days X back
flat E of Clam Shell Shore   Large form of arrowhead 2
or more days   Woodcock at the spring under
clam-shell. Campanula aparinoides ap. 3 or 4
days   The clover heads are turned brown & dry &
white weed is also drying up. I think that that is the

water dock just opening XXX in J.P. Brown's meadow.
Disturbed 2 broods of partridges this Pm–One ⅓
grown flying half a dozen rods over the bushes–yet the
old as anxious as ever rushing to me with the courage
of a hen. Columbines still–   What is that Potamogeton
well out at E guttata ditch? a few 3 4 or 5 small green
floating leaves–about 2 inches long.
–short stout
peduncle &
cylindrical spike–immersed leaves numerous linear
³⁄₁₆ inch wide wavey margined 4 to 6 or 7 inch long
–pellucid brown. & pointed. ap. sessile.

Lygodium palmatum *hardly* yet in flower I should
say–for the most very green & tender atop & not much
flatted out. Saw a pretty large hawk with narrow & long
wings–black tipped beneath–and white rump–Light
beneath–circling over the ministerial swamp with a
loud shuffling jay like–& some what flicker like sound.
                    Sat July 8th
    Pm to Assabet Bathing Place–
    Melilots a day or 2–   Spiranthes Gracilis a day or
2–? XXX   A Lysimachia Stricta? by Birch fence in path
beyond Shad-bush meadow–with whorls of 3 leaves–&
spike about 8 inches long–about June 26th–lower half
now out of bloom ¼ in bloom, upper quarter budded.
Ludwigia ap XXX   The *4th* & *5* ult were the hot Bathing
days thus far   thermometer at 98–& 96
respectively   Sium almost. say 9th XXX
                    8 Pm
    Full moon by boat to Hub. Bend.
    There is wind making it cooler–& keeping off
fog–delicious on water–   The moon reflected from the
rippled surface like a stream of dollars –   I hear a
few toads still–see a bat how long?   The bull frogs
trump from time to time–   It is commonly a full round
errr-err-err-err (gutturally & increasing in volume) &

then coarsely trilled?) *er-er-er / er-er-er / -er-er-er /*
Occasionally varied like the looing of a bull. The
whippoorwills are heard & the baying of dogs.

The R. nitida I think has some time done the–lucida
generally now ceasing–& the Carolina? just begun.

The middle Lechea not quite.

Sunday July 9th

Pm Fair Haven Hill via Hub. Bathing.

V. vacillans berry 4 or 5 days–common
blue-huckleberry XXX. Hubbard aster some days Is it
not Tradescanti like?–begins to blossom low in the
grass. Hypericum corymbosum not yet. Tansy by RR.
causeway a day or more. Chenopodium album XX

Examined a lanceolate thistle which has been
pressed & lain by a year–   The papers being taken off
its head sprang up more than an inch & the downy
seeds began to fly off.

Monday July 10th

Took up one of the small tortoise eggs which I
buried June 15th. The eye was remarkable developed
in the colorless & almost formless head one or 2 large
dark circles of the full diameter–   A very distinct
pulsation where the heart should be & along the neck
was perceptible–but there seemed to be no body but a
mass of yellow yolk.

Pm to Hub. Close–

Spotted pyrola–& Walden
Gaultheria ap 2 or 3 days in open ground.   some
choke-berry leaves in dry places are now red–some
locust leaves & elm leaves yellow. Lycopus sinuatus a
day or 2   platanthera lacera in one place ap. a week.
Stow's strawberry meadow ditch. Ludwigia palustris
same place ap 3 or 4 days   Pycnanthemum
lanceolatum 2 or 3 days. Polygala cruciata Hub. close 2
or 3 days   I find that most of the wild gooseberries are
dried up & blackened. Solidago stricta ap. tomorrow or

next day. Northern wild red cherry ripe ap some days.
Low blackberry XXX

A seriocarpus? in Poor house meadow with linear,
or narrow-spatulate, entire blunt leaves.

The following are the birds I chanced to hear in this
walk–(did not attend much)–   The seringos on fences
–link of bobolink–crow oven bird–tanager–che-wink
–huckleberry bird pretty often & loud–flicker
cackle–woodthrush–robin?–(Before 3 pm)   Then
red-eye–veery trill–catbird rigmarole–&c &c–

This is what I think about birds now generally   See a
few hawks about.

Have not heard owls lately not walking at night
Crows are more noisy prob. anxious about young.
Hear phebe note of chicadee occasionally–otherwise
    inobvious.
Partridge young ⅓ grown
Lark not very common but sings still.
Have not heard conqueree of blackbird for about a
    month methinks
Robin still sings & in morning–& Song sparrow
    – heard one conqueree July 11th chattering flocks
    now of females & young over river   Baywing
    See no downy woodpeckers–nor nuthatches
Crow b. birds occasionally chatter–
Hear flicker rarely.
Rush sparrow common & loud.
Saw a snipe within 2 or 3 days–& July 11th
Woodcock seen within " "
Think I have heard Pine warbler within a week.
Cuckoo & Quail from time to time
Barn swallow bank swallow &c numerous with their
    young for a week or 2
I hear the plaintive note of young blue birds
Chip sparrow in morning.
Purple finch about & sings.

Martin lively.
Warbling vireo still–& Wood Thrush–& red-eye &
    tanager all at midday
Catbird's rigmarole still.
Chee wink sings–(& veery trill from out shade
Whippoorwill at evening
Sum Yellow bird & yel– throat rarely–
Goldfinch oftener twitters over
Oven bird still–
Ev. forest note I think still.
Night warble of late
Rarely a full bobolink
Kingbird lively.
Cherry bird commonly heard.
Think I saw turtle dove within a day or 2
    The singing birds at present are
(villageous) robin–chipbird–warb-vireo–swallows
(Rural) song-sparrow–flicker–king bird–Goldfinch–link
    of bobolink–cherry bird–
(Sylvan) Red eye–tanager–woodthrush–chee-wink
    –veery–ovenbird–all even at midday   Catbird full
    strain–whippoorwill–crows
                    Tuesday July 11 '54
                    Pm by boat to Fair Haven
White Geum prob. about the 5th (not the 3d)
    Pontederia now makes a handsome show   The
female redwings & their young now fly in small
chattering flocks over the river. The smallest flowered
hypericum several days–have I mentioned it?
    Purple utricularia well out since the 5th say 7th X
The black high blue berries are a trifle earlier smaller &
acid. The R. lucida still common   Utricularia cornuta
at Fair Haven ap 2 days XXX   The water target is
common off this shore   Hypericum corymbosum in
front of Lee's Cliff–a day or 2 XXX. The drought is very
obvious on these rocks now–which are so verdurous in

spring. The Ivy (toxicodendron), arenaria serpyllifolia
&c are quite sere & brown. Pennyroyal–thimble
berries–& ferns also are withering. Some huckleberries
quite as if dried on a pan   Ampelopsis out 3 or 4 days
on the rock. Parietaria ap 2 or 3 days against rock
– Handsome now from these rocks the bay (on the s
side of Fair Haven at the inlet of river)–with its spit
of shining pads–   Lobelia
inflata a day or
more XXX   Veronica
serpyllifolia about done
large burr-reed leaves   There is much
afloat & lodged in the
middle of the river at Clam-shell bend–   Did the wind
tear it up? I heard Conants cradle cronchrunching the
rye behind the fringe of bushes in the Indian
field.   reaping begun.

Sun set when I was off Nut meadow   A straight edge
of massy cloud had advanced from the SSE & now
stretched overhead from WSW to ENE and after sunset
reflected a soft fawn? colored? light on the landscape
lightning up with harmonious light the dry parched &
shorne hill sides–The soft mellow fawn colored light
seeming to come from the earth itself.

July 12th

Pm to Dodge's Brook–
The early cotton grass is now about gone from
Hubbard's Close. With this month began the reign of
river *weeds obstructing the stream*. Potamogetons–&
heartleaves &c now for a *long* time covered with
countless mosquito cases?–   They catch my oars &
retard the boat–   A rail will be detained a month by
them in mid stream. & tortoises Sternothiaerus or
E picta 4 or 5 or more in a row lie along it   Many
young–barn? swallows (They are a darker crescent on
the breast & long tail feathers not grown) sit in flocks
on the bared dead willows over the water & let me

float within 4 or 5 feet– Birds do not distinguish a man sitting in a boat.

I see a green bittern wading in a shallow muddy place–with an awkward teetering fluttering pace. Button bush XXX. Observed a pickerel in the Assabet about a foot long–headed up stream–quasi transparent (such its color) with darker & lighter parts contrasted–very still while I float quite near– There is a constant motion of the pectoral fins & also a waving motion of the ventrals ap. to resist the stream, and a slight waving of the anal ap to preserve its direction – It darted off at last by a strong sculling motion of its tail. See White maple leaves floating bottom up covered with feathery aphides.

A lilium Canadense (at Dodge Brook corner by road) approaching Superbum 4½ feet high with a whorl of 4 flowers _⌐⌐ & 2 more above somewhat pyramidal. ⋊ & petals recurved.
Thursday July 13th 54

2 Pm to Bare Hill Lincoln by RR–

Have heard a faint locust-like sound from crickets a week or 2. In the midst of July heat & drought– The season is trivial as noon. I hear the hot weather & noonday birds–redeye–tanager–wood-pewee &c Plants are curled & withered. The leaves dry ripe like the berries. The point of a lower leaf of a smooth sumach is scarlet–& some geranium leaves Many birch leaves are yellow & falling. Leaves are very much eaten–of some kinds hard to find a perfect specimen–unless of a firm texture– The Pyrus arbutifolia is very thick & glossy dark green– The tupelo leaf is pretty firm & perfect–not *so* glossy–more or less winding & the shoots are zigzag or winding. Polygonum hydropiper XXX at Baker swamp Thoroughwort tomorrow or next day XXXX. Scutellaria lateriflora some days at least– The chestnuts now in full bloom–are conspicuous from the hills–(Bare Hill). like a yellowish or creamy tinged rime. V. vacillans on Bare Hill ripe enough to pick now consid. in advance of huckleberries. sweeter than last & grow in dense clusters. The V. Pennsylvan.–is soft & rather thin & tasteless–mountain & springlike–with its fine light blue bloom very handsome simple & ambrosial– This–vacillans–is more earthy like solid food. Many of the huckleberries here on the hill top have dried black & shrivelled before ripening.

Boys go after the cows now about 5½ o clock   Decodon not distinctly flower budded yet–

Gnaphalium pearly–well out say yesterday XXX   If there is an Interregnum in the flowers it is when berries begin.

Scent the bruised leaves of the fragrant goldenrod along the Lincoln road now

What I have called S. arguta XXX at Walden v. radical leaves also an aster perhaps Diplopappus umbellatus at Baker swamp will open in a few days

Friday July 14th

awake to a day of gentle rain–very much needed –none to speak of for nearly a month methinks. The cooler & stiller day has a valuable effect on my spirits.

Pm– Over the Hill to Brown's watering place. It holds up from time & then a fine misty rain falls. It lies on the fine reddish tops of some grasses thick & whitish like morning cobwebs. The stillness is very soothing. This is a summer rain. The earth is being bedewed. There is no storm or violence to it. Health is a sound relation to nature. Anychia plenty by the Watering Place (with the Amphicarpaea) but calyx ap. not expanded–. Amphicarpaea not yet. Penthorum 3 or 4 days ap. XXX   Xyris ap 3 or 4 days in meadow close by. Hardhack 2 or 3 days XXX   A hedyotis still   Elodea tomorrow XXX

The red capsules of the hypericum Ellipticum here & there   This one of the Fall-ward phenomena in still rainy days.

Sat. July 15

Pm to Hub. Bridge Causeway via river.
XXX Rained still in forenoon, now cloudy

Fields comparatively deserted today & yesterday –hay stands cocked in them on all sides–Some being shorn are clear for the walker. It is but a short time that he has to dodge the haymakers– This cooler–still cloudy weather after the rain is very autumnal & restorative to our spirits– The robin sings–still–but the goldfinch twitters over oftener–& I hear the link link of the bobolink (one perfect strain!) and the crickets creak more as in the fall– All these sounds dispose our minds to serenity– Perhaps the mosquitoes are most troublesome such days in the woods if it is warm enough. We seem to be passing or to have passed a dividing line between spring & autumn–& begin to descend the long slope toward winter. on the shady side of the hill I go along Hubbards Walls toward the bathing place–stepping high to keep my feet as dry as may be–(all is stillness in the fields) The calamint (pycnanthem muticum) standing by the wall with its hoary upper leaves–full of light even this cloudy day–& reminding of the fragrance which I know so well is an agreeable sight. I need not smell it. it is a balm to my mind to remember its fragrance–

I hear a bay wing on the wall near-by sound far away–a fainter song spar– strain somewhat– I see its open mouth & quivering throat yet can hardly believe the seemingly distant strain proceeds from it–yaw yaw / twee twee / twitter twitter–te twee twe tw tw tw & so ends with a short & rapid trill– Again I am attracted by the Clam shell reach of the river running E & W–as

seen from Hubbard's fields–now beginning to be
smoothed as in the fall– First next the meadow is the
broad dark green
rank of pickerel
weeds &c &c
(polygonum &c)
then the light
reflecting edging
of pads–& then
the smooth still
cloud reflecting   water. My thoughts are driven

inward–even as clouds and trees are reflected in the
still smooth water– There is an inwardness even in
the mosquitoes hum–while I am picking blueberries in
the dank wood.

Rhexia near the R. Copallina–ap yesterday XXX   The
flicker still & the veery full & maryland yel throat. &
nut hatch   Many birds begin to fly in small flocks like
grown up broods–   Green grapes & cranberries also
remind me of the advancing season–   The former are
as large as ripe cranberries–the latter as big as
peas–though the vines are still full of blossoms.
Cymbidiums are quite fresh–& pogonias linger still.
Drosera rotundifolia end of Hubbard bank wall Corner
road–some days–perhaps a fortnight–for it was nearly
out on the 2nd its lower flowers first & now dry.

The stems an leaves of various asters & golden-rods
which ere long will reign along the way begin to be
conspicuous. Amaranthus hybridus several days at
least–   It has come out quite fair–& warm–   There are
many butterflies yellow & red about the A. incarnata
now

Sunday July 16th

A thick fog began last night & lasts till late this
morning. first of the kind methinks

Pm via RR. & Pond to Saw Mill Brook–

Many yellow butterflies & red on clover & yarrow
– Is it the yel– winged or savannah sparrow with
yellow alternating with dark streaks on throat–as well
as yel over eye–reddish flesh colored legs & 2 light bars
on wings? S nemoralis yesterday XXX

Woodcock by side of walden in woods.

Methinks there were most devils needles a month
ago. Lycopus virginicus by target meadow a day or two
may be as long as the other elsewhere. Ludwigia
palustris grows there   Goodyera repens tomorrow.
XXX   Polygala verticillata ap. some days. The Rhus
toxicodendron leaves are turned clear light yellow in
some places in others many dried & brown. Mimulus
ringens at Saw Mill Brook, ap 2 days. XX   The large?
circaea it is the lutetiana though the flowers are white
ap 2 or 3 days. Trientalis ash col fruit.

After the late rains & last nights fog it is *somewhat*
dogdayish & there is a damp–earthy mildewy scent
to the ground in wood paths   Aralia nudicaulis
berries well ripe. The polygala sanguinea
heads in the grass look like sugarplums.

Monday July 17

Last night & this morning another thick
Dog-dayish fog– I find my chamber full
this morning. It lasts till 9 Am–

11 Am by river to Fair Haven–

I go to observe the lilies. I see a rail lodged in the
weeds with 7 tortoises on it–another with 10–another
with 11 all in a row sunning now at midday hot as it is
– They are mostly the painted tortoise. Apparently no
weather is too hot for them thus to bask in the sun.
The pontederia is in its prime alive with butterflies
yellow & others– I See its tall blue spikes reflected
beneath the edge of the pads on each side–pointing
down to a heaven beneath as well as above– Earth
appears but a thin crust or pellicle. The river was at its

lowest thus far prob. on the 13th ult. The rains
succeeding the drought have now raised it a little. &
this forenoon though a little air is stirring the water is
smooth & full of reflections here & there–as if there
had been oil in those rains–which smoothed it. In that
hottest & driest weather about the 4th ult–there was
yet considerable air stirring. Methinks that about *this*
time the waters begin to be more glassy dark &
smooth.

The cuckoo *caws* at midday–

At Purple Utricularia shore–there are within a circle
of 4 or 5 rods diameter 92 lilies fairly open & about half
a dozen which *appear* to have already partly closed   I
have seen them far more numerous   I watch them for
an hour & a half

At 11–45	92 fairly open
" 12	88
12¼	75
12½	46
12¾	26
1	4 which are more or less

stale. By about 1½ they are all shut up & no petal is to
be seen up & down the river unless a lily is broken off
– You may therefore say that they shut up between
11½ & 1½–though almost all between 12 & 1. I think that
I could tell when it was 12 o clock within half an hour
by the lilies   One is about an hour about it. The petals
gradually draw together & the sepals raise themselves
out of the water and follow. They do not shut up so
tight but that a very little white appears at the apex.
Sometimes a sepal is held back by a pad or other weed
leaving one side bare–   Many fall over on their sides
more or less, but none withdraw under water as some
have said. The lilies reach from the waters edge where
they are raised 2 or 3 inches above the surface out 5 or
6 rods to where the water is 4 ft deep & then suceed

the *small* yellow lily. Meanwhile large yellowish devils needles–coupled are flying about & repeatedly dipping their tails in the water–   Why are not all the white lily pads red beneath?

On the muddy bottom under the pads & between their stems are countless red bugs crawling about –   The birds are quite lively at this hour of noon–the robin–red-eye–wood-pewee–martins & king birds –&c   The cuckoo is a very neat slender & graceful bird. It belongs to the nobility of birds. It is elegant.

Here and there a phalanx of bluish green *large* bullrushes rises near the shore–and all along a troop of pontederias–parted & often surrounded by a testudo of pads. I feel an intense heat reflected from the surface of the pads. The rippled parts of the stream contrast with the dark smooth portions–   They are separatated as by an invisible barrier–   Yet when I paddle in to the smoothness I feel the breeze the same. I see where a juncus militaris has grown up through a white lily pad and stands two feet above it–   Its hard sharp point pierced it instead of lifting it off the water–   It reminds me of the Saladin's cutting a silk handkerchief in the air with his cimetar. This continual snapping of the pads which I hear appears to be made underneath–& *may be* produced by minnows darting at the insects which feed on them.

At Cardinal shore Lobelia Cardinalis a day or more XXX–   Pycnanthemum incanum ap. several days. It also is hoary at top. Staghorn sumach in fruit. The fall of hellebore & cabbage has begun–   The former lies along yellow & black & decaying. The stinging spotted flies are very troublesome now–   They settle in the hollows of the face. & pester us like imps. The clams lie on their edges or ends like buds or bulbs crowded together. Desmodium acuminatum at Conant orchard grove perhaps 2 or 3 days One 4 feet high, its leaves making a flat wicket, a foot from the ground.

Agrimony here almost done. Dip. Cornifolius a day or more XXX   I was surprised by the loud humming of bees &c &c in the bass tree–Thought it was a wind rising at first. Methinks none of our trees attract so many.

I am surprised to see crossing my course in middle of Fair Haven Pond great yellowish devils' needles –flying from shore to shore–from Island to Baker's farm & back, about a foot above the water–some against a head wind   Also yellow butterflies –Suggesting that these insects see the distant shore & resolve to visit it–   In fact they move much faster than I can toward it–yet as if they were conscious that they were on a journey–flying for the most part straight forward. It shows more enterprise & a wider range than I had suspected. It looks very bold   If devils needles cross Fair Haven, then man may cross the Atlantic. Seeing him I am remind of Horace's lines about the breast of triple brass. Pasture thistle on Lee's Cliff 3 or 4 days   Woodbine on rocks begun to redden there–   I start 2 green bitterns in different places amid the weeds by the shore–   In Conants meadow just beyond Wheeler's–The smaller fringed orchis not quite reached by the mowers   It may have been out 4 or 5 days   It is a darker purple for being so exposed–None yet opening in the shade. Aralia racemosa at Spring a short time. The sarothra tomorrow XXXX   The late rose not *fairly* begun along the river now where lucida is leaving off.

Tuesday July 18th

5 Am Up Turnpike

A hay making morning fog–through & above which the trees are glorious in the sun. The elm leaves ap. to be drinking the moisture along the dusty debauched

highway–some of them yellowing   Whence these fogs
& this increase of moisture in the air? The king-bird
–songspars–& quail are lively. The centaurea not
yet–   I think I have not heard a Night-warbler for a
fortnight   Erigeron Canadense XXX. Erigeron
Strigosum I must call the other.

                              Pm to Sam Barretts by boat
& Old Wheeler House.

   A hot midsummer day–with a sultry mistiness in
the air suddenly revealed   The river smooth & still
with a deepened shade of the elms on it–like midnight
its bed curtains shoved aside had a sultry languid
look–   The atmosphere now imparts a bluish or
glaucous tinge to the distant trees. A certain
debauched look as the highway in the morning.
–NB & shadows on land and water beginning to have a
peculiar distinctness & solidity–   This a crisis in the
season   After this the foliage of some trees is almost
black at a distance–   I do not know why the water
should be so remarkably clear & the sun shine through
to the bottom of the river–making it so
plain   Methinks the air is not clearer nor the sun
brighter yet the bottom is unusually distinct & obvious
in the sun. There seems to be no concealment for the
fishes. On all sides as I float along the recesses of the
water & the bottom are unusually revealed–& I see the
fishes & weeds & shells. I look down into the sunny
water. In midsummer, when its foliage is thickest &
stems most concealed the Salix Purshiana is most
beautiful–   Its leafy sails are now all set concealing its
spars & it appears to float in light masses buoyantly on
the water–

   Methinks the asters & golden rods begin–like the
early ripening leaves, with mid-summer heats. Now
look out for these children of the sun. When already
the fall of some of the very earliest spring flowers has
commenced.

The Island is now dry & shows few flowers   Where I
looked for early spring flowers I do not look for
midsummer ones. Such such places are now
parched–& withering. Blue vervain–ap a day XX   one
circle is open a little below the top. As I go along the
Joe Smith road I see some of the lower leaves of the
white vervain turned a faint mulberry color–   Brooks
has let out some of his pigeons which stay about the
stands or perches to bait others–   Wild ones nest in
his woods quite often. He begins to catch them the
middle of august.

I found so many berries on that rocky road–between
and about the careless farmer's houses & walls–that
the soil seemed more fertile than where I live–every
bush and bramble bears its fruit–the sides of the road
are a fruit garden– –blackberries–huckleberries
–thimble berries fresh & abundant–no signs of
drought   all fruits in abundance–the earth
teems   What are the virtues of the inhabitants that
they are thus blessed? Do the rocks hold moisture–or
are there no fingers to pluck them? I seem to have
wandered in to a land of greater fertility–some
upcountry eden. Are these the delectable mountains
– It is a land flowing with milk and honey. Great
shining blackberries peep out at me from under the
leaves upon the rocks. There the herbage never
withers–   There are abundant dews.

Now come the dews and fogs to save the berries–&
the transplanted trees.

Elecampane will ap open in 2 or 3 days   begins to
show some yellow–   Choke cherry XXXX though not
dark. say a week later   By the elecampane & the
Wheeler house to my great surprise growing
abundantly in the road the Monarda Fistula–ap a
week at least. 3 or more feet high with a few heads
containing a whorl of large very showy showy crimson
flowers with crimsoned bracts in whorls beneath–with

a balm or summer savory or sweet marjoram fragrance
– These things out of the heavenward north-west.
Perhaps it is Wood's variety ξ mollis–   It cannot be the
Didyma for the corollas is not more than 1⅜ inches
long.

2 common milkweeds I do not identify   1st ap. A.
syriaca of L. & Big. nectaries "with an oblique ridge on
each side of the fissure; horns long with a slender
point as high as the nectaries; leaves gradually acute.
It appears to be A cornuti of Gray–but what does he
mean by leaves "with a slight point"   can he refer to
the mucronate leafed kind? Ap. A. Cornuti of Wood,
but in his plate he gives the short stout recurved horn
of the mucronate kind–V. if the heads are spinous. as
A. Cornuti.

Then there is a common with many thick elliptic
short petioled leaves (up RR June 25) mucronated
–stout stemmed–   Is it Purpurascens of Big? It is not
dark purple. Not Purpurascens of Gray when he says
the pedicels are only about 2ce the length of the
divisions of the corolla & that only the lower leaves are
mucronate–   Are the pods smooth?

This side the sun flower house against woods in
road just beyond large pine Hedyotis longifolia a good
while tufted–but without striae in throat many
flowered

We have very few bass trees in Concord–but walk
near them at this season & they will be betrayed
though several rods off by the wonderful susurrus of
the bees &c which their flowers attract–   It is worth
going a long way to hear–   I was warned that I was
passing one in two instances on the river–the only two
I passed–by this remarkable sound–   At a little
distance is like the sound of a waterfal or of the
cars–close at hand like a factory full of looms. They
were chiefly humble bees–& the great globose tree was
all alive With them–   I heard the murmur distinctly

15 rods off–   You will know if you pass within a few
rods of a bass tree at this season in any part of the
town by this loud murmer like a waterfall which
proceeds from it.

July 19th 54

Pm to Beck Stows & Walden–

Alisma ap a day or more XXX   Polyg. careyi
tomorrow   In moores swamp I pluck cool though not
very sweet large red raspberries in the shade making
themselves dense thickets. Wild holly berries a day or
2 XXX. The *throttled* sound of a cuckoo from out the
shade of a grove–

How lustily the poison dog wood grows–5 feet from
the ground this year & still growing covered with a rich
glaucous bloom–   The more smothering furnace like
heats are beginning–& the *locust* days. Crotalarias but
few–ap a day or 2 only. The tall wand-like large leaved
Desmodium canadense. some days at least on the dry
rough sunflower field. Black choke berry several days.
High Blue berries scarce–but a few half an inch or
more in diameter.

Ap. a catbird's nests in a shruboak lined with root
fibres with 3 green blue eggs.

Erigeron Annuum perhaps 15 rods or more just
beyond the Hawthorn bridge on right hand–a new
plant–prob last month NB Thinner leaves than the
strigosum. The white cotton-grass now & how long? at
Beck stows ap. to be the Eriophorum gracile? I see no
rusty ones

In the maple swamp at Hubbards Close the great
cinnamon ferns are very handsome now in tufts falling
over in handsome curves on every side–A rank
undergrowth about 3 feet high completely hiding the
dead leaves   Some are a foot wide & raised up 6 feet
long. Clintonia berries in a day or 2. I am surprised to
see at Walden a single aster patens with a dozen
flowers fully open–a day or more.

smooth sumach berries XXX   The anychia shows
some small pods–prob. flowered about July
1st   Lechea minor shows stamens X
     A wood thrush tonight. Veery within 2 or 3 days.
                    July 20th
     A very hot day–a bathing day   warm days about this
     Pm to Hub. Bath. That long narrow sparganium
which is perhaps the smaller one growing long in our
river, stands thick with the heart-leaf–& potamogeton
in the middle in shallow places–   Methinks there
begins to be a bluish skum on the water at this
season–some what stagnant looking. This may be the
oil which smooths it. The large potamogeton in
midstream is 10 feet long. There is an immense
quantity of clams there in the middle where it is 4 feet
deep. I dived & took up 4 large ones in one hand at the
first grip   Now and for several days I have seen on the
leaves of the red & black oaks minute caterpillars
feeding with very small pearly dew-drop like ova near
them partly hatched. Skunk cabbage fruit some
days–cut by the mowers
     A muttering thunder cloud in NW–gradually rising
–& with its advanced guard hiding the sun–& now &
then darting forked lightning–   The wind rising
ominously also drives me home again. At length down
it comes upon the thirsty herbage beating down the
leaves with grateful tender violence. & *slightly* cooling
the air–but all the thunder & lightning was in its–van.
How soon it swept over & we saw the flash in the SE.
Corn in blossom these days
                    July 22nd
     The hottest night–the last.
     It was almost impossible to pursue any work out of
doors yesterday–   There are but few men to be seen
out–   You were prompted often–if working in the
sun–to step into the shade to avoid a sun stroke. At

length a shower passing in the west slightly cooled the
air. The domestic animals suffer much. Saw a dog
which had crawled into a corner & was ap. dying of
heat. Fogs almost every morning now–   First *noticed*
the dry scent of corn fields a week ago.

Now clouds have begun to hang about all day
–which do not promise rain–   As it were the morning
fogs elevated but little above the earth and floating
through the air all day.

Pm to Assabet Bath

Centaurea–one or 2 flowerets XXXX–   There is a cool
wind from east which makes it cool walking that way
while it is melting hot walking westward.–   Spear
leaved thistle ap several days–some being withered.
The larger pinweed ap a few days–prob. same date
with the minor. its lower leaves dull red those of
L. minor equally red or brighter. Some Amelanchier
obovata leaves a light dirty scarlet. Boehmeria prob
2 or 3 days at L. ciliata Corner road. Zizania a day
XXX with a handsome light green panicle a foot or
more long–a long slender stem & corn-like leaves
frequently more than an inch wide. Diervilla
leaves dull red & green   The Large primrose
lower leaves a clear dark red   The Epilobium
coloratum lower leaves very dark red. Gerardia
flava–ap 2 or 3 days. Lupine Hillside up RR. near
fence–also S. odora a day or 2 XXX there & what I will
call S. puberula?–to-morrow. S altissima on RR. a day
or 2 XXX   When the flower buds of the Boehmeria just
ready to open are touched with a pin the stamens
spring out remarkably scattering their pollen.

Sunday July 23d

Pm to Walden via Hub. Grove & Fair Haven Hill

Carrot by RR. sometime–say 10 days. Eupatorium
purpureum XXX–   There is a a peculiar light reflected
from the shorn fields as later in the fall–when rain and

coolness have cleared the air. Eupatorium pubescens
tomorrow XXX. The white orchis at same place 4 or 5
days at least–spike 1¾ X 3 inches–

I see small flocks of song sparrows &c rustle along
the walls & fences–   L. ciliata ap several days corner
causeway right side–   Boehmeria there also–   Since
the 19th have heard locusts oftener. A. acuminatus at
Radula swamp in a day or 2   Is my 3 leaved L. stricta?
at radula swamp common A. radula? a day. XXX–   Saw
yesterday on edge of Lee House meadow a low blue?
bery bush–with large oblongish black berries & narrow
leaves with little or no bloom–conspicuous calyx ap
between v. vacillans & v. corymbosum.   some
elsewhere 2½ feet high.

I also have seen on Fair Haven Hillside near W.
spring a sort of larger V. Pennsylvanicum with oblong
black berries & conspicuous calyx.

Lespedeza capitata. Lupine bank a day XXX   C.
pumila berries some time. Hazel leaves in dry places
have begun to turn yellow & brown. Lespedeza
violacea ap. several days. I see broods of partridges
later than the others now the size of the smallest
chickens. Onoclea green fruit conspicuous–   See a
thunder cloud coming up in N.W. but as I walk & wind
in the woods, loose the points of compass & can not
tell whether it is travelling this way or not–   At length
the sun is obscured by its advance guard.–but as so
often the rain comes leaving thunder & lightning
behind.

July 24

The last 4 or 5 days it has been very hot–& have been
threatened with thunder showers every afternoon
which interfered with my long walk though we had not
much– –   Now at 2 pm I hear again the loud thunder &

see the dark cloud in the west–   Some small and
nearer-clouds are floating past–white against the
dark-blue distant one. Burdock–prob 20th XXX

July 25

A decided rain storm today & yesterday–Such as we
have not had certainly since May. Are we likely ever to
have 2 days rain in June & the 1st half of July? There is
considerable wind too.

Pm to Bare Hill Lincoln via RR.

High blackberries a day or 2 XXX–   The middle
umbelet of the bristly aralia in some places also a day
or more. S. bicolor tomorrow XXX

I still see the cracks in the ground in old pastures
made last winter. The turtle dove dashes away with
a slight note from midst of open pastures
– Diplopappus umbellatus just beyond Baker
Swamp –on right hand of road prob about 10 days say
July 15–

I see some oak sprouts from the stump 6 feet
high–   Some are now just started again after a pause
–with small red leaves as in the spring–   Clematis ap a
day or 2

Hedyotis longifolia on Bare hill still–   Decodon not
yet but will ap. open in 2 or 3 days.

The rain has saved the berries–   They are plump &
large. The long chestnut flowers have fallen & strew
the road. Arabis Canadensis Sickle pod still in flower
–& with pods not quite 2 inches long. Pennyroyal a day
or 2

Hear a woodthrush–   Desmodium nudiflorum a
week at least–   Have I not noticed it before? I now
start some packs' of partridges old & young–going off
together–without mewing

Saw in woods a toad dead leaf color with black
spots.

Wednesday July 26

P hydropiperoides first obvious–   mikania a day or 2
– Lilies open about 6 Am.

Pm to Lime Kiln via Rudbeckia

Ate an early apple from one of my own
trees   Amaranthus ap. 3 or 4 days. The under sides of
its lower leaves are of a rich pale lake-color–   I see
these in Hosmer's onion garden where he is weeding
& am most attracted by the weeds   This appears to
have nothing to do with their maturity since very
young & fresh ones are so. One reason why the lately
shorn fields shine so and reflect so much light is that a
lighter colored & tender grass which has been shaded
by the crop taken off is now exposed and also a light &
fresh grass is springing up there–   Yet I think it is not
wholly on this account but in a great measure owing to
a clearer air after rains which have succeeded to misty
weather. I am going over the hill through Ed. Hosmer's
orchard–when I observe this light reflected from the
shorn fields contrasting affectingly with the dark
smooth Assabet reflecting the now dark shadows of
the woods–

   The fields reflect light quite to the edge of the
stream–   The peculiarity of the stream is in a certain
languid or stagnant smoothness of the water–and of
the bordering woods in a dog day density of shade
–reflected darkly in the water–   Alternate cornel
berries a day or 2. XXX   To day I see in various parts of
the town the yellow butter flies in fleets in the road–on
bare damp sand. (not dung) 20 or more collected
within a diameter of 5 or 6 inches–in many places
– They are a greenish golden sitting still near together
& ap headed one way if the wind blows. At first
perhaps you do not notice them but as you pass along
you disturb them, and the air is suddenly all alive with

them fluttering over the road–& when you are passed
they soon settle down in a new place–   How pretty
–these little greenish golden spangles–   Some are a
very pale greenish yellow. The farmer is not aware how
much Beauty flutters about his wagon. I do not know
what attracts them thus to sit near together–like a fleet
in a haven. Why they collect in groups–   I see many
small red ones elsewhere on the seriocarpus &c &c.
Rudbeckbeckia ap 3 or 4 days at least XXX only the
middle flowers yet for most part

Rusty cotton-grass how long. Green grapes have for
some days been ready to stew.

Dip. linarifolius XXX   Aster Dumosus XXX

Almost Every bush now offers a wholesome &
palatable diet to the wayfarer–large & dense clusters of
v. vacillances–largest in most moist ground sprinkled
with the red ones not ripe–Great high blue berries
–some nearly as big as cranberries–of an agreeable
acid–huckleberries of various kinds some shining
black–some dull *black*–some blue–& low black berries
of 2 or more varieties. The broods of birds just
matured find thus plenty to eat. Gymnadenia maybe 5
or 6 days in swamp SE of lime kilns one without any
spurs. It is a windy day & hence coarse in respect to
birds like yesterday–yet almost constantly I hear borne
on the wind from far mingling with the sound of the
wind–the Z-ing of the locust scarcely like a distinct
sound. Vernonia begun in center a day.

Friday July 28th

Clethra XXX–   Methinks the season culminated
about the middle of this month–That the year was of
indefinite promise before– –but that after the 1st
intense heats we postponed the fulfillment of many of
our hopes for this year–& having as it were attained
the ridge of the summer–commenced to descend the
long slope toward winter–the afternoon & down hill of

the year–   Last evening it was much cooler–& I heard a
decided fall sound of crickets–
Partridges begin to go off in packs–
Lark still sings–& robin
Small sparrows still heard.
Kingbird lively–
Veery & woodthrush (?) not very lately–nor ovenbird.
Red-eye & chewink common–
Night warbler & ev. forest note not lately
Cherry bird common–
Turtle dove seen.

July 29

Pm   Berrying to Brooks Clarks'

Richweed how long? Amaranthus hypochondriacus
ap. some days with its interesting spotted leaf–lake
beneath. purple spike–amid the potatoes

Sunday July 30

Crescuta not long. Desmodium Canadense is to be
found at Clamshell Hill oaks–   I have found the new
Rudbeckia in 5 distinct and distant parts of the town
this year–Beyond Alms house–Arethusa meadow
–Sam. Wheeler meadow Abel. Hosmer Meadow–&
J. Hosmer meadow–also in last place beyond ditch the
rusty cotton grass is now common. Cicuta bulbifera ap
a week or more. Is that goose grass near yel. thistles–?
Opened one of the snap turtle's eggs at Dugan desert
laid June 7th   There is a little mud turtle squirming in
it ap. perfect in outline shell & all–but all *soft* & of one
consistency–a bluish white–with a mass of yellow yolk
(?) attached. Perhaps it will be month more before it is
hatched. There are some of what I will call the
clustered low blackerries on the sand just beyond the
Dugans desert– –   The are commonly a few larger
grains in dense clusters on very short peduncles & flat
on the sand–clammy with a cool sub-acid taste. Small
rough sunflowers ap 2 days

I have seen a *few* new fungi within a week. The tobacco pipes are still pushing up white amid the dry leaves–sometimes lifting a canopy of leaves with them 4 or 5 inches.

Bartonia ap some days. A. undulatus I have called it (though it is conspicuously serrate & not distinctly wing petioled–beneath–A. Cordifolius??) ap 3 or 4 days   Bunchberries. Mt. sumack ap 2 or 3 days XXX

Nabalus albus ap 3 or 4 days. Mulgedium ap 4 or 5 days   Barn swallows still

July 31st '54

Blue-curls XXX–   Wood thrush still sings
– Desmodium rotundifolium XXX. Lespedeza hirta say 26th ult at Heywood Peak.

Aug 1st 54

6 Am on River–   B. Beckii XXX   Bass prob. out of bloom about a week. Corrallorhiza some days at Flint's Pond.

Pm. To Peters

Sunflower XXX–   meadow haying begun for a week. Erechthites begun for 4 or 5 days in Moore's swamp – 2 turtle doves in the stubble beyond. Hieracium Canadense–ap a day or 2   Do not see stamens of thyme-leaved pinweed but *perhaps*? petals? Ground nut well out. XX

Wednesday Aug 2nd   Surveying in Lincoln

S. lanceolata 2 or 3 days. Decodon XXX
– Polyg– arifolium in swamp   Chenopod. hybridum prob now–open   surveyed E. part of Lincoln.

5 Pm to Conantum on foot–

My attic chamber has compelled me to sit below with the family at evening for a month. I feel the necessity of deepening the stream of my life–   I must cultivate privacy. It is very dissipating to be with people too much. As C. says, it takes the edge off a man's thoughts to have been much in society–   I can

not spare my moonlight & my *mts* for the best of man I
am likely to get in exchange–

   I am inclined now for a pensive evening walk
– Methinks we think of spring mornings & autumn
evenings– I go via Hubbard Bath. Chelone say 2 days
X at Conants meadow beyond Wheelers– July has
been to me a trivial month– It began hot–& continued
drying–then rained some toward the middle–bringing
anticipations of the fall–& then was hot again about
the 20th– It has been a month of haying–heat–low
water & weeds– Birds have grown up & flown more or
less in small flocks; Though I notice a new sparrow's
nest & eggs & perhaps a cat bird's eggs lately– The
woodland quire has steadily diminished in volume–

   At the bass I now find that that memorable hum has
ceased–& the green berries are formed Now
blueberries–huckleberries & low blackberries are in
their prime. The fever bush berries will not be ripe for
2 or 3 weeks.

   At Bittern Cliff the G. Quercifolia? ap 4 or 5 days at
least. How interesting the small alternate cornel-trees
–with often a flat top a peculiar ribbed & green
leaf–& pretty red stems supporting its harmless blue
berries–inclined to drop off– The Sweet-viburnum
not yet turning. I see ap. a thistle down over the river
at B. Cliff–it is borne toward me but when it reaches
the rock some influence raises it high above the rock
out of my reach– What a fall-like look the decayed &
yellow leaves of the large sol seal hav in the thickets
now! These with skunk cab. & Hellebore–suggest that
the early ripeness of leaves–&c has somewhat normal
in it–that there is a fall already begun. Eupatorium
sessilifolium one or 2 stamens ap for 2 days XXX its
smooth leaf distinguishes it by the touch from the
sun-flower–

I sat on the Bittern Cliff as the still eve drew on
– There was a man on Fair-Haven furling his sail &
bathing from his boat– A boat on a river whose
waters are smoothed and a man disporting in it–how it
harmonizes with the stillness & placidity of the
evening! Who knows but he is a poet–in his yet
obscure but golden youth? Few else go alone in to
retired scenes without gun or fishing rod. He bathes in
middle of the Pond while his boat slowly drifts away
– As I go up the hill surrounsded by its shadow while
the sun is setting I am soothed by the delicious
stillness of the evening. Save that on the hills the
wind blows   I was surprised by the sound of my own
voice– It is an atmosphere burdensome with
thought– For the first time for a month at least I am
reminded that thought is possible. The din of
trivialness is silenced. I float over or through the deeps
of silence. It is the first silence I have heard for a
month– My life had been a River Platte tinkling over
its sands but useless for all great navigations–but now
it suddenly became a fathomless ocean. It shelved off
to unimagined depths.

I sit on rock on the hill top–warm with the heat of
the departed sun–in my thin summer clothes– Here
are the seeds of some berries in the droppings of some
bird on the rock– The sun has been set 15 minutes & a
long cloudy finger stretched along the northern
horizon is held over the point where it disappeared.
– I see dark shadows formed on the S side of the
woods E of the river– The creaking of the crickets
becomes clear & loud & shrill–A sharp tinkling like rills
bubbling up from the ground. After a little while the
western sky is suddenly suffused with a pure white
light against which the hickories further east on the
hill show black with beautiful distinctness– Day does

not furnish so interesting a ground   A few sparrows
sing as in the morning & the spring–also a peawai & a
cheewink. Meanwhile the moon in her first quarter is
burnishing her disk– Now suddenly the cloudy finger
& the few scattered clouds glow with the parting salute
of the sun–the rays of the sun which has so long sunk
below the convex earth are reflected from each cloudy
promontory–with more incomparable brilliancy than
ever.

   The hard hack leaves stand up so around the stem
that now at 1st starlight I see only their light
undersides a rod off– Do they as much by day? The
surface of the forest on the E of the river–presents a
singularly cool & wild appearance–cool as a pot of
green paint–stretches of green light & shade
–reminding me of some lonely *mt* side. The
night-hawk flies low–skimming over the ground
now– How handsome lie the oats which have been
cradled in long rows in the field–¼ of a mile
uninterruptedly.

   The thick stub ends so evenly laid are almost as rich
a sight to me as the graceful tops– A few fireflies in
the meadows– I am uncertain whether that so large &
bright & high was a firefly or a shooting star   Shooting
stars are but fireflies of the firmament. The crickets on
the Causeway make a *steady* creak–On the dry pasture
tops an *interrupted* one. I was compelled to stand to
write where a soft faint light from the western sky
came in between 2 willows.

   Fields today sends me a specimen copy of my
"Walden"   It is to be published on the 12 inst.

Friday Aug. 4th

   Pm via Turnpike to Smith's Hill

   A still cloudy day with from time to time a gentle
augusst rain– Rain & mist constrict our horizon & we
notice near & small objects   The weeds–fleabane &c

begin to stand high in the potatoe fields–over topping
the potatoes–this hard hack interests me with its
bedewed pyramid. Rue is out of bloom   Sicyos ap. in a
few days   The buttonwoods are much improved this
year–& may recover–   Sonchus in one place out of
bloom   Purple Gerardia ap. XX by brook. The
autumnal dandelion is now more common. NB
Ranunculus aquatilis var fluviatilis white petals with a
yellow claw small flowers somewhat like heart-leaf fls.
on surface of Hosmer ditch W. end by turnpike. A new
plant–Say July 1st   Is it open in sunny weather?

The lower leaves of the sharp angled Lycopus are a
dull red–& those of the elodea are a fine clear
somewhat crimson red–   Fragrant everlasting ap X

The swamp blackberry on high land ripe a day
or 2. I hear the pigeon woodpecker still
–*wickoff-wickoff-wickoff-wickoff* from a neighboring
oak–   See a Late rose still in flower. On this hill
–(Smith's) the bushes are black with huckleberries.
They droop over the rocks with the weight and are
very handsome. Now in their prime Some glossy
black–some dull black–some blue–& patches of v.
vacillans intermixed.

Hieracium paniculatum in woods by Saw Mill Brook
a day or 2 XXX–   The leaves of some weeds perhaps
golden rods are eaten in a ribbon character like some
strange writing–ap. half way through the leaf–often
along the edge   This for some time. Goodyera
pubescens a day or 2 XXX   Hieracium scabrum ap. 2
or 3 days X   It is already fall in low swampy woods
where the cinnamon fern prevails–   There are the
sight & scent of beginning decay. I see a new growth
on oak sprouts 3 to 6 inches–with reddish leaves as in
spring–   Some whole trees show the lighter new
growth at a distance.–above the dark green. Cannabis
Sativa ap. XXX.

After sunset–a very low thick & flat white fog like a
napkin on the meadows which ushers in a foggy night.

Sat Aug 5th '54

8½ Am by boat to Coreopsis Bend.

A general fog in the morning–dispersed by 8
o'clock– At first the air still & water smooth–afterward
a little breeze from time to time–judging from my sail
from the N.N.E. A plattoon of haymakers has just
attacked the meadow grass in the Wheeler meadow
– Methinks the river's bank is now in its most
interesting condition– On the one hand are the light
lofty & wide-spread umbels of the sium–pontederias
already past their prime–white lilies perhaps not
diminished in number–heart leaf flowers &c   On the
other the S. Purshiana full foliaged but ap. already
slightly crisped & imbrowned or yellowed with
heat–the button bush in full blossom–& the mikania
now covering it with its somewhat hoary bloom, The
immediate bank is now most verdurous–& florid
–consisting of light rounded masses of verdure and
bloom–& the river slightly raised by the late rains takes
all rawness from the brim. Now then the river's brim is
in perfection after the mikania is in bloom & before
the Pontederia & pads & the willows are too much
imbrowned–and the meadows all shorne. But already
very many pontederia leaves and pads have turned
brown or black– The fall in fact begins with the first
heat of July–Skunk cabbage–hellebores–convallarias
–pontederias–pads &c–ap. to usher it in– It is one
long acclivity from winter to midsummer–& another
long declivity from midsummer to winter. The
mower's scythe however spares a fringe of to him
useless or noxious weeds along the rivers edge–such
as sium–woolgrass–various sedges & bullrushes
–pontederias & polygonums.

The pontederia leaves have but a short life the
spring so late & fall so early.

Smaller flowers I now observe on or by the river are yel– lilies both kinds–the larger p. (hydropiperoides) with slender white spikes–and the small front rank rose-colored one–the bidens Beckii 3 to six or 7 inches above the surface–on that very coarse stout-stemmed somewhat utricularia-like weed which makes dense beds in the water–the 3 water utricularia–especially the purple–the cardinal flower–water-asclepias–and a few late-roses– As I go past the White Ash–I notice many small cob-webs on the bank–shelf above shelf –promising a fair day. I find that we are now in the midst of the meadow haying season–& almost every meadow or section of a meadow has its band of half a dozen mowers and rakers either bending to their manly work with regular & graceful motion–or resting in the shade–while the boys are turning the grass to the sun. I passed as many as 60 or 100 men thus at work today– They stick up a twig with the leaves on on the river's brink as a guide for the mowers that they may not exceed the owners bounds– I hear their scythes cronching the coarse weeds by the river's brink as I row near– The horse or oxen stand near at hand in the shade on the firm land waiting to draw home a load–anon– I see a plattoon of 3 or 4 mowers one behind the other diagonally advancing with regular sweeps across the broad meadow–& ever and anon standing to whet their scythes–Or else having made several bouts they are are resting in the shade on the edge of the firm land– In one place I see one sturdy mower stretched on the ground amid his oxen in the shade of an oak–trying to sleep or I see one wending far inland with a jug to some well-known spring.

There is very little air stirring today–& that seems to blow which way it listeth– At Rices bend the river is for a long distance clogged with weeds–where I think my boat would lodge in mid stream if I did not more

than guide it–the potamogeton leaves almost bridge it
over–and the burr reed blades rise a foot or more
above the surface–   The water weeps or is strained
through–   Though yesterday was rainy–the air today is
filled with a blue haze–   The Coreopsis is many fairly
but yet freshly out. I think not more than a week–from
1 foot to a foot & a half high–some quite white,
commonly the petals reflexed a little–just on the edge
of or in the water–   The meadow grass not yet cut
there–   In crossing the meadow to the Jenkins'
spring–at noon I was surprised to find that the dew
was not off the deep meadow grass–but I wet the legs
of my pants through. It does not get off them during
the day   I hear these days still those familiar notes–of
a vireo? *somewhat* peawai like–2 or more *whe-tar che*.
Near Lee's (returning) saw a large bittern pursued by
small birds alight on the shorne meadow near the
pickerel weeds–but though I rowed to the spot he
effectually conscealed himself–   Now Lee and his men
are returning to their meadow haying after dinner &
stop at the well under the black oak in the field–   I too
repair to the well when they are gone & taste the flavor
of black strap on the bucket's edge. As I return down
stream I see the haymakers now raking with hand or
horse rakes into long rows or loading–one on the load
placing it & treading it down while others fork it up to
him–and others are gleaning with rakes after the
forkers–   All farmers are anxious to get their meadow
hay as soon as possible for fear the river will rise–   On
the 2nd ult Hagar told me he had done all his haying
–having little or no meadow–& now the chief business
was to kill weeds in the orchard &c. Formerly they
used to think they had nothing to do when the haying
was done & might go a-fishing for 3 weeks.

    I see very few whorld or common utricularias–but
the purple ones are exceedingly abundant on both

sides the river ap. from one end to the other. The
broad pad field on the SW side of Fair Haven is
distinctly purpled with them. Their color is peculiarly
high for a water-plant. In Sudbury the huckleberries
&c appeared to be dried up– At Lee's Cliff–I meet in
the path a woodchuck–probably this year's one–which
stood within 7 feet & turned the side of its head to me
as if deaf of one ear–& stood listening till I advanced
– A very large flock of black birds–perhaps grackles &
cowbirds–& maybe? young red-wings–with a roar of
wings flying from this side the river to that & alighting
on the sedge & willows & ground.

Aug. 6 '54

Pm to Tarbel Hills by boat–

Rather cool with a strong wind–before which we
glide. The rippled surface of the water & The light
under sides of the white maples in rounded masses
bordering the stream–and also the silvery tops of the
swamp-white oaks–give a pleasing breezy aspect to the
shores &c– Surprised to see the Hibiscus just out
XXX–nearer Flint's & also at Ball Hill bend–ap. always
earlier in those places–

I noticed yesterday that the fields of juncus militaris
on the S side of Fair Haven–showed a stripe 6 or 8
inches wide next the water & bounded by a very level
line above of a different color more or less reddish or
as if wet–as if there had been a subsidence of the water
to that extent–Yet it has actually risen rather– The
sun is quite hot today but the wind is cool–& I
question if my thin coat will be sufficient. Methinks
that after this date there is commonly a vein of
coolness in the wind–

The Great Meadows are for the most part shorne
– Small light green sensitive ferns are springing up
full of light on the bank. I see some smaller White
maples–turned a dull red–crimsonish. a slight blush

on them   Grape-vines–the downy undersides of their
leaves turned up by the wind–are methinks more
conspicuous now at a distance along the edge of the
meadow–where they round & mass the trees &
bushes–Long irregular bowers here & there marked
with the white-downy undersides of the leaves. The
wind is very unsteady & flirts our sail about to this side
& that–

We prefer to sail today (Sunday) because there are
no haymakers in the meadow.

Landed at Tarbell's Hills– I am more pleased with
the form of the ground there than with anything else
–With the huckleberry hills–& hollows–the cow paths
& perhaps the old cornhills–   There are very agreeable
slopes & undulations–& the light is very agreeably
reflected from the barren surface of the earth–   It is at
length cloudy–& still behind the hills–& very grateful is
this anticipation of the fall–cool-ness & cloud–& the
crickets steadily chirping in mid-afternoon   The
huckleberries are somewhat shrivelled & drying
up.– As I look westward up the stream–the oaks &c
on Ponkawtasset are of a very dark green almost
black–which methinks they have worn only since
midsummer–. Has this anything to do with the bluish
mistiness of the air? or is it an absolute deepening of
their hue? We row back with 2 big stones in the stern.
Interesting here & there the tall & slender Zizania
waving on the shore with its light panicle 18 inches or
more in length. Krigia–is it again?

Aug 7th

It is inspiriting at last to hear the wind whistle &
moan about my attic–after so much trivial summer
weather–& to feel cool in my thin pants.

Do you not feel the fruit of your spring & summer
beginning to ripen, to harden its seed within you–   Do
not your thoughts begin to acquire consistency as well
as flavor & ripeness–   How can we expect a harvest of

thought who have not had a seed time of character
– Already some of my small thoughts–fruit of my
spring life, are ripe, like the berries which feed the 1st
broods of birds,–and other some are prematurely ripe
& bright like the lower leaves of the herbs which have
felt the summer's drought–

Seasons when our mind is like the strings of a harp
which is swept–& we stand and listen. A man may hear
strains in his thought far surpassing any oratorio–

Sicyos XXX   –Pm *to Peters*–Beck Stow's &
Walden–

Liatris ap XXX– Still autumnal–breezy with a cool
vein in the wind–so that passing from the cool &
breezy into the sunny & warm places you begin to love
the heat of Summer– It is the contrast of the cool
wind with the warm sun. I walk over the pin-weed
field. It is just cool enough–in my thin clothes– There
is a light on the earth & leaves as if they were
burnished– It is the glistening autumnal side of
Summer– I feel a cool vein in the breeze–which
braces my thought–& I pass with pleasure over
sheltered & sunny portions of the sand where the
summers heat is undiminished–& I realize what a
friend I am losing. The pin weed does not show its
stamens–I mean the L. Thymifolia–It was open prob.
about July 25. This off side of summer glistens like a
burnished shield. The waters now are some degrees
cooler–winds show the undersides of the leaves– The
cool nocturnal creak of the crickets is heard in the
midafternoon– Tansy is ap. now in its prime & the
early golden-rods have acquired a brighter yellow–

From this off side of the year–this imbricated slope
with alternating burnished surfaces & shady ledges
–much more light & heat is reflected (less absorbed)
methinks than from the springward side. In
midsummer we are of the earth–confounded with it &
covered with its dust   Now we begin to erect ourselves

somewhat & walk upon its surface. I am not so much
reminded of former years, as of existence prior to
years– From Peters I look over the great meadows.
There are 60 or more men in sight on them–in squads
of half-a dozen far & near–revealed by their white
shirts– They are alternately lost & reappear from
behind a distant clump of trees. A great part of the
farmers of Concord are now in the meadows. & toward
night great loads of hay are seen rolling slowly along
the rivers bank–on the firmer ground there–& perhaps
fording the stream itself–toward the distant barn
–followed by a troop of tired haymakers. The very
shrub oaks & hazels now look curled & dry in many
places– The bear oak acorns on the former begin to
be handsome– Tansy is in *full blaze* in some warm
dry places– It must be time methinks to collect the
hazel nuts & dry them–many of their leaves are turned.
The jersey-tea fruit is blackened. The Bushy gerardia is
ap. out in some places. XXX. Blue berries pretty thick
in Gowing's swamp–some have a slightly bitterish
taste. A wasp stung me at one high blue berry bush on
the fore finger of my left hand–just above the 2nd
joint– It was very venomous   a white spot with the
red mark of the sting in the centre while all the rest
of the finger was red soon showed where I was stung
–& the finger soon swelled much below the joint so
that I could not completely close the finger–& the
next finger sympathized so much with it–that at first
there was a *little* doubt which was stung. These
insects are effectively weaponed– But there was not
enough venom to prevail further than the finger.
Trillium berry

Aug 8th '54

Pm to Annursnack via Assabet

A great spider ¾ inch long with large yel marks on
the sides–in middle of a flat web. This is a day of

sunny water. As I walk along the bank of the river I look down a rod & see distinctly the fishes and the bottom. The cardinals are in perfection–standing in dark recesses of the green shore, or in the open meadow. They are fluviatile & stand along some river or brook–like myself   I see one *large white* maple crisped & tinged with a sort of rosaceous tinge–just above the Golden Horn–   The surface is very glassy there. The foliage of most trees is now not only most dense–but a very dark green–the swamp wht. oak –clethra &c–   The S. purshiana is remarkable for its *fine* & narrow leaves (feathers?) of a very light or yellowish green– –as if finely cut against the dark green of other trees–yet not drooping or curved downward–but remarkably concealing its stems.

Some silky cornel leaves are reddish next water. Very many leaves on hill are crisped & curled with drought. Black-cherry ripe XXX   The meadow hay is sprinkled here & there on the river. On Annursnack I scare up many turtle doves from the stubble.

Hear a supper horn–(J. Smith's (?)) far away blown with a long drawn blast–which sounds like a strain of an Æolian Harp. The distance has thus refined it. I see some slight dun clouds in the east horizon perhaps the smoke from burning meadows

Wednesday Aug 9th To Boston

Walden Published. Elder berries XXX. Waxwork yellowing X

Aug 10th

4½ Am to Cliffs–   A high fog–   As I go along the RR–I observe the darker green of early mown fields–   A cool wind at this hour over the wet foliage–as from over *mt* tops & uninhabited earth. The large primrose conspicuously in bloom.   does it shut by day? The woods are comparatively still at this season–   I hear only the faint peeping of some robins–(a few song

sparrows on my way)–a wood pewee–kingbird–crows
–before 5–or before reaching the Springs. Then a
chewink or 2–a cuckoo–jay–& later returning–the link
of bobolink & the goldfinch–

That is a peculiar and distinct hollow sound made
by the pigeon woodpecker's wings as it flies past near
you. The aralia Nudicaulis is another plant–which for
some time–& perhaps more generally than any yellows
the forest floor with its early fall–or turning–as soon as
its berries have ripened–along with Hellebore–Skunk
cabbage–Convallarias &c. Ambrosia XXX– at length as
I return along the back road–at 6½ the sun begins to
eat through the fog.

The tinkling notes of gold-finches & bobolinks
which we hear now a days are of one character–&
peculiar to the season. They are not voluminous
flowers–but rather nuts of sound. ripened seeds of
sound. It is the tinkling of ripened grains in Nature's
basket.– It is like the sparkle on water–a sound
produced by friction on the crisped air.

For a day or 2 I have inclined to wear a thicker or fall
coat.

Aug 10th continued 54

Pm   Clematis Brook via Conantum–

A cloudy afternoon & rather cool–but not
threatening rain soon–   Dangle berries ripe how long?
one of the handsomest berries. On the S.W. side of
Conant's Orchard Grove–saw from 20 rods off some
patches of purple grass Poa hirsuta ac. to Russel now
in bloom abundant. In the J. Hosmer Hollow.–which
painted a stripe of hill side next the woods for half a
dozen rods in length. It was as high colored and
interesting though not so bright as the patches of
rhexia. On examination I found it to be a kind of grass
a little less than a foot high with but few green blades
–& a fine spreading purple top in seed–but close at

hand it was but a dull purple & made but little
impression on the eye–was even difficult to detect
where thin– But viewed in a favorable light 15 rods
off–it was of a fine lively purple color enriching the
earth very much. It was the more surprising because
grass is commonly of a sobre & humble color. I was
charmed to see the grass assume such a rich color–&
become thus flower-like. Though a darker purple its
effect was similiar to that of the rhexia. Hardly any dog
days yet– The air is quite clear now.

A. macrophyllus–near beaked hazel by roadside
some time. That sort of sweet William? Pink with
viscidness below the joints but not pubescent against
the Minott House how long

The arum triphyllum fallen some time & turned
quite white– A. Cornuti leaves begun to yellow–&
brakes &c. R. Toxicodendron along the Minott House
ditch in the midst of its fall. Almost all its leaves *burnt
brown* & partly yellow.

1st muskmelon in garden.

Mr Loomis says that he saw a mocking bird at Fair
Haven Pond today

Aug 11th

Pm to Assabet Bath– I have heard since the 1st of
this month the *steady*-creaking cricket. Some are
digging early potatoes– I notice a new growth of red
maple sprouts–small reddish leaves surmounting light
green ones. The old being dark green– Green lice on
birches. A. Tradescanti 2 or 3 days in low ground
–flowers smaller than A. Dumosus–densely racemed
with short peduncles or branchlets–calyx scales
narrower & more pointed. Ammannia humilis NB A
New Plant) perhaps 3 weeks at NE end of Wheeler's
brush fence meadow–like an erect isnardia i.e.
Ludwigia palustris–with small-wrinkled yellowish
petals with a purplish vein.

Sat Aug 12th 54

watermelon–X

Pm to Conantum by boat

Methinks I heard a few toads till about the middle of
July– To day there is an uncommonly strong wind
against which I row–yet in shirt sleeves trusting to sail
back– It is SW. I see 12 painted tortoises on a rail only
5 feet long–& perhaps some were scared off before I
observed them. The Bidens Beckii yellows the side of
the river just below the Hub bath–but is hardly yet in
fullest flower–generally. I see Goldfinches now a days
on the lanceolate thistles ap. after the seeds. It takes
all the heat of the year to produce these yellow
flowers   It is the 3 o'clock pm. of the year when they
begin to prevail–when the earth has absorbed most
heat–when melons ripen & early apples & peaches
– The cranberry cheeks begin to redden– Vib. dent.
berries XXX– Hazel nut husks now have a reddish
edge–being ripe–   Is not this a sign? It is already the
yellowing year– Vib nudum berries generally
green–but some higher & more exposed of a deep fiery
pink on one cheek & light green on the other–and a
very few–dark purple or without bloom black already. I
put a bunch with only 2 or 3 black ones in my hat the
rest pink or green. When I got home more than half
were turned black–& ripe!! A singularly sudden
chemical change. Another cluster which had no black
ones was a third part turned. It is surprising how very
suddenly they turn from this deep pink to a very dark
purple or black–When the wine which they contain is
mature. They are a very pretty irregularly elliptical
berry–one side longer than the other–& particularly
interesting on account of the mixture of light-green
–deep pink–& dark purple & also withered berries in
the same cyme. The wind is autumnal & at length
compels me to put on my coat–   I bathe at Hubbards

– The water is rather cool comparatively– as I look down stream from SW to NE I see the red undersides of the *wht* lily pads about ½ exposed–turned up by the wind to angle of 45° or more– Those hemispherical red shields are so numerous as to produce a striking effect on the eye–as of an endless array of forces with shields advanced–Sometimes 4 or 5 rods in width

– Off Holden Woods a baffling counter wind as usual (when I return) but looking up stream I see the great undulations extending into the calm from above where the wind blows steadily. I see no maples changed yet along *this* stream. There are but few haymakers left in the meadows. On Conantum saw a cow looking steadily up into the sky for a minute– It gave to her face an unusual almost human or wood-god Fawn-like expression–& reminded me of some frontispieces to Virgil's bucolics– She was was gazing upward steadily at an angle of about 45°

– There was only some downy clouds in that direction. It was so unusual a sight that anyone would notice it– It suggested adoration.– The woodbine on rocks in warm & dry places is now more frequently turned a few leafets bright scarlet–

The now quite common golden rods fully out–are what I have–called–stricta & also the more strict puberula?– The arguta and odora are not abundant enough to make an impression– The S. nemoralis is not yet generally out.

The *common* asters now are the *patens* dumosus –radula–& D. umbellatus.

This is a famous year for huckleberries &c They are now drying up for the most part before spoiling. The bushes on Conantum are quite black with them– They are clustered like v. vacillans apparently – High blackberries are in prime. And I see some *great* low blackberries on long peduncles lifted above

the huckleberries–composed of great grains.–as large
as the largest high blackberries–   Pokeberries XXX also
poke stems are purple–not yet peduncles. Plucked a
small hieracium scabrum–hairy–? which I may have
called Gronovii.

I think I should not notice the shadow of conantum
Cliff now–perhaps because the grass is so sere &
russet–   It should be a tender green–

For Birds–

I think that I begin to see a few more hawks than of
late. A white-rumped today–

Partridges fly in packs–

Blue birds sound oftener plaintively

Larks are still seen

Blackbirds fly in great flocks

Robin peeps occasionally

Song sparrow sings clearly in morning &c

Hear Pig. woodpeckers' *wickoff* still occasionally

Pigeons begin to be seen–

Hear rush sparrow still

No seringos for some time

Turtle doves common in small flocks in stubble

Wht bellied swallows still

Barn swallows still

Perhaps chip-sparrows are silent

Have not heard a woodthrush since last week of July–

Catbird & thrasher done singing–

Chewink still heard

Wood-pewee   "

No night warble hear one at eve Aug 14–or tweezer–or
    Ev. forest note– –nor veery–

Kingbird twitters still

No red eyes hear one today nor tanagers heard since
    5th ult.

Goldfinch common

Cherry bird heard

The night-hawk squeaks at sunset & the whippoorwill
    sings Aug 14th

The screech owl screams at evening

Cuckoo heard

Gold robin sometimes heard partially

Aug 13th

1st *marked* Dog-day–sultry & with misty clouds. For
10 days or so we have had comparatively cool fall-like
weather–

I remember only with a pang the past spring &
summer thus far. I have not been an early riser
– Society seems to have invaded and overrun me–   I
have drank tea & coffee–& made my-self cheap and
vulgar–my days have been all noon tide without
sacred mornings & evenings. I desire to rise early
henceforth–to associate with those whose influence is
elevating–To have such dreams & waking thoughts
that my diet may not be indifferent to me.

Pm to Bare Hill Lincoln via RR–

I have not chanced to hear the bullfrogs trump
much if any since the middle of July. This is a quite
hot day–again after cooler weather–   A *few* small red
maples about blush now a dull red–   For about a
month I think I have particularly noticed the light
undersides of leaves–especially maples–   I see small
flocks of grass-birds–&c   In Macintosh's field
(pasture) some dwarf acalypha some time out. The
erechthites down begins to fly.   some of these plants
are 6 feet high. I see where the pasture thistles have
ap. been picked to pieces for their seeds? by the gold
finch? and the seedless down strews the ground–

Huckleberries begin to be wormy–but are still sound
on Bare Hill. Now the *mts* are concealed by the
dog-day haze–and the views of dark ridges of forest

one behind the other separated by misty valleys
– Squirrels have begun to eat hazel nuts–& I see Their
dry husks on the ground turned reddish-brown

The change decay & fall of the brakes in woods &c is
perhaps more autumnal than any sight– They make
more show than the aralia. Some are quite brown &
shrivelled–others–yellow–others yellow & brown
–others yellow, brown, & green–making a very rich &
particolored or checkered work as of plaited
straw–bead or strawwork–or ivory– Others are still
green with brown spots. In respect to these and many
other plants of this size & habit it is already fall. They
stand yellow & yellowing all through the woods
–None perhaps so conspicuous as the brake– At
thrush alley was surprised to behold how many birch
leaves had turned yellow–every other one–while clear
fresh leather colored ones strewed the ground with a
pretty thick bed under each tree– So far as the
birches go it is a perfect autumnal scene there–

Aug 14th

No rain–only the dusty road spotted with the few
drops which fell last night–but there is quite a high &
cool wind this morning.

Since August came in we have begun to have
considerable wind as not since may at least. The roads
now a days are covered with a light colored powdery
dust this yesterday several inches deep–which also
defiles the grass & weeds and bushes–& the traveller is
deterred from stepping in it. The dusty weeds &
bushes leave their mark on your clothes.

Mt ash berries orange?–& its leaves half yellowed in
some places–

3 Pm to Climbing Fern with E. Hoar.

It takes a good deal of care & patience to unwind
this fern without injuring it– Sometimes same frond
is half leaf–half fruit. E. talked of sending one such leaf

to G. Bradford to remind him that the sun still shone
in America. The uva-ursi berries *beginning* to turn
             6 Pm to Hub Bath–& Fair Haven Hill
   I notice now that saw like grass paspalum
ciliatifolium seed where the mowers have done
– The swamp blackberries are quite small and rather
acid. Though yesterday was quite a hot day–I find by
bathing that the river grows steadily cooler as yet for a
fortnight & though we have had no rain here. Is it
owing Solely to the cooler air since August came in
both day & night–or have rains in the SW cooled the
stream within a week? I now standing on the shore see
that in sailing or floating down a smooth stream at
evening–it is an advantage to the fancy to be thus
slightly separated from the land. It is to be slightly
removed from the commonplace of earth. To float
thus on the silver plated stream–is like embarking in a
train of thought itself– You are surrounded by water
which is full of reflections–& you see the earth at a
distance which is very agreeable to the imagination.
   I see the blue smoke of a burning meadow
   The clethra must be one of the most conspicuous
flowers not yellow at present. I sit ¾ up the hill. The
crickets creak strong & loud now *after sun-set*. No
word will spell it. It is a short strong regular singing
sound as of a thousand exactly together–though
further off some alternate–repeated regularly & in
rapid time perhaps 2ce in a second. Methinks their
quire is much fuller & louder than a fortnight ago
– Ah! I need solitude. I have come forth to this hill at
sunset to see the forms of the *mts* in the horizon–to
behold & commune with something grander than
man– Their mere distance & unprofanedness is an
infinite encouragement– It is with an infinite
yearning & aspiration that I seek solitude–more &
more resolved & strong–but with a certain genial

weakness that I seek society ever. I hear the night hawk squeak–& a whippoor-will sing. I hear the tremulous squealing scream of a screech owl in the Holden woods–sounding somewhat like the neighing of a horse–not like the snipe. Now at 7¾ perhaps ½ hour after sunset–the river is quite distinct & full of light in the dark landscape a silver strip of sky–of the same color & brightness with the sky–   As I go home by Haden's I smell the burning meadow–   I love this scent   It is my pipe. I smoke the earth.

Tuesday Aug 15th

5¼ Am to Hill by boat.

By 5½ the *fog* has with drawn from the channel here & stands southward over the Texas Plain. 40 50 feet high

C. Sericea berries at the hill landing a day or 2   Some birds after they have ceased to sing by day continue to sing faintly in morning now as in spring –   I hear now a warbling vireo–a robin half strain–a golden-robin whistles– –blue birds warble–Pig. woodpecker not to mention the tapping of a woodpecker–& the notes of birds which are heard through the day–as Wood peawai–song-sparrow –cuckoo &c. On the top of the hill I see the goldfinch eating the seeds (?) of the Canada thistle–   I rarely approach a bed of them or other thistles nowadays but I hear the cool twitter of the goldfinch about it. I hear a red squirrels reproof too as in spring from the hickories. Now just after sunrise–I see the western steeples with great distinctness–tall white lines–   The fog eastward over the great meadows appears indefinitely far–as well as boundless–   Perhaps I refer it to too great a distance. It is interesting when the fluviatile trees begin to be seen through it, & the sun is shining above it. By 6 o'clock it has risen up too much to be interesting.

The button bush is now nearly alltogether out of
bloom–so that it is too late to see the rivers brink in its
perfection– It must be seen between the blooming of
the mikania & the going out of bloom of the button
bush–Before you feel this sense of lateness in the year
–before the meadows are shorn–and the grass of hills
& pastures is thus withered & russet–

9 Am–

Walk. all day with W.E.C. NW in to Acton & Carlisle–
A Dog-day–comfortably cloudy & cool–as well as
still– The river meadows where no mowing–have a
yellowish & autumnal look–Especially the wool-grass.
I see large flocks of bobolinks on the Union
turn-pike Are the darker ones with some yellowish (?)
on side heads–Young red-wings or male bobolings
changing? Forded the Assabet at the bathing place
– Saw carrion fl. berries just begun to turn–say in a
day or 2– Pan. cornel berries XXX on College Road.
Many of the trees in Barretts orchard on Annursnack
–touch the ground all around like a dish cover–&
weighed down with fruit–and the branches are no
thicker over head than around– Is not this the best
form for an apple tree–a hollow hemisphere–nearly
resting on the earth–the branches equally dispersed
over the superficies–& light and air equally admitted.

Hills & pastures are now dry &
slippery– They seem as completely
russet as in Winter– I associate the mist
of this dog-day with the burning of meadows
– Crossed from top of Annursnack to top of
Strawberry Hill–past a pigeon bed. Measured the great
chestnut– At about 7 feet from ground the smallest
place I could find it is 14¾ feet in circumference–at 6 ft
from ground 15¹⁄₁₂ feet in circ. at 5 feet 15⁴⁄₁₂ at one foot
from ground not including some bulgings–22 feet in
circ. It branches first at about 9 feet from ground–

   The top has some dead limbs–& is not large in prop.
to trunk–   There are great furrows in the bark.
Desmodium marilandicum on Strawberry Hill by wall
some days out–   We took our dinner on the N side of
the wall on top of the Hill–   The dog-day haze
conceals the distant hills & mts–but some new &
nearer elms &c stand out with new distinctness
against it   It is remarkable how far & widely the smoke
of a meadow burning is visible–& how hard to locate.
That in the meadow near Joe Merriams half a dozen
miles off which has lasted some days appears to
possess the whole east horizon–as if any man who
lived 2 or 3 miles east of this must smell it & know all
about–but most who live within a mile of it may not
have noticed it. It impresses me as if all who dwell in
the eastern horizon must know of it & be interested in
it–as if it were a sort of public affair & of moment to a
whole town–yet hardly the next neighbors observe it
–& the other day when I passed within half a mile of it
it did not make nearly so great a show as from this
very distant eminence. The white smoke is now seen
slanting upward across half a township–& gradually
minglled & confounded with the haze of the day–so
that it may even seem to have produced the latter
–   West by Nagog is a dense dark almost black smoke
& another less dark in the south–   The owner of the
meadow little thinks how far the smoke of his burning
is seen by the inhabitants of the country & by
travellers–filling their horizon and giving a character
to their day–Shutting out much sky to those who dwell
half a dozen miles away. So far a mans deformities are
seen by & affect his fellows. They help to blot out the
sky to those dwell far away. Looking from this
Strawberry Hill to the long range behind Wm Brownes
N.E. by E I see that it & other hills are marked finely by
many parrallel lines ap. the edges of so many
terrasses–arranging the crops & trees in dark lines–as

if they were the traces of so many lake shores.
Methinks this is an almost universal phenomenon.
When farthest inland we are surrounded by countless
shores or beaches–terrace above terrace. It is the
parrallelism of green trees bushes & crops–which
betrays them–at a distance–   The locomotive whistle
far S.W. sounds like a bell   Lycopodium dendroideum
fallen ap some days. From this hill we steered NE
toward the E point of a wood in the direction of
Hutchinson's perhaps 2 miles off–   Before starting on
this walk I had studied the map to discover a new walk
& decided to go through a large wooded tract W & NW
of the Paul Dudley's House where there was no road
–there at last to strike east across the head of Spencer
brook meadow perhaps to the old Carlisle road. A mile
& a half NE of Strawberry Hill 2 or 3 large & very
healthy & perfect sassafrass trees–(3 large at least)
very densely clothed with dark green lemon? or
orange? tree shaped leaves–Singularly healthy. This
half a mile or so west of the Dudley House.
Comparatively few of the leaves were of the common
form i.e. 3 lobed but rather simple. There was
much *mt* sumach close by
turning scarlet –& sweet ferns also
browning & yellowing. Keeping on through a
somewhat swampy upland–we fell into a path–which
Channing preferring though it lead us through woods
widely out of our course westward–I soon correctd it
–& descending through swampy land at length saw
through the trees & bushes into a small meadow
completely surrounded by woods in which was a man
haying only 8 or 10 rods off. We felt very much like
Indians stealing upon an early settler–&–naturally
inclined to one side to go round the meadow through
the high blue-berry bushes. The high blue berries were
from time to time very abundant–but have acquired a
dead & flat taste–lost their raciness–   Soon after we

followed an indistinct path through a dense birch wood–leading quite out of our course i.e. westwardly – We were covered from head to foot with green lice from the birches–especially conspicuous on dark clothes–but going through other woods soon brushed them off again. At length when I endeavored to correct my course by compass–it pointed so that I lost my faith in it–& we continued to go out of our way–till we came out on a side hill immediately over looking a stream & mill & several house–& a small mill pond undoubtedly on the Nashoba in the N. part of acton on the road to Chelmsford. We were completely lost & saw not one familiar object. At length saw steeples which we thought Westford–but the monument proved it Acton– Took their bearing–calculated a new course–& pursued it at first ENE then E–& finally SE –along rocky hill sides covered with weeds where the fall seemed further advanced than in concord–with more autumnal colors–through dense oak woods & scrub oak–across a road or two–over some pastures –through a swamp or 2 where the cinnamon fern was as high as our heads & the dog wood now fruiting was avoided by C– After travelling about 5 miles for the most part in woods without knowing where we were–we came out on a hill from which we saw far to the South the open valley at head of Spencer Brook

In the meanwhile we came upon another pigeon bed where the pigeons were being baited–a little corn &c being spread on the ground–& at the first the bower was already erected. What I call S. arguta is an exceedingly handsome–a pyramidal head with rather horizontal branchlets with a convex surface of erect flowers–quite a splendid flower it would be in a garden. A miser XXX In Carlisle on high land that kind of viburnum–with smaller darker with rusty patches & less oblong berries & more obtuse leaves –(at both ends)–a large spreading bush 8 or 9 feet high

at least. Russell said it was the V. prunifolium–but the
leaves are not sharply serrate but nearly entire only
crenate at most commonly short & broad–The
peduncle not ½ inch long–   Was it S. *ulmifolia* in the
Ammania woodpath out? XXX or altissima?

At Eve. Mr Russell showed his microscope at Miss
Mackay's–   Looked at a section of Pontederia leaf–saw
what answered to the woody fiber & the cells on each
side ⟨drawing⟩ also the starch in potatoe–lime
in ⟨drawing⟩ Rhubarb–fern seeds–so called–&
lichen do of which last there were 50 or 60 in one little
wart o   o this size. The power of this glass was 900
diameters. All the objects were transparent and had a
liquid look–crystalline–& reminded me of the moon
seen through a telescope– –   They suggested the
significance or insignificance of size & that the moon
itself is a microscopic object to us–so little it concerns
us.

Aug 16   8 Am to Climbing fern with
John Russell.

He says that my winkle fungus is a boletus of
Linnaeus–polyporus of others–auricularia (ear-like)
now. My beautiful purple grass now in flower the Poa
hirsuta.

Peppermint has just begun X. Walked along the
Dennis shore–   That sedge by edge of river with 3
ranked linear leaves ⟨drawing⟩ is Dulichium
spathaceum   My ⟨drawing⟩ wool-grass is a Trichophorum.
Says that in Chelmsford they rub the pigeon bait with
the S. odora to attract pigeons. That fuzzy topped
sedge with slender spikes in straw colored ovate
heads–arranged umbel-like ⟨drawing⟩ he thought
scirpus [prob. cyperus] ⟨drawing⟩ strigosus.
A. puniceus a day or 2 ⟨drawing⟩ XXX. That
saw-like spiked grass ⟨drawing⟩ which is an
autumnal sight in ⟨drawing⟩ the mown fields is
Paspalum ciliatifolium. Choke-cherry leaves are now

many reddened. Scirpus capillaris turned yellow only
2 or 3 inches high now covers the sand on Lupine hill.
A Bluet still. A. Longifolius a day or 2 XXX   A
pear-formed puff ball–Lycoperdon (in
Yellow thistle meadow–) now dry buff-colored.

That concave chocolate colored one   I have
is a Lycoperdon bovi–(something) from being in
pastures   That potamogeton in Nut meadow brook at
the watering place beyond Jennie's is p– Claytoni with
many long linear pellucid immersed leaves ½' wide–&
some floating. My staghorn lichen is the Borreri–   The
former grows on the ground & is more like a Cladonia.
A Laevis 2 or 3 days if I have not mentioned it before
– Viola pedata again. Saw the variolaria on the white
pines on Harrington Road–   Hypnum riparium in the
Harrington trough. Uva Ursi berries reddened XXX
–but R. says not ripe or soft till spring & Opegrapha
like arab characters   Showed me the Prussian eagle in
the stem of the brake–   A. corymbosus? some time by
this road (Russell thought it Cordifolious but the
flowers are white & petioles not winged–   In the
T. Wheeler pasture–showed me the Cladonia
rangiferina (the common white one)–the C. sylvestris
(the green one with it) also the furcata & spoke of the
alpina as common in woods.

This day & yesterday and when I was last on the
river the wind rose in the middle of the day–blowing
hardest at noon–quite hard–but went down toward
night. Pointed out an Erigeron strigosum with out
rays. He had read of it as a var. Some had small rays
–Leaves narrower above Rogers house. on right.

Pm

With Russell to Fair Haven by boat–

That coarse somewhat B. Beckii looking weed
standing upright under water in the river is–Hornwort
Ceratophyllum echinatum. That moss on the button

bushes–is a fontinalis or else dichelyma   a coarser species is on the bridges. Cannot see the fruit now–for some reason–   On the rock at Bittern Cliff–the Parmelia detonsa. R. mistook a black pony in the water with a long mane behind some weeds for a heron. Nuphar lutea pads nearly all eaten & mere skeletons remaining.

Saw where a partridge had dusted herself at a wood chuck's hole. Methinks that for about 3 weeks past the light undersides of the upper leaves of maples–swamp oaks &c &c have been permanently conspicuous–while in June to mid of July they were observable only when there was more wind than usual–   As if owing to the dry weather & heat–those leaves were permanently held up like those of the hard hack &c various weeds & shrubs on dry land–perhaps had risen in the night and had not vitality enough to fall again–. Now accordingly I see the dark green uppersides of the lower leaves –alone and various agreeable shades of green thence upward. Now is the season to observe these various shades–especially when the sun is low in the west.

At the steam mill sand bank–was the distinct shadow of our shadows–1st on the water then the double one on the bank bottom to bottom one being upside down–3 in all –one on water, 2 on land or bushes. R. showed me the ginseng in my collection. Thinks that one of my Maine asters is a northern form of the Cordifolius. No haymakers in meadows now

Princes feather how long? Woodcock in garden. Polygonum dumetorum XXX at Bittern Cliff.

Aug. 18th

Warbling vireo in morning–one–   B. connata? or cernua? near boats place XXX–former if lower leaves are 3 parted.

Russell thought it was the S. discolor or else

Eriocephala which I saw–not sericea which is not
common–   Also that my cone bearing one was
S. Humilis. Barratt the best acquainted with them

That the R. triflorus was badly described. That we
had 3 gooseberries–the common smooth–the prickly
fruited–& the prickly branched.

Said we had 2 strawberries–the virginiana & the
vesca–the last not uncommon–

That the thalictrum dioicum was only about a foot
high. That the seed of Flowering Fern was heavy &
hence it fell in circles & so grew.

That the C. crus-galli was a var of the White thorn.
Best time for sea-side flowers mid. of July–for Wht *mts*
4th of July

Robbins of Uxbridge best acquainted now with the
Potamogetons. Tuckerman thought it would be
impossible to arrange them at present European
specimens being inaccessible or fragmentary–   That
the Smaller Sparganium was my taller one of the river
& should rather be called *minor*–being only narrower–

That we had but one urtica hereabouts. Of the
Rose-colored water lily in a pond hole in Barnstable
–Into which Parker stript & went–& the farmer dug it
all up & sold it.

The spanish moss–is a lily–tillansia–so named by
Linnaeus–(because it dislikes moisture–as much as his
friend Tillans the sea.

All these spots on my collection of leaves–crimson
&c are fungi–   The transparent globes on the hornwort
are an alga *nostoc.*

Almost impossible to find fishworms now it is so
dry–   I cannot find damp earth anywhere–but where
there is water on the surface or near.

Pm Over Great Meadows

A Great drought–now for several weeks   The
haymakers have been remarkably uninterrupted this

year–by rain– Corn & potatoes are nearly spoiled
– Our melons suffer the more because there was no
drought in June & they ran to vine which now they
cannot support–Hence there is little fruit formed &
that small & dying ripe– Almost everywher if you dig
into the earth you find it all dusty– Even wild black
cherries & choke cherries are drying before fairly
ripe–all shrivelled. Many are digging potatoes ½
grown Trees & shrubs recently set out–and many old
ones are dying. A good time to visit swamps &
meadows– I find no flowers yet on the
Amphicarpaea. In a ditch behind Peter's a small
Cistuda Blandingii swimming off rapidly– Its shell is
4¼ inches long by 3¼ wide in rear 3 wide in front
–And its depth is nearly 2 inches. with a slight dorsal
ridge–which the large one has not I distinguished it
from the E. guttata at first glance by its back being
sculptured concentrically about the rear side–leaving a
smooth space within ½ inch in diameter–my large one
is almost entirely smooth on back being sculptured
only ⅛ of an inch wide on circumference of each scale.
It has small rather indistinct yellow spots somewhat
regularly arranged in the middle of each scale. Head
peppered with dull yellow spots above. Head, legs, &
tail, black above Head light yellow beneath–& also
legs about roots passing into a dirty white. It is a very
restless & active turtle–Not once inclosing itself or
using its valve at all–at once walking off when put
down keeping its head–legs–& tail out–continually
running out its neck to its full extent and often
bending it backward over the shell–. Its neck with the
loose skin about it has a squarish form. Readily turns
itself over with its head when on its back– Upper
shell black–Sternum light brown with a large black
blotche on the outside after part of each scale–& about
½ its area–5 claws on fore feet–4 & a rudiment or

concealed one on hind feet– In this small one the sculptured part occupies nearly the whole scale & is from ½ to ¾ inch wide–while in the large one it is only ⅛ of an inch wide–a mere border– Ap. as it grows the smooth rear is extended or shoves forward & a portion of the sculptured part scales off.

In this ditch an interesting green jelly–conferva like at a little distance–perhaps a kind of frog spawn–but without any *eyes* in it   Of various forms floating–often a sort of thick ring–made of a hollow cylinder. Was that a proserpinacea in that ditch with all but 2 or 3 small leaves at top–pectinate? Saw there the large semi pellucid waved heart shaped–rad. leaves of the heart-leaf–green & purplish. sometimes all purplish –more delicate than the waved rad. leaves of Yel lilies &c a dimple of leaves   We can walk across the Great Meadows now in any direction– They are quite dry – Saw a snipe   Even the pitcher plant leaves are empty. are covered with spatular sun-dew   There are 15 or 20 haymakers here yet–but almost done– They and their loads loom at a distance. Men in their white shirts look taller & larger than near at hand.

I have just been through the process of killing the cistude for the sake of science–but I cannot excuse myself for this murder–& see that such actions are inconsistent with the poetic perception–however they may serve science–& will affect the quality of my observations. I pray that I may walk more innocently & serenely through nature– No reasoning whatever reconciles me to this act– It affects my day injuriously– I have lost some self respect– I have a murderer's experience in a degree– The bobolinks alight on the wool-grass– Do they eat its seeds? The Zizanaia on the N side of the river near the Holt–or meadow watering place is very conspicuous & abundant.

NB   Surprised to find the Ludwigia Sphaerocarpa
ap. some time out–(Say Aug. 1st) in a wet place–about
20 rods off the bars to the path that leads down from
near Pedricks–2 to 2½ feet high–with a thick but
unbroken bark about the base much like the decodon
–no petals–yellowish seed vessels. I think I saw a
mocking bird on a black cherry near Pedrick's Size of
& like a cat bird bluish black side head–a white spot on
closed wings–lighter breast & beneath–but he flew
before I had fairly adjusted my glass–   There were
brown thrashers with it making their clicking note.
The leaves of the panicled cornel are particularly
curled by the heat & drought showing their lighter
under sides–   Low blackberry vines generally are
reddening–& already give an october aspect to some
dry fields–where the early potentilla grows–as that
plain of Pedrick's

At Beck stows on New Bedford Road–   What I had
thought a utricularia–ap. to be Myriophyllum
Ambigiuum–one is floating long & finely capillary
leaves with very few emersed & pectinate–another var
is on the mud short with linear or pectinate leaves
–   Perhaps they are the vars–*natans*–& *limosum*. The
last out some days–the 1st perhaps hardly yet.–   The
Green Bittern there leaving its tracks on the mud.
The S. nemoralis is now abundantly out on the Great
fields.

Aug 19th

Pm–to Flints Pond via RR–with Mr Loomis

The hills & fields generally have such a russet
withered–wintry look that the meadows by the RR–ap.
to have got an exceedingly fresh & tender green–   The
near meadow is very beautiful now–seen from the R.R.
through this dog-day haze which *softens to velvet* its
fresh green of so many various shades–blending them
harmoniously darker & lighter patches of grass–& the

very light yellowish green of the sensitive fern which
the mowers have left. It has an indescribable beauty to
my eye now which it could not have in a clear day. The
haze has the effect both of a wash or varnish and of a
harmonizing tint– It destroys the idea of definite
distance which distinctness suggests. It is as if you had
painted a meadow of fresh grass springing up after the
mowers– –here a dark green–there lighter–& then
again the yellowish onoclea–then washed it over with
some gum like a map–& tinted the paper of a faint
misty blue–

   This is an effect of the dog-days. There is now a
remarkable drought–some of whose phenomena I
have referred to during several weeks past–q.v. Of
large forest trees the red maples ap. to suffer most
– Their leaves are very generally wilted & curled
showing the under sides–Perhaps not only because
they require so much moisture, but because they are
more nearly ripe–& there is less life & vigor in them.
– The P. grandidenta perhaps suffers equally & its
leaves hang down wilted–even many willows. Many
white birches long since lost the greater part of their
leaves which cover the ground sere & brown as in
autumn. I see many small trees quite dead–birches &c.
I see amalanchier leaves scarlet–& black birch &
willow yellowing. Various ferns are yellow & brown.
When I see at the brick-sand cutting how thin a crust
of soil & darker sand only 3 or 4 feet thick–there is
above the pure white sand which ap. to compose the
mass of the globe itself–and this ap. perfectly dry I am
surprised that the trees are not all withered–& wonder
if such a soil could sustain a large growth– After
digging through ordinary soil & yellow sand 3 or 4 feet
you come to a pure white sand very evenly abruptly &
distinctly separated from the former–& this is laid
open to the depth of 10 feet–I know not how much

deeper it extends–So that the forest grows as it would in a wholly artificial soil made on a rock perchance– I presume you would not now anywhere on these plains find any moisture in that 4 feet crust–& there is never any in the sand beneath. I am surprised to see how shallow & dry all the available earth is there–in which the forest grows.

So like tinder is everything now that we passed three places within a mile where the old sleepers heaped up by the track had just been set on fire by the engine –In one place a large pile.

Plenty of P. arifolium in the ditch in the 2d field.

Some barberries are red–& some thornberries   A linear leaved Epilobium in Bakers i.e. Mackintoshe's swamp

Flints Pond has fallen very much since I was here–the shore is so exposed that you can walk round –which I have not known possible for several years–& the outlet is dry– There is such a haze we see not further than over Annursnack which is blue as a *mt* But Walden is not affected by the drought. Lobelia dortmanna is still abundantly in flower–& hedge hyssop–&c some clethra. There is a good deal of wind–but I see where the waves have washed 10 feet further within an hour or two over the S shore. The wet sand is covered with small bird tracks–perhaps peetweets–& is marked all over with the galleries of some small creatures–(worms or shell fish perhaps) of various sizes–some quite large–which have passed under the surface like a meadow mouse– Are not these food for the water birds?– I find growing densely there on the SE shore–& at the *Ball* shore –where it ap. to have been covered with water recently –the myriophyllum tenellum–another species of that of which I found 2 vars yesterday–perhaps since Aug 1st   A new plant.

The *Balls* again *somewhat* stale left high & dry ap. a month ago. Some 5 inches in diameter.

I find here & there washed up what I take to be the inner scales of a tortoise–and in one place where it fitted over the edge of the shell _____ –thin & transparent like isinglass or parchment.

This is one traced

Plucked about 4½ one bunch of vib. nudum berries *all* green, with very little pink tinge even.   when I got home at 6½ 9 were turned blue–the next morning 30. It seems that they do not always pass through the deep pink stage. They are quite sweet to eat like raisins

I noticed these birds in this walk–

A lark–which sang.

White bellied swallows–on Tel. wire.

Barn   "   I think

Night hawks which squeaked

Heard a chewink–*chewink*

Saw cherry-birds flying lower over Heywood meadow like swallows–ap. for flies. & heard them cricket like.

Kingbirds quite common–twittering, one on Tel. wire.

Blue birds saw & heard

Chicadees lisping note

Jays–scream

A wood cock–in wood path–goes off with rattling sound.

Wilson's thrush's *yorrick*

Saw crows

Grouse

Song sparrows–chirp

Grass bird–& perhaps another sparrow

Gold finch–heard–

Sunday Aug 20 '54

I hear no trilling of birds early.

5¼ Am to Hill. I hear–a gold-robin–also faint *song* of
com. robin. Wood pewee (fresh)–red wing black-bird
with fragmentary trill–bobolinks–(The males ap.
darker & by themselves.) King birds–nuthatch heard
–yel– throated vireo heard & saw–on hickories–(Have I
lately mistaken this for red-eye?) Goldfinch–Slate col
hawk (with white-rump & black wingtips)   The grape
leaves even at this hour after a dewy night are still
many of them curled upward showing their light
undersides & feel somewhat crisped by the drought
– This I think is one with that permanent standing up
of the leaves of many trees at this season.

Prinos berries have beg. to redden XXX   When the
red-eye ceases generally then I think is a crisis– The
wood land quire is dissolved. That if I remember–was
about a fortnight ago. The concert is over– The
pewees sit still on their perch along time returning
to the same twig after darting at an insect. The
yel– throated vireo is very restless darting about– I
hear a sound as of green pignuts falling from time to
time & see & hear the chickaree thereabouts.!!

Pm Up Assabet by boat to Bath.

A warm but breezy day wind W by S. Water clear &
sunny– I see much of my fresh water sponge just
above the Island.–attached to the bottom–rocks–or
branches under water. In form it reminds me of some
cladonia lichens for it has many branches like a
lichen–being a green porous spongey substance with
long slender pointed fingers or horns–pointed upward
or outward–the thickest about–½ inch in diameter &
emits a peculiar penetrating strong rank scent like
some chemicals. The whole mass perhaps 8 or 10
inches in diameter. When raised to the surface it

slowly sinks again. The bottom of the S. branch is in many places almost covered with the short cut leaves of the sium–as I call it. On the sandy bottom in midstream (muscle shoals) a dozen rods above the Rock I notice a small? green clam which must be the same with or similar to that which Perkins showed me in Newburyport. It has bright green rays from the eye (?) on a light green ground–   Found in pure sand. Saw 3. The rays show through to the inside–   It is handsomer without than the common. Some chicadees on the p. pines over water near the hemlocks look longer than usual hanging back downward–   See a strange bird about size of cedar bird–also on the p. pine–perhaps greenish olive above whitish or ashy beneath with a yellow vent & a dark line on side head

Saw a wood pewee which had darted after an insect over the water in this position in the air   It often utters a continuous–pe-e-e

The P. Amphibium at Assabet rock ap. several days rising 4 or more *ft* above water–   In many places I notice oaks stripped by caterpillars nowa-d-ays. Saw yesterday one of those great light green grubs with spots. I see today many–more than ½ dozen large wood tortoises on the bottom of the river–some ap. 8 to 9 inches long in shell–some with their heads out. Are they particularly attracted to the water at this season. They lie quite still on the bottom. Off Dodge's Brook saw a fish lying on its side on the surface with its head downward slowly steering toward the shore with an undulating motion of the tail. Found it to be a large sucker which had ap. been struck by a king fisher? (or heron?) & got away–(The mill is not agoing today Sunday)   It had been seized near the tail which for 3 inches was completely flayed & much torn –lacerated a part of the caudal fin being carried off. It

had also received a severe thrust mid way its body
–which had furrowed its side & turned down a large
strip of skin. It was breathing its last when I caught
it It was evidently too powerful for the bird which
had struck it– I brought it home & weighed &
measured it. It weighed 2 lbs & 2 ounces & was 19¼
inches long Above it was a sort of blue black or slate
color darkest on the head–with blotches of the same
extending down its sides which were of a reddish
golden passing into white beneath. There were a few
small red spots on the sides just behind the gills. It
had what I should call a gibbous head
but no horns–a line of fine mucous pores above &
below eye– Eyes at least 1½ inches apart– Great
corrugated ears on the lower lip. Fins all dark like the
back. Nostrils double– Opercula not golden– Irides
golden– Scales on lat. line 65 about? those near tail
gone with skin Fin rays as I counted–P. 17–V 10–A 9
–D. 13 C. some wanting. I think it must have been a
Kingfisher it was so much lacerated at the tail. Looking
down on it it was very broad at base of head tapering
thence gradually to tail. It had a double bladder
nearly 6 inches long by 1 inch+
at widest part Now at 4 Pm hear a
croaking frog near the waters edge–sounding like the
faint quacking of a duck with more of the r in it
–something like *crack–grack grack*–rapidly repeated
– Though I knew that I must be within 3 feet of it as I
looked from the boat upon the shore, I could see
nothing–but several times I interrupted him & caused
him to jump. It is surprising how perfectly they are
concealed by their color even when croaking under
one's eyes. It was R. palustris–though I did not see it
when it croaked. I after heard them further off just
before sunset–along the edge of the river–& saw that I
had often mistaken their note for that of a cricket. So

similar are these 2 earth sounds. The cricket like note of this little frog in the meadow ushers in the evening. A man tells me today that he once saw some black snakes eggs on the surface of a tussock in a meadow just hatching–some hatched– The old one immediately appeared & swallowed all the young. Assabet quite low– Those beds of dirty green ostrich-feather potemogetons are much exposed & dry at top

I perceive quite a number of furrows of clams in the sand all leading from the side toward the middle of the river–with the clams at that end. Can they be going down now? They have not moved op. Hub. bath. where they are in middle as well as by shore   Their position in the furrows is on their sharp edges with what I will call their 2 eyes forward.

We had a very little drizzling rain on the 4th ult–& I think that was the last drop.

There is so thick a bluish haze these dog-days that single trees ½ mile off seen against it as a light colored background stand out distinctly a dark mass–almost black–as seen against the more distant blue woods. So also when there is less haze the distinct wooded ridges are revealed one behind another in the horizon.

Aug 21st

Pm to Conantum via Hub. Bath.

Leaves of small hypericums beg. to be red

The river is warmer than I supposed it would become again–yet not so warm as in July– A small wary dipper–solitary dark colored–diving amid the pads–The same that lingered so late on the Assabet. Red choke berries are dried black–ripe some time ago. In Hub's Meadow bet. the two woods I cannot find a pitcher plant with any water in it. Some of the Hub.

aster are still left–against the upper Hub. wood by the shore which the mowers omitted. It looks like a var. of A. Tradescanti, with longer less rigid–& more lanceolate toothed cauline leaves–with fewer & more distant branchlets–& the whole plant more simple & wand-like. The bayonet rush has not generally blossomed this year–What has–long ago

Have noticed winged grass-hoppers or locusts a week or more. Spikenard berries are now mahogany color. Trillium berries bright red. I see a woodchuck at a distance–cantering like a fat pig–ludicrously fat–first one end up then the other– It runs with difficulty. The fever bush berries are partly turned red–perhaps prematurely. Now say is hazel-nut time. I think that my A. Corymbosus–at least the early ones, are A. cordifolius–since Wood makes this to vary to white & to have a flexuous stem. I see robins in small flocks & pig. wood-peckers with them. Now see in pastures tufts of grass which have been pulled up by cattlle, withered. quite thickly strewn. Spiranthes cernua a day or 2– Brought home a great Eupatorium Purpureum from Miles' swamp–(made species *fistulosum* by Barratt. It is 10½ feet high & 1 inch in diameter–said to grow to 12 feet. The corymb. 18½ inches wide X 15 inch deep. the largest leaves 13 X 3 inches. The stem hollow throughout– This I found to my surprise when I undertook to make a flute of it trusting it was closed at the leaves–but there is no more pith there than elsewhere– It would serve many purposes as a water pipe &c Prob. the Indians knew it & used. They might have blowed arrows through a straight one– It would yield an available hollow tube 6 feet long.

Did I see the yel. red-poll back–Head not conspicuously reddish.

Aug 22

The haze accompanied by much wind is so thick
this forenoon that the sun is obscured as by a cloud. I
see no rays or sun-light.

A bee–much like a honey-bee cutting rounded
pieces out of rose leaves

Pm. to Great Meadows on foot
along bank in to Bedford meadows–thence to
Beck-Stows & Gowing's swamp.

Walking may be a science–so far as the direction of a
walk is concerned. I go again to the great meadows–to
improve this remarkably dry season–& walk where in
ordinary times I cannot go– There is no doubt a
particular season of the year when each place may be
visited with most profit & pleasure–and it may be
worth the while to consider what that season is in each
case.

This was a prairial walk. I went along the river &
meadows from the first–crossing the red bridge road
to the Battle Ground. In the Mill Brook–behind Jone's
was attracted by one of those handsome high colored
masses of fibrous pink roots of the willow in the water.
It was 3 or 4 feet long 5 or 6 inches wide & 4 or 5 inches
thick–Long parrallel roots nearly as big as a crow quill
with innumerable short fibres on all sides–all forming
a dense mass of a singular bright pink color– There
are 3 or 4 haymakers still at work in the great meadows
–though but very few acres are left uncut   Was
surprised to hear a phoebes pewet–pewee & see it   I
perceive a dead mole in the path half way down the
meadow. At the lower end of these meadows–bet. the
river & the firm land are a number of shallow muddy
pools or pond holes where the yellow lily & pontederia
–Lysimachia stricta–Ludwigia sphaerocarpa &c &c
grow where ap. the surface of the meadow was floated
off some spring–& so a permanent pond hole was

formed in which even in this dry season there is
considerable water left. The great roots of the yel. lily
laid bare by the floating off of the surface crust last
spring–2½ or 3 inches in diameter & a yard or more of
visible length–look like great great serpents or hydras
exposed in their winter quarters–   There lie now as
they have fallen on the mud little heaps or collections
of the singularly formed seed-vessels of the pontederia
–as they have fallen on the mud directly under the
nodding but bare spikes. In these shallow muddy
pools but a few inches deep & few feet in diameter I
was surprised to observe the undulations produced by
some pretty large fishes endeavoring to conceal
themselves–   In one little muddy basin where there
was hardly a quart of water caught half a dozen little
breams and pickerel only an inch long as perfectly
distinct as full grown–& in another place where there
was little else than mud left breams 2 or 3 inches long
still alive. In many dry hollows were dozens of *small*
–breams–pickerel & pouts–quite dead & dry.
Hundreds if not thousands of fishes had here perished
on account of the drought–

Saw a blue heron–(ap a young bird–of a brownish
blue) fly up from one of these pools–& a stake driver
from another–& also saw their great tracks on the mud
& the feathers they had shed. some of the long narrow
white neck feathers of the heron   The tracks of the
heron were about six inches long.

Here was a rare chance for the herons to transfix the
imprisoned fish. It is a wonder that any have escaped.
I was surprised that any dead were left on the mud but
I judge from what the book says that they do not touch
dead fish. To these remote shallow & muddy pools
–usually surrounded by reeds & sedge–far amid the
wet meadows–to these then the blue heron resorts for
its food. Here too is an abundance of the yel– lily on

whose seeds they are said to feed. There too are the
paths of muskrats. In most of the small hollows
formed by the crust being carried off in the spring–the
proserpinacea grows abundantly–   There are now
hopping all over this meadow small rana palustris &
also some more beautifully spotted *halecina* or shad
frogs. There is a pretty strong wind from the NNW
– The haze is so thick that we can hardly see more
than a mile. The low blue haze around the *distant*
edge of the meadow looks even like a low fog (i.e. at a
sufficient distance). I find at length a pitcher plant
with a spoonful of water in it–   It must be last night's
dew–   It is wonderful that in all this drought it has not
evaporated. Arum berries ripe XXX   High blue berries
pretty thick, but now much wilted & shrivelled.

Thus the drought serves the herons &c–confining
their prey within narrower limits–& doubtless they are
well acquainted with suitable retired pools far in the
marshes to go a-fishing in–

I see in Pedrick's bushy & weedy meadow dense
fields of S. arguta–stricta or puberula? & altissima &c
now in its prime–   Corn stalks begin to be cut &
stacked–it is so dry.

I hear that Brooks' meadow (it is what I called the
burning by Joe Merriam's) is on fire–& cannot be put
out. Are not most Ardeas (herons & bitterns) seen at
this season?

Wednesday Aug 23d '54

Pm to Gowing's swamp & Hadlock meadows. I
improve the dry weather to examine the middle of G's
swamp. There is in the middle an open pool 20 or 30
feet in diameter nearly full of sphagnum & green froth
on the surface (frog-spittle) and what other plants I
could not see on account of the danger in standing on
the quaking ground. Then a dense border a rod or
more wide of a peculiar rush (?) with clusters of seed

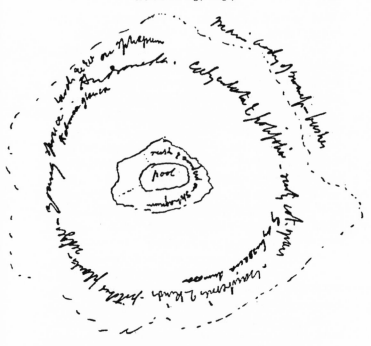

vessels 3 together now going to seed a yel. green
–forming an abrupt edge next the water this one a
dense bed of quaking sphagnum–in which I sink 18
inches in water, upheld by its matted roots where I
fear to break through–   On this the spatulate sundew
abounds. This is marked by the paths of muskrats,
which also extend through the green froth of the pool.

Next comes half a dozen rods wide a dense bed of
Andromeda Calyculata The A. polifolia mingled with
it–the rusty cotton grass–cranberries the common &
also V. Oxycoccus–pitcher plants–sedges & a few
young spruce & larch here & there–All on sphagnum
–which forms little hillocks about the stems of the
andromeda–

Then ferns, now yellowing, high blue-berry bushes

–&c &c &c–on the bushy & main body of the swamp –under which the sphagnum is now dry & white.

NB   I find a new cranberry on the sphagnum amid the A. Calyculata–V. Oxycoccus–of which Emerson says, it is the "common cranberry of the north of Europe" cranberry of commerce there found by "Oakes on Nantucket, in Pittsfield, and near Sherburne–"   It has small now purplish dotted fruit flat on the sphagnum–some turned scarlet partly, on terminal peduncles–with slender thread like stems & small leaves strongly revolute on the edges–

One of the Miss Browns (of the factory quarter) speaks of the yel– flowered asclepias in that neighborhood. Crossed the Brooks or Hadlock –meadows–which have been on fire–(spread from bogging–)–several weeks. They present a singularly desolate appearance–   Much of the time overshoes in ashes & cinders.–   yellowish peat ashes in spots here & there–The peat beneath still burning–as far as dry –making holes sometimes 2 feet deep they say. The surface strewn with cranberries burnt to a cinder. I seemed to feel a dry heat under feet–as if the ground was on fire, where it was not–

It is so dry that I walk lengthwise in ditches perfectly dry full of the proserpinacea now beginning to go to seed–which usually stands in water–Its pectinate lower leaves all exposed. On the baked surface –covered with brown paper conferva–

Aug. 24 '54

Pm to Fair Haven Pond by boat

A strong wind from the SSW–which I expect will waft me back. So many pads are eaten up & have disappeared that it has the effect of a rise of the river drowning them. This strong wind against which we row is quite exhilirating after after the stiller summer. Yet we have no rain–& I see the blue haze bet. me &

the shore 6 rods off–   The bright crimson red
undersides of the great white lily pads turned up by
the wind in broad fields on the sides of the stream–are
a great ornament to the stream–   It is not till august
methinks that they are turned up conspicuously. Many
are now turned over completely. After august opens
–before these pads are decayed, (for they last longer
than the nuphars of both kinds–) the stronger winds
beg. to blow & turn them up at various angles–turning
many completely over–& exposing their bright
crimson (?) red under sides with their ribs v. p 303-304
–   The surface being agitated the wind catches under
their edges & turns them up & holds them commonly
at an angle of 45°. It is a very wholesome color, & after
the calm summer–an exhilirating sight–with a strong
wind heard & felt–cooling & condensing your
thoughts. This has the *effect* of a *ripening* of the
leaf–on the river. Not in vain was the underside thus
colored–which at length the august winds turn up–

    The soft pads–eaten up mostly–the pontederias
crisped & considerably blackened–only a few flowers
left–   It is surprising how the maples are affected by
this drought–Though they stand along the edge of the
river–they ap. to suffer more than any trees–   Their
leaves–(and also those of the alders & hickories–and
grapes & even oaks more or less) are permanently
curled & turned up in the upper ¾ of the trees–So that
their foliage has a singularly glaucous hue–in rows
along the river   At a dist. they have somewhat of the
same effect with the silvered tops of the swamp
white-oak. The sight suggests a strong wind constantly
blowing. I went ashore & felt of them. They were more
or less crisped & curled permanently. It suggests what
to a slight extent occurs every year. On the Cliffs–So
many young trees & bushes are withered that from the
river it looks as if a fire had run over them. At Lee's

Cliff larger ash trees are completely sere & brown
–burnt up–   The White pines are particolored
there

Now methinks hawks are *decidedly* more common
–beating the bush & soaring. I see two circling over the
Cliffs. See a blue heron standing on the meadow at
Fair Haven Pond. At a dist. before you only the 2
waving lines appear– ⌒⌒⌒ & you would
not suspect the long neck & legs.

Looking across the pond–the haze at the waters
edge under the opposite woods looks like a low fog. To
night, as for *at least* 4 or 5 nights past, and to some
extent I think a great many times within a month–the
sun goes down shorn of his beams–half an hour before
sunset–round & red–high above the horizon. There are
no variegated sunsets in this dog-day weather.

Aug 25

I think I never saw the haze so thick as now at 11 am
looking from my attic window–   I cannot quite
distinguish J. Hosmers house–only the dark outline of
the woods behind it. There appears to be as it were a
thick fog–over the Dennis plains–   Between me &
Nawshawtuct is a very blue haze like smoke–Indeed
many refer all this to smoke.

Tortoise eggs are now a-days dug up in digging
potatoes–

Pm

Up Assabet–by boat–to Bath–

I think that the p. hydropiperoides is now in its
prime. At the poke-logan op. the bath place–the pools
are nearly all dry & many little pollywogs an inch long
lie dead or dying together in the moist mud. Others
are covered with the dry-brown paper conferva
–   Some swamp white oaks are yellowish &
brown–many leaves–   The vib. nudum berries in
various stages–green–deep-pink–and also deep blue

not purple or ripe–are very abundant at Shad-bush meadow–   They ap. to be now in their prime–& are quite sweet but have a large seed. Interesting for the various colors on the same bush & in the same cluster–   Also the chokeberries are very abundant there–but mostly dried black.

There is a *large field* of rhexia there now almost completely out of bloom–but its scarlet leaves reddening the ground at a distance supply the place of flowers.

We still continue to have strong winds in the middle of the day. The sun is shorn of his beams by the haze before five o'clock Pm–round & red–& is soon completely concealed ap. by the haze alone. This blue haze is not dissipated much by the night–but is seen still with the earliest light.

Aug 26th

For a week we have had warmer weather than for a long time before–yet not so warm nearly as in July. I hear of a great many fires around us far & near both meadows and woods–In Maine & New York also – There *may* be some smoke in this haze–but I doubt it.

Pm to Dugan Desert

I hear part of a phoebe's strain as I go over the rail road bridge–   It is the voice of dying summer. The pads now left on the river are chiefly those of the white lily. I noticed yesterday where a large piece of meadow had melted & sunk on a sandy bottom in the Assabet –& the weeds now rose above the surface where it was 5 feet deep around. It is so dry that I take the left at the RR bridge & go through the meadows along the river. In the hollows where the surface of the meadow has been taken out within a year or 2–spring up Pontederias & lilies–proserpincea–polygonums –ludwigia palustris &c &c. Nasturtium hispidum still in

bloom & will be for some time. I think I hear a
red-eye   Rudbeckia–the small one–still fresh–   The
Poa hirsuta is left on the upper edge of the meadows
(as at J Hosmer's)–as too thin & poor a grass beneath
the attention of the farmers–   How fortunate that it
grows in such places–& not in midst of the rank
grasses which are cut–   With its beautiful fine purple
color–its beautiful purple blush–it reminds me &
supplies the place of the rhexia now about done
–   Close by or held in your hand its fine color is not
obvious–it is but dull. but a distance with a suitable
light.   it is exceedingly beautiful. It is at the same time
in bloom. This is one of the most interesting
phenomena of–august–   I hear these afternoons the
faint cricket-like note of the R. palustris squatting by
the side of the river–easily confounded with that of the
interrupted cricket–only the last is more ringing &
metallic. How long has it been heard? The choke
cherry leaves are some of them–from scarlet inclining
to crimson. Rad. leaves of the yel. thistle spot the
meadow–   Opened one of my snap. turtle's eggs   The
egg was not warm to the touch. The young is now
larger & dark colored shell & all–more than a
hemisphere & the yolk which maintains it is much
reduced. Its shell very deep hemispherical fitting close
to the shell of the egg–& if you had not just opened the
egg you would say it could not contain so much. Its
shell is considerably hardened–its feet & claws
developed & also its great head, though held in for
want of room–   Its eyes are open–it puts out its head
–stretches forth its claws–& liberates its tail though all
were enveloped in a gelatinous fluid. With its great
head it has already the ugliness of the full grown–& is
already a hieroglyphic of snappishness. It may take a
fortnight longer to hatch it.

How much lies quietly buried in the ground that we wot not off– We unconsciously step over the eggs of snapping turtles slowly hatching the summer through. Not only was the surface perfectly dry & trackless there but black berry vines had run over the spot where these eggs were buried & weeds had sprung up above. If Iliads are not composed in our day, snapping turtles are hatched & arrive at maturity. It already thrusts forth its tremendous head (for the first time in this sphere)–& slowly moves it from side to side (–opening its small glistening eyes for the first time to the light–) expressive of dull rage as if it had endured the trials of this world for a century– When I behold this monster thus steadily advancing toward maturity –all nature abetting–I am convinced that there must be an irresistible necessity for mud turtles. With what tenacity Nature sticks to her idea! These eggs not warm to the touch–buried in the ground–so slow to hatch–are like the seeds of vegetable life.

Grapes ripe. XXX owing to the hot dry weather. Passing by M. Miles' he told me he had a mud turtle in a box in his brook–where it had lain since the last of April–& he had given it nothing to eat.

He wished he had known that I caught some in the spring & let them go– He would have bought them of me. He is very fond of them– He bought one of the 2 which Ed. Garfield caught on Fair Haven in the spring.   paid him 75 cents for it. Garfield was out in his boat & saw 2 fighting on the pond–approached carefully & succeded in catching both & getting them into the boat– He got them both home by 1st carrying one along apiece, then putting him down & while he was crawling off going back for the other. One weighed 43 or 4 lbs & the other 47. Miles gave me the shell of the one he bought which weighed 43–or 4– It is 15⅝ inches long X 14½ broad–of a roundish form–broadest backward– The smaller ones I have seen are longer in proportion to their length & the points larger also. The upper shell is more than 4½ inches deep & would make a good dish to bail out a boat with. Above it is a muddy brown–composed of a few great scales   He said he had no trouble in killing them– It was of no use to cut off their heads. He thrust his knife through the soft thin place in their sternum & killed them at once. Told of one Artemas (?) Wheeler of Sudbury who used to keep 15 or 20 in a box in a pond hole & fat them & eat them from time to time–having a great appetite for them. Some years ago–in a Jan. thaw many came out on the Sudbury meadows & a cold snap suddenly succeeding–a great many were killed. One man counted 80 or more dead–some of which would weigh 80 to 100 lbs. Miles himself found 2 shells on his river meadow of very large ones. Since then they have been scarce. Wheeler he thought used to go a-hunting for them the 2nd (?) of May. It increases my respect for our river to see these great products of it. No wonder the Indians made much of them. Such great shells must have made convenient household utensils for them.

Miles once saw a large bull-frog jump at & catch a green snake 10 inches long which was sunning along the edge of the water–& hold it cross wise in its mouth–but the snake escaped at last.

Even the hinder part of a mud-turtle's shell is scolloped one would say rather for beauty than use.

Pigeons with their *quivet* dashed over the Dugan Desert– Hear by Tel.graph that it rains in Portland & New York–

In the evening some lightning in the horizon & soon after a *little* gentle rain which

Aug 27

I find next day has moistened the ground about an
inch down only. But now it is about as dry as ever.

Pm To Pine Hill via Turnpike
& Walden–

Small B. Chrysanthemoides some time by turnpike.
The leaves of the smallest hypericum are very many of
them turned–to a somewhat crimson red–sign of the
ripening year–

What I have called the cast steel soap gall–about
1 inch in diameter handsomely variegated with a dirty
white or pale tawny on a crimson ground.

Hard and perfectly smooth. Solid & hard except a
very small cavity in the center containing some little
grubs– –Full of crimson juice (which runs over the
knife & has stained this page & blues my knife with its
acid.) for an eighth of an inch from the circumference.
Then lighter colored–v. p 304   Many red-oak acorns
have fallen   The great green acorns in broad shallow
cups–   How attractive these forms! No wonder they
are imitated on pumps–fence–& bed posts. Is not this
a reason that the pigeons are about? The yel. birch is
yellowed a good deal–the leaves spotted with green
–   The dogs bane a clear yellow. The cinnamon ferns
hardly begin to turn or fall. The lice on the birches
make it very disagreeable to go through them. I am
surprised to find the brook & ditches in Hubbard's
Close remarkably full after this long drought–when so
many streams are dried up. Rice & others are getting
out mud in the pond hole op. Breeds–   They have cut
down straight through clear black muck–perfectly
rotted–8 feet & it is soft yet further. Button bushes
Andromeda proserpinacea–hard-hack–&c &c grow
atop. It looks like a great sponge. Old trees buried in it.
On the walden road some maples are yellow–& some

chestnuts brownish-yellow & also sere. From
Heywoods Peak I am surprised to see the top of Pine
Hill wearing its October aspect–Yellow with changed
maples–& here and there faintly blushing with
changed red maples. This is the effect of the drought
–   Among other effects of the drought I forgot to
mention the fine dust which enters the house & settles
everywhere–& also adds to the thickness of the
atmosphere. Fences & roadside plants are thickly
coated with it. I see much froth on alders. As I go up
Pine Hill gather the shrivelled v. vacillans berries
–many as hard as if dried on a pan   They are very
sweet & good and not wormy like the huckleberries.
Far more abundant in this state than usual owing to
the drought. As I stand there I think I hear a rising
wind rustling the tops of the woods–& turning see
what I think is the rear of a large flock of pigeons. Do
they not eat many of these berries? Hips of the early
rose changed. Some vib. lentago berries–turned
blue–before fairly reddening. Blue stemmed G-rod a
day or 2. When I awake in the morning I remember
what I have seen & heard of snapping turtles & am in
doubt whether it was a dream or reality. I slowly raise
my head & peeping over the bed-side see my great
mud turtle shell lying bottom up under the table
–showing its prominent ribs–& realize into what world
I have awaked. Before I was in doubt how much
prominence my good Genius would give to that fact.
That the first object you see on awakening should be
an empty mud-turtle's shell!! Will it not make me of
the earth earthy? or does it not indicate that I am
of the earth earthy? What life–what character this has
shielded–which is now at liberty to be turned bottom
upward. I can put specimens of all our other turtles
into this cavity. This too was once an infant in its egg.

When I see this, then I am sure that I am not
dreaming, but am awake to this world. I do not know
any more terrene fact. It still carries the earth on its
back. Its life is bet. the animal & vegetable–like a seed
it is planted deep in the ground–& is all summer
germinating. Does it not possess as much the life of
the vegetable as the animal?

Would it not be well to describe some of those
rough–all day walks across lots–As that of the 15th ult
– Picking our way over quaking meadows & swamps
–& occassionly slipping into the muddy batter midleg
deep–jumping or fording ditches & brooks–forcing our
way through dense blueberry swamps–where there is
water beneath & bushes above–then brushing through
extensive birch forests all covered with green lice
–which cover our clothes & face–then under larger
wood relieved, more open beneath–steering for some
more conspicuous trunk   Now along a rocky hill side
where the sweet fern grows for a mile–then over a
recent cutting–finding our uncertain footing on the
cracking tops & trimmings of trees left by the
choppers–   Now taking a step or 2 of smooth walking
across a high way–   Now through a dense pine wood
descending–into a rank dry swamp where the
cinnamon fern rises above your head–with isles of
poison dog wood–   Now up a scraggy hill–covered
with shrub oak–stooping & winding ones way–for half
a mile–tearing ones clothes in many places & putting
out ones eyes–& find at last that it has no bare brow
but another slope of the same character–   Now
through a corn field diagonally with the rows–now
coming upon the hidden melon patch seeing the
back-side of familiar hills & not knowing them. The
nearest house to home which you do not know
–seeming further off–than the farthest which you do

know– In the spring defiled with the froth on various bushes. &c &c &c– Now reaching on higher land some open–pigeon place–a breathing place for us.

I suppose that is a puff ball–about 2 inches through (on the ground) roundish brownish cracked. pale wash leather color–with a handsome variegated slate color within–not yet dusty–contrasting with the outside.

Aug 28

Much cooler this morning making us think of fire – This is gradually clearing the atmosphere–& as it is about as dry as ever I think that haze was not smoke –quite as dry as yesterday.

Pm– By Great meadows & Bedford meadows to Carlisle Bridge– Back by Carlisle & Concord side across lots to school house– Improve the continued drought to go through the meadows

There is a cool east wind (it has been E a good deal lately in this drought) which has cleared the air wonderfully–revealing the long concealed woods & hills in the horizon & making me think of November even– And now that I am going along the path to the meadow in the woods beyond Peters–I perceive the fall shine on the leaves & earth–i.e. a great deal of light is reflected through the clearer air which has also a vein of coolness in it–

Some crotalaria pods are now black & dry & rattle as I walk. The farmers improve this dry spell to cut ditches & dig mud in the meadows & pond holes– I see their black-heaps in many places– I see on the Great Meadows circular patches–the stubble of a coarse light green sedge–ap– cut grass–of various dimensions which look as if they had been brought from other places & dropped there in the spring. Yet they are very numerous & extensive–running into one another–yet with a rounded or coarsely crenate edge

– In fact they prob. cover the greater part of the
meadow   It must be that the cut grass merely spreads
in circles. There are some in the meadow near the
Kibbe place. It makes firm ground– Between there are
the dark colored patches of cranberries–ferns & finer
grasses (?) of such singular forms as are used in lace
work–like the spaces left between circles
–suggesting that this is the ground
work–on which the other is dropt. Or does
the cut-grass? incline to grow in this circular manner?

The meadow is drier than ever–& new pools are
dried up– The breams from 1 to 2½ inches long lying
on the sides–and quirking from time to time–a dozen
together where there is but a pint of water on the mud
are a handsome but sad sight–pretty green jewels
–dying in the sun– I saved a dozen or more by putting
them into deeper pools. Saw a whole school of little
pouts hundreds of them 1½ inches long–many dead
–all ap. fated to die & some full grown fishes. Several
hair worms 4 or 5 inches long in this muddy water.
The muddy bottoms of these pools dried up is cracked
into a sort of regular crystals. In the soft mud the
tracks of the great bittern & the blue heron– Scared
up one of the former–& saw a small dipper on the
river. Just after entering the Bedford meadows,
(travelling N.) for perhaps a mile in length & the width
of the meadow the surface on all sides had been lifted
or tilted up–showing the blue edges of the soil–so that
there was hardly a level square rod & here & there
permanent pools were made in it.–giving the aspect of
waves 2 feet high or more with numerous holes &
trenches & making it very difficult to mow it–as well as
to walk over it. I do not know why it should have
happened there more than elsewhere– Found the
Ludwigia sphaerocarpa down that way.

It seems that the upper surface of the victoria regia

is "a light green" & the under "a bright crimson"–ac. to Schomburg. its discoverer–   In this it is like our *wht* lily pads.

We did not come to a fence or wall for about 4 miles this pm. Heard some *large* hawks whistling much like a boy high over the meadow.

Observed many of those cast steel soap galls from a tenth of an inch to an inch in diam. on a Quercus ilicifolia–   They are attached to the outer edge of the cup–commonly filling the space between 2 acorns & look as if they had merely lodged between them dropping out readily–though they are slightly attached to one cup. I see some not much bigger than a pins head, in the place, & reminding me, of those small abortive acorns which so often grow on the cup of the small chinquapin–   May not these galls be connected with those–and be also an abortive acorn? I have 3, of medium size, on the edge of one acorn cup, & not occupying more than ⅓ its circumference –unsupported by any neighboring cup–the middle one the smallest–being ap. crowded. Ap. the insect deposits its egg in the edge of the cup–& this egg as in all galls–is, I should say, at once the seed of vegetable & of animal life–it produces the vegetable gall–& is the seed of it–also the animal. May it not be regarded as the seed of the gall, as well as the ova of the insect? Moles make heaps in meadows

In my experience–at least *of late years*–all that depresses a man's spirits–is the sense of remissness –duties neglected–unfaithfulness–or shamming –impurity–falsehood–selfishness inhumanity, & the like–

From the experience of late years I should say that a man's seed was the direct tax of his race–   It stands for my sympathy with my race–   When the brain

chiefly is nourished, & not the affections–the seed
becomes merely excremental.

Saw a bushel of hazel nuts in their burrs which
some boy had spread on the ground to dry behind
Hodgman's. Observed yesterday–in a pool in what was
Heywood's Peat meadow S of but near Turnpike–ap. a
utricularia very small with minute forked green
leaves–& bladders on bare threads rooting in mud at
bottom–ap out of bloom. Also ap another kind with
long stems–many black bladders & no *obviously* green
leaves–filling the pools–in Hubs close.

Aug 29

A cool morning with much *fog.* more than yesterday
– Have not had much during the warmer part of the
drought methinks.

Cattle are driven down from up country– Hear the
drovers *whoa whoa whoa* or *whay whay whay*

Where I walked yesterday it ap. as if the whole
surface of the meadow had been at one time lifted
up–but prevented by shores or bushes or ice–from
floating off–then broken up by wind & waves–& had
finally melted & sunk irregularly–near where it rose. I
repeated stepped into the long crack-like intervals
between the cakes–

When our meadows are flooded in the spring–& our
river is changed to a sea–then the gulls–the sea birds
come up here to complete the scene. Or are they
merely on their way eastward–?

Were not those large & often pointed rocks
occasionally seen on the meadows brought there by
the floating meadow–& so dropped broad end down?

Pm to Darby Bridge neighborhood & Front of
Tarbel's.

It is a great pleasure to walk in this clearer
atmosphere, though cooler. How great a change &

how sudden from that sultry & remarkably hazy
atmosphere to this clear–cool autumnal one–in which
all things shine–& distance is restored to us. The wind
blew quite hard in the midst of that haze–but did not
disperse it   Only this cooler weather with a steady east
wind has done it. It is so cool that we are inclined to
stand round the kitchen fire a little while these
mornings–though we sit & sleep with open windows
still. I think that the cool air from the sea has
condensed the haze–not blown it off. The grass is so
dry & withered–that it caught fire from the locomotive
4 or 5 days ago near–the widow Hosmers & the fire ran
over 40 or 50 rods–threatening the house–Grass which
should have afforded some pasturage–   The cymes of
elder berries–black with fruit are now conspicuous

Up RR. Poison sumac berries begin to look ripe–or
dry–of a pale straw color. The zizania is pretty
abundant in the river–in rear of Joseph Hosmer's–   A
small what his father calls partridge hawk killed many
chickens for him last year–but the slate-colored hawk
never touches them–   Very many water plants
–pontederias–lilies–zizania &c &c are now going to
seed prepared to feed the migrating water fowl &c
–   Saw a hop-horn beam (ostrya) on which every leaf
was curiously marked with a small rather triangular
brown spot (eaten) in the axils of the veins next the
midrib–oppositely or alternately–   Underside–lower
leaves of lycopus virginicus lake color–   I see where
the squirrels ap. have stripped the p. pine cones
–scattering the scales about–   Many birds now adays
resort to the wild black cherry trees–as here Front of
Tarbel's   I see them continually coming & going
directly from & to a great distance   Cherrybirds
–robins–& king birds. I enjoy the warmth of the sun
now that the air is cool–& Nature seems really more
genial. I love to sit on the withered grass on the sunny

side of a wall. My mistress is at a more respectful
distance–for by the coolness of the air I am more
continent in my thought & held aloof from her–while
by the genial warmth of the sun I am more than ever
attracted to her. I see a boy already raking cranberries.
The moss-rose-hips will be quite ripe in a day or 2.
N.B   Found a new & erect Euphorbia (hypericifolia)
on the slope just E of his lizzard ditches. prob open
first in July. still in bloom & pretty   At Clam Shell Bank
the barn swallows are very lively filling the air with
their twittering now at 6 pm–   They rest on the dry
mullein tops then suddenly all start off together as
with one impulse & skim about over the river–hill–&
meadow. Some sit on the bare twigs of a dead apple
tree–   Are they not gathering for their migration? Early
for several mornings I have heard the sound of a flail
–   It leads me to ask if I have spent as industrious a
spring & summer as the farmer–& gathered as rich a
crop of experience–   Let the sound of my flail be
heard, by those who have ears to hear, separating the
kernel from the chaff all the fall & winter–& a sound no
less cheering it will be. If the drought has destroyed
the corn, let not all harvests fail. Have you
commenced to thresh your grain. The lecturer must
commence his threshing as early as august–that his
grain may be reduced to fine flour for his winter
customers   The fall rains will make full springs & raise
his streams sufficiently to grind his grist. We shall hear
the sound of his flail–all the fall early & late–   It is
made of tougher material than hickory–& tied together
with some thing stronger than an eel-skin. For him
there is no husking bee–but he does it all alone & by
hand–at evening. with the barn door shut–   For him
too I fear there is no patent corn sheller–but he dries
his work by hand ear by ear on the edge of a shovel
over a bushel–on his hearth–& after he takes up a

handful of the yellow grain & lets it fall again while he blows out the chaff–and he goes to bed happy when his measure is full.

Channing has come from Chelsea beach this evening–with–Euphorbia polygonifolia in flower –Bayberry in fruit–Datura in flower–staghorn sumac fruit–Chenopodium (It seems not to be made a distinct species, though very mealy) scarlet pimpernel still in flower–Salsola Kali (–the prickly plant) & ap. Solidago sempervirens.

Aug 30

Another great fog this morning–which lasts till 8½ –   After so much dry and warm weather cool weather has suddenly come–& this has produced these 2 larger fogs than for a long time–Is it not always so?

Hear a warbling vireo faintly. on the elms.

Pm to Conantum via Clamshell Hill & meadows.

The clearness of the air which began with the cool morning of the 28th ult– makes it delicious to gaze in any direction–   *Though there has been no rain*, the valleys are emptied of haze, and I see with new pleasure to distant hill-sides & farm houses–& a river reach shining in the sun–& to the *mts* in the horizon. Coolness & clarity go together. What I called S. altissima a simple slender one with a small head some time–Perhaps not to be distinguished. Crossed the river at Hub's Bath–   Ap. as many clams lie up as ever. The 2 river polygnums may be said to be now in prime   The hydropiperoides has a peculiarly slender waving spike. The B. Beckii made the best show I think a week ago–though there may be more of them open now–they are not so widely open.

Was not that a meadow hen which I scared up in 2 places by the river side–of a dark brown like a small

woodcock–though it flew *straight* & low I go
along the flat Hosmer shore to Clamshell Hill– The
sparganium seed balls beg. to brown & come off in the
hand– The Ammannia humilis is quite abundant on
the denuded shore there–& in John Hosmers meadow
–now turned red. & so detected–reddening the
ground–

Are they not young henhawks which I have seen
sailing for a week past–without red tails?

I go along through J. Hosmer's meadow near the
river, it is so dry– I see places where the meadow has
been denuded of its surface within a few years 4 or
5 rods in diameter–forming shallow platters–in which
the Lysimachia stricta–*small* hypericums–lindernia
–gratiola–pipes ammannia &c grow. I walk dry shod
quite to the phalanxes of bull rushes–of a handsome
blue green or glaucous color.

The colors of the rain-bow rush are now pretty
bright. The floating mill-foil at purp. utric. shore with
red stems. Blue-eyed grass still   Dogwood leaves have
fairly begun to turn– A *few* small maples are scarlet
along the meadow   A dark brown or black shining oval
or globular fruit of the skunk-cabbage–with prominent
calyx-filaments & style–roughening it is quite
handsome like a piece of carved ebony. or bog wood? I
see its small green spathes already pushing up.

The berries are about all dried up or wormy–(I am
on conantum)–though I still eat the dried blueberries
– There are now none to pluck in a walk–unless–it be
black cherries–and apples.

I see Brown thrashers on the black cherry tree–&
hear their sharp clicks like a squirrel. Hazel nut time
about a week ago–to be in advance of the squirrels– I
see the dried reddened burrs & shells under every
bush where they have been. The Bidens frondosa

some time   Distinguished by its being fairly pinnate
with from 3 to 5 leafets. I notice the rad. leaves of
primrose. The huckleberries are so witherd & brown in
many places owing to the drought that they appear
dead–and as if they were some which had been broken
up by the pickers–or as if burnt. Some white-ash trees
have suffered more than any others I have noticed–on
Cliffs their leaves being quite brown & sere

Minott Pratt here this eve–   He tells me he finds a
white hard hack–bay berry–in Holden's pasture–& on
the Old Carlisle road C. florida near Bateman's pond.
–& what Russell thought a rare hedysarum
somewhere   Pratt once caught a mud turtle at Brook
Farm which weighed 46 lbs.

Aug 31st

Warmer this morn & considerably hazy again.
Wormwood pollen yellows my clothes commonly.

Ferris in his Utah–crossing the plains in '52 says that
on "Independence Rock–near the Sweetwater "at a
rough guess, there must be 35,000 to 40000" names of
travellers".

Pm To Lincoln   Surveying for Wm Peirce–   He says
that several large chestnuts appear to be dying near
him on account of the drought–   Saw a meadow said
to be still on fire after 3 weeks–fire had burned holes
1½ feet deep–was burning along slowly at a
considerable depth. P. brought me home in his wagon
–   Was not quite at his ease & in his element, i.e.
talked with some reserve though well behaved, unless
I approached the subject of horses. Then he spoke
with a will & with authority–betraying somewhat of the
jocky. He said that this dry weather was "trying to
wagons. It loosened the ties" (?) If that was the
word   He did not use blinders. nor a check rain
–   Said A horse's neck must ache at night which has

been rained up all day– He said that the outlet of
Flint's Pond had not been dry before for 4 years & then
only 2 or 3 days– Now it was a month.

Notwithstanding this unprecedented drought our
river–the main stream has not been very low. It may
have been kept up by the reservoirs– Walden is
unaffected by the drought & is still very high. But for
the most part silent are the water courses when I walk
in rocky swamps where a tinkling is commonly heard.

At 9 this evening I distinctly & strongly smell smoke
I think of burning meadows, in the air in the village.
There must be more smoke in this haze than I have
supposed– Is not the haze a sort of smoke, the sun
parching & burning the earth?

Sep 1st

A misty morning followed by a still cloudy misty
day–through which has fallen a very little rain this
fornoon already– Now I notice a few faint *chipping*
sparrows–busily picking the seeds of weeds in the
garden– Are they the Savannah spars?– They show
no white in tail–Yet I see no yellow on brows. Small
feathers on back–centered with black & edged with
pale brown (?) Inner vanes of wing quills bay. Crown
without chestnut Brown slash from angle of mouth
backward– Do not the sparrows now commonly
begin to feed on seeds of weeds in gardens?

Pm along river to E. Hosmers–

A very little mizzling– The A. Tradescanti is
perhaps *beginning* to whiten the shores or moist
banks– I see a fine (reddish) topped grass in lowlands
whitened like a thin veil with what it has caught of this
dewy rain– It wets my feet much. The C. sericea
berries are now in prime–of dif. shades of blue lighter
or darker & bluish white. They are so abundant as to
be a great ornament to our causeways & river side

–   The white berried too is now in prime–but drops off–   The vib. dentatum berries are smaller & duller. The vib. lentago are just fairly begun to have purple cheeks.

Even this rain or mizzling brings down many leaves of elms & willows &c The first *to notice* since the fall of the birches which began so long ago. Saw 2 wild ducks go over–another said they were large grey ducks–also that Simon Brown's boy had got a young wild duck which came home from the river with the tame ones–

Sep. 2nd

The 2nd still misty mizzling & rainy day–   We all lie abed late–   Now many more sparrows in the yard larger than chip-birds & showing ashy under sides as they fly–A *part* the same as yesterdays. Are they Savannah's or Baywings, or both? I see but the *slightest touch* of white in the tail of any. Those clear ashy beneath are cinereous about the shoulders above. A tree sparrow too? Though I do not see the spot. Heard a faint warble from one the next Pm at about 6 Pm. on apple trees

Opened one of my snap turtles eggs. The young alive but not very lively with shell dark greyish black –Yolk as big as a hazel nut–tail curled round and is considerably longer than the shell. & slender   3 ridges on back–one at edges of plates on each side of dorsal which is very prominent as There is only the traces of a dorsal ridge in the old. Eye open. V. p 313

Pm by boat to Purp. Utric. Shore

Still & cloudy all shut in but no rain. The flags are turned yellow along the river quite an autumnal scene with commonly a strip of green left in their centers –   The sparganium not changed. The pontederias half of them, are brown and crisp–of pads only the *wht* lily are conspicuous–   The buttonbushes are generally yellowing, i.e are of an autumnal yellowish green. The blackwillows are decidedly crisped & yellowish. The interrupted fern begins to yellow. The aut. dandelion is conspicuous on the shore.

How handsome ripe grapes with the bloom on them! this rubbed off they show purple or black. I find some quite sweet which have ripened on a rock. They are a noble fruit to the eye. The waxwork is fairly yellow on all hands–now is the time to gather it. Ivy leaves on some plant are yellow–scarlet & dull red –beside green.

I see wht lilies wide open at 2½ Pm– They are half open even at 5 Pm in many places–this moist cloudy day–& thus late in their season– Still a few pontederias also. I see dogsbane still in flower

The B. Beckii is oftenest eaten? off just below the blossoms. Saw what I think must be a solitary wood? duck–started it several times driving it before me up the river–getting within 20 rods. It uttered a shrill quacking each time. Bathed at Hubbards. The water is surprisingly cold on ac. of the cool weather & rain.–but especially since the rain on yesterday morning– It is a very important & remarkable Autumnal change. It will not be warm again probably–

To my great surprise I find this morn (sep 3d) that the little unhatched turtle which I thought was sickly & dying & left out on the grass in the rain yesterday morn–thinking it would be quite dead in a few minutes– I find the shell alone–& the turtle a foot or 2 off vigorously crawling–with neck outstretched –holding up its head & looking round like an old one. & feet surmounting every obstacle– It climbs up the nearly perpendicular side of of a basket with the yolk attached. They thus not only continue to live after they are dead–but begin to live before they are alive.

Are those large rigid green clusters the dried fertile flowers of the black ash.? The keys are formed & ap ripe.

The moderate mizzling rain of yesterday & today is the first–(excepting the slight shower in the eve of the 26th ult) since that moderate one of Aug 4th. Yet this brings down leaves cools the rivers & ponds & brings back ducks & other migratory birds. I see 2 or 3 large plump sparrows hopping along on the button bushes & eating the mikania blossoms–sometimes perching on the lower mossy stems & uttering a faint chip–with crown distinctly divided by a light line–& another light line over eye–light throat & vent–ashy? breast & beneath without spot. Is it not the white throated sparrow?

Observed a large clam at the Bath place–(where they have not gone down) ap. quite old, with sort of wartlike protuberances–as if the shell were worn in to hollows while the harder parts were prominent. The shell, where worne, green. The end shaggy with a kind of moss or alga.

A sort of A longifolius some days by millbrook on Lowell road–but with *not long* loose green tipped scales. i.e. not squarrose–Call this A. tenuifolius for present (It may be carneus).

2 leaved sol seal berries red. X

I have not allowed enough prob. for the smoke mixed with the haze in the late drought–   The fires in woods meadows have been remarkabley numerous & extensive all over the country the earth & vegetation have been so dry–especially along railroads–& on *mts* & pine plains   Some meadows are said to have been burned 3 feet deep!–   On some *mts* it burns all the soil down to the rock–   It catches from the locomotive –from sportsmen's wadding–& from burning brush & peat meadows. In all villages they smell smoke

especially at night–   On Lake Champlain the pilots of
steam boats could hardly see their course & many
complained that the smoke made their eyes smart &
affected their throats. Bears it is said have in some
instances been compelled to migrate.

Index of MS Volume

THOREAU wrote his index in both ink and pencil, and made additions and corrections in both mediums. All revisions are accepted; they are not reported in the tables of Alterations or Emendations. Some entries have been realigned, and page numbers of this edition have been supplied in braces.

MS Volume XVII

On last fourteen pages of MS volume

EDITORIAL APPENDIX

Annotations

ANNOTATIONS provide several kinds of information: sources of direct quotations and identifiable allusions; completion of references to authors and books; translations of passages in foreign languages; identification of obscure or archaic terms not included in *Webster's Ninth New Collegiate Dictionary* (1991); contexts for topical references; significant biographical facts that pertain to the Journal; and identification of persons and places not included in *Merriam-Webster's Biographical Dictionary* (1995) and *Webster's New Geographical Dictionary* (1984). Local residents of note and those whose association with Thoreau was significant are annotated. Prominent and frequently mentioned local places and landscape features are named on the map which follows the Annotations (pp. 378-379). The map coordinates provide approximate locations of other significant features noted in the Annotations. More detailed geographic portrayals of Thoreau's Concord are Herbert W. Gleason's map accompanying the 1906 edition of the Journal, and Mary Gail Fenn, *Thoreau's Rivers*, Thoreau Society Booklet no. 27 (Geneseo, N.Y.: The Thoreau Society, 1973). Scientific nomenclature is annotated only when Thoreau's spelling varies from that of his sources or when some other amibiguity exists in the entry; for detailed information about Thoreau's botanical terminology, see Ray Angelo, "Botanical Index to the Journal of Henry David Thoreau," *Thoreau Quarterly* 15 (1983; reprint, Layton, Utah: Peregrine Smith, 1984). A more recent version of Angelo's text is available on the Internet at ⟨http://www.herbaria.harvard.edu/~rangelo/BotIndex/WebIntro.html⟩.

In general, information given in the text is not repeated in the Annotations, and only the first appearance of a name (which may be located in the Index) is annotated fully. Short-title references to works Thoreau read are expanded in the Bibliography that follows the Annotations, and the edition Thoreau used is cited whenever possible. Where his edition is unknown, the Bibliography lists either his probable source (for example, the edition Emerson owned) or one that could have been available to him. Translations are by the staff of the Thoreau Edition unless otherwise noted. Thoreau's errors and substantive alterations of quotations are indicated. Contextual punctuation appears outside of quotation marks when ambiguity would result from using the standard form. The following abbreviations and short titles are used throughout this section:

Angelo	Ray Angelo, "Botanical Index to the Journal of Henry David Thoreau," *Thoreau Quarterly* 15 (1983; reprint, Layton, Utah: Peregrine Smith, 1984)
Days	Walter Harding, *The Days of Henry Thoreau* (New York: Alfred A. Knopf, 1970)
"Field Notes"	"Field Notes of Surveys Made by Henry D. Thoreau Since November 1849," MS in Concord Free Public Library; facsimile published in Kenneth Walter Cameron, *Thoreau's Canadian Notebook and Record of Surveys: Selected Chapters from Transcendental Climate* (Hartford, Conn.: Transcendental Books, 1967), pp. 413-549
Higginson	Thomas Wentworth Higginson, *Cheerful Yesterdays* (Boston: Houghton, Mifflin and Company, 1898)
Journal 3	Henry D. Thoreau, *Journal 3: 1848-*

	1851, ed. Robert Sattelmeyer, Mark R. Patterson, and William Rossi (Princeton: Princeton University Press, 1990)
Journal 4	Henry D. Thoreau, *Journal 4: 1851-1852*, ed. Leonard N. Neufeldt and Nancy Craig Simmons (Princeton: Princeton University Press, 1992)
Journal 5	Henry D. Thoreau, *Journal 5: 1852-1853*, ed. Patrick F. O'Connell (Princeton: Princeton University Press, 1997)
Journal 6	Henry D. Thoreau, *Journal 6: 1853*, ed. William Rossi and Heather Kirk Thomas (Princeton: Princeton University Press, 2000)
1906	*The Journal of Henry David Thoreau*, ed. Bradford Torrey and Francis H. Allen, 14 vols. (Boston: Houghton Mifflin and Company, 1906)
Walden	Henry D. Thoreau, *Walden*, ed. J. Lyndon Shanley (Princeton: Princeton University Press, 1971)

MS Volume XVII

3.14-15 The ... lyre.: Despite his deep reservations about the increasing industrialization and technological changes he observed in Concord, T was fascinated by what he describes as the aeolian-harp-like sounds of the telegraph wires. The telegraph lines were strung in Concord on August 28, 1851, and T first mentioned their musical quality a few days later on September 3 (*Journal 4*, p. 35). See also 4.15 and *Journal 5*, p. 79.

4.23 F. Browne: Francis (Frank) Brown (or Browne) (1830-1900) was Emerson's nephew, the son of Mrs. Emerson's sister Lucy Jackson Brown. He was an avid amateur naturalist whom T often consulted.

5.14 Channing: T's friend William Ellery Channing the Younger (1817-1901) lived opposite the Thoreaus on Main Street in Concord and frequently accompanied T on his walks and boating excursions. He was a poet and the nephew of the Reverend William Ellery Channing. Throughout the Journal, T refers to him as "C.", "Ch.", or "W.E.C."

6.5-15   Columella . . . him.:   Lucius Junius Moderatus Columella was a first-century agricultural writer whose *De Re Rustica* was included in a collection of Latin agricultural writers titled *Rei Rusticae Auctores Latini Veteres*. The Latin phrases T quotes appear on p. 163; "de rusticis rebus" means "matters of husbandry." Hipparchus, a Greek astronomer and mathematician of the second century B.C., is credited with the first systematic use of trigonometry.

8.32-9.1   At . . . sure.:   In *Wilson's American Ornithology*, p. 30, Alexander Wilson describes this bird's presence even in severe winters outside of Philadelphia; he calls it the gold-winged woodpecker. It is also known as a flicker.

10.4-11   I . . . babboons.:   The Kansas-Nebraska Act, introduced by Democratic Senator Stephen A. Douglas of Illinois, was passed by the U.S. Senate on March 3, 1854, by the House on May 22, and was signed into law on May 30. By establishing that the new territories of Kansas and Nebraska could make their own decisions regarding slavery, the Kansas-Nebraska Act explicitly repealed the 1820 Missouri Compromise, which had prohibited slavery in territories north of the 36° 30″ line. Its passage was seen as a victory for the pro-slavery forces in Congress, and abolitionists throughout New England were enraged. Angelina Grimké Weld, for example, wrote in a letter to a friend: "The passage of the Nebraska Bill, though expected, nevertheless falls *heavily* upon every heart which beats for liberty. It seems to have aroused the slumbering North as no other slave enactment ever did before" (*Liberator* 27, no. 1042 [July 7, 1854], p. 106). For a detailed account of the events surrounding the passage of the Kansas-Nebraska Act, see David M. Potter, *The Impending Crisis, 1848-1861*, completed and edited by Don E. Fehrenbacher (New York: Harper and Row, 1976), chaps. 4-8.

10.21-24   De Quincy . . . Esquimaux.:   "The Philosophy of Herodotus," in Thomas De Quincey's *Historical and Critical Essays*, 1:130.

13.1   Cadmus: Cadmus, son of Agenor, King of Phoenicia, and brother of Europa, introduced the use of letters into Greece.

14.5-11   We . . . hollows.:   T often skated with Channing, Hawthorne, Emerson, and his sister Sophia.

15.26-28   "the . . . fall.":   Arnoldus Montanus, "Description of New Netherland," in *The Documentary History of the State of New-York*, p. 121, reads "and grow again by the fall".

16.1 Sleepy Hollow: According to his "Field Notes," p. 509, T in spring 1854 surveyed woods and land in Sleepy Hollow, a Concord cemetery located on the Bedford Road just northeast of the center of Concord (Map, C-4). T is buried there.

18.29-19.23 Kane ... snow.": Elisha Kent Kane, *The U.S. Grinnell Expedition in Search of Sir John Franklin*, pp. 48, 66, 165, 166, 341-342. See also Annotation 76.14.

21.23 Rufus Hosmer: T's contemporary and friend (1809-1860).

21.26 R.W.Es gate: R.W.E. is Ralph Waldo Emerson (1803-1882).

24.7-8 F. linaria ... F hiemalis: *Fringilla linaria* and *Fringilla hiemalis. Fringilla linaria* is the common redpoll (see Annotation 68.19-23); *Fringilla hiemalis* (correctly spelled *hyemalis*) is the dark-eyed junco. T also calls it the snowbird and the slate-colored snowbird.

24.10-18 In ... readmitted.: T undoubtedly refers to his *Walden* manuscript, the seventh and eighth drafts of which he was finishing in early 1854. Later in March he begins to send printer's copy to his publisher, James T. Fields. See 50.36-51.7, 59.35-60.6, and Annotations 49.3 and 259.27.

24.20 Minott's hillside: George Minott (1783-1861), a farmer who was a great favorite of both Emerson's and T's, lived with his sister Mary on the Lexington Road opposite Emerson. He appears frequently in the Journal as a source of anecdotes about Concord and natural history. See 29.6-9 and 47.29-36.

25.5-9 A ... him.: Witherel is probably E. W. Wetherell, a Concord farmer. See 1906, 10:398-399, for T's description of this man, whose intimacy "with mud and its inhabitants" T admires. Marshall Miles (1820-1890), a farmer and pencil maker, lived southwest of Concord in the vicinity of the Old Marlboro Road (Map, D-2).

28.20-29.4 I ... underside.: In January and February 1854, T was adding to and revising the final manuscripts of *Walden*, particularly passages in two chapters, "The Pond in Winter" and "Spring." Journal passages like this one reflect T's interest in describing the effect of the spring thaw on the pond. See J. Lyndon Shanley, *The Making of* Walden *with the Text of the First Version* (Chicago: University of Chicago

Press, 1957), and Ronald Earl Clapper, *The Development of Walden: A Genetic Text* (Ph.D. diss., University of California, Los Angeles, 1967).

29.6   Ch.:   Channing; see Annotation 5.14.

31.2-5   Ac. . . . night.:   George B. Emerson, *A Report on the Trees and Shrubs Growing Naturally in the Forests of Massachusetts*, p. 494.

33.34-34.3   I . . . overboard.":   T may be referring to Michael Flannery, formerly of County Kerry, Ireland, a laborer whom T occasionally aided. According to Harding, T loaned Flannery money, wrote letters home on his behalf, and submitted a petition in order to reimburse him for prize money his employer had kept (see *Days*, p. 313).

34.10-11   "in . . . ice":   T slightly misquotes Sir John Richardson, who wrote in *Fauna Boreali-Americana* (p. 115): "Musquash, watsuss, or wachusk, also peesquaw-tupeyew (the animal that sits on the ice in a round form). CREE INDIANS."

34.14-22   Boiled . . . correct.:   Edward Tuckerman, *An Enumeration of North American Lichenes*, p. 42. "Franklin's Journey" refers to Sir John Franklin's *Narrative of a Journey to the Shores of the Polar Sea;* see also Annotation 76.14. T also refers to Mayne Reid's *The Young Voyageurs*, pp. 294-297.

34.24-25   Peter . . . flooded.:   Peter Hutchinson (1799-1882), a free Black and renowned pig butcher, had built his cabin on property that bordered the Great Meadows. T refers to Hutchinson and "Peter's Path" (Map, B-4,5) throughout the Journal.

36.18   Chinese lady: T may refer to Ida Pfeiffer's *A Lady's Voyage Round the World*, pp. 63-64, where Pfeiffer describes the mincing walk of Chinese women whose feet have been bound since childhood.

38.21-24   Godwin . . . &c.:   John Goodwin (1803-1860) was a local hunter and fisherman with whom T often conversed; according to Horace Hosmer, he was "a stout, square built man of medium height, a hunter, trapper, day laborer &c. He had double teeth all round and when moderately full of rum, would take a cracker, and a glass tumbler (such as was used in bar rooms) and take a bite alternatively from each" (*Remembrances of Concord and the Thoreaus: Letters of Horace Hosmer to Dr. S. A. Jones*, ed. George Hendrick [Urbana: University of Illinois Press, 1977], p. 112). See also 100.25-101.5 and 183.10-16, and Annotation 95.4-14.

39.22   C.:   Channing; see Annotation 5.14.

39.24-33   My ... him–:   Undoubtedly William Ellery Channing, T's frequent walking companion, whose "coarseness & vulgarity" T describes in a Journal entry for April 12, 1852 (*Journal 4*, pp. 440-441). See Annotation 5.14 and *Journal 5*, p. 183.

41.5-28   To ... Col.:   Harris is Thaddeus William Harris (1795-1856), a noted entomologist who taught natural history at Harvard from 1837 to 1842 and served as the College Librarian from 1831 until his death. Clark is Alvan Clark (1804-1887) of Cambridgeport, Massachusetts, whose company, Alvan Clark & Sons, manufactured telescopes for a number of U.S. institutions, including one in 1854 for Amherst College, as T notes. The Amherst College telescope was equipped with a clock drive and was the first equatorial refractor built by Clark. T mentions his delight with the purchase of his own telescope a number of times in *Journal 8* (see 43.21-25, 52.31-32, 61.20-24, 80.1-2, and 209.7-8).

41.5   C.:   Channing; see Annotation 5.14.

42.14   Wilson ... sing: *Wilson's American Ornithology*, p. 223.

49.3   Got ... Walden–:   T refers to the first page proofs for *Walden.* He had been correcting his *Walden* manuscript all winter and had by this time sent some copy to the printer (J. Lyndon Shanley, *The Making of* Walden *with the Text of the First Version* [Chicago: University of Chicago Press, 1957], p. 32). See 50.36-51.7 and 59.35-60.6 for T's continuing remarks about his composition process, and see Annotations 24.10-18 and 259.27 for additional information regarding the publication of *Walden.*

49.20-21   Had ... scale.:   Allusion to Kane, *The U.S. Grinnell Expedition in Search of Sir John Franklin.*

50.21-33   Read ... '54.:   Étienne Geoffroy Saint-Hilaire (1772-1844) was a French naturalist whose theory of organic unity held that the same plan of structure prevails throughout the animal kingdom. The article T quotes from is "Life and Doctrine of Geoffroy St. Hilaire" (pp. 89, 90, 92, 93, 95, 97). Baron Georges Jean Léopold Nicolas Frédéric Cuvier (1769-1832) founded comparative anatomy.

51.14   Farmers: Probably Jacob B. Farmer, one of the Concord residents who liked to share their stories and discoveries with T. T recorded many of his conversations with Farmer in his Journal; they often discussed birds and their nests and eggs. Farmer collected birds' eggs; he once gave T what he called the seringo's egg, and his discovery of a screech owl's nest at Farmer's Swamp led T there in search of the bird. See 1906, 7:206-208, 7:422, 7:444-445, 9:16-17, 9:457, and 9:459 for T's accounts of his encounters with Farmer.

52.10-13   Haris ... Tipula.:   For Harris, see Annotation 41.5-28. The *New England Farmer*, published in Boston from 1848 to 1871, was a periodical devoted to agriculture, horticulture, and related arts and sciences.

53.26-28   Jardine ... flock–:   Sir William Jardine (1800-1874) was a British naturalist who devoted himself especially to ornithology. He wrote many memoirs of naturalists that appeared as prefaces to volumes of their work, including "Life of Alexander Wilson, Ornithologist" in the 1832 and 1840 editions of *Wilson's American Ornithology*. He also provided the notes for the 1852 edition, from which T quotes (p. 575).

54.12-13   All ... Hosmer.:   T recorded his survey for Abel Hosmer on April 4, 1854, in his "Field Notes," p. 510.

54.29-30   Surveying ... Green's: According to his "Field Notes," p. 510, T surveyed a "woodlot in Concord & Carlisle" for Samuel Hoar on April 5, 1854.

55.17   the ... Admetus: As punishment for killing Cyclops, Apollo was sent by Zeus to serve Admetus, king of Pherae; he tended Admetus's flocks for nine years.

55.24-30   I ... man–:   T's employer was Samuel Hoar (1778-1856), for whom T surveyed a woodlot on April 5. Hoar, a lawyer for T's father's pencil manufacturing firm and one-time judge on the Massachusetts Supreme Court, was Concord's leading citizen as well as Justice of the Peace. His difficult, rigid personality is well documented.

57.25-31   At ... lecture.:   T refers to Ralph Waldo Emerson's lecture on France at the Concord Lyceum on April 4, 1854.

62.3-4   Wilson ... blossoms.:   *Wilson's American Ornithology*, p. 79.

62.8   Pm ... Lincoln: According to his "Field Notes," p. 510, T surveyed property for Oliver W. Esty of Lincoln on April 11, 1854.

62.15   Surveying ... Lincoln.:   According to his "Field Notes," p. 510, T surveyed for Schuyler Parks of Lincoln on April 12, 1854.

62.26-27   Orpheus ... trees: Orpheus, son of Oeagrus and the Muse Calliope, charmed all of nature with his playing upon the lyre given him by Apollo; his music was so lovely that "rivers ceased to flow" and "mountains moved to listen to his song" (*Lemprière's Classical Dictionary of Proper Names Mentioned in Ancient Authors*, revised by F. A. Wright [London: Routledge and Kegan Paul Ltd, 1963], p. 430).

63.9   F juncorum: *Fringilla juncorum*, the field or rush sparrow.

63.13   "like . . . cup":   Source unlocated.

63.33-64.1   On . . . stream.:   The *Boston Evening Herald* for April 8, 1854, reports a drowning that is likely the one to which T refers. Following the heading "Body Found" the article reads: "Coroner Wright, of Concord, was called on Wednesday to view the body of an Irishman, found in Concord river, in the town of Lincoln. He was five feet six inches high, about 40 years of age, and had been in the water a long time; had black hair and a goatee, and wore a black vest, white shirt, plaid frock coat, black pants, &c. No papers or money were found on him. The coroner did not think it necessary to hold an inquest."

64.29   winkle-like fungus: In pencil, T identifies the "winkle-like fungus" as *auricularia*. A winkle is a marine snail with a spiral shell.

66.30-33   Johnson . . . them.":   Edward Johnson, *A History of New-England*, p. 214.

68.9-10   The . . . Institution.:   The Smithsonian Institution was founded by Congress in 1846 with an endowment of more than $500,000 from the estate of the British scientist James Smithson (1765-1829). Joseph Henry, the founding Secretary of the Smithsonian, established data-collecting programs with voluntary observers around the country. A program to collect meteorological data systematically by obtaining weather reports from a national network of observers began in 1848; many of these observers, who numbered several hundred by 1852, wired in their bulletins. In spring 1851, the Smithsonian distributed to scientists around the country "a circular titled 'Registry of Periodical Phenomena,' which invited 'all persons who may have it in their power, to record their observations [of 'periodical phenomena of Animal and Vegetable life'], and to transmit them to the Institution'" (Bradley P. Dean, introduction to *Wild Fruits: Thoreau's Rediscovered Last Manuscript*, ed. Bradley P. Dean [New York: W. W. Norton and Company, 2000], pp. x-xi). T never visited the Smithsonian, but he corresponded with zoologist

Spencer Fullerton Baird (1823-1887), who supervised the collection of natural history specimens as the Institution's assistant secretary and museum curator from 1850 to 1878, when he succeeded Joseph Henry as its Secretary.

68.12-17 Dod ... it.": According to the 1855 Concord census, Jonathan M. Dodd, 54, was a broker. He lived on Main Street not far from the Thoreaus, and his property extended to the Sudbury River at the back. John Brown Merchant may be John Brown Jr. (1818-1891), son of John and Sarah Brown of Concord.

68.19-23 linaria ... April.: *Linaria* is one of several names T uses for what is now called the common redpoll, *Carduelis flammea*. See *Journal 5*, Annotation 394.36-395.1, for a more extensive discussion of this bird. For F. hiemalis, see Annotation 24.7-8.

69.4-11 Was ... tail.: The golden-crowned thrush and wood wagtail are nineteenth-century names for the ovenbird, *Seiurus aurocapillus*. The "aquaticus" refers to the aquatic thrush and the aquatic wood-wagtail, contemporary names for the northern waterthrush, *Seiurus noveboracensis*. The song of T's mysterious "night warbler" is the ovenbird's flight song. See *Journal 5*, Annotation 55.23.

69.15-21 Saw ... b (?): In entries dated April 18, 20, 23, and 25, T uses letters "a", "b", "b'", and "c" to distinguish the various warblers he sees. On April 23, he decides that c, first described on April 20 (73.30-31), is probably the "Myrtlebird" or "Yellow-rump" warbler (79.12-13). On April 25, he first tentatively identifies b' as the "*golden crested wren*" (83.35-84.1); some time later, probably on or after May 7, he revises "*golden*" in pencil to "Ruby". Later in the entry he decides that warblers a, b, and b' are all the same bird, the golden-crested wren (84.21-23); again he revises "Golden" to "Ruby" in pencil. On May 7, T concludes that what he has been calling the golden-crowned is really the ruby-crested wren, but he is finally left with a doubt that he has seen both birds (103.28-34).

Wilson's American Ornithology describes the ruby-crowned wren, also known as the ruby-crowned kinglet, on pp. 55-56, and the golden-crested wren, also known as the golden-crested kinglet, on pp. 84-87.

71.32 P. grandid.: *Populus grandidentata*.

76.14 We ... Franklin–: Sir John Franklin (1786-1847) headed several expeditions to the Arctic in the first half of the nineteenth century. T read both Franklin's *Narrative of a Journey to the Shores of the Polar Sea* and Kane's account of the search for Franklin's party (see 18.29-19.23).

83.23-84.2   Heard ... flycatcher.:   See Annotation 69.15-21.

84.10   lieferungs: Installments, consignments.

86.12-13   SW ... of):   Roger Williams in "A Key into the Language of America," which T read, describes the southwest wind as "the pleasingest, warmest wind in the climate, most desired of the Indians, making fair weather ordinarily; and therefore they have a tradition, that to the southwest, which they call Sowwaniu, the Gods chiefly dwell; and hither the souls of all their great and good men and women go" (*Collections of the Massachusetts Historical Society*, p. 218).

86.34   F Brown's: See Annotation 4.23.

86.36-37   W calls dusky: *Wilson's American Ornithology*, p. 391.

90.1-5   Though ... thought.:   T could be referring to a number of ongoing Indo-European conflicts. The Crimean War had begun in 1853 between Russia and Turkey, and in 1854, Britain and France allied with Turkey and declared war on Russia. In 1853, the United States sent naval squadrons to Japan, formally demanding a trade agreement; the Treaty of Kanagawa was signed in 1854.

90.6-8   Forbes ... snow.):   James D. Forbes, *Travels through the Alps of Savoy*, pp. 242-243. Forbes does not say what caused his guides to lose the skin "off their faces." In a discussion of solar radiation, pp. 214-215, he writes, "the sun's rays have an intensity and energy at great heights, which they entirely want on the plains. At first, this might be supposed imaginary, or to result from the reflection of the heat by the snow. On a station ... where there is no permanent snow, this error is avoided; and no one who has compared the effect of a single day's exposure amongst the Alps, in discolouring the hands and face, with that of the hottest weather at Paris or Marseilles, will be disposed to question the former assertion."

91.16-22   At ... itself.:   The April 25, 1854, meeting of the American Institute Farmers' Club was reported in the *New-York Daily Tribune* two days later. At the meeting, a Mr. Scott mentioned "Spurry" as one of the "noxious weeds of this vicinity" that was "never found growing anywhere except in sand." He reported seeing a man inquiring about the seed of that plant to "sow upon drifting sand, to hold it together, where nothing else would grow" (p. 5).

95.4-14   I ... penobscots.: Two Hayneses, sometimes nicknamed "the lame Haynes" and "Heavy Haynes" but rarely identified by their given names, appear often in T's Journal. Hunters, fishermen, and frequenters of the tavern, they and John Goodwin (see Annotation 38.21-24) are among the members of the Concord community with whom T felt an affinity. See 100.25-101.5 and 183.9-16 for two more extensive accounts of T's meetings with Goodwin and a Haynes.

98.32-99.5   I ... rhyme.: The report that triggered T's negative response to scientific associations is not known. In a Journal entry for March 5, 1853, T expressed his discontent with the American Association for the Advancement of Science. He had been provoked by a circular letter inviting him to become a member, and in December 1853 he declined to join the organization. See *Journal 5*, pp. 469-470, and *The Correspondence of Henry David Thoreau*, ed. Walter Harding and Carl Bode (New York: New York University Press, 1958), pp. 309-310.

100.25-101.5   Rembering ... out–: See Annotations 38.21-24 and 95.4-14 for identification of Goodwin and Haynes.

103.28-35   A ... same.: *Wilson's American Ornithology*, pp. 55-56, 84-87. See Annotation 69.15-21.

106.13   Hollowell Place: See *Walden*, pp. 82-83, for T's depiction of the Hollowell Place and his account of how he almost came into "actual possession" of it (Map, D-3).

106.26   melainai: T's transliteration of μελαιναι (dark, black).

106.31-33   Only ... θαλασσα.: Of the poets T may have in mind, Homer applies words meaning "dark" or "stormy" to ocean waves, deep water, and the surface of the sea roughened by winds. Although the Black Sea was known to the ancient Greeks as the Euxine Pontos (Hospitable Sea), Euripides uses the phrase ποντος μελας (black sea) as a descriptor for it. T's "mlaine" is an incomplete transliteration of μελαινη; T questions the ending of the Greek version that follows "mlaine" and alters it from η to α. The correct form is μελαινα θαλασσα.

108.33-34   Nat Hist Rooms: The Museum of Natural History in Boston.

109.15-16   Harris ... Botany: Harris is identified at Annotation 41.5-28. "Hovey's Magazine" is *The Magazine of Horticulture, Botany, and All Useful Discoveries and Improvements in Rural Affairs*, ed. C. M. Hovey (Boston: Hovey and Company, 1835-1868). "Big's Botany" is Jacob Bigelow's *Florula Bostoniensis* or his *American Medical Botany*.

110.18-19 The ... note: The current scientific name for Wilson's thrush (also known as the tawny thrush and the veery) is *Catharus fuscescens*. More than once in his Journal T describes the bird's song as "yorrick." In a footnote to "Natural History of Massachusetts," he writes of the veery: "This bird ... is one of the most common in the woods in this vicinity, and in Cambridge I have heard the college yard ring with its trill. The boys call it '*yorrick*,' from the sound of its querulous and chiding note, as it flits near the traveller through the underwood" (*The Dial: A Magazine for Literature, Philosophy, and Religion* 3 [July 1842]: 26).

112.16 Rices: Israel Rice (1788?-1873), a Sudbury farmer with whom T held occasional conversations about weather and birds, appears several times in T's Journal. T once borrowed a boat from him and described him as "very obliging" and unassuming–"Thanks & compliments fell off him like water off a rock." See *Journal 4*, p. 417; *Journal 5*, pp. 76-77; and 1906, 8:177 and 10:325.

116.17-20 Now ... 37): T refers to an 1837 entry in a notebook in which he and his sister Sophia and brother John kept references to and descriptions of various birds from September 1836 to March 1842. This manuscript notebook is in the Berg Collection of the New York Public Library and is described in William L. Howarth's *The Literary Manuscripts of Henry David Thoreau* (Columbus: Ohio State University Press, 1974), pp. 306-307.

122.4 Have ... Sylva: Thomas Nuttall, *The North American Sylva*. T borrowed this work from the Society of Natural History Library when he was in Boston on May 9, 1854.

122.17 Pm ... S.: Sophia Thoreau (1819-1876), T's sister, was an amateur botanist who often accompanied him on local excursions.

127.34-35 but ... Storer: D. Humphreys Storer and William B. O. Peabody, *Reports on the Fishes, Reptiles and Birds of Massachusetts*, p. 213.

128.28-30 If ... it.: T alludes to a popular rendition of a Hindu myth, in which "the tortoise Chukwa supports the elephant Maha-pudma, which in its turn supports the world" (*Brewer's Dictionary of Phrase and Fable*, 15th ed., revised by Adrian Room [New York: HarperCollins, 1995], p. 1087).

129.11-16 Storer . . . has.: Storer and Peabody, *Reports on the Fishes, Reptiles and Birds of Massachusetts*, p. 213.

134.28 S: Possibly T's sister Sophia, with whom he went boating on May 16. An artist, Sophia sometimes supplied T with color terminology. For example, describing the sunset, T writes in *Journal 6*: "the patches of clear sky are a glorious cobalt blue as sophia calls it" (p. 234).

137.34-138.1 Cob-webs . . . washing: T often refers to cobwebs and other gauzy substances in nature as the work of fairies, and he passed this expression along to the local children who shared his forest walks. Louisa May Alcott remembers T telling her as a young girl that "a cobweb was a handkerchief dropped by a fairy" (Madeleine B. Stern, introduction to *The Selected Letters of Louisa May Alcott*, ed. Joel Myerson and Daniel Shealy [Boston: Little, Brown and Company, 1987], p. xix). See 202.28 for T's characterization of cobwebs as "little napkins of the fairies"; see also *Journal 1*, ed. Elizabeth Hall Witherell et al. (Princeton: Princeton University Press, 1981), p. 448, where T describes the fog as "Dew cloth–and fairy napkin" in his poem "Fog."

144.9-10 a . . . forever: Allusion to the answer to the first question in the Westminster Catechism, "What is the chief end of man?" "Man's chief end is to glorify God and to enjoy him forever" (*Shorter Catechism*).

146.16-23 The . . . kindred.: The "red-bird," which T also refers to as the "red election" in *Journal 2: 1842-1848*, ed. Robert Sattelmeyer (Princeton: Princeton University Press, 1984), p. 50, and the "red Election-bird" in *A Week on the Concord and Merrimack Rivers*, ed. Carl F. Hovde, William L. Howarth, and Elizabeth Hall Witherell (Princeton: Princeton University Press, 1980), p. 57, is probably the scarlet tanager. In his descriptions of the bird T repeatedly notes the contrast between the tanager's bright red plumage and the dark forest background, an image vividly captured in his May 20, 1853, Journal entry: "It flies through the green foliage as if it would ignite the leaves" (*Journal 6*, p. 139).

146.17 election days: On Election Day, traditionally the last Wednesday in May, the Governor of Massachusetts was both elected and inaugurated. Election Day was also a school holiday in New England in the early 1800s, and, according to

Edward Jarvis, "a day of great expectation and exhilaration" for boys, who celebrated it by fishing and hunting, especially shooting birds and destroying their eggs (*Traditions and Reminiscences of Concord, Massachusetts, 1779-1878*, ed. Sarah Chapin [Amherst: University of Massachusetts Press, 1993], pp. 145-147). See also Alice Morse Earle, *Customs and Fashions in Old New England* (New York: Charles Scribner's Sons, 1893), pp. 225-226.

147.22-23 to . . . Lind: Jenny Lind (1820-1887) was a popular soprano known as "the Swedish Nightingale." See *Journal 6*, Annotation 112.36-113.2, for T's reference to Lind's 1850-1852 U.S. tour sponsored by P. T. Barnum.

149.21-26 My . . . kind??: Gray, *A Manual of the Botany of the Northern United States*, p. 125. Neither Bigelow's *Florula Bostoniensis* nor his *American Medical Botany* lists the "Rubus triflorus."

149.27 daw-bugs: Variant of "dor bug," a beetle that flies with a buzzing sound.

152.2-3 Round . . . Cornel: "Cornel" is the common name for *Cornus*. "Round-leaved" and "panicled" are two types of cornel.

152.28 Slippery: The slippery elm (*Ulmus rubra*).

155.29-30 Saw Mr Holbrook: Probably Colonel Joseph Holbrook (b. 1797), who owned the Holbrook Coffee House on the north side of Main Street from 1846 to 1869.

156.35-157.2 The . . . temperature?: The *Boston Evening Transcript* announced the impending annual eclipse in its May 25, 1854, edition: "The annular eclipse of the sun tomorrow afternoon, will begin at Boston at 27 minutes and 12 seconds past 4 o'clock, and continue 2 hours, 20 minutes, 21 seconds. The duration of the ring will be one second less than two minutes." In its May 27 edition, the paper published a short description of the phenomenon: "The sky was overcast at the beginning of the eclipse, but at intervals, and at the precise moment of the greatest obscuration, the sky in that part of the heavens became entirely clear, and the phenomenon could be witnessed without the aid of smoked glass. At the period that the two bodies reached the annular point, the scene was sublime and beautiful, the ring was perfect, presenting not a single ring of fire but a series of rings in all the colors of the most brilliant prism, more varied and gorgeous than any rainbow we ever witnessed. After the breaking of the ring on the sun's upper rim, it was seen only occasionally, thick clouds constantly passing over the two bodies entirely obscuring them. At the close of the eclipse the heavens were entirely obscured. During the greatest obscuration there was a considerable diminution of light, a slight fall in the mercury, and a gloomy aspect was imparted to objects on the surface of the earth, like a sudden twilight."

160.6-16   Saw ... spirits.:   James E. De Kay, *Zoology of New-York*, Part 3, pp. 38-39, and Storer and Peabody, *Reports on the Fishes, Reptiles and Birds of Massachusetts*, pp. 227-228. The *Coluber eximius* is commonly called the chequered adder, the milk snake, the chicken snake, the house snake, and the thunder and lightning snake.

163.31-166.4   These ... me.:   Edward G. Loring, a Massachusetts Probate Court Judge and U.S. Slave Commissioner, issued a warrant for the arrest of the fugitive slave Anthony Burns. Burns, a runaway from Alexandria, Virginia, had been living and working in Boston since his arrival in the city in the spring of 1854. Upon discovering his whereabouts, his owner Charles F. Suttle demanded that Burns be returned, in accordance with the provisions of the Fugitive Slave Law. Burns was duly arrested on May 24, two days after the passage of the Kansas-Nebraska Act, which had touched off strong protests by prominent abolitionists. On the evening of May 26, Thomas Wentworth Higginson, Bronson Alcott, and other activists attempted to rescue Burns from the Boston Court House where he was being held, but the plan failed; and Commissioner Loring rendered Burns to Suttle on June 2. Burns's freedom was later purchased, and he moved to Canada after studying at Oberlin College (see Albert Von Frank, *The Trials of Anthony Burns: Freedom and Slavery in Emerson's Boston* [Cambridge: Harvard University Press, 1998], pp. 302-305; Stanley W. Campbell, *The Slave Catchers: Enforcement of the Fugitive Slave Law, 1850-1860* [Chapel Hill: University of North Carolina Press, 1970], pp. 124-130; and Higginson, pp. 147-159). T comments extensively on Burns's arrest, attempted rescue, and trial in *Journal 8*, and the speech he delivered on July 4, 1854, at an antislavery rally in Framingham was heavily culled from his Journal entries. That speech was subsequently published as "Slavery in Massachusetts." For T's additional references to the Burns trial and the Fugitive Slave Law, see 175.25-36, 184.28-185.28, 195.17-196.17, 198.4-200.8, 203.12-204.9, 205.26-206.36, 207.23-36, 210.5-21, and 211.11-14. See also *Journal 3*, pp. 203-209, for

T's comments regarding the rendition of the fugitive slave Thomas Sims in 1851.

166.10-19 Saw ... nest.: The animal T describes is the ring-tailed cat, a relative of the raccoon, found in wooded and brushy areas throughout southern California. Its current scientific name is *Bassariscus astutus.*

167.24-25 The ... flowers: Angelo identifies this as the wild pink, *Silene caroliniana* (p. 135).

168.11 Old Election: According to Edward Jarvis, the activities connected with Election Day, traditionally the last Wednesday in May, ceased in 1821 (*Traditions and Reminiscences of Concord, Massachusetts, 1779-1878*, ed. Sarah Chapin [Amherst: University of Massachusetts Press, 1993], p. 147). See Annotation 146.17.

169.18-23 Hear ... head–: T's representation of the bird's song is described in a footnote in the 1906 edition of the Journal as a "good rendering of the song of the black-throated green warbler" (6:321). His description of the bird matches ornithologist Edward Howe Forbush's description of the black-throated green warbler: "bright, lemon-yellow sides of head and pure black throat," whose song "*[z]ee zee zu zi* and *zi zi zi zi zee zu zi*" is "sometimes rendered 'trees, trees, murmuring trees'" (*Natural History of the Birds of Eastern and Central North America* [Boston: Houghton Mifflin Company, 1939], p. 429). T mentions the "evergreen forest note" again on June 12 and 18, July 10 and 28, and August 12 (see 188.3-4, 209.10, 226.10, and 246.9).

173.4-5 This ... Manna"–: In October 1852 T borrowed the first volume of William Kirby and William Spence's *An Introduction to Entomology* from the Boston Society of Natural History Library. He copied several passages into his Fact Book. Part of the passage he titled "Ephemerae" reads: "the season of different harvests is not better known to the farmer, than that in which the Ephemerae of a particular river are to emerge, is to the fishermen. ... Between the 10th & 15th of August is the time when those of the Seine & Marne, which Reaumur described, are expected by the fishermen, who call them *Manna*" (*Thoreau's Fact Book in the Harry Elkins Widener Collection in the Harvard College Library*, ed. Kenneth Walter Cameron [Hartford, Conn.: Transcendental Books, 1966], 1:128).

173.15 Blake & Brown: T's friends and admirers Harrison Gray Otis Blake and Theo Brown, two distinguished residents of Worcester, a town celebrated for its strong intellectual tradition. Blake was a Harvard alumnus, a longtime schoolteacher, and a "leading liberal spirit" in Worcester. He had been a frequent correspondent of T's since 1848; T wrote his longest, most philosophical and revealing letters to him. Blake's circle of friends in Worcester included Theo Brown, a tailor by vocation and the "freshest and most original mind" of the town. Blake and Brown took walks with T, exchanged visits with him, and arranged lectures for him in Worcester, often in the parlors of Blake's school. See *Days*, pp. 231-233; Robert D. Richardson Jr., *Henry Thoreau: A Life of the Mind* (Berkeley: University of California Press, 1986), pp. 327-328; and Annie Russell Marble, *Thoreau: His Home, Friends and Books* (New York: Thomas Y. Crowell and Co., 1902), pp. 151, 254-255.

175.31-32   attack ... House: On May 26, 1854, an unorganized mob of Bostonians and prominent abolitionists, led by some members of the Boston Vigilance Committee, gathered at the Court House for the purpose of rescuing the fugitive slave Anthony Burns, who was being held there under the authority of the Fugitive Slave Law. The incident became violent when the crowd stormed its way inside and one federal guard, James Batchelder, was killed. Guards pushed the would-be rescuers back outside, where they dispersed. Burns was later rendered to his owner, Charles F. Suttle of Alexandria, Virginia. Thomas Wentworth Higginson and others were tried and acquitted by a federal grand jury for their role in the botched rescue attempt, which Higginson called "one of the very best plots that ever–failed" (p. 150). See Annotation 163.31-166.4. For more information about the raid, see Higginson, pp. 147-166; Frederick C. Dahlstrand, *Amos Bronson Alcott: An Intellectual Biography* (Rutherford, N.J.: Fairleigh Dickinson University Press, 1982), pp. 235-236; Albert Von Frank, *The Trials of Anthony Burns: Freedom and Slavery in Emerson's Boston* (Cambridge: Harvard University Press, 1998), pp. 62-70; and Charles Emery Stevens, *Anthony Burns: A History* (1856; reprint, New York: Negro Universities Press, 1969), pp. 29-47.

181.23-27   Herndon ... country".:   William Lewis Herndon and Lardner Gibbon, *Exploration of the Valley of the Amazon*, p. 251.

182.19   Indian locket: In one of a series of commonplace books into which he copied information about Native Americans, T refers twice to a "green locket" that he had collected (Pierpont Morgan Library, MA 600, pp. 77, 124). He may be thinking of that locket, which he also calls a gorget. It is not included among the objects in T's collection of artifacts that is now owned by the Peabody Museum of Archaeology and Ethnology at Harvard University.

183.10-16   Haynes . . . muskrats.:   See Annotations 38.21-24 and 95.4-14 for identification of Goodwin and Haynes.

183.16-184.5   Find . . . ult.:   T records many observations of the greater purple fringed orchis (*Habenaria fimbriata*) in his Journal, using a number of variations of the plant's full name. See *Journal 5*, pp. 100-101, for an earlier example of T's rapture over this plant, where he calls it "unexpectedly beautiful" and the "most striking & handsome large wild flower of the year."

185.32   seringo: T's coinage for both a sound made by various birds and (as here) a species of sparrow (see *Journal 3*, Annotation 314.29).

186.18   Mrs Brown: Lucy Jackson Brown was Emerson's sister-in-law and the mother of T's friend Francis Brown, who is mentioned throughout the Journal.

190.12   Garfield: Daniel Garfield (1784-1867) was a Concord farmer whose property was located west of Conantum (Map, D-3).

192.4   Mr Bacon: Austin Bacon, of Natick, Massachusetts, was an amateur naturalist who exchanged visits with T (see *Days*, p. 350).

192.5   Sisymbrium . . . Big.:   *Sisymbrium amphibium*, marsh yellow cress, is described on p. 253 of Bigelow, *Florula Bostoniensis*.

192.27-30   Caught . . . ones.:   T sent this cicada to Harvard librarian Thaddeus William Harris (see Annotation 41.5-28) on June 25; writing back on June 27, Harris identified it as a female, a specimen new to him and different from his "specimens of *Cicada septemdecim*" and from "all the other species" in his collection. He asked T to send more specimens of both sexes to help him determine whether the specimen was "merely a variety or a different species" (*The Correspondence of Henry David Thoreau*, ed. Walter Harding and Carl Bode [New York: New York University Press, 1958], p. 329).

193.5-6   I . . . hydrometer.:   A hydrometer is an instrument for determining a liquid's gravity and strength. T's "skater insect" is probably a water strider (*Gerris remigis*), an insect-eating water bug whose long, slender legs enable it to skim over the surface of quiet waters; it is also known as the water skater or pond skater. In *A Report on the Insects of Massachusetts*, which T read, Harris characterizes the "Geometers," or *Geometrae*, one of the eight groups of moths he describes (pp. 330-343); in his description of another group, *Pyralides*, he mentions "*Hydrocampa*," one kind of *Pyralides* whose caterpillars "live in the water upon aquatic plants" (p. 344). "Hydrometer" may be T's conflation of these two terms.

195.30   Missouri compromise: See Annotation 10.4-11.

198.18   anthony Burns: Anthony Burns (1834-1862), a fugitive slave from Alexandria, Virginia, was rendered to his owner Charles F. Suttle on June 2, 1854, in compliance with the Fugitive Slave Law of 1850. He was the last fugitive to be returned to slavery from the state of Massachusetts. See Annotations 163.31-166.4 and 175.31.

198.19-24   I . . . imagined–:   T alludes to John Milton's description of hell in *Paradise Lost* (Philadelphia: Johnson and Warner, 1808), I:230-237.

199.21   Art . . . interrupted: Hippocrates's aphorism "Life is short, the Art long" (*Hippocrates*, vol. 4, Loeb Classical Library, p. 99) finds expression in the works of many writers whom T read.

199.29   tintimmarre: "a confused noise, uproar, clamour, racket, hubbub, clatter" (*Oxford English Dictionary*, 1970).

203.17-18   "gilding . . . alchemy.":   William Shakespeare, *Poems*, Sonnet 33, l. 4.

204.32-33   The . . . ripe.:   As T notes in "Huckleberries," Sebastian Rasles, who "was making a Dictionary of the Abenaki Language in 1691," says that the Abnaki Indian name for July means "when the blueberries are ripe" (*The Natural History Essays*, ed. Robert Sattelmeyer [Salt Lake City: Peregrine Smith Books, 1980], p. 234). This information appears on pp. 477-478 of Rasles's *A Dictionary of the Abnaki Language, in North America*.

206.29   Garrison . . . Parker: William Lloyd Garrison (1805-1879), Wendell Phillips (1811-1884), and Theodore Parker (1810-1860) were prominent abolitionists in the antislavery movement.

207.23-29   What . . . men–:   T alludes to "organized emi-

gration"–sending settlers who supported the Free-Soil movement to the territories that were allowed to choose between
free labor and slavery by the Kansas-Nebraska Act (see Annotation 10.4-11). To prevent the expansion of slavery, Eli Thayer
of Worcester, a member of the Massachusetts legislature,
founded the Massachusetts Emigrant Aid Society to facilitate
emigration of New Englanders to Kansas Territory. The char-
ter for the organization was signed by the governor on April
26, before the House had even begun debates on the Kansas-
Nebraska bill. By the end of July, the first group of New England settlers had arrived in Kansas. See Samuel A. Johnson,
*The Battle Cry of Freedom: The New England Emigrant Aid
Company in the Kansas Crusade* (Lawrence: University of
Kansas Press, 1954), pp. 3-32; and Kenneth S. Davis, *Kansas: A
Bicentennial History* (New York: W. W. Norton and Company,
1976), pp. 37-71. See also Annotation 210.5-7.

208.3-4   I. Dugan: Likely Isaac Dugan (b. 1814), a son of
Thomas and Jane (Jenny) Dugan. The Dugans were African-
American residents of Concord, living off the Old Marlboro
Road, southwest of Concord (Map, D-2). The area near the
Dugan house by Nut Meadow Brook was a favorite haunt
of T's.

208.17   Daniel Foster: The Reverend Daniel Foster (1816-
1864) of East Princeton, Massachusetts, was one of "a few exceptions to Thoreau's disdain for the clergy" (*Days*, p. 322).
He served briefly (1851-1852) as minister of the Second Con-
gregational (Trinitarian) Church in Concord; his wife, Dora,
was a close friend of Sophia Thoreau's. As T records in his
Journal, at least one of the statements Foster made in a ser-
mon pleased him: "'Thank God there is no doctrine of election with regard to Nature, we are all admitted to her'" (*Journal 4*, p. 292). Foster later became a prominent antislavery
lecturer, was an associate of John Brown's in Kansas, and finally commanded a company of black troops in the Civil
War. He was killed in action near Richmond, Virginia, in September 1864. See *Journal 3*, pp. 204-205, for T's praise of Foster's abolitionist prayer at the Boston Harbor when the fugitive slave Thomas Sims was returned to slavery in Georgia.

209.7-18   Examined . . . warbler?:   The blue yellow-back
warbler (*Sylvia pusilla*) is described on p. 270 in *Wilson's
American Ornithology.* T later positively identifies his
"*tweezer* bird" as *Sylvia Americana*, a name other ornitholo-
gists give for Wilson's *Sylvia pusilla* (1906, 8:384).

210.5-7   It ... wanted–:   The Free-Soil Party, a minor but influential political party in the pre-Civil War period, was organized to prevent the extension of slavery in the southwestern territories acquired from Mexico. Launched in August 1848 by members of the abolitionist Liberty Party, the antislavery Whigs, and New York's Free-Soil Democrats, the new party called for "free soil, free speech, free labor, and free men." Its presidential nominee, the former U.S. president Martin Van Buren, pulled 10 percent of the popular vote in the November 1848 election, and the party elected a number of congressmen. Support for the party was reduced by half in the 1852 election; in 1854 the remaining Free-Soilers were absorbed into the newly formed Republican Party. See also Annotation 207.23-29.

210.8-9   godly ... discovered: Thomas Carlyle writes in *On Heroes, Hero-Worship, and the Heroic in History*: "Cromwell's *Ironsides* were ... men fearing God; and without any other fear. No more conclusively genuine set of fighters ever trod the soil of England, or of any other land" (p. 347). On his dated reading list for April 15, 1841 (Henry E. Huntington Library manuscript HM 13201), T notes that he read the proof sheets of Carlyle's book that came from England, probably sent by Emerson, who was in England at the time. In his 1847 essay "Thomas Carlyle and His Works," T comments specifically on Carlyle's sympathetic depiction of Cromwell as a man of "action" and "endeavor" (*Early Essays and Miscellanies*, ed. Joseph J. Moldenhauer et al. [Princeton: Princeton University Press, 1975], pp. 245, 250-251).

211.20-25   Heard ... beneath–:   T's new bird is most likely the yellow-breasted chat (*Icteria virens*), a member of the warbler family.

212.34-213.4   In ... young.:   John Tanner, *A Narrative of the Captivity and Adventures of John Tanner*, p. 311; and William Smellie, *The Philosophy of Natural History*, p. 139: "Fishes receive no aid from their parents."

216.18   Texas house: The Thoreau family moved to a newly constructed residence on Texas Street (now Belknap Street) in Concord in 1845. Except for the two years he lived at Walden Pond and a year he resided with the Emerson family during Emerson's absence, T lived in the Texas house with his family from 1845 to 1850, when the Thoreaus purchased a residence on Main Street (see *Days*, pp. 177-178).

216.26   P. Hutchinson: See Annotation 34.24-25.

216.30-32 The ... forward.: *Lechea thymifolia*, or thyme-leaved pinweed, is described on p. 49 in Gray, *A Manual of the Botany of the Northern United States.*

217.35-218.1 The ... Tempes.: Tempe, a valley in Thessaly, between Mount Olympus and Ossa, has been described by poets as "the most delightful spot" on earth, "with continually cool shades and verdant walks, which the warbling of birds rendered more pleasant and romantic, and which the gods often honored with their presence" (*Lemprière's Classical Dictionary of Proper Names Mentioned in Ancient Authors*, revised by F. A. Wright [London: Routledge and Kegan Paul Ltd, 1963], p. 613).

218.30 C.: Channing; see Annotation 5.14.

220.20-23 A ... purple: Alphonso Wood, *A Class-Book of Botany*, pp. 337-338.

234.22-23 It ... cimetar.: T alludes to a scene in Sir Walter Scott's *The Talisman*, in which the Sultan Saladin, ruler of Egypt, demonstrates to King Richard I of England his skill and the excellence of his scimitar by slicing both "a cushion of silk and down" and a "sort of veil" (*The Complete Works of Sir Walter Scott*, vol. 5 [New York: Conner and Cooke, 1833], pp. 88-89).

235.20-21 Seeing ... brass.: Horace writes in Ode 3, "To Virgil setting out for Greece": "Oak and triple bronze must have girt the breast of him who first committed his frail bark to the angry sea" (*The Odes and Epodes*, Loeb Classical Library, p. 13).

237.23-24 Are ... mountains-: T alludes to the "Delectable Mountains" in John Bunyan's *The Pilgrim's Progress* (New York: John Tiebout, 1811): "a most pleasant mountainous country, beautified with woods, vineyards, fruits of all sorts, flowers also, with springs and fountains, very delectable to behold" (p. 112).

237.24 It ... honey.: Allusion to Exodus 3:8.

237.32-238.5 By ... long.: Wood describes *Monarda fistulosa* and *Monarda didyma* in *A Class-Book of Botany*. Infraspecies *mollis* appears under *Monarda fistulosa* and is designated ξ (p. 417).

238.6-22 2 ... smooth?: *Asclepias syriaca* (named by Linnaeus) is described by Bigelow, *Florula Bostoniensis*, pp. 101-102, as follows: "Stem simple; leaves lance-oblong, gradually acute ... Nectaries red, truncated obliquely inward, and cleft with an oblique ridge on each side of the fissure."

Gray's description of *Asclepias cornuti* in *A Manual of the Botany of the Northern United States*, p. 366, includes the phrase "with a slight point." Wood describes *Asclepias cornuti* on pp. 458 and 459 of *A Class-Book of Botany;* the plate T refers to is on p. 458.

The corolla of *Asclepias purpurascens* is described by Bigelow in *Florula Bostoniensis*, p. 103, as "of a dark crimson purple" with "Nectaries of the same colour"; T's description of the pedicels and lower leaves of *Asclepias purpurascens* matches Gray's in *A Manual of the Botany of the Northern United States*, p. 367.

247.26-29 Wednesday ... Lincoln.: According to his "Field Notes," p. 511, on August 2, 1854, T surveyed an acre of swamp woodland in the east part of Lincoln for Albert Hagar.

247.35 C.: Channing; see Annotation 5.14.

250.30-31 Fields ... inst.: James T. Fields (1817-1881), an influential figure in the literary world, was a partner in the Boston publishing firm Ticknor and Fields and editor of the *Atlantic Monthly*. *Walden* was actually published on August 9.

253.34-35 that ... listeth: Allusion to John 3:8.

259.27 Walden Published.: *Walden* was published in the U.S. by Ticknor and Fields of Boston on August 9, 1854, in an edition of two thousand copies selling for one dollar each (see *The Cost Books of Ticknor and Fields and Their Predecessors: 1832-1858*, ed. Warren S. Tryon and William Charvat [New York: The Bibliographical Society of America, 1949], pp. 289-290). T's terse announcement in his Journal belies his excitement about its publication: Emerson remarks in a letter to his friend George Bradford later in August that T "is walking up & down Concord, firm-looking, but in a tremble of great expectation" (*The Letters of Ralph Waldo Emerson*, vol. 4, ed. Ralph L. Rusk [New York: Columbia University Press, 1939], p. 460).

260.29 Russel: The Reverend John Lewis Russell (1808-1873) of Salem, Massachusetts, was a well-known amateur botanist; he was appointed Professor of Botany and Horticultural Physiology at the Massachusetts Horticultural Society in 1833 and later became a fellow of the American Academy of Arts and Sciences. During Russell's three-day visit in mid-August 1854, T showed him all around Concord, examining local specimens with him and consulting him on botanical identifications. See Angelo, pp. 22-23. One of Russell's scientific papers, "Visit to a Locality of the Climbing Fern" (*Magazine of Horticulture* [March 1855]: 126-134), was based on his botanical excursion with T on August 16.

261.21 Mr Loomis: Eben J. Loomis (1828-1912), a mathematician for the *American Ephemeris and Nautical Almanac* in Cambridge, became friends with the Thoreaus in the summer of 1853 when Mrs. Thoreau invited him and his new wife Mary Wilder Loomis, who was a close friend of T's aunts Maria and Jane, to spend part of their honeymoon in Concord. T and Loomis spent much time together during the couple's subsequent visits, including the summer of 1854 (see *Days*, pp. 350-351).

266.33-267.2 3 ... America.: E. Hoar could be either Edward Sherman Hoar (1823-1893) or his sister Elizabeth (1814-1878), both amateur naturalists and the children of T's neighbor Samuel Hoar. T more likely refers here to Elizabeth since Edward lived in California from 1849 to 1857. He did visit Concord in 1852, but no visit is recorded for the summer of 1854. George Bradford (1807-1890), a founding member of the Brook Farm community and a longtime friend of Emerson's, moved to Concord and opened a private school in 1844. During the summer of 1854 he was in Europe.

269.9 W.E.C.: Channing; see Annotation 5.14.

271.13 Paul Dudley's: Paul Dudley (1799-1882) was a farmer in Acton.

272.23 C–: Channing; see Annotation 5.14.

273.1 Russell: See Annotation 260.29.

273.6-7 Miss Mackay's: Miss Mackay is probably Frances Mary Mackay of Concord.

276.3 Barratt: Joseph Barratt (1796-1882) of Middletown, Connecticut, was the author of *Salices Americanae*.

276.15 Robbins: James Watson Robbins (1801-1879), a physician of Uxbridge, Massachusetts, was a serious amateur botanist interested in aquatic plants, especially Potamogeton. Robbins corresponded with several botanists, including Tuckerman, Gray, and Wood, whose work T read; he also wrote the Potamogeton section of the fifth edition of Gray's *A Manual of the Botany of the Northern United States* (Finding Aid, Thomas Morong Papers, Library of the Gray Herbarium, Harvard University).

276.25-27 The ... sea.: T could have known this story

from any number of botanical sources. Edwin Way Teale gives a version in his *North with the Spring* (New York: Dodd, Mead and Company, 1951): "*Tillandsia* . . . is an airplant manufacturing its own food. . . . Contrary to Linnaeus's opinion, Spanish moss thrives best in moist surroundings. The Swedish scientist was so convinced that this airplant disliked moisture that he named it after Elias Tillands, a student with such an aversion to water that he once walked more than 1,000 miles around the head of the Gulf of Bothnia rather than make the relatively short crossing from shore to shore" (pp. 60-61).

276.35 A . . . weeks: This is the first of several observations T made about the severity of the summer's drought. See also 281.16-21, 289.19-22, 300.1-6, 309.10-11, 310.3-6, 310.22-311.14, and 314.27-315.5.

284.3-7 On . . . Newburyport.: Henry Coit Perkins (1804-1873), a Newburyport, Massachusetts, physician and amateur naturalist, offered T his first look through a high-power microscope when they met in December 1850 through Thomas Wentworth Higginson (see *Days*, p. 285). See *Journal 3*, p. 161, for T's description of the specimens Perkins showed him, including a "green clam shell."

285.18-19 Fin . . . wanting.: T uses standard abbreviations for the positions of fish fins: P for pectoral, V for ventral, A for anal, D for dorsal, and C for caudal.

287.14-17 I . . . stem.: Wood describes *Aster corymbosus* and *Aster cordifolius* in *A Class-Book of Botany*, pp. 318-319.

287.21-26 Brought . . . throughout: In May 1841 Joseph Barratt published *Eupatoria Verticillata*, a broadside describing species and varieties of the genus *Eupatorium* he had collected. He named one of his species *Eupatorium fistulosum* (trumpetweed), to be distinguished from Linnaeus's "original" *Eupatorium purpureum* (sweet-scented Joe-Pye weed), which Barratt claimed to be "a different plant, presenting also several interesting varieties." T's reference to the plant's maximum height of twelve feet comes from Gray's description of *Eupatorium purpureum* in *A Manual of the Botany of the Northern United States* (p. 192).

289.31-33 I . . . fish.: *Wilson's American Ornithology*, p. 556.

289.36-290.1 Here . . . feed.: According to Nuttall, the heron "occasionally feeds upon the seeds of the pond lilies"

(*A Manual of the Ornithology of the United States and of Canada: The Water Birds*, p. 44).

292.3-8 I . . . Sherburne–": Emerson, *A Report on the Trees and Shrubs Growing Naturally in the Forests of Massachusetts*, p. 406.

292.12 factory quarter: T probably refers to the area west of Concord where many mills and factories were built in the early 1800s. In *Concord: American Town* (Boston: Little, Brown and Company, 1947), Townsend Scudder refers to "Factory Village–West Concord–making Donnets flannels, lead pipe, harness, pails, chairs, and other commodities" (p. 194).

297.21 M. Miles': Marshall Miles; see Annotation 25.5-9.

304.1-4 It . . . pads.: Sir Robert Hermann Schomburgk (1804-1865), a British explorer, discovered the water lily *Victoria regia* in 1835 during his travels to British Guiana. An article in the Worcester, Massachusetts, *Daily Transcript* for August 24, 1854, quotes Schomburgk's description of the upright margins of the water lily's leaves as "on the inside light green . . . on the outside . . . of a bright crimson." T was fascinated with this lily; in his eulogy for T, Emerson noted that T "expected to find yet the *Victoria regia* in Concord" (Joel Myerson, "Emerson's 'Thoreau': A New Edition from Manuscript," in *Studies in the American Renaissance*, ed. Joel Myerson [Boston: Twayne Publishers, 1979], p. 45).

307.20 by . . . hear: Allusion to Matthew 11:15.

307.24-308.3 The . . . full.: The Lyceums in Concord and other New England towns engaged lectures for the fall and winter each year. T undoubtedly has in mind his own upcoming lecture series, which he undertook following the publication of *Walden*.

310.9-14 Minott . . . lbs.: Minot Pratt (1805-1878), a farmer, bee-keeper, and amateur botanist, moved to Concord after living for four years in the experimental community of Brook Farm. Pratt later engaged in the establishment of alien plants in Concord. See Angelo, p. 25. See *Journal 5*, pp. 359-364, for T's bee-hunting trip with Pratt. See Annotation 260.29 for identification of Russell.

310.18-21 Ferris . . . travellers.": Benjamin G. Ferris, *Utah and the Mormons*, p. 22.

310.19-20 "at . . . be: To the left of this line, at the inner margin of MS page 449, T used orange wax to attach two clippings, one on top of the other, from the September 1, 1854, issue of the *Boston Evening Transcript*. The article on top was clipped from p. 2:

A Dry August. The meteorological correspondent of the Traveller gives the following interesting information: In the month of August the quantity of rain which fell in Boston was very small, or 0.58 of an inch only, the least in any August since 1828, when it was but three-eighths of an inch. The wettest August was 1826, in which 12.10 inches of water fell. The driest was 1828, when the quantity of rain was only 3-8ths (0.37) of an inch.

At the Observatory at Cambridge, the fall of rain last month was even less than in Boston in August, 1828, viz: 0.35 inch, and from July 25th to September 1, (37 days) it was 0.446 inch only. In August, 1853, the fall at the Observatory was 8.59 or 24 times as large as that in the month just ended.

The article on the bottom was clipped from p. 1:

The Season in 1754. A correspondent of the Portland Advertiser furnishes an interesting article upon the drought. He says: "We have amused ourselves recently, in looking back to our past annals for seasons of dearth, to find a parrellel for "this most unparalleled state of the weather," and many a complaint starts out from the past years through Parson Smith's invaluable journal, to encourage us to hope, almost against hope, that we shall survive the present drought, and again behold the earth smiling in freshness and beauty." We copy the record of the year 1754, just one hundred years ago, from Parson Smith's journal:

1754, July 1st. "I have no grass growing in my mowing ground, and there is no feed on the Neck; the reasons are the open winter, three weeks early drought, and the grasshoppers." 22d. "There is a melancholy drought." October 26th. "A great storm; the earth is filled with water."

Ninety years ago the following record was made:

1764, June 25th. "It is as melancholy dry a time as ever I saw." July 5th. "As great a drought as in 1749." August 1st. "Drought awfully continues." 12th. "No feed on the Neck for a great while." 16th. "The drought increases." Now for the usual alternation. Aug 19th. "Storm of rain." 31st. "Marvellous growing time; surprising change on the face of the earth." Sept. 24th. "The earth has a most beautiful green face." Oct. 6th. *The grass is better set than in the spring.*"

Fifteen of the years between 1722 and 1764, are mentioned on account of the drouth that prevailed. The writer closes his communication with the following deductions. He says:

These well attested facts prove, 1st, that we live in an exceedingly dry climate; that we are continually subject to droughts. 2d, that the early and latter rains seldom fail. 3d, that notwithstanding these contingencies, the earth yields to us an abundant supply for our wants and luxuries; that we need patient and faithful husbandry, and perhaps some new and improved modes of culture to meet the peculiar condition of our atmospheric influences, and to counteract them; and 4th, and above all, the folly, the futility, nay, the wickedness of the constant and yearly murmurings and complainings of the dealings of providence in those particulars which are the results of our peculiar climate, and to which our vegetable kingdom is wisely adapted.

310.22   Pm . . . Peirce–:   T recorded his survey of a house lot for William Peirce on August 31, 1854, in his "Field Notes," p. 512.

314.27-315.5   I . . . migrate.:   Newspapers in late August and early September of 1854 continued their reports on the prevailing summer drought and the raging forest fires in the country. An article in the August 31, 1854, edition of the *New-York Tribune* described the fires in Vermont (where Lake Champlain is located), Maine, Massachusetts, New Hampshire, Rhode Island, and other parts of the country: "the green mountains of Vermont are a tower of fire by night and a pillar of smoke by day, stopping the passage of the locomotive through the valleys–the mountain sides and old pine plains of Massachusetts are equally carbonized. . . . New-York is swept from sea to lake. . . . the very earth of northern Ohio is turned to cinders." The next day the newspaper published a letter describing the fires' effects on humans and animals: "The woods are on fire in every direction, the smoke is so dense as to render it impossible to discover objects at the distance of twenty rods, the air is full of burning cinder and ashes. . . . Wild beasts are leaving the forests or being burned up. Bears are seen wandering about the fields in the day time". An article in the September 2 edition of the *New-York Daily Times*, "Fires and Bears at the White Mountains," also reported that the "extreme drouth [in New Hampshire] brings down the bears from their mountain homes."

BIBLIOGRAPHY

Barratt, Joseph. *Eupatoria Verticillata. Specimens to Illustrate the North American Verticillate Species and Varieties of the Genus Eupatorium: With Synonymes and References.* Middletown, Conn., 1841.

———. *Salices Americanae. North American Willows.* Middletown, Conn.: Charles H. Pelton, Printer, 1840.

Bigelow, Jacob. *American Medical Botany, Being a Collection of the Native Medicinal Plants of the United States.* 3 vols. Boston: Cummings and Hilliard, 1817-1820.

———. *Florula Bostoniensis: A Collection of Plants of Boston and Its Vicinity, with Their Generic and Specific Characters, Principal Synonyms, Descriptions, Places of Growth, and Time of Flowering, and Occasional Remarks.* 2d ed., enl. Boston: Cummings, Hilliard, and Company, 1824.

Carlyle, Thomas. *On Heroes, Hero-Worship, and the Heroic in History.* London: James Fraser, 1841.

Columella, Lucius Junius Moderatus. *De Re Rustica.* In *Rei Rusticae Auctores Latini Veteres, M. Cato, M. Varro, L. Columella, Palladius.* [Heidelbergae]: Ex Hier. Commelini typographio, 1595.

De Kay, James E. *Zoology of New-York, or the New-York Fauna; Comprising Detailed Descriptions of All the Animals Hitherto Observed within the State of New-York, with Brief Notices of Those Occasionally Found near Its Borders, and Accompanied by Appropriate Illustrations.* 5 vols. Albany: W. and A. White and J. Visscher, 1842.

De Quincey, Thomas. *Historical and Critical Essays.* 2 vols. Boston: Ticknor, Reed, and Fields, 1853.

Emerson, George B. *A Report on the Trees and Shrubs Growing Naturally in the Forests of Massachusetts.* Boston: Dutton and Wentworth, State Printers, 1846.

Ferris, Benjamin G. *Utah and the Mormons: The History, Government, Doctrines, Customs, and Prospects of the Latter-

Day Saints. From Personal Observation during a Six Months' Residence at Great Salt Lake City. New York: Harper and Brothers, 1854.

Forbes, James D. *Travels through the Alps of Savoy and Other Parts of the Pennine Chain with Observations on the Phenomena of Glaciers*. Edinburgh: Adam and Charles Black, 1843.

Franklin, John. *Narrative of a Journey to the Shores of the Polar Sea, in the Years 1819, 20, 21, and 22*. Philadelphia: H. C. Carey and I. Lea [etc.], 1824.

Gray, Asa. *A Manual of the Botany of the Northern United States, from New England to Wisconsin and South to Ohio and Pennsylvania inclusive*. Boston: James Munroe and Company, 1848.

Harris, Thaddeus William. *A Report on the Insects of Massachusetts, Injurious to Vegetation*. Cambridge: Folsom, Wells, and Thurston, 1841.

Herndon, William Lewis, and Lardner Gibbon. *Exploration of the Valley of the Amazon, Made under Direction of the Navy Department*. Washington: Robert Armstrong, Public Printer, 1854.

Johnson, Edward. *A History of New-England. From the English planting in the Yeere 1628. untill the Yeere 1652*. London: N. Brooke, 1654.

Kane, Elisha Kent. *The U.S. Grinnell Expedition in Search of Sir John Franklin: A Personal Narrative*. New York: Harper and Brothers, 1854.

Kirby, William, and William Spence. *An Introduction to Entomology: Or Elements of the Natural History of Insects*. 4 vols. London: Longman, Hurst, Rees, Orme, and Brown, 1815.

"Life and Doctrine of Geoffroy St. Hilaire." *The Westminster Review* 61 (January 1854): 84-100.

Montanus, Arnoldus. "Description of New Netherland." *The Documentary History of the State of New-York*. Ed. E. B. O'Callaghan. Vol. 4. Albany: Charles van Benthuysen, Public Printer, 1851. 113-132.

Nuttall, Thomas. *A Manual of the Ornithology of the United States and of Canada: The Water Birds*. Boston: Hilliard, Gray, and Company, 1834.

———. *The North American Sylva; or, A Description of the Forest Trees of the United States, Canada and Nova Scotia*. 3 vols. Philadelphia: Robert P. Smith, 1853.

Pfeiffer, Ida. *A Lady's Voyage Round the World: A Selected Translation from the German of Ida Pfeiffer.* Trans. Mrs. Percy Sinnett. New York: Harper and Brothers, 1852.

Rasles, Sebastian. *A Dictionary of the Abnaki Language, in North America.* In *Memoirs of the American Academy of Arts and Sciences,* new ser., vol. 1 (1833): 370-574.

Reid, Mayne. *The Young Voyageurs, or The Boy Hunters in the North.* Boston: Ticknor, Reed, and Fields, 1854.

Richardson, John. *Fauna Boreali-Americana; or The Zoology of the Northern Parts of British America: Containing Descriptions of the Objects of Natural History Collected on the Late Northern Land Expeditions, under Command of Captain Sir John Franklin.* London: John Murray, 1829.

Shakespeare, William. *The Poems of Shakespeare.* London: William Pickering, 1842.

Smellie, William. *The Philosophy of Natural History.* Ed. John Ware. Boston: Hilliard, Gray, and Company, 1836.

Storer, D. Humphreys, and William B. O. Peabody. *Reports on the Fishes, Reptiles and Birds of Massachusetts.* Boston: Dutton and Wentworth, State Printers, 1839.

Tanner, John. *A Narrative of the Captivity and Adventures of John Tanner.* Ed. Edwin James. New York: G. and C. and H. Carvill, 1830.

Tuckerman, Edward. *An Enumeration of North American Lichenes, with a Preliminary View of the Structure and General History of These Plants, and of the Friesian System.* Cambridge: John Owen, 1845.

Williams, Roger. "A Key into the Language of America." *Collections of the Massachusetts Historical Society.* 1st ser., vol. 3 (1794; reprint 1810): 203-239.

Wilson, Alexander. *Wilson's American Ornithology, with Notes by Jardine: To Which Is Added a Synopsis of American Birds, Including Those Described by Bonaparte, Audubon, Nuttall, and Richardson; by T. M. Brewer.* New York: H. S. Samuels, 1852.

Wood, Alphonso. *A Class-Book of Botany, Designed for Colleges, Academies, and Other Seminaries.* 23d ed., rev. and enl. Boston: Crocker and Brewster, 1851.

This map of the Concord area was drawn by Theo Baumann, of the Australian National University, using the following contemporaneous and current maps: H. F. Walling's (1852), a reconnaissance survey of 1886, Herbert Wendell Gleason's (1906), and the topographic sheets of the U.S. Geological Survey (1950, 1958).

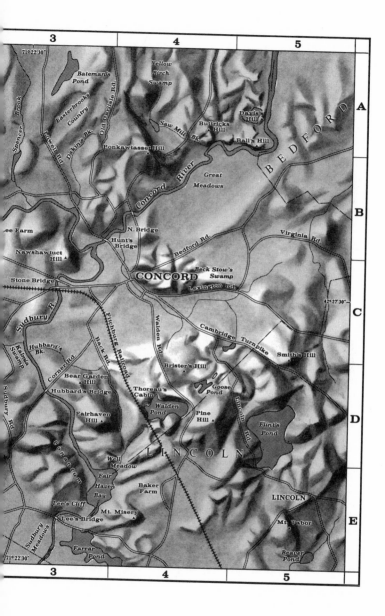

Index

Notes on Illustrations

Page of MS Volume XVII following page 414

This page contains the brief Journal entry Thoreau made on August 9, 1854, to record *Walden*'s publication (see p. 259). The book had been nine years in the making and Thoreau held considerable hope for its success, but in this laconic entry he reveals nothing of the feelings evoked by the event.

Rowse Portrait of Thoreau

This likeness of Thoreau, which is now in the Concord Free Public Library, was drawn in late summer or early fall 1854 by Samuel Worcester Rowse, a young portrait painter from Maine. Rowse was boarding with the Thoreaus while he worked on a portrait of Emerson. Eben Loomis, a guest at the Thoreaus' during this time, wrote an account of the circumstances surrounding the drawing's creation: "For two or three weeks he did not put a pencil to paper; but one morning at breakfast, he suddenly jumped up from the table, asked to be excused and disappeared for the rest of the day. The next morning he brought down the crayon, almost exactly in its present form, scarcely another touch was put upon it" (Thomas Blanding and Walter Harding, "A Thoreau Iconography," in *Studies in the American Renaissance*, ed. Joel Myerson [Boston: Twayne Publishers, 1980], p. 3). Loomis found Rowse's the most satisfactory of the few likenesses of Thoreau, because "it represents Henry just as he was in that summer" (p. 4). Thoreau's sister Sophia also considered it a good portrait because it revealed the poet in her brother (p. 3).

Broadside Depicting Anthony Burns

The arrest, trial, and return of the fugitive slave Anthony Burns inspired Thoreau's extensive antislavery tirade in the Journal during May and June. Burns was arrested in Boston on May 24, 1854. Following a trial, in which he was defended by Richard Henry Dana Jr., and an unsuccessful rescue attempt by Thoreau's friends Bronson Alcott and Thomas Wentworth Higginson, Burns was turned over to his owner and returned to slavery in Alexandria, Virginia. His freedom was later purchased by abolitionists. He attended Oberlin College in the late 1850s and eventually moved to St. Catherine's, Canada, where he served as a Baptist minister until his death in 1862. See Albert Von Frank, *The Trials of Anthony Burns: Freedom and Slavery in Emerson's Boston* (Cambridge, MA: Harvard University Press, 1998).

This broadside was printed by R. M. Edwards in 1855. Around the portrait of Burns, based on a daguerreotype made by Whipple & Black, Edwards represented various incidents of Burns's life as a slave and as a free man (reproduced from Library of Congress negative number LC-USZ62-90750). See the Historical Introduction, pp. 405-407, and Annotations 163.31-166.4, 175.31, and 198.18.

Page of MS Volume XVII

Thoreau drew this representation of Gowing's Swamp in his August 23, 1854, Journal entry. The Journal includes many of Thoreau's sketches of natural phenomena; this one is unusual for its size and for the care with which Thoreau locates and names the various plants growing in the swamp on this date. The summer's drought made it possible for him to walk into the middle of the swamp and document the plants he saw there. See p. 291, where the drawing has been reduced to fit the printed page.

Acknowledgments

For permission to refer to, copy, and publish manuscript and other material, the editor is indebted to the Pierpont Morgan Library, New York; the Concord Free Public Library, Concord, Massachusetts; the Houghton Library, Harvard University; the Huntington Library, San Marino, California; the Library of Congress, Washington, D.C.; and the Thoreau Society, Lincoln, Massachusetts.

Contributions of time, expertise, and good will were made by Ray Angelo, Kimberly Bell, Michael Berger, Barbara Brunhuber, Daria D'Arienzo, Jennifer Etherton, Sheila Evans, Bradley Fletcher, Julie A. Frost, Janet Gabler-Hover, Danielle Garland, Madeline Gibson, Gloria Polizzotti Greis, Pitt Harding, Derrick Harris, Derek Katz, Colette McHarry Kenworthy, Leigh Kirkland, John Finley Kiser, Betty Koed, Allan Kulikoff, Christopher Lapeyre, James E. Lapeyre, Sarah Mace, Ian Marshall, Thomas L. McHaney, Joel Myerson, Ralph Norris, Kelli Olson, Dianne Piper-Rybak, Jason Price, Elaine Saino, Clare Sigrist, Bradley Smith, Kevin P. Van Anglen, Mike Volmar, Leslie Wilson, Jacque Wilson-Jordan, Croft Yjader, and Deborah Zak.

The staff of the Thoreau Edition is grateful to John Morris for his services as a programmer and a consultant.

Material assistance was generously provided by the National Endowment for the Humanities, the Albert and Elaine Borchard Foundation, Inc., the Ellis L. Phillips Foundation, the National Trust for the Humanities, Princeton University, the Department of English and the Davidson Library at the University of California, Santa Barbara, the Department of English and the College of Arts and Sciences at Georgia State

University, the Universities Research Association, the Department of English and the University Libraries at Northern Illinois University, and the Division of Arts and Humanities at Pennsylvania State University, Altoona.

Ms. Petrulionis would like to thank Georgia State University for a travel grant that allowed her to conduct work on this volume at the Pierpont Morgan Library.

Editorial Contributions

PRELIMINARY transcriptions were prepared by Carolyn Kappes and Lorna Carey Mack, and reviewed by Ms. Mack. All tasks of establishing the text and apparatus were done by Ms. Petrulionis with the assistance of Thoreau Edition staff members. Preliminary apparatus was reviewed by Heather Kirk Thomas. Ms. Petrulionis wrote the Historical Introduction; Ms. Thomas reviewed it. Mariane Schaum prepared copy for the index. Text, apparatus, introductions, and index for the volume were reviewed by Noelle A. Baker, Robert Sattelmeyer, and Ms. Schaum of the Journal Office at Georgia State University and by Louisa Dennis, Elizabeth Marshall Dubrulle, Minka Misangyi, Mary Lamb Shelden, and Lihong Xie of the Textual Center. Elizabeth Hall Witherell reviewed copy throughout work on the volume.

Historical Introduction

Journal 8: 1854 is edited from the 467-page manuscript volume that Thoreau numbered "XVII" and kept from February 13 to September 3, 1854. As is characteristic of his journalizing from 1850 on, Thoreau attends most carefully during these six and a half months to the natural phenomena of the passing seasons as winter gives way to spring, spring to summer, and summer to the first hints of fall. In this volume he shows himself to be an increasingly confident taxonomist, creating lists which distill his observations about plant leafing and seasonal birds, and he continues to be enthralled by what he observes, as evidenced when he delights in the antics of mud turtles and romanticizes bedewed cobwebs as "a faery's washing" (p. 138). Two particularly significant public events take place in his life this summer, but Thoreau notes these in his Journal with only a line each. On July 4, 1854, at an antislavery rally at Framingham, Massachusetts, Thoreau appeared for the first time in the company of prominent abolitionists, delivering as heated a statement against slavery as he had yet made. And on August 9, 1854, Ticknor and Fields published *Walden*, the book Thoreau had been working on since 1846 and which had initially been advertised in the endpapers of *A Week on the Concord and Merrimack Rivers* in 1849.

Apart from the Framingham rally and the publication of *Walden,* the outward circumstances of Thoreau's life during this period were unremarkable. He lived at home with his parents, his sister Sophia, and his aunt, Louisa Dunbar, at their residence on Main Street in Concord. His mother, Cynthia Dunbar Thoreau, took in boarders, so the household often included additional inhabitants; Samuel Rowse, who drew a portrait of Thoreau in late summer or early fall 1854, was one of these (see Notes on Illustrations, p. 389, and the second illustration, following p. 414).

As he had been doing since 1849, Thoreau continued to earn money by surveying–during the period covered he surveyed in every month but July–and in the Journal he provides occasional glimpses of his employers. With wry insight, Thoreau describes the "profound silence" of Concord's leading citizen, Samuel Hoar, for whom he surveyed property on April 5. Despite their lifelong acquaintance and Thoreau's friendship with his children Elizabeth and Edward, Hoar maintained a reserve that Thoreau took in stride: "I treated him simply as if he had bronchitis & could not speak–just as I would a sick man a crazy man or an idiot– The disease was only an unconquerable stiffness in a well-meaning & sensible man–" (p. 55). On April 12 Thoreau mentions the noontime gin drinking of Schuyler Parks, who hired him to survey a woodlot in Lincoln (p. 62).

Thoreau's habitual walking companion during this time was William Ellery Channing the Younger, usually referred to in the Journal as "C.", "Ch.", or "W.E.C." Thoreau alludes to Channing's coarse behavior throughout his Journal, and he doubtless has Channing in mind when he complains in the March 12 entry, "My companion tempts me to certain licences of speech–i.e, to reckless & sweeping expressions which I am wont to regret that I have used" (p. 39). Nevertheless, Channing remained a steadfast friend throughout Thoreau's life. In *Journal 8* Thoreau records a memorable cross-country excursion that they took together on August 15 (pp. 269-273).

Thoreau's relationship with Ralph Waldo Emerson, which had become distant and uncomfortable as early as the summer of 1850, continued to be tense. *Journal 8* records but a single conversation between the two men–a one-line statement about Emerson's sighting of a particular bird (p. 41). In March Thoreau circulated a petition asking Emerson to "read to the Lyceum as many of the lectures which he has read abroad the past winter as may be convenient for him" (March 30, 1854; Houghton Library, Harvard University, bMS AM 1280 [676]); still, his veiled references to Emerson in the Journal suggest the depth of his frustration with his former mentor. In the April 8 entry he comments on Emerson's lecture on France, one of the lectures Emerson gave in response to the petition: "At the Lyceum the other night I felt that the lecturer had chosen a theme too foreign to himself & so failed to interest me as much as formerly–" (p. 57). A week later, Thoreau bristled, most likely at Emerson, "When I meet one of my neighbors these days who is ridiculously stately being offended–I say in my mind Farewell–. I will wait till you get your manners off– . . . You are so grand that I cannot get within ten feet of you" (p. 67). For his part, Emerson praised both Thoreau and *Walden* during this period, but his journal rivals Thoreau's for its silence as to the tenor of their relationship. In March 1854, Emerson offered his assistance in securing a British publisher for *Walden*, but this professional favor did not serve to repair the damaged friendship.

In addition to his routine activities in Concord, Thoreau traveled to Boston and Cambridge on three occasions in the spring and summer of 1854, but he took no extended trips. On March 13, he visited his friend Thaddeus William Harris, Harvard's librarian and an esteemed entomologist. Harris introduced him to Alvan Clark, owner of a well-known telescope manufactory; Thoreau had bought a small spyglass earlier that day, and Clark verified its quality for him (see Annotation 41.5-28). Thoreau had previously studied nature primarily with the naked eye, but his interest in telescopes became obvious as early as March 1853: "Would it not be well to carry a spy glass in order to watch these shy birds–such as ducks & hawks–?" (*Journal 6*, p. 48). On February 19, 1854, he made an exasperated comment that anticipates his acceptance of the need for a better lens: "Who placed us with eyes between a microscopic and a telescopic world?" (p. 13). Thoreau's decision to buy the spyglass and his immediate satisfaction with it provide a further example of an evolving "concern for accurate measurement and description" (*Journal 6*, Historical Introduction, pp. 372-373). On April 10, Thoreau elaborated on the philosophy of simplicity that had compelled him to postpone this purchase: "I bought me a spy-glass some weeks since. I buy but few things–and those not till long after I began to want them–so that when I do get them I am prepared to make a perfect use of them and extract their whole sweet" (p. 61). Thoreau delighted in his new lens, especially when it revealed as a bald eagle a bird that he had mistaken for a hawk (p. 59): "I think I have got the worth of my glass now that it has revealed to me the white-headed eagle" (p. 80).

Thoreau returned to Boston on May 9, and in addition to examining the birds at the Society of Natural History, he visited again with Harris. Finally, on August 9, Thoreau picked up copies of *Walden* at the office of Ticknor and Fields in Boston.

Thoreau's reading as reflected in his Journal during this period includes various works of natural history, travel, and history (see Bibliography, pp. 374-376). He engages actively with his sources, comparing his experience with their descriptions and commenting on their limitations. He uses the botanical texts of

Bigelow and Gray as well as *Wilson's American Ornithology* primarily to confirm and supplement his sightings and descriptions rather than to form his opinions. Thoreau's confidence in his own ability to observe and judge natural phenomena is that of a peer, rather than a student: in an entry for May 28, comparing his observations of the checkered adder with Storer's, he comments that Storer must have been describing a preserved specimen because the colors he attributes to it are faded (p. 160), and in a June 21 entry he describes his own experience with "2 old pouts tending their countless young close to the shore" to counter Smellie's assertion that "fishes take no care of their young" (pp. 212-213).

Thoreau also uses the travel literature he is reading comparatively. Each time he relates events from Kane's account of Franklin's expedition, for example, he compares Franklin's experiences with his own in the Concord winter: in an entry dated April 26, after describing the golden bleakness of early spring, he writes, "We are far north with Sir John Franklin" (p. 76).

During these months, Thoreau was also keeping two commonplace books for reading notes. One, which he used from 1851 to 1857, contains excerpted passages describing natural phenomena and scientific observations and ideas. The other, which he kept from late 1853 or early 1854 until the end of 1854, includes passages from sources about Native Americans. For the passages from the period of *Journal 8* in the first of these commonplace books, see Kenneth Walter Cameron, *Thoreau's Fact Book in the Harry Elkins Widener Collection in the Harvard College Library,* vol. 1 (Hartford, Conn.: Transcendental Books, 1966), from "Eagles" on p. 176 through "Loon" on p. 197. For a list of the books Thoreau quoted during this time in the second commonplace book, also known as "Indian Book 8," see Suzanne Dvorak Rose, "Tracking the Moccasin Print: A Descriptive Index to Henry David Thoreau's Indian Notebooks and a Study of the Relationship of the Indian Notebooks to Mythmaking in *Walden*" (Ph.D. diss., University of Oklahoma, 1994), pp. 387-436.

As with the volumes preceding it, *Journal 8* contains a wealth of information on Concord's natural history. In minute detail, Thoreau records his observations of nature, often expanding his descriptions into or combining them with laconic statements about human shortcomings as compared to nature's steadier conduct. He registers a sighting of at least one wildflower blooming, berry ripening, or leaf yellowing in nearly every daily entry, including entries raging against slavery, and he maintains his disciplined reporting of seasonal phenomena during a record drought in late summer.

A typical Journal entry for a summer day in 1854 is several pages long; the spring and summer entries exhibit Thoreau's now routine practice of marking the names of maturing plants with a series of Xs and entering two short slashes (//) in the margin beside lines containing phenological information he wanted to locate later. In late May, Thoreau compiled information about the leafing of trees and shrubs that he had been recording in the Journal since April 20. He filled five manuscript pages with a closely written list that organized the plants he had observed in "the order of their leafing" (see Textual Note 292.5-32 for a description of a draft of a small portion of this list). At the top of the manuscript page, Thoreau wrote in pencil "With Correction in pencil from 55–6–7–& 8–", and nearly every entry on the list is followed by a pencilled comment. In order to appreciate Thoreau's extensive work on this list, readers should compare the text on pp. 149-154 with the Later Revisions for those pages. Thoreau had noted times of leafing in his Journal as early as 1852, and in an entry for May 15, 1853, he included a much less extensive list of trees and shrubs in the order of their leafing (*Journal 6*, pp. 125-126). This attention to leafing culminates in an impressive table Thoreau created, probably in 1860, that he titled "Leafing of trees & shrubs in 52 ... 60" (Pierpont Morgan Library, MA 610); in it he lists almost two hundred species, with information from his observations during the years 1852 to 1860.

In June, Thoreau caught a cicada and sent it to his entomologist friend Thaddeus Harris to examine; Harris's response on June 27 indicates his appreciation of Thoreau's skill as a naturalist. Harris thanked Thoreau for both his letter and the specimen, "for the letter, because it gives me interesting facts concerning Cicadas; and for the specimen because it is *new* to me, as a species or as a variety." In addition, he wrote, "I should be very glad to get more specimens and of both sexes" (*The Correspondence of Henry David Thoreau*, ed. Walter Harding and Carl Bode [New York: New York University Press, 1958], p. 329).

Thoreau's summer ramblings also give rise to an obsession with turtles, particularly snapping turtles, also called mud turtles. As a naturalist, he reveled in their weight and size, their coloration, and their predictably hostile behavior as he thrust his hand into the water, struggling to catch and bring one into his boat. He carefully measured their plates, described the shells' size and markings, and noted each detail of individuality. More than once, he compared his specimens to those in Storer's *Reports on the Fishes, Reptiles and Birds of Massachusetts*. While his comments initially centered on the turtles' physical qualities, ultimately

Thoreau achieved a Transcendental level of illumination in their presence. In late August he brought a turtle shell home and slept with it in his room. The next morning he awoke and peered at it: "That the first object you see on awakening should be an empty mud-turtle's shell!! Will it not make me of the earth earthy? or does it not indicate that I am of the earth earthy?" (p. 300).

A turtle's life in the muddy bottom of Heywood Meadows intrigued Thoreau, and much as he "was determined to know beans" in *Walden* (p. 161), in *Journal 8*, he resolved to decipher the turtle. As a scientist, Thoreau attempted to inspect the turtles that snapped "mechanical like a spring" (p. 131). He anthropomorphized their "rage" (p. 126), "vigilant eyes" (p. 127), "spiteful face" (p. 128), and "insensitivity" (p. 131). Thoreau recounted stories from local farmers who hunted and ate turtles; he seemed prone to agree with those who maintained that this creature's robotic snapping was instinctive and not necessarily provoked by outside stimuli. Late in the summer, as he examined an unhatched turtle in the egg, its symbolic dimension unfolded. His hours of observation and musing about this creature culminated in the realization that the turtle represented a reptilian example of nature's single-mindedness, a principle that he had noted in the formation of the sand foliage on March 2 (pp. 25-26). He remarked in an August 26 entry celebrating Nature's persistence, "When I behold this monster thus steadily advancing toward maturity–all nature abetting–I am convinced that there must be an irresistable necessity for mud turtles. With what tenacity Nature sticks to her idea!" (p. 297).

Thoreau believed that a true understanding of the inhabitants of nature was based on observing live specimens in their environments, although he

realized that studying a dead specimen was more convenient and might be preferable from a scientific point
of view. On May 28, when "tempted to kill a rare
snake," Thoreau reminded himself that "this is not the
means of acquiring true knowledge" (p. 162); likewise,
on August 18 he reproached himself for killing the *Cistuda blandingii* (Blanding's Turtle) "for the sake of science" (p. 278). Although his reputation as a naturalist
had generally worked to his advantage when neighbors shared their findings (occasionally of new species) with him, Thoreau was repulsed in April when a
local man brought him a two-headed calf to examine,
mistakenly thinking he would be interested in the
oddity: "I felt nothing but disgust at the idea–& began
to ask myself what enormity I had committed to have
such an offer made to me" (p. 73).

Unquestionably, the revisions to the final drafts of
Walden and the book's subsequent publication represent Thoreau's most noteworthy literary achieve-
ments in 1854. J. Lyndon Shanley, Ronald Earl Clapper,
and Robert Sattelmeyer, who have all studied the composition history of *Walden*, have determined that in
early 1854 Thoreau added significant material to a
number of the book's chapters, including "Economy,"
"Higher Laws," "Brute Neighbors," "The Pond in Winter," and "Spring." To give just one example, Thoreau
mined his Journal entries of March 2 and 5 in rework-
ing the sand foliage description in "Spring" (see Cross-
References to Published Versions 25.18-19 through
26.9-12 and 30.20-21 through 30.22-23, and *Walden*,
pp. 304-309).

Two Journal entries written in March reveal Thoreau's preoccupation with his ongoing revisions to the
Walden manuscript. On March 1, he noted that "In
correcting my mss–which I do with sufficient phlegm.
I find that I invariably turn out much that is good along

with the bad, which it is then impossible for me to distinguish" (p. 24). On March 31, he grumbled about the imperfections of his revision process: "When I have sent off my MSS to the printer certain objectionable sentences or expressions are sure to obtrude themselves on my attention with force–though I had not consciously suspected them before. My critical instinct then at once breaks the ice & comes to the surface" (p. 51).

On the back paste-down endpaper of the manuscript volume from which *Journal 8* is edited, Thoreau continued this editorial self-appraisal:

My faults are

Paradoxes–saying just the opposite–a style which may be imitated–

Ingenious–

Playing with words–getting the laugh–not always simple strong & broad–

Using current phrases–& maxims when I should speak for myself–

Not always earnest–

In short–in fact–alas! &c

Want of conciseness–

On March 16, Thoreau signed an indenture for the publication of *Walden* with Ticknor & Fields. He noted in the Journal on March 28 that he had received the first proofs from the publisher, but he did not finish sending copy to Ticknor & Fields until some time in late April or May. Horace Greeley, editor of the *New-York Tribune* and Thoreau's unofficial literary agent, wrote to Thoreau on March 23 and promised his support for the new book. Since first meeting Thoreau in 1843, Greeley had become an ardent supporter of Thoreau's literary endeavors, and he kept his pledge to promote *Walden* by publishing chapters from the book in the *Tribune* on July 29. A number of other papers, including the *Boston Evening Transcript*, the *Boston Commonwealth*, the *Boston Traveller*, the *New York Evening Post*, and the *Oneida Circular*, carried pre-publication notices of and excerpts from *Walden*.

In May, Thoreau was contacted by Charles Scribner, who wanted to include Thoreau in his forthcoming *Encyclopedia of Literature*, a request that no doubt increased Thoreau's confidence in himself as an author. When the volume appeared in 1855, it reprinted portions of *Walden* chapters including "Economy," "Visitors," and "Brute Neighbors." The book's editors, George and Evert Duyckinck, described Thoreau as "a humorist in the olden English sense of the word" (see Gary Scharnhorst, *Henry David Thoreau: An Annotated Bibliography of Comment and Criticism before 1900* [New York: Garland, 1992], p. 42).

One week prior to *Walden*'s debut, Thoreau received a sample copy of the book, an occurrence he entered matter-of-factly in the Journal (p. 250). The book's publication also elicited a typically understated entry: "Wednesday Aug 9th To Boston *Walden* Published. Elder berries XXX. Waxwork yellowing X" (p. 259; see the first illustration, following p. 414). Emerson, however, described his friend's anticipatory mood with regard to the book's reception. On August 28, Emerson wrote to George Bradford that Thoreau was "walking up & down Concord, firm-looking, but in a tremble of great expectation" (*The Letters of Ralph Waldo Emerson*, vol. 4, ed. Ralph L. Rusk [New York: Columbia University Press, 1939], p. 460).

After Thoreau picked up his copies of *Walden* from Ticknor and Fields on August 9, he distributed them to friends and family, including Bronson Alcott, H.G.O. Blake, Thomas Wentworth Higginson, Spencer Fullerton Baird, William Ellery Channing, and Lidian Emerson. *Walden* received a good deal of attention–Ticknor and Fields promoted it heavily–and enjoyed a largely favorable critical reception. Although some reviewers were quick to label the book an impractical production from an odd recluse and the conservative clergy protested what they regarded as its pantheism, most reviewers responded warmly to Thoreau's call for simplicity and economic reform. On the day *Walden* was published, a reviewer in the *Boston Daily Bee* exhorted readers to "Get the book," assuring them, "You will like it. It is original and refreshing; and from the brain of a *live* man" (see Scharnhorst, *Henry David Thoreau*, p. 26).

In addition to the attention brought on by *Walden*'s publication, Thoreau's alliance with the organized abolitionist movement made headlines in July. At a highly publicized Independence Day rally sponsored by the Massachusetts Anti-Slavery Society, Thoreau joined activists William Lloyd Garrison, Wendell Phillips, Sojourner Truth, and others before a gathering estimated to be in the thousands to attack the institution of slavery in general and the 1850 Fugitive Slave Law in particular. The timing of this year's antislavery meeting worked to the abolitionists' advantage. New Englanders were in a rage over the recent passage of the Kansas-Nebraska Act (see Annotation 10.4-11); and on May 24 the fugitive slave Anthony Burns had been arrested in Boston and incarcerated in the courthouse, an act which precipitated an impassioned outburst from Thoreau in his Journal and which may have influenced his decision to speak at the antislavery meeting. During the week of Burns's trial, Thoreau's abolitionist friends Bronson Alcott and Thomas Wentworth Higginson took part in a failed rescue attempt, which Thoreau characterized in his Journal on June 4 as a "heroic attack" (p. 175). Ultimately, efforts to free or purchase Burns failed, and on June 2 he was returned to his owner, Charles F. Suttle, and taken back to Virginia (see Annotation 163.31-166.4).

At the rally, Thoreau most likely read only a portion of the address he had composed for the occasion; in the *Liberator* on July 7, William Lloyd Garrison characterized the speech as "racy and ably written." In the full version published in the *Liberator* on July 21, Thoreau denounced state and federal officials, called for disunion, and came closer than he ever had to advocating violence: "my thoughts are murder to the state," he proclaimed, in a line taken from the Journal entry of June 16 (p. 200; see also "Slavery in Massachusetts," *Reform Papers*, ed. Wendell Glick [Princeton: Princeton University Press, 1973], p. 108). In composing the text of his speech, Thoreau combined portions of several Journal entries written from May 29 through June 19 with material about the fugitive slave Thomas Sims from his 1851 Journal. Thoreau extensively reworked his Journal passages, which were filled with fury about Burns and the Federal Slave Commissioner Edward G. Loring, who had presided over Burns's trial, to craft them into his speech; in order to appreciate fully the scope of Thoreau's editorial revisions, readers should consult the Later Revisions (164.5 through 166.4, 182.7 through 185.28, 196.9 through 199.35, 200.30, and 204.7 through 207.36). Notwithstanding the strong rhetoric of his July Fourth speech, Thoreau maintained a habitual reticence about recording in the Journal his emotional reactions to events. The entry for the July 4 event–"8 Am to Framingham" (p. 221)–is as understated as that for the publication of *Walden*. And in the weeks following, when the speech, entitled "Slavery in Massachusetts," was published in the *Liberator* and other papers, Thoreau remained silent on the subject in his Journal.

Although he was gratified by the recognition he received this summer, Thoreau expressed near-desperation over his lack of time alone; his Journal entries from later in the summer convey a growing diffidence regarding his public persona. He seems to resent the need to commune with others at all, even his family: "My attic chamber has compelled me to sit below with the family at evening for a month. I feel the necessity of deepening the stream of my life– I must cultivate privacy. It is very dissipating to be with people too much. . . . I can not spare my moonlight & my *mts* for the best of man I am likely to get in exchange–" (pp. 247-248). The month-long drought, which forced him out of his hot quarters, may have affected his mood, however; when the weather cooled a few days later, so did his rancor: "It is inspiriting at last to hear the wind whistle & moan about my attic–after so much trivial summer weather–" (p. 256). In a letter to his friend H.G.O. Blake written the day before *Walden*'s publication, Thoreau voices an ironic, Wordsworthian regret about the public nature of his summer: "Methinks I have spent a rather unprofitable summer thus far. I have been too much with the world, as the poet might say." Thoreau vowed to "get away from men"; he wrote: "They very rarely affect me as grand or beautiful; but I know that there is a sunrise and a sunset every day" (*The Correspondence of Henry David Thoreau*, p. 330).

Journal 8 chronicles a pivotal period in Thoreau's life. At the volume's conclusion on September 3, he was thirty-seven years old and had received acclaim as an author, notoriety as an abolitionist, and increasing respect as a natural scientist. His participation in public life during these months, however, reinforced his understanding of the personal and creative tolls exacted by such interaction, and he realized yet again that for him fulfillment came at the sacrifice of conventional obligations and rewards. Despite the satisfaction he derived from his public accomplishments, Thoreau begrudged the hours and days spent away from the woods: "Ah! I need solitude," he lamented on August 14 (p. 267). For the remainder of his life, while he continued to involve himself in the world as a writer, lecturer, and surveyor, Thoreau protected and savored his identity as a solitary observer and recorder of nature.

SOURCES

The standard biographical source for details of Thoreau's life and literary activities during 1854 is Walter Harding, *The Days of Henry Thoreau* (New York: Alfred A. Knopf, 1965; Princeton: Princeton University Press, 1982); the standard edition of Thoreau's correspondence is *The Correspondence of Henry David Thoreau*, ed. Walter Harding and Carl Bode (New York: New York University Press, 1958). The best intellectual biography is Robert D. Richardson Jr., *Henry Thoreau: A Life of the Mind* (Berkeley: University of California Press, 1986); intellectual biography is also the focus of a lengthy essay in Robert Sattelmeyer's *Thoreau's Reading: A Study in Intellectual History with Bibliographical Catalogue* (Princeton: Princeton University Press, 1988), which in addition lists all books and articles Thoreau is known to have read or borrowed. Information relevant to Thoreau's surveying activities can be found in the facsimile of his "Field Notes of Surveys Made by Henry D. Thoreau Since November 1849" published in Kenneth Walter Cameron, *Transcendental Climate* (Hartford: Transcendental Books, 1963), 2:413-549, and in *A Catalog of Thoreau's*

Surveys in the Concord Free Public Library, ed. Marcia Moss (Geneseo, N.Y.: The Thoreau Society, 1976).

Writings about Thoreau and Emerson's relationship, and by and about Thoreau's companions and visitors, include Harmon Smith, *My Friend, My Friend: The Story of Thoreau's Relationship with Emerson* (Amherst: University of Massachusetts Press, 1999); William Ellery Channing, *Thoreau: The Poet-Naturalist* (Boston: Roberts Brothers, 1873); and "The Selected Letters of William Ellery Channing the Younger (Part Two)," ed. Francis B. Dedmond, in *Studies in the American Renaissance*, ed. Joel Myerson (Charlottesville: The University Press of Virginia, 1990), 159-241.

Kenneth Walter Cameron, in *Thoreau's Fact Book in the Harry Elkins Widener Collection in the Harvard College Library*, 3 vols. (Hartford, Conn.: Transcendental Books, 1966-1987), and Suzanne Dvorak Rose, in "Tracking the Moccasin Print: A Descriptive Index to Henry David Thoreau's Indian Notebooks and a Study of the Relationship of the Indian Notebooks to Mythmaking in *Walden*" (Ph.D. diss., University of Oklahoma, 1994), provide access to the manuscript volumes in which Thoreau kept extracts of his reading.

In addition to William Howarth's *The Book of Concord: Thoreau's Life as a Writer* (New York: Viking Press, 1982) and the works by Richardson and Sattelmeyer, relevant studies of Thoreau's scientific knowledge include Laura Dassow Walls, *Seeing New Worlds: Henry David Thoreau and Nineteenth-Century Natural Science* (Madison: University of Wisconsin Press, 1995); Michael Berger, *Thoreau's Late Career and "The Dispersion of Seeds": The Saunterer's Synoptic Vision* (Rochester, N.Y.: Camden House, 2000); Leo Stoller, "A Note on Thoreau's Place in the History of Phenology," *Isis* 47 (1956): 172-181; John Hildebidle, *Thoreau: A Naturalist's Liberty* (Cambridge, Mass.: Harvard Uni-

versity Press, 1983); William Rossi, "Poetry and Progress: Thoreau, Lyell, and the Geological Principles of *A
Week*," *American Literature* 66 (June 1994): 276-300;
and Ray Angelo, "Botanical Index to the Journal of
Henry David Thoreau," *Thoreau Quarterly* 15 (1983; reprint, Layton, Utah: Peregrine Smith, 1984). A more
recent version of Angelo's text is available on the
Internet at ⟨http://www.herbaria.harvard.edu/~rangelo/
BotIndex/WebIntro.html⟩.

Important studies of the Journal as a work in its own
right as well as in relation to Thoreau's life and other
writings include Howarth, *The Book of Concord*;
H. Daniel Peck, *Thoreau's Morning Work: Memory and
Perception in* A Week on the Concord and Merrimack
Rivers, *the Journal, and* Walden (New Haven: Yale
University Press, 1990); and Sharon Cameron, *Writing
Nature: Henry Thoreau's Journal* (New York: Oxford
University Press, 1985).

Studies of the composition and public reception of
Walden include J. Lyndon Shanley, *The Making of
Walden: With the Text of the First Version* (Chicago:
University of Chicago Press, 1957); Stephen Adams and
Donald Ross Jr., *Revising Mythologies: The Composition of Thoreau's Major Works* (Charlottesville: University Press of Virginia, 1988); and Robert Sattelmeyer, "The Remaking of *Walden*," in James Barbour
and Tom Quirk, eds., *Writing the American Classics*
(Chapel Hill: University of North Carolina Press, 1990),
53-78. Also useful are William Rossi, "The Journal and
Walden," in Walden *and "Resistance to Civil Government,"* ed. William Rossi, 2d ed. (New York: W. W. Norton, 1992), 249-254; Steven Fink, *Prophet in the Market-
place: Thoreau's Development as a Professional Writer*
(Princeton: Princeton University Press, 1992); Gary
Scharnhorst, *Henry David Thoreau: An Annotated Bibliography of Comment and Criticism before 1900* (New

York: Garland, 1992); and Ronald Earl Clapper, "The Development of *Walden*: A Genetic Text" (Ph.D. diss., University of California, Los Angeles, 1967). Also relevant are the historical introductions to *Walden*, ed. J. Lyndon Shanley (Princeton: Princeton University Press, 1971), 359-377, and *Journal 6: 1853*, ed. William Rossi and Heather Kirk Thomas (Princeton: Princeton University Press, 2000), 366-380.

Thoreau's abolitionism and his participation in the July Fourth rally at Framingham are discussed in Wendell Glick, Textual Introduction to "Slavery in Massachusetts" in *Reform Papers* (Princeton: Princeton University Press, 1973), 331-335; Sandra Harbert Petrulionis, "Editorial Savoir Faire: Thoreau Transforms His Journal into 'Slavery in Massachusetts,'" *Resources for American Literary Study* 25 (1999): 206-231; Barry Kritzberg, "Thoreau, Slavery, and Resistance to Civil Government," *Massachusetts Review* 30 (winter 1989): 535-565; Robert C. Albrecht, "Conflict and Resolution: 'Slavery in Massachusetts,'" *ESQ* 72 (1973): 179-188; and Alfred A. Funk, "Henry David Thoreau's 'Slavery in Massachusetts,'" *Western Speech* 36 (summer 1972): 159-168.

Historical scholarship regarding the Anthony Burns case and the New England abolitionist climate at the time is voluminous; especially helpful are Albert Von Frank, *The Trials of Anthony Burns: Freedom and Slavery in Emerson's Boston* (Cambridge: Harvard University Press, 1998); Charles Emery Stevens, *Anthony Burns: A History* (1856; reprint, New York: Negro Universities Press, 1969); Jane H. Pease and William H. Pease, *The Fugitive Slave Law and Anthony Burns: A Problem in Law Enforcement* (Philadelphia: J. B. Lippincott, 1975); Samuel Shapiro, "The Rendition of Anthony Burns," *Journal of Negro History* 44 (January 1959): 34-51; David R. Maginnes, "The Case of the Court

House Rioters in the Rendition of the Fugitive Slave Anthony Burns, 1854," *Journal of Negro History* 56 (January 1971): 31-42; "Trial of Anthony Burns," *Proceedings of the Massachusetts Historical Society* (January 1911): 322-334; and Thomas Wentworth Higginson, *Cheerful Yesterdays* (1898; reprint, New York: Arno Press, 1968).

Textual Introduction

Journal 8: 1854, like other volumes in this edition of Thoreau's Journal, is edited from a holograph manuscript, conservatively emended, and printed in clear text. The text is accompanied by an Editorial Appendix that includes Annotations and an Index and that provides relevant historical and textual information as well as a table of Cross-References to Published Versions. This Textual Introduction describes the pertinent characteristics of the manuscript and the principles and procedures followed in the editing of this volume of Thoreau's Journal.[1]

THE JOURNAL TEXT, 1854

The present volume prints the text of one Journal volume, numbered XVII, which Thoreau kept from February 13 through September 3, 1854. During this period Thoreau continued the practice established by 1851 of treating the Journal as an integral work in itself, and the volume is intact, with no excisions of material that was used for other purposes.[2] Thoreau usually marked Journal passages he used in another work by drawing a vertical line in pencil through each. (These lines are easily distinguished from the broader blue vertical lines that H.G.O. Blake drew through passages he excerpted for use in his four volumes of selections from the Journal published between 1881 and 1892.) In

[1] A more comprehensive description of the editorial practices and policies of this edition of the Journal may be found in the Textual Introduction to *Journal 1: 1837-1844* (Princeton: Princeton University Press, 1981), pp. 614-643; see also the General Introduction to the same volume, pp. 578-591.

[2] See the Textual Introduction to *Journal 3: 1848-1851* (Princeton: Princeton University Press, 1990), pp. 499-500, for a discussion of the transition from Thoreau's earlier use of the Journal in drafting literary works in progress.

Journal 8, Thoreau drew use marks through passages he used in *Walden*, "Slavery in Massachusetts," and "Huckleberries" as well as through many passages containing information about the state of plants he was observing. The other significant later use that Thoreau made of the material in *Journal 8* is indicated by marginal list marks (generally two short parallel vertical marks, occasionally a question mark) indexing observations of natural phenomena, some of which he later transcribed into lists and charts of natural history data.

PHYSICAL DESCRIPTION OF MANUSCRIPT

MS Volume XVII

Pierpont Morgan Library (MA 1302:23); first entry dated February 13, 1854, and last entry dated September 3, 1854. No leaves have been removed; volume has been rebound by Morgan Library.

Mottled yellow-brown/dark brown boards; restored tan leather spine with three sets of double gold rules. 235 leaves, with paste-down and free front endpapers and paste-down back endpaper, paged "1-453" and "461", "463", "465", "467", "457", "459", "455" in pencil by Thoreau on rectos; 14 index pages at end of volume. Front paste-down endpaper contains Thoreau's pencilled number "17" in upper left corner; front free endpaper contains pencilled number "23" in upper right corner, not by Thoreau. Index, in ink with pencilled additions, appears on pp. "461"-[462], "463"-[464], "465"-[466], "467"-[468], "457"-[458], "459"-[460], and "455"-[456] (pages are numbered in this sequence; index text is continuous). Top of draft letter to "Mr. Hosmer" containing list of early May plants on recto hinged on MS p. "423" (see Textual Note 292.5-32); two clippings from *Boston Evening Transcript* waxed onto MS p. "449" (see Annotation 310.19-20 and Textual

sounds like a train of an election bell.
The distance has thus refined it. I see some
slight dun clouds in the east horizon perhaps
the smoke from burning meadows

Wednesday Aug 9th To Boston
Walden Published.   Elder berries & xx Waxwork yellowing x

Aug 10th
4½ am to Cliffs - A high fog. As I go
along the R.R. I observe the darker green of early
mown fields - a cool wind at this hour
over the wet foliage - as from an uninhabited
uninhabited earth. The large primrose conspicuously in bloom. Does it shut by day? The woods
are comparatively still at this season. I hear only
the faint peeping of some robins - (a few song sparrows
on my way) - a wood pewee - kingbird - crows - before
5 - or before reaching the Springs. Then a
thrush or 2 - a cuckoo - jay - & later returning - the link of bobolink & the goldfinch -
That is a peculiar and distinct hollow sound
made by the pigeon woodpeckers' wings as it
flies past near you. The aralia nudicaulis
is another plant - which for some time - &
perhaps more generally than any - yellows the
forest floor with its early fall - or turning -
as soon as its berries have opened - along with the
Hellebore - Skunk cabbage - Convallaria &c.

Page of MS volume XVII

Rowse portrait of Thoreau

Broadside depicting Anthony Burns

in standing on the quaking ground. Then
a dense border of ...
so peculiar ...
of red and ...
going west ...
an abrupt ...
this one ...
quaking ...
which ...
...

This is marked by the path muskrats which also
extent through the green parts of the pool.
Next comes, a dense bed of Andromeda Calyculata
... The A. polifolia mingled with it — the
rust cotton grass — & cranberries — The
common & also V. Oxycoccus — pitcher plants — sedge
& a few young spruce & larch here & there —
All on sphagnum — which forms little hillocks
about the stems of the andromeda
... ferns, now yellowing, high blueberry bushes —
&c &c &c. — on the ... main body of the
swamp — under which the sphagnum is
now dry & white.

NB I find a new cranberry on the sphagnum and
the A. Calyculata — V. Oxycoccus — of which
Emerson says it is ... The common

Page of MS volume XVII

Note 310.19-20). Back paste-down endpaper contains Thoreau's pencilled list of "My faults" (see Historical Introduction, p. 403), his notes about publication of *Walden* ("Walden Published Wednesday Aug. 9th '54") and distribution of *A Week on the Concord and Merrimack Rivers* ("Sent Fields 12 copies of the 'Week' Oct 18th 54"), and H.G.O. Blake's pencilled memo, "Left off at Feb. 22d Page 22d / 13 17 27 29 33", referring to his selection of excerpts. Leaves are greenish laid paper, 23.8 x 19.2 cm, lined, with stationer's mark "Goodwins" inside circle with wheat sheaf. Nonauthorial contents are H.G.O. Blake's label in black ink on front board, "Feb. 13th–Sept. 2d 1854. /17.", pencilled number "23" in upper right corner of front free endpaper, pencilled "MA 1302-23" on p. [2], Blake's use marks throughout the volume and his memo noted above on back paste-down endpaper.

A list of winter phenomena with dates from December 1849 to January 1855 that was originally laid in MA 1302:23 has been removed to a separate cloth folder that is also accessioned as MA 1302:23.

LEVEL OF TEXT REPRESENTED

In keeping with the editorial policy of this edition, copy-text for *Journal 8* is the final form of Thoreau's original state of composition, incorporating all current changes of text (reported in the table of Alterations), with as little editorial interpolation and emendation as is necessary to make ambiguous or erroneous material intelligible. The original level of text is to be distinguished from preliminary versions, from later revisions made to the Journal text, and from later transcriptions and adaptations of Journal text for other purposes.

In cases where alterations, even though extensive, were clearly or presumably made at the time of original composition, such changes are treated as current and incorporated into the text. Because Thoreau often wrote several days' worth of dated entries in one sitting, the editor has treated any botanical or phenological cross-reference as current Journal when it is written in ink and references an entry up to five days forward. Occasionally Thoreau returned to earlier entries to make additions, corrections, and revisions; these changes were sometimes made in connection with his use of Journal passages in other writing projects. In accordance with the editorial policy first applied in *Journal 4*, all substantive revisions not accepted as current are included in the list of Later Revisions found in the Editorial Appendix.[3]

Later versions of Journal material Thoreau used in other works are not considered as Journal text, although they may be of use in resolving unclear readings in the Journal. All passages of Journal text later incorporated into published writings are listed in the table of Cross-References to Published Versions found in the Editorial Appendix. In addition to these passages there are extant extensive transcriptions, some considerably revised, of passages on Thoreau's moonlight walks from 1850 to 1854. These transcriptions were made in August and September 1854 in preparation for a lecture and a never-completed literary project.[4]

EDITORIAL POLICIES AND PROCEDURES

The text of this edition of Thoreau's Journal is based on a diplomatic transcription, prepared by editorial staff, of a photocopy of the holograph manuscript. The

[3] See the Textual Introduction to *Journal 4: 1851-1852* (Princeton: Princeton University Press, 1992), p. 651, for a discussion of the rationale for the change of policy from recording selected later revisions, which was followed in *Journals 1-3*.

[4] See William L. Howarth's "Successor to *Walden*? Thoreau's

editor and the staff of the Thoreau Edition read the transcripts and preliminary textual tables at least four times against photocopy and at least once against the holograph manuscript in the Pierpont Morgan Library. In addition, both the volume editor and the Editor-in-Chief consulted the holograph manuscript to resolve problems that arose in the course of editing. The editor and the Thoreau Edition staff have also thoroughly proofread the computer printout of the transcripts and tables. At each stage in the composition of the book, proof has received multiple readings against the edited transcripts and tables. In accordance with guidelines established by the Modern Language Association's Committee on Scholarly Editions, this volume has been inspected by an independent textual expert, Professor Richard D. Rust.

Like all other volumes in *The Writings of Henry D. Thoreau, Journal 8* is printed in clear text, with no editorial interpolations in the text. Above the clear text of each page, a running head corresponding to the date of the entry in the text below has been provided. To avoid the ambiguities created by hyphenating compound words at the ends of lines, the text is printed with a ragged right-hand margin.

EDITORIAL APPENDIX

Each of the sections of apparatus in the Editorial Appendix is explained in a headnote. The sections that report editorial decisions–Textual Notes, Emendations, Alterations, and End-of-Line Hyphenation–are described in more detail below.

'Moonlight–An Intended Course of Lectures,'" *Proof* 2 (1972): 89-115, for an extended discussion of this material, and Howarth's *The Literary Manuscripts of Henry David Thoreau* (Columbus: Ohio State University Press, 1974), pp. 333-354, for a description of the extant transcriptions and portions of lecture draft.

Textual Notes

The Textual Notes describe and explain significant features of the manuscript and editorial decisions that require more explanation than is provided by the Textual Introduction and the tables. An asterisk marking an entry in the tables indicates a textual note.

Emendations

This table provides a sequential list of all substantive editorial changes to the text. It also lists alternative readings of words especially difficult to decipher in the manuscript.

The general emendation policy is conservative, and the text has been altered only when the original form was judged to be misleading or distracting to the reader. Emended readings derive from one or more of the following authorities: identical or analogous forms in the text; later versions of the text in manuscript or in print; Thoreau's sources or reference works; the editor's judgment.

Since the text is sparingly emended, it preserves many of the anomalies associated with a handwritten document which the author never prepared for publication. Errors of fact, spelling, and grammar; inconsistencies in spelling, capitalization, punctuation, and word division; and occasional lacunae in entries are all permitted to stand if they do not seriously affect the sense of a passage. Certain recurring idiosyncrasies of Thoreau's handwriting and spacing in the manuscript that are not meaningful or are not susceptible to typographic reproduction are normalized and not reported in the table of Emendations.[5] All of Thor-

---

[5] For a detailed description of categories of emendation and normalization, see the Textual Introduction to *Journal 2: 1842-1848* (Princeton: Princeton University Press, 1984), pp. 480-482.

eau's drawings are reproduced: most of them are actual size, although a few have been reduced to fit the printed page. They are positioned to correspond as closely as possible to their location on the manuscript page.

Alterations

This table provides a sequential list of all revisions to the Journal which editorial judgment has determined to be current. Only alterations affecting meaning are reported. For relatively simple changes, the table merely lists the altered and original forms, without specifying the means of alteration (e.g., 107.30 on] in; 141.3 islands] an island). More complex changes are more extensively described, with editorial notation italicized (e.g., 233.22-23 & ... off] *interlined with a caret and* petal *preceded by cancelled* white; 311.7-9 But ... heard.] *written vertically in margin with an arrow for position*). Insignificant alterations, such as cancelled false starts, corrections of meaningless misspellings, or re-formed letters or words, are not reported.

End-of-Line Hyphenation

When Thoreau's end-of-line hyphens in the manuscript divide compound words (e.g., sea- / shore), the words must be resolved to one of two forms: closed (seashore) or hyphenated (sea-shore). If the evidence from Thoreau's practice in the same manuscript volume, in later versions of the passage, or in manuscript volumes that immediately precede or follow the one included in *Journal 8* is not conclusive, analogous forms and spellings in contemporaneous dictionaries have been considered. If the evidence remains inconclusive in a particular instance, the hyphen is retained. All compounds hyphenated at the ends of lines in the manuscript have been resolved to the forms that appear in the table; no new end-of-line hyphens have been introduced.

Textual Notes

THE TEXTUAL NOTES report significant features of the manuscript and sources for editorial emendations. Contextual punctuation appears outside of quotation marks when ambiguity would result from using the standard form.

MS Volume XVII

11.26 completely: "& completely" in MS. T first wrote "faded & completely withered"; he cancelled "faded" but neglected to cancel the "&".

27.26 fungus?: T originally wrote "fungus? puff ball?"; he cancelled "puff ball" without cancelling the question mark that followed the phrase.

32.15 Septemmber: T originally wrote "November"; he then cancelled "Nove" and interlined "Septem" above.

37.25 ozit ozit ozit: Below the first "ozit", T made four marks. Their function is not clear.

48.31-32 either . . . woodcock: T originally wrote "either a snipe or a woodcock"; he later cancelled "either a snipe or" in pencil; still later, in ink, he cancelled "a woodcock" and interlined "prob. a snipe".

52.9 wink: As in MS. The 1906 Journal (6:181) emends to "ring with".

58.35 note.: T originally wrote "A turtle dove. The willow near Miles tomorrow or next day *if fair*– That at the bridge equally early." He then wrote "went off with a slight whistling note." and marked the phrase with a line indicating that it should follow "dove". He neglected to cancel the superfluous period following "note".

76.25 martin.: T interlined "& a little of the warble of the martin." with a caret which he placed between the preceding word "it" and the period that follows "it". He neglected to cancel this superfluous period.

82.33 this: T originally wrote "this & the gooseberry"; he cancelled "the gooseberry" but neglected to cancel the "&". He also interlined *"very much more"* with a caret and then cancelled the phrase.

92.23-93.10 Wht maple . . . Mouse-ear 29th: T wrote this plant list on two MS pages, "137" and [138]. It appears in four columns on p. 137 and in two columns on p. 138. The first and second columns on p. 137 are printed as 92.23-31, the third and fourth columns as 92.32-93.6. The two-column list on p. 138 is printed as 93.7-10.

92.26-28   Sedge ... 20.:   T revised the original order of these entries by numbering them in ink in the left margin. Initially, "Earliest willows   12 fairly begun not common till ap. 20." preceded "Sedge   11".

104.3   it ... meadow.–:   "it.–& the meadow" in MS. T interlined "& the meadow" with a caret which he positioned to the right of the dash.

105.20   hawk: Under this word, T drew three diagonal lines to connect "hawk" to "(Saw one at Boston next day–" on the following line.

115.6-7   The ... others: T interlined this material and wrote seven dashes following "others", probably to connect this information to the index marks he placed in the right margin.

116.6   On ... &c: T placed a series of dashes under this line, probably to separate it from the paragraph that follows.

150.16-17   Viburnum ... Nudum: In MS, the mark that connects "lentago" and "Nudum" is a dotted line in the shape of a close parenthesis.

151.35   ? Norway pine: "? Norway   ″ ″ in MS. T origi-nally wrote "? Norway   ″ ″ below "Pitch pine", with the ditto marks aligned under "pine". Between these two entries, he interlined "?? Bear berry not seen" and added two addi-tional sets of ditto marks following "? Norway   ″ ″, under "not" and "seen".

152.11   ?? Clethra seen late: In MS, T cancelled this entry in pencil. Following it, on the same line, he wrote "v forward" in pencil. Later in the list of plants, T interlined "Clethra May 14–55" in pencil.

153.7   ? Large ... observed.:   In MS, T cancelled this entry in pencil. Following it he wrote "Greater part on common May 15–55".

159.7   low: As in MS. The 1906 Journal (6:307) emends to "high".

159.11   is   feet: T left a blank space between "is" and "feet" for a number he neglected to supply.

177.11   Pm. .... Place: In MS, these words appear on the same line with "street–", following a large blank space.

179.34   Joe: "J.oe" in MS. T added "oe" to "J." without cancelling the period.

212.34   ap.:   T interlined "One has some wounds ap." with a caret placed between "parents" and the period that follows "parents". He neglected to cancel this superfluous period.

215.32-33   XXX . . . unless: In MS, T drew a line that extends from "XXX" to the space between "house" and "unless", perhaps to indicate the transposition of "XXX" with "RR above red house".

228.30   Pyrus: "P.yrus" in MS. T added "yrus" to "P." without cancelling the period.

231.26   dry.:   In MS, "dry." is followed by "The" on the same line at the end of the page. An ink smudge covers part of the word. On the next page, T begins a new paragraph with "The".

235.11-12   some . . . wind: In MS, T interlined this phrase below "about a foot above" and above "yellow butterflies–" with no mark for position. It could fit equally well following "water–" or "butterflies–".

265.5   Cuckoo heard: "Cuckoo   ″   " in MS. Originally this entry in the list of birds followed "Cherry bird heard", with the ditto marks aligned under "heard". Between these two entries, T interlined "The night-hawk squeaks at sunset & the whippoorwill sings Aug 14th" and "The screech owl screams at evening".

281.13-15   A . . . swamp: Following this addition, T wrote four dashes, probably to connect this line to the index marks he placed in the right margin.

288.28-29   Was . . . it: Preceding this interlined sentence, T wrote three dashes, probably to connect it to the index marks he placed in the left margin.

291.1   {drawing}:   To the right of the drawing, T wrote "Main body of swamp–bushes". In a spiral within the drawing, he wrote the following: "Andromeda, Calyculata & polifolia–rusty cot. grass–cranberries 2 kinds–pitcher plants–sedges–young spruce–larch &c &c on sphagnum". Within this spiral, he wrote "Kalmia glauca" and "Gaylussacia dumosa". At the center, T made another drawing of a "pool" surrounded by the words "rush & sundew on sphagnum". Under this smaller drawing, he wrote in pencil "V aug. 30 '56" (1906, 9:34-46). See the fourth illustration, following p. 414.

292.5-32   cranberry . . . are: A pencilled plant list, written on a narrow strip torn from a draft of a letter from T to "Mr. Hosmer" dated May 3, 1854, is hinged on MS page "423", which begins with "cranberry" and ends with "are". This list is part of a draft for the long plant list at MS 220.3-224.26 (149.33-154.12). Two dates are legible on the pencilled list, May 7 and May 10. All of the plants listed for May 7 are included in the May 7, 1854, Journal entry, although that entry also includes a few other plants (101.6-105.12). All of the plants listed for May 10 are included in the May 10, 1854, Journal entry (109.25-113.7).

293.35   Cliffs–:   "Cliffs–& at Lee's" in MS. T cancelled "at Lee's" without cancelling the "&".

294.2-3   The . . . there: Following this interlineation, T wrote five dashes, probably to connect this line to the index marks he placed in the right margin.

299.28   remarkably: In MS, part of this word is blotted by a brown stain caused by the "crimson juice" of the "cast steel soap gall" (299.10) that, as T notes at 299.15, "has stained this page".

310.19-20   "at . . . be: Waxed on in the left margin of MS page "449" next to this line are two clippings from the *Boston Evening Transcript* of September 1, 1854. See Annotation 310.19-20.

312.28   old.:   T interlined "which is very prominent as There is only the traces of a dorsal ridge in the old." with a caret placed between "dorsal" and the period that follows "dorsal". He neglected to cancel this superfluous period.

Index of MS Volume

318.28   (v. no *16*–p 384): T refers to an entry in his MS volume 16; see 1906, 6:66.

323.35   Mr Hoar: T originally wrote "Mr Hoar"; "Hoar" has been erased, but the word can still be discerned.

Emendations

THIS table lists all editorial changes made from the text other than normalized features described in the Textual Introduction (pp. 418-419), and it reports resolutions of ambiguous manuscript features. Numbers at the left margin key the entry to page and line; if the number is marked with an asterisk, the emendation is discussed in a Textual Note. The emended reading appears to the left of the bracket, and the original reading appears to the right; editorial descriptions are italicized. A wavy dash (~) to the right of the bracket replaces the word to the left of the bracket in cases where only punctuation is emended. A virgule (/) indicates the end of a line.

MS Volume XVII

3.14	telegraph] telegrap *in MS*
3.29	red–spot] *possibly* red-spot
4.13	quite] quit *in MS*
4.15	telegraph] telegrap *in MS*
5.13	It must be] It must *in MS*
5.33	in itself] intself *in MS*
8.2	high] *possibly* High
8.22	thaw & freeze] & thaw freeze *in MS (see Alteration 8.22)*
9.23	when] went *in MS*
9.33	squirrel] squir / rel *in MS*
11.26	the] the & *in MS (see Textual Note 11.26)*
11.26	completely] complete / ly *in MS*
14.6	dark] *possibly* dusk
14.7	pleasant] *added*
14.13	those] *possibly* these
14.31	&] *possibly* or
16.21	architectural] achitectural *in MS*
16.25	accordingly] according / ly *in MS*
17.19-20	on an average] *possibly* as an average
18.31	climate!"] *quotation mark added in pencil*
22.6	rose-briar] ~. *in MS*

25.6	thought] though *in MS*
25.20	even] *possibly* ever
26.26	& large pyrola–] –& large pyrola *in MS*
27.25	jelly] jilly *or* gilly *in MS*
* 27.26	fungus?] ~?? *in MS*
30.9	andromeda are] andromedare *in MS*
30.20	even] *possibly* ever
31.35	consists] consits *in MS*
33.30	wreathe] weathe *in MS*
34.18	somewhat] *possibly somewhat*
37.35	sprayey] sprayy *in MS*
39.27	more] mere *in MS*
40.12	they] (~ *in MS*
41.16	object] *possibly* ~?
41.20	enlarge] enlage *in MS*
46.32	far] *possibly* for
47.14	hang] hand *in MS*
47.33	there to] *possibly* their to
49.7	a wave] *possibly* as wave
50.5	At] A *in MS*
51.21	yesterday] yester / day *in MS*
52.35	fringed] finged *in MS*
53.33	avoid] avid *in MS*
54.26	familiar] fimiliar *in MS*
58.6	it a toad] it *and* toad *cancelled in MS*
58.33	syllables] syllabes *in MS*
* 58.35	note.] ~.. *in MS*
59.18	arabis laevigata?] *interlined with no mark for position*
60.13	of autumn] f autumn *in MS*
61.6-7	open? Ac. . . . 9th] Ac. . . . 9th *interlined with a caret preceding* ?
63.6	bird] *possibly* ~.
63.35	Pond] P. *in MS*
66.6	wings] winds *in MS*
67.24	ridiculously] riduclously *in MS*
67.36	introduce] interduce *or* intorduce *in MS*
73.10	large] lage *in MS*
74.7	Frogs] Froogs *in MS*
75.1-2	night-hawk like] night-hawlike *in MS*
75.5	At] Aat *in MS*
75.19	prevail] pevail *in MS*
75.35	bundles] bundless *in MS*

* 76.25	martin.] ~.. *in MS*
78.16	one] on *in MS*
79.12	Yellow-rump] Yellow-rum *in MS*
80.28	directly] diretly *in MS*
81.16	earlier] ear / lier *in MS*
81.18	earlier] ealier *in MS*
82.13	grackles] glackles *in MS*
82.15	in 1 or 2] *possibly* in or 2
* 82.33	this] this & *in MS*
83.33	which] with *in MS*
84.14-15	and . . . boots] *interlined with a caret following* yet.
85.7	brown] browng *in MS*
86.4	red] read *in MS*
88.11	tomorrow . . . 1st–] earliest v. May 1st tomorrow– *in MS (see Alteration 88.11)*
88.29	is] his *in MS*
92.32	Saxifrage Ap. 13] Ap. *interlined above* 13 *in MS*
93.30	Cliff] Ciff *in MS*
93.35	cannot] can / not *in MS*
97.11	shining] shinging *in MS*
100.19	& coming] & oming *in MS*
103.4	part] pat *in MS*
*104.3	it & the meadow.–] it.–& the meadow *in MS*
104.13	where] *preceded by uncancelled* whery *in MS*
104.35	water or other] wate other *in MS*
106.2	changing] chanding *in MS*
106.14	smacking] smaking *in MS*
110.12	careless] carless *in MS*
110.24	unmistakeable] unmis / takeable *in MS*
111.36	Sudbury] Sud *in MS*
112.19	above] abover *in MS*
112.19	meadows] meads *in MS*
112.28	haste] hast *in MS*
113.5	meadow] meade *in MS*
113.21	at Mr] aMr *in MS*
115.4	up] ap *in MS*
115.7	others] *followed by seven dashes in MS (see Textual Note 115.6-7)*
115.9	indistinctly] indistinct / ly *in MS*
115.31	Brook] B *in MS (see Alteration 115.31)*

116.1	Brook] B. *in MS (see Alteration 116.1)*
*116.6	On . . . &c] *underlined with a series of dashes in MS*
116.29	broad] *followed by a caret in MS*
116.32	grown] grow *in MS*
117.9-10	balm of gilead & *wht* maple] & balm of gilead *wht* maple *in MS (see Alteration 117.9-10)*
117.26	ring] *possibly* sing
119.1	Ministerial] Min. *in MS*
119.8-9	more erect] morerect *in MS*
119.11	so] *possibly* too
121.13	is] ~) *or* is I *in MS*
121.21	leafets] leafeats *in MS*
122.1	there] thre *or* ther *in MS*
123.11	Golden . . . nest] *interlined with no mark for position*
123.22	returned] retuned *in MS*
123.27	an inch] ainch *in MS*
125.1	flesh] fesh *in MS*
125.27	just] justt *in MS*
126.15	rough] rouch *in MS*
128.27	didnt] did / nt *in MS*
130.16	put] puut *in MS*
134.29	S of] *possibly* So of
135.9	begin] *underlined twice in MS*
136.12-13	the C. . . . late] *interlined with a caret following about*
139.21	completely] complety *or* complely *in MS*
141.19	Rubus] ubus *interlined in pencil*
143.21	Bayberry] *revised in pencil from* Barberry
143.34	possess] possesse *in MS*
144.20	syllable] syllablbe *or* syllablle *in MS*
146.35	spread] pread *in MS*
148.7	sun rises] rises *in MS*
150.9	Ap. 27] p. *added in pencil*
151.35	Norway pine ″ ″] Norway ″ ″ ″ *in MS (see Textual Note 151.35)*
154.32	handsome] hand / some *in MS*
155.23	they] thy *in MS*
157.2	Bethlehem] behlehem *or* Behlehem *in MS*
158.1	small] *underlined twice in MS*

158.14	NB] *added in margin with no mark for position*
158.26	night] *possibly* ~–
158.27	ring] *possibly* sing
160.14	45] 4.5 *in MS*
162.4	Fair Haven] F. H. *in MS*
164.14	all] *cancelled in MS*
164.19	afforded] affrded *in MS*
164.25	*Man*] *underlined twice in MS*
164.25	*Slave*] *underlined twice in MS*
165.10	*She's*] *underlined three times in MS*
165.11	*Protection*] *underlined twice in MS*
165.12	*Freedom of Massachetts*] *underlined twice in MS*
167.25	deserves] deseres *in MS*
170.10	crisped] criped *in MS*
171.10	lesson] lession *in MS*
172.25	*Great . . . Ephemerae*] *underlined twice in MS*
173.14	*3d*] *underlined twice in MS*
174.18	distinct] distint *in MS*
175.1	bleached] blach *in MS*
*177.11	Pm. . . . Place] Street . . . Place *in MS*
177.19	they] thy *in MS*
177.25	They] The *in MS*
178.4	afternoon] after / noon *in MS*
178.6	large–] *followed by uncancelled* viote *or* liote
*179.34	Joe] J.oe *in MS*
182.5	there] *possibly* then
182.34	reclining] recling *in MS*
183.15	there] *possibly* then
184.13	sings] *possibly* rings
185.24	*men*] *underlined twice in MS*
186.20	At] A *in MS*
187.5	dispersed] dispered *or* dispesed *in MS*
187.27	after] afte *in MS*
189.19	My] May *in MS*
189.27	budded] bubbed *in MS*
189.28	irregular] irrugular *in MS*
190.7	farmers] farmes *in MS*
190.9	dragging] dogging *or* dagging *in MS*
192.16	that only] thonly *in MS*

193.8   NB] *added in margin with no mark for position*

195.3   NB] *added in margin with no mark for position*

195.4   NB] *added in margin with no mark for position*

196.8   flower] flow *in MS*

198.24   such] sush *in MS*

199.9   they] thy *in MS*

200.4   put] pust *or* purt *in MS*

200.17   Peak] P. *in MS*

201.4-5   a rank one] a rank *cancelled in MS*

201.33   they next day they] thy next day thy *in MS*

202.7   perfectly] perfetly *in MS*

202.12   singing] *possibly* ringing

202.15   flower] flow *in MS*

203.4   them] *possibly* then

205.16   broad] boad *in MS*

205.19   *perhaps*] pehaps *in MS*

205.35   majority] *preceded by uncancelled* to *added in margin*

206.29   politicians] poticians *in MS*

207.33   petition] petion *in MS*

208.17   made] mad *in MS*

208.26   *immediately*] im- / mediately *in MS*

210.18   respectable] respetable *in MS*

211.28   There] The *in MS*

212.12   shuts] shouts *in MS*

*212.34   ap.] ap.. *in MS*

213.28   peculiar] pecluair *in MS*

214.20   woods] wods *in MS*

216.9   clear] *possibly* clean

217.27   Pm. to Cliffs] *interlined below* 1st *in MS*

218.29   Pond] P. *in MS*

218.32-33   sundew some days] sundew some daws *in MS*

220.22-23   However . . . purple] *interlined with no mark for position*

221.24   picked] piked *in MS*

222.12   3rd] *possibly* 2nd

224.8   Haven] H. *in MS*

226.27   & their young] young *interlined in pencil* (*see Alteration 226.27*)

227.1	toxicodendron] toxiodendron *in MS*
227.5	Parietaria] *first* i *added in pencil*
228.4	awkward] awward *in MS*
*228.30	Pyrus] P.yrus *in MS*
232.14	Brook] B *in MS*
233.36	then] *possibly* there
234.33	They] The *in MS*
235.9	Fair Haven] F. H. *in MS*
*235.11-12	some . . . wind] *interlined with no mark for position*
236.15	NB] *added in margin with no mark for position*
236.17-18	This . . . distance–] *added vertically in margin with no mark for position*
239.20	scarce] scace *in MS*
239.26	NB] *added in margin with no mark for position*
239.31	handsome] hand / some *in MS*
241.33	Fair Haven] F. H. *in MS*
242.15	Fair Haven] F. H. *in MS*
243.24	in] *possibly* a
244.13	reflect] rflect *in MS*
245.10	flowers] flows *in MS*
246.13	Brooks] *possibly* Brook
247.17	Flint's] F. *in MS*
248.29	hav] *possibly* has
249.6	evening!] *possibly* ~?
251.7	NB] *added in margin with no mark for position*
251.9	flowers] flows *in MS*
251.20	They] y *added in pencil*
251.24	Brook] B. *in MS*
252.28	heat] *possibly* heats
254.8	commonly] com / monly *in MS*
255.10	roar] *possibly* soar
256.1	Grape-vines–] *dash above dash in MS*
256.7	unsteady] undsteady *in MS*
257.5	lower] loower *in MS*
257.8	swept] *possibly* swift
258.35	yel] yell *in MS*
262.10	hardly] hard / ly *in MS*
263.10	extending] exting *in MS*
263.29	dumosus] dunosus *in MS*

264.10   begin] bein *in MS*
*265.5   Cuckoo heard] Cuckoo   " *in MS*
267.3   Fair Haven] F. H. *in MS*
267.25   singing] *possibly* ringing
271.16   Hill] H *in MS*
271.23   close] lose *in MS*
272.7   I lost] Iost *in MS*
273.23   flower] flow *in MS*
274.7   Lycoperdon] Lyco / perdon *in MS*
274.10   linear] liner *in MS*
275.10   undersides] undesides *or* underides *in MS*
275.10   maples] mapes *in MS*
278.9   Of] *possibly* of
279.18   At] A *in MS*
279.18   Road] Rod *in MS*
279.19   thought] *final* t *added in pencil*
279.29   Pond] P. *in MS*
281.15   swamp] *followed by four dashes in MS (see*
                Textual Note 281.13-15)
283.24   Assabet] *preceded by uncancelled* A *in MS*
285.19-20   I think . . . tail.] *written vertically in margin*
                with no mark for position
286.12   clams] *possibly* clam
286.13   op.] *possibly* ap.
286.28   beg.] beg *in MS*
287.9   mahogany] mahog. / any *in MS*
288.21   high] hig *in MS*
288.28   Was] *preceded by three dashes in MS (see*
                Textual Note 288.28-29)
292.25   beginning] beging *in MS*
292.30   Fair Haven] F. H. *in MS*
293.11   303-304] 439 *in MS*
*293.35   Cliffs–] *followed by* & *in MS*
294.3   there] *followed by five dashes in MS (see*
                Textual Note 294.2-3)
294.7   Haven] H. *in MS*
294.25   now a-days] now a-d-ays *in MS*
297.27   Fair] F. *in MS*
297.34   Miles] Mile *in MS*
298.26   sunning] *possibly* running
299.18   304] 440 *in MS*
301.20   our] *possibly* an
303.4   there] *possibly* these

303.29-30	& here . . . it.] *interlined with no mark for position*
305.23	sunk] rung *or* sung *in MS*
307.7	N.B] *added in margin with no mark for position*
307.17	me] *followed by* is *cancelled in pencil*
309.31	tree] *possibly* trees
310.11	florida] floride *in MS*
311.2	Flint's] F *in MS*
311.29	or] *possibly* on
*312.28	old.] old.. *in MS*
312.28	313] 453 *in MS*
313.23	remarkable] remark / able *in MS*
314.12	another] anothe *in MS*

Alterations

THIS table reports Thoreau's substantive alterations to the text. Several types of changes, discussed in the Textual Introduction, p. 419, are not reported. Numbers at the left margin key the entry to page and line; if the number is marked with an asterisk, the alteration is discussed in a Textual Note. The revised reading appears to the left of the bracket, and the original reading appears to the right; editorial descriptions are italicized. A wavy dash (~) to the right of the bracket replaces the word to the left of the bracket in cases where only punctuation is altered.

MS Volume XVII

3.33	small] *interlined above cancelled* long
4.2	on] *interlined with a caret*
4.5-6	viz . . . woodpecker] *interlined with a caret*
4.23	Browne] e *inserted*
5.2	estimate] estimation
5.11	have to] *interlined with a caret*
5.28	Indian] indian
5.28	on . . . side] *interlined with a caret*
6.2	as it were] *interlined with a caret*
6.5	saying that] *followed by cancelled* it
6.11	C.] *interlined with a caret*
6.14	gives . . . of] *interlined above cancelled* enumerates
7.3	width] *followed by cancelled* of th
7.13	entrance–] ~.
7.14	in . . . places] *interlined with a caret*
7.19	as if] *preceded by cancelled* making
7.22	channel] *interlined above cancelled* gallery
7.23	they . . . &] *interlined with a caret*
7.36	In these] *preceded by cancelled* The pan
8.21	January] *preceded by cancelled* February
8.22	thaw & freeze] freeze *marked for transposition with* & thaw *(see Emendation 8.22)*
8.23	(root of ρεω)] *interlined with a caret*

8.23	ρεω] *preceded by cancelled* reo
8.30	insects] *preceded by cancelled* black *and followed by cancelled* with
8.34	a] an
9.8	pads] *followed by cancelled* there
9.9	ice] *followed by cancelled* there
9.13-14	floating . . . surface] *interlined with a caret*
9.18	full] *interlined with a caret*
9.20	more or less] *interlined with a caret*
9.23	wind–] ~.
9.27	with . . . sound] *interlined with a caret*
9.29	seen . . . ice] *interlined with a caret*
9.33	high] *interlined with a caret*
9.35	walnuts] wal *inserted*
10.2	in effect] *interlined with a caret*
10.4	some of the] *interlined with a caret*
10.25	black] *preceded by cancelled* I am
10.27	handsome lanceolate] *interlined with a caret*
10.29	strongly] *interlined with a caret*
10.33	block–] *followed by cancelled* I ha
10.35	the] *inserted*
11.9	silvery] *interlined with a caret*
11.16	12 feet high] *interlined with a caret*
11.17	sassafras] young *interlined with a caret and cancelled*
11.23	open] *interlined with a caret*
11.25-26	4 or 5] *interlined with a caret*
* 11.26	completely] *preceded by cancelled* faded
11.33-34	or very rarely] *interlined with a caret*
11.34	the . . . instance] *interlined with a caret*
11.34	there] *preceded by cancelled* yet
12.17	or so] *interlined with a caret*
12.29	Ah] ah
12.30	ponder] *preceded by cancelled* study
13.7	printed] *preceded by cancelled* written
13.11-14	The . . . crevices?] *interlined above and below*
13.14	Fair] fair
13.32	are] *inserted with a caret*
13.36	wht] *interlined with a caret*
14.1	The] I
14.12	no . . . winter] *interlined with a caret*

14.31	to &] *interlined with a caret*
14.32	broad] *interlined with a caret*
15.17	black?] ? *inserted*
15.18	wings] *preceded by cancelled* 1st
15.22	amid] *preceded by cancelled* look
16.3	regularly] *preceded by cancelled* & be
16.10	He] he
16.11	Flints] flints
16.17-18	or N westerly] *interlined with a caret*
17.4	a mere] an mere
17.4	mere] *interlined*
17.4-6	This . . . snow] *added*
17.20	*On*] *inserted*
17.20	it] *inserted*
17.25	Found] found
17.26	from . . . feet] *interlined with a caret*
17.27	open] *interlined with a caret*
17.29-30	level . . . oak] *interlined with a caret*
17.32-33	and . . . NW] *interlined*
18.10	green] *interlined with a caret*
18.20-21	20 rods] *interlined with a caret*
18.22	yellow sandstone] *interlined with a caret above cancelled* granite
19.3-4	refers to] *interlined above cancelled* quotes
19.4	suggesting] *preceded by cancelled* saying
19.26	Fair] fair
19.30-31	The . . . far] *interlined with a caret*
20.4	an] *interlined*
20.8-9	They . . . look.] *interlined above*
20.14	the] *interlined with a caret*
20.18	on] in
20.25	male] *preceded by cancelled* female
20.25	a] the
21.34	some . . . diameter] *interlined with a caret*
21.35	gnawed off &] *interlined with a caret*
22.4-5	or . . . creature] *interlined with a caret*
23.36	1 about Thanksgiving] *preceded by cancelled* 1 in T
24.3	&] *inserted and altered from* in
24.21	Minott] *followed by cancelled* sits
24.22-23	in his Grandfather] *interlined with a caret and* Grandfather *preceded by cancelled* fathers predecessor

24.27	hill] *preceded by cancelled* s side
24.30	soft] *interlined with a caret*
25.5	Corner] corner
25.7-9	It ... him.] *added*
25.22	sharp] *interlined with a caret*
25.23	itself–] ~.
25.25	Mixed] *interlined above cancelled* Cla
25.26	being] *added in margin*
25.34-35	is ... the] *interlined with a caret above cancelled* is
25.35	a] *preceded by cancelled* this
26.6	inwardly–] ~.
26.16	a ... day] *interlined*
26.22	ditches &] *interlined with a caret*
26.23	dirty] *inserted*
26.26	& large pyrola] *interlined with a caret*
26.30	bruised] *interlined with a caret*
27.6	& ... walls] *interlined with a caret*
27.12-13	slowly stretching himself] *interlined with a caret*
27.24	its globe] *interlined with a caret*
27.25	of others (?)] *interlined*
27.26	see] *interlined above cancelled* find
* 27.26	fungus?] *followed by cancelled* puff ball
27.27	10 or 12] *interlined with a caret above cancelled* so many
27.27	like a star] *interlined with a caret*
28.1	within ... inches] *interlined below*
28.4	*vacillans.*] *added*
28.5	woody fibres] woody fibers
28.11	large] *inserted*
28.12	sort] *preceded by cancelled* for
28.12-13	⅞ ... diam.] *interlined with a caret*
28.17	but ... coffin] *interlined with a caret*
28.17-19	Also ... bark] *interlined below*
28.24-25	It ... inches] *interlined*
28.27	5] 6
28.29	in flakes] *interlined with a caret*
29.31	the] they
30.1-2	I ... pebbles] *interlined above*
30.4	water] *preceded by cancelled* dark *interlined with a caret*
30.6	& sluggish] *interlined with a caret*

30.14	doubtful–] ~.
30.21	crystal] *interlined with a caret*
30.26	loose] *interlined with a caret*
31.1	Pm . . . pond] *added*
31.10	covered] *preceded by cancelled* full of ice or
31.21	is] &
31.24	increased] *preceded by cancelled* direct
31.29	East] east
32.7-8	All . . . (?)] *interlined with a caret*
32.9	deciduous] *preceded by cancelled* their
32.13	not] *interlined with a caret*
* 32.15	Septemmber] November
32.18-19	commonly . . . diameter] *interlined with a caret*
33.12	Saw] *preceded by cancelled* Heard
33.15	dry] *interlined with a caret*
33.16	spring] *interlined above cancelled* year
33.20-21	same color] *interlined with a caret*
33.26-27	melt . . . ice &] *interlined with a caret*
34.19	or starch] *interlined with a caret*
34.24	gulls?] ? *inserted*
34.28	very] *interlined with a caret*
34.32	or speckled] *interlined with a caret*
34.33	incline to] *interlined with a caret*
35.2-4	The . . . water] *interlined with a caret*
35.11	a] *interlined above cancelled* the
35.12	the shore] a shore
36.10	Corner] corner
36.21	It] it
36.22	at] *interlined above cancelled* on
36.26	the] a
36.31	narrow] *interlined with a caret*
36.34	child-like] *interlined with a caret*
36.35	repeatedly] *interlined with a caret*
37.8	showing the nails] *interlined with a caret*
37.18	spring–] ~.
37.25-26	the . . . &c &c] *interlined below*
37.29	also] *interlined with a caret*
37.31	a . . . sand.] *added*
37.34	pleasant] *interlined with a caret*
37.35	forth burst] *marked for transposition*
38.1	gradual but sure] *interlined with a caret*
38.10	with wet] *interlined with a caret*

38.15-16	blown . . . that] *interlined with a caret*
38.16-17	no . . . place–] *interlined with a caret*
38.17	distant] *interlined with a caret*
38.22	ago–] ∼.
38.24	says . . . &c] *interlined with a caret*
38.25	where] Where
38.30	Up . . . woods] *interlined with a caret*
38.30	Up] to
38.35-36	on . . . ?] *interlined with a caret*
39.12	especially] *interlined with a caret*
39.23	Hill] hill
39.28	concerning] *interlined above cancelled* toward
40.8	Bedford] bedford
40.11	deciduous] *interlined with a caret*
40.26	like?] ∼–
41.13	takes 2] *followed by cancelled* for
41.22	As] as
42.2	Raw . . . rain.] *added*
42.4	on the grass] in the grass
42.13	without] &
42.15-16	Saw . . . hole.] *interlined with a caret*
42.17	Peter's] peter's
43.11	Am– . . . morning.] *added and* Am– *added in margin*
43.20	an] *added in margin*
43.28	heads] *followed by cancelled* which
43.30	i e] or
43.30	They] *preceded by cancelled* They
43.34	& heard] *interlined with a caret*
43.37	A] The
44.2	too] *added in margin*
44.20-21	a . . . one] *interlined with a caret*
44.23	flooded] *interlined with a caret*
44.24	angry] *interlined with a caret*
44.33-34	could . . . years?] *added*
45.18	Lupine Hill] lupine hill
45.20	with ice] *interlined with a caret*
45.24	very regularly] *interlined with a caret*
45.25	apparently] *interlined with a caret*
45.34	& windy] *interlined with a caret*
46.4	poised] *preceded by cancelled* with
46.5	midway] *interlined with a caret*

46.15   lines] *preceded by cancelled* white

46.18   entirely] *interlined with a caret*

46.21   Bay]   bay

46.26   motionless] *interlined with a caret*

46.34   rose]   arose

47.7   about . . . bridges] *interlined with a caret*

47.8   Rather]   rather

47.10   teraced] *interlined with a caret*

47.13-14   & regular] *interlined with a caret*

47.21   now] *interlined with a caret*

47.29   confesses to] *interlined above cancelled* tells

47.31   said] *interlined above cancelled* thought

47.32-33   that . . . there] *interlined with a caret*

47.35   answered] *followed by cancelled* that

48.2   melting] *preceded by cancelled* fast

48.6-7   or 20] *interlined with a caret*

48.14   open] *interlined with a caret*

48.20   high]   a

48.20   near] *interlined above cancelled* by

48.26-27   Mar . . . meadow] *added*

48.29   Pm . . . Pond] *added*

48.30   Coldest]   coldest

49.3   Got . . . Walden–] *added*

49.8   air] *followed by cancelled* shaped like

49.8-9   outline of the] *interlined above cancelled* (curve of the)

49.12   black beaked] *interlined with a caret*

49.13   low] *added in margin*

49.20-22   Had . . . Cliffs] *added*

49.24   hour] *interlined above cancelled* morning or day

50.6   & . . . of] *interlined with a caret*

50.8   ¼+]   + *inserted*

50.18   sun–]   ~.

50.21   Etienne]   Ettienne *and preceded by cancelled* Geo

50.27   but]   by on

50.35   Weather . . . drizzling] *added*

51.12   sweet] *interlined with a caret*

51.20   after] *followed by cancelled* more than

51.28   smooth] *interlined above cancelled* still

51.28   ice] *preceded by cancelled* It

51.30	dripping] *interlined above cancelled* overhanging
51.32	at] *preceded by cancelled* on the
51.34	impression] *preceded by cancelled* sense
51.34	it] It
51.35-36	The bark of] *interlined with a caret*
51.36	Poplar] Poplars
52.2	red] *interlined with a caret*
52.12	one of the] *interlined above cancelled* a
52.16	Farmer's] farmer's
52.24	drifts] *inserted*
52.34	Hosmer] hosmer
53.3	The] the
53.6	in the ditch] *interlined with a caret*
53.6-7	in the brook] *interlined with a caret*
53.12	most] *preceded by cancelled* of it
53.25	of the ducks] *interlined with a caret*
53.36	–of] –a
54.1	ice] *interlined with a caret*
54.15	Has] has
54.22	(the goshawk)] *interlined with a caret*
54.26-28	This . . . yesterday.] *added*
55.9	an] a *and preceded by cancelled* the
55.10	marsh] *interlined with a caret*
55.12	be–] ~.
55.14	The] the
55.21	writing] *preceded by cancelled* wit
55.32	warm] warming
55.35	yesterday–] ~.
56.1-2	The . . . rods] *interlined with a caret*
56.24-25	probably . . . 2] *interlined below*
57.21-22	the warmer . . . out] *interlined with a caret*
58.1	hazels] *preceded by cancelled* alder
58.5	frog?] ? *inserted*
58.7	quacking] quaking
58.11	Nut Meadow Brook] nut meadow brook
58.11	or rather heard] *interlined with a caret*
58.12	plunge] *interlined above cancelled* leap
58.17-18	though . . . me–] *interlined with a caret*
58.23	Heart-leaf] heart-leaf
58.31-32	did . . . spawn?] *interlined above*
58.35	went . . . note.] *marked for repositioning (see Textual Note 58.35)*

59.5	say the 10th] *interlined with a caret*
59.18	arabis laevigata?] *interlined (see Emendation 59.18)*
59.22	was . . . hawk &] *interlined with a caret*
59.24-25	in . . . glass] *interlined with a caret following it with cancelled caret following* crows
59.25	I] *preceded by cancelled* then it
59.28-29	It . . . hawk.] *added*
59.34	Hazel . . . open.] *added*
60.4	rapidly] *interlined with a caret*
60.18	for] *preceded by cancelled* since
60.19	catkinned] catkin
60.21	(before bursting)] *interlined with a caret*
60.23	glowing] *interlined with a caret*
60.28	chirping] *preceded by cancelled* somewhat
60.31-32	where . . . water] *interlined with a caret*
60.35	Hill] hill
61.6-7	Ac. . . . 9th] *interlined with a caret (see Emendation 61.6-7)*
61.25	dead] *interlined with a caret*
61.35	like the hazel] *interlined with a caret*
62.10	Evening] *preceded by cancelled* Ap 12th
62.14	12th] 11th
62.18-19	It . . . day] *interlined above*
62.22	stirring] *interlined with a caret above cancelled* with mixing
62.24	man] *followed by cancelled* was like
62.28-29	he . . . rocks] *interlined with a caret*
63.2	Book] book
63.12	amid] *preceded by cancelled* or ol
63.17	faint] *interlined with a caret*
63.25	large] *interlined with a caret*
63.34	5] *followed by cancelled* of
64.4	pretty] *preceded by cancelled* quite
64.5	peduncles] *followed by cancelled* are
64.8	15 . . . 18] *interlined with a caret*
64.9	fusty] *interlined with a caret*
64.10	brown] *interlined with a caret*
64.15	present] *interlined with a caret*
64.18	NW] SW
64.18	on a . . . shore] *interlined with a caret*
64.19	perfectly erect] *interlined with a caret*
64.22	& effective] *interlined with a caret*

64.25-26	The . . . russet] *added and* the russet *altered from* The russet
64.29	winkle-like] *interlined with a caret*
64.30	somewhat] *preceded by cancelled* with *and followed by cancelled* concentric
64.33-35	saw . . . stump.] *interlined with a caret*
65.4	more] 3
65.8	rising] –
65.9	stumps & other] *interlined with a caret*
65.11	their relatives] *interlined with a caret*
65.15	6] 5
65.23	yellow] *interlined with a caret*
65.28	some] *interlined above cancelled* The
65.35	somewhat] *interlined with a caret*
66.1	& whitish] *interlined with a caret*
66.2	on the wings] *interlined with a caret*
66.24-25	they . . . chip] *interlined with a caret*
66.26	limbs] *preceded by cancelled* twigs
66.27	the 13th first] *interlined with a caret*
66.36	of yesterday] *interlined with a caret*
67.16	least–] ~.
67.25	Farewell] farewell
68.12	the broker] *interlined with a caret*
68.17	made a] made a a
68.20	were the] were a
68.25	sound] *interlined above cancelled* noise
68.31-33	The . . . buds.] *interlined with a caret*
69.5	The golden crowned] *interlined with a caret*
69.7	over the snow] *interlined with a caret*
69.11	forked] *interlined with a caret*
69.11	male] *interlined with a caret*
69.12	breast & underparts] *interlined with a caret*
69.12	are] is
* 69.15	–a–] *interlined with a caret*
69.18	bluish] *interlined with a caret*
69.19	yellowish] ish *inserted*
69.20	wing] wings
69.20-21	b (?)] *interlined with a caret*
69.27	with rounded tail] *interlined with a caret*
70.18-19	though . . . snow] *interlined with a caret*
70.19	least] *preceded by cancelled* the
70.26	I] *preceded by cancelled* I think
70.26	by an eddy] *interlined with a caret*

70.27-28	a foot . . . mill] *interlined with a caret*
70.29	to explore] *interlined with a caret*
70.33-35	From . . . stream.] *added*
71.1	crescent of] *interlined with a caret*
71.4	shone] *followed by cancelled* of
71.6	a] *interlined with a caret*
71.8	catch] catches
71.12-13	or fair weather] *interlined with a caret*
71.29-30	A . . . snow] *added*
71.36	resting] *uncancelled* floating *interlined above*
72.9	there–] ~.
72.13	4] 3
72.16	it] has
72.21	hole] *added*
72.26	humilis?] ? *inserted*
72.28	male–] ~.
73.5	as . . . snow] *interlined with a caret*
73.6	blue-bird–] ~.
73.9-10	I think . . . it.] *interlined with a caret*
73.22	Guinea-hen] guinea-hen
73.28-29	Saw . . . female (?)] *interlined below*
73.31	–c–] *interlined with a caret*
74.2-3	& now . . . them.] *interlined below and* different *preceded by cancelled* more
74.4-5	The . . . today.] *interlined below*
74.13	seen with] *interlined above cancelled* when
74.15	4 Pm] *added in margin*
74.16	[they . . . buds]] *interlined with a caret following cancelled* Shadbush buds
74.17	spiraea–] *interlined with a caret*
74.18	blossom?] *interlined with a caret*
74.19	blossom?] *interlined with a caret*
74.21	say 22nd] *interlined with a caret*
74.24	or air] *interlined with a caret*
74.25	on] *preceded by cancelled* on pitch pine
74.30	one or two] *interlined with a caret*
75.8	little] *interlined with a caret*
75.15	her] *interlined with a caret*
75.34-35	with . . . bundles] *interlined with a caret*
76.2	shrub or tree] *interlined above cancelled* plant

76.2	out] in
76.6	behind–] *followed by cancelled* (The begin
76.11	those] *interlined with a caret*
76.12	golden] *interlined with a caret*
76.13-14	& . . . twigs] *interlined with a caret*
76.25	& . . . martin.] *interlined with a caret (see Textual Note 76.25)*
76.27	many] *interlined with a caret*
76.27	Brookfield] brookfield
77.6	even] *interlined with a caret*
77.13	Missouri] missouri
77.14	not evergreen merely] *interlined with a caret*
77.15-17	Nuphar . . . dilapidated] *interlined with a caret*
77.17	narrow] *interlined with a caret*
77.18	&c&c] *added in margin below cancelled* sweet flag *interlined with a caret*
77.20-21	clover . . . flag] *interlined with a caret*
78.1	in the morning] *interlined with a caret*
78.5-6	So . . . them.] *interlined with a caret*
78.11-12	their . . . breasts] *interlined with a caret*
78.12	on the] on then
78.16	were] was
78.24	are] *followed by cancelled* still
78.28	light] *preceded by cancelled* white
78.35	morning] *interlined above cancelled* water
79.2	brush] brushing
79.5	It] At
79.8	on] *preceded by cancelled* where
79.12-13	was . . . 20th?] *interlined with a caret*
79.15-16	or whistling] *interlined with a caret*
79.17	yel] *interlined with a caret*
79.34	they] *interlined with a caret*
80.2	turns] *interlined above cancelled* his motions
80.7	circling or rather] *interlined with a caret*
80.19	2] *interlined above cancelled* some
80.24	his *red*] the *red*
80.24	*bill*–] ~.
80.25-26	very . . . sides] *interlined with a caret*
80.27	& unhesitatingly] *interlined with a caret*
81.7	meadow–] ~.

81.7	red-] *interlined with a caret*
81.10	–b'–] *interlined with a caret*
81.12	was . . . 26] *interlined with a caret*
81.13	dull] *interlined with a caret*
81.13	(?)] *added in margin*
81.18	saxifrage–] ~.
81.19	A] *preceded by cancelled* The
81.20	any] a
81.24	drooping] *interlined with a caret*
81.26	small] *interlined with a caret*
81.29	Monday] *added*
82.2	open] *interlined with a caret*
82.2	up] *interlined with a caret*
82.4	of] *interlined with a caret*
82.5	52 &] *interlined with a caret*
82.5	53] *followed by cancelled* & 4
82.12	in company] *interlined with a caret*
82.12	slaty] slate
82.14	swamp] *added in margin*
82.16	low & broad] *interlined with a caret*
82.16	coned] *interlined with a caret*
82.23	Also] also
82.25	alders] *interlined with a caret*
* 82.33	this] *very much more interlined with a caret and cancelled*
82.33	is] *preceded by cancelled* the gooseberry *(see Textual Note 82.33)*
83.2	upright] *interlined with a caret*
83.3	terminal] *interlined with a caret above cancelled* stems
83.8	a maple] an maple
83.8	There] there
83.12	very *large*] very *interlined with a caret*
83.19	barn] *interlined above cancelled* bank
83.19	v 29th] *interlined with a caret*
83.23	yes] *interlined with a caret*
83.23	v. n. page] *interlined with a caret*
83.26-27	& seems] *preceded by cancelled* &
83.27	very] *preceded by cancelled* a
83.29-31	some . . . note.] *interlined with a caret*
83.34	whitish] *interlined with a caret*
84.2	flycatcher.] *followed by cancelled* or the heim

84.13	great] *interlined with a caret*
84.14-15	and . . . boots] *interlined with a caret (see Emendation 84.14-15)*
84.20	Saw] *followed by cancelled* my
84.26-27	& . . . him.] *added*
84.33	his] *interlined above cancelled* its
84.33	Begins] begins
84.36-85.1	His . . . thrasher.] *interlined with a caret and* His *altered from* his
85.3	Our] *preceded by cancelled* The
85.12	Nature] nature
85.31	ferruginous] *preceded by cancelled* more
85.36	delicious] *interlined with a caret*
86.23	Hubbards] hubbards
86.33	with notch] *interlined below*
86.35-36	except . . . faded.] *interlined with a caret*
87.29	like song sparrow] *interlined with a caret*
88.2	& low] *interlined with a caret*
88.9-10	Prob. T. Stricta] *interlined above cancelled* arabis laevigata
88.11	v. May 1st] *interlined with a caret (see Emendation 88.11)*
88.13	The early . . . green] *interlined above*
88.17	rising] *interlined with a caret*
88.17	in the west] *interlined with a caret*
89.9	sun–] ~.
89.22	Genius] genius
89.30-31	a little idleness] *interlined with a caret*
89.31	& death] *interlined with a caret*
90.9	the rise . . . of] *interlined with a caret*
90.9-10	though unsteady &] *interlined with a caret above cancelled* does not attain
90.13	surely] *interlined above cancelled* gradually
90.16	expect] *interlined above cancelled* am inclined to believe
90.16	or] of
90.27	of] *interlined above*
90.36-91.1	thought . . . grass] *interlined with a caret*
91.4	&c] *inserted*
91.19	His] his
91.27	barn] *interlined above cancelled* chimney
91.36	a-Maying] *interlined with a caret*
91.36	to-day] *hyphen inserted*

92.3	He] he
92.9	alighted] lighted
92.10	a few] *interlined with a caret above cancelled* the
92.13	just] *interlined with a caret*
92.16	Its] its
92.21	& judge] *interlined above*
* 92.26-28	Sedge . . . 20.] *marked for transposition*
92.27	Earliest] Early
92.29	hazels 12] *preceded by cancelled* P. tremuloides 12
92.31	Crowfoot] *preceded by cancelled* Cowslip
93.7	26] 25
93.8	Fern] fern
93.15	6 . . . RR.] *added*
93.27	highscented] *preceded by cancelled* am
93.32-33	forward–] ~.
93.33	Snakes] *preceded by cancelled* alders
94.9	with . . . up] *interlined with a caret*
94.13	Now] now
94.21	in this order] *interlined with a caret*
94.23-24	v . . . is.] *interlined with a caret*
94.24-25	red . . . here] *interlined with a caret*
94.25-26	(but . . . forward)] *interlined with a caret*
94.26-27	& . . . 27] *interlined with a caret*
94.29	young shoots] *interlined with a caret*
94.30-31	as . . . next] *interlined below*
94.32	v May 5] *interlined with a caret*
94.34	Saw] *preceded by cancelled* I th
95.11	Haynes] *preceded by cancelled* In
95.15-16	the . . . broad] *interlined below*
96.3	leafing] *followed by cancelled* as much as
96.7-9	making . . . gooseberry.] *interlined with a caret*
96.14	Stow's] stow's
96.19	wool] wood
96.29-30	(& the . . . dist.] *interlined below*
96.35	Late] late
97.1	? Probably Pears] *interlined*
97.3	Dwarf or sand-cherry] *interlined*
97.6	May . . . all] *interlined below*
97.8	Some] *added*
97.13	Sweet Fern] sweet fern

97.16	expanding] *interlined with a caret above cancelled* showing
97.17	hang] hand
97.28	herbs] *preceded by cancelled* plants
97.32	season's] 's *inserted*
99.2	wooden as] *followed by cancelled* that of
99.8	The . . . concealed] *interlined with a caret*
99.12	F. hiemalis] F. *inserted*
99.13	bold] *interlined with a caret*
99.22	it] in
99.23	& startling] *interlined with a caret*
99.24	crowfoot] *interlined with a caret*
99.34-35	female . . . long] *interlined above*
100.1	female] *preceded by cancelled* white
100.6	already] *interlined with a caret above cancelled* who
100.16	Musketaquid] musketaquid
100.25	1st–& Goodwin] & *inserted under dash*
100.30	erect] *interlined with a caret*
100.31	scanning] *preceded by cancelled* low ranging the
101.6	7] 6
101.21-23	The . . . river.] *added*
101.24	May-day] may-day
101.30	Hill] hill
101.30	leaves] leaved
101.30	of the] *interlined with a caret*
101.30	seal] *followed by cancelled* leaves *interlined with a caret*
102.1	great] *interlined with a caret*
102.5	man] *followed by cancelled* blesses the
102.8-9	It . . . to the sun] *interlined with a caret*
102.11	or north] *interlined with a caret*
102.15	nothing] *preceded by cancelled* there
102.20-21	already . . . back] *interlined with a caret*
102.22	sweet-gale] *preceded by cancelled* deep
102.23-28	& the A. . . . faces.] *interlined*
102.34	tender] *interlined with a caret*
102.35	*already . . .* wind] *interlined with a caret*
102.36	clothed] &
103.11	are] *interlined with a caret*
103.20-21	except . . . later.] *interlined with a caret and* leaf *preceded by cancelled* leaf

103.28-30	This . . . crest–] *interlined below*
103.31	saw] *preceded by cancelled* & he
103.32-34	I did nt . . . two?] *interlined*
103.36	Alders–] *preceded by cancelled* You
103.36	of all kinds] *interlined with a caret*
103.36	are] &
104.3	& the meadow] *interlined with a caret (see Textual Note 104.3)*
104.6	interval] in *interlined with a caret*
104.7	between] *preceded by cancelled* a
104.19	rolling] *interlined with a caret*
104.32	scarlet–] ~.
104.33	landscape] sandscape
105.5	or deepens] *interlined with a caret*
105.5	the *mts*] *interlined with a caret*
105.9-11	& . . . buds?] *interlined and* are *interlined with a caret*
105.13	8th] 7th
106.4	globe] *interlined above cancelled* earth
106.11	–no] *preceded by cancelled* no track
106.13	found myself] *interlined with a caret above cancelled* was
106.13	quite a sea] *interlined above cancelled* the midst of the highest waves
106.15	yet . . . time] *enclosed in parentheses and uncancelled* mingled with *interlined above*
106.28	about . . . high &] *interlined with a caret*
106.31	Only] only
106.32	color of the] *interlined with a caret*
106.33	μελαινα] μελαινη
106.35-107.1	How . . . world!] *interlined below*
107.2	impulse] *preceded by cancelled* wind
107.4	so great an] *interlined with a caret above cancelled* this
107.8	toward] *interlined with a caret above cancelled* at
107.8	after] *interlined with a caret above cancelled* on
107.11	small] *interlined with a caret*
107.12	though I] *interlined with a caret*
107.21-22	more flower-like] *interlined with a caret*
107.25	houstonias] *interlined with a caret and preceded by interlined and cancelled* & some little

107.26-28   whose ... sod.] *interlined with a caret;* as
interlined below cancelled like *and* low
followed by cancelled amid

107.30   on] in

107.31-32   open ... downward] *interlined with a caret*

107.34-35   as ... breath.] *interlined below*

108.14   loose] *interlined with a caret*

108.19   were] *interlined with a caret*

108.20   their] *preceded by cancelled* I c

108.24   & ... together] *interlined with a caret*

108.26   again] *interlined with a caret*

109.22   he] *preceded by cancelled* our snow flea

109.24   Planted melons.] *added*

109.26   chip-bird] *preceded by cancelled* steady

109.28   X?] *inserted*

109.33   think] thinks

109.34   a] an

109.34   damp] *interlined with a caret*

109.36   also] *interlined with a caret*

110.1-2   their ... leaves] *interlined with a caret*

110.4   suddenly] *interlined with a caret*

110.6-7   & ... birches] *interlined with a caret*

110.12   careless] *preceded by cancelled* most

110.14   indeed] *interlined with a caret*

110.15   alone] along

110.15-16   which ... larger] *interlined with a caret*

110.16   now] *interlined with a caret*

110.16-18   The ... green] *interlined with a caret*

110.18   wilson's] *preceded by cancelled* thrush

110.28   quite within] *preceded by cancelled* just

110.35   Knoll–] ~.

111.8   where] *preceded by cancelled* well

111.17   dull] *interlined with a caret*

111.19   of] or

111.20   Were] *preceded by cancelled* Could

111.24   Boston] boston

111.28   in blossom] *interlined with a caret*

111.30   amid ... &c] *interlined with a caret*

111.31   & pushed] *interlined with a caret*

112.1   meadows] *preceded by cancelled* be

112.9   A] a

112.10   House] house

112.14   2 or 3] *interlined with a caret above
cancelled* a

112.14	days] day *and followed by cancelled* or 2
112.15	shoots] *interlined with a caret*
112.16	He] *preceded by cancelled* While talking
112.23	forenoon] *preceded by cancelled* day
112.27	sprinkle] *preceded by cancelled* rain
112.30	meadow] *preceded by cancelled* pasture
112.30	or near] *interlined with a caret*
112.31	fairly] *interlined with a caret*
112.32	sprinkling] spring
112.33	Bittern] bittern
113.14	*comparitively*–] ~.
113.21	at Mr Brooks'] *interlined with a caret*
113.22-23	May . . . these] vib Dentatum–if that is it–with cornel like leaves at Talls Island *interlined below and cancelled*
113.26	open slowly] *interlined below*
113.30	young] *added in margin*
113.31	″ Red] ″ *added in margin*
113.32	″ White?] ″ *added in margin*
113.33	Alders generally] Amelanchier oblongifolia *interlined above and cancelled*
113.36	2 . . . Gileads] *interlined and* 2 *added in margin*
114.1	Some] *added in margin*
114.10	(I . . . one)] *interlined with a caret*
114.14-15	It . . . flowers] *interlined*
114.22	berry &] berry)
114.26	XXX] *followed by cancelled* earlier than elsewhere no
114.27	place] places
114.28	say just started] *interlined above*
114.33	The] *interlined above cancelled* or
115.1	an] a
115.1	open] *interlined with a caret*
115.1	or gauze] *interlined with a caret*
115.3	slender] *interlined with a caret*
115.5	a foot high] *interlined with a caret*
*115.6-7	The . . . others] *interlined below and young interlined with a caret*
115.16	on] *interlined above cancelled* at
115.17	distant] *interlined with a caret*
115.21	a] *preceded by cancelled* an
115.25	maple] maples

115.31	at . . . Brook] *interlined with a caret (see Emendation 115.31)*
115.34	Everett's] everett's
115.35	& . . . woods] *interlined with a caret*
116.1	i.e. . . . Brook] *interlined with a caret (see Emendation 116.1)*
116.6	to Island &c] *added in margin*
116.7	There . . . east] *interlined with a caret*
116.16-17	the . . . Brook] *interlined with a caret*
116.17	haste?] ~–
116.22	great] *interlined with a caret*
116.23	also] *preceded by cancelled* their
116.29-30	of . . . wind.] *interlined with a caret*
116.31-32	wet & glossy] *interlined with a caret and* wet *marked for transposition with* & glossy
116.32	full] Full
117.4	indigenous] *interlined above cancelled native*
117.6	when . . . flower] when they leaf *marked for transposition with* flower
117.6	leaf] *interlined above cancelled* flower
117.9-10	balm . . . maple] & balm of gilead *marked for transposition with wht* maple *and* tr *written in margin (see Emendation 117.9-10)*
117.10	2] 3 *interlined with a caret and cancelled*
117.11	to] are
117.14-15	probably . . . extent] *interlined with a caret*
117.15	But . . . all] *added*
117.15-16	V . . . inst] *written vertically in margin*
117.20-23	thunder . . . daughter] *interlined with a caret*
117.21	rainbow] *interlined with a caret*
117.25	old] *interlined above cancelled* very
117.26	before–] ~.
117.31	(but] *preceded by cancelled* the
117.35	Sweetbriar . . . generally–?] *added*
118.8-9	very . . . yet] *interlined with a caret*
118.9	thickly] *interlined with a caret*
118.15	brink] bring
118.17	fairly] *interlined with a caret*
118.24	yellow-bird] &
118.24	& the] –the
119.3	buds] *preceded by cancelled* or

119.5-6	only . . . dies] *interlined with a caret*
119.22	Blue] blue
119.27	The] the
119.35	begin to be] *interlined with a caret*
120.2	flower] *interlined above cancelled* leaf
120.4	flocks–] ~.
120.5	sounds–] ~.
120.6	rusty] *interlined with a caret*
120.11	all] *interlined with a caret*
120.20	in a] *interlined with a caret*
120.30	no. no.] *interlined with a caret*
121.11-12	unless . . . currant?] *interlined with a caret*
121.15	Gaylusccia] gaylusccia
121.15	to leaf] *interlined with a caret*
122.6	periods–] ~.
122.8-9	no . . . acid] *interlined with a caret*
122.9-10	The . . . words] *interlined above and* & higher colored *interlined with a caret*
122.12	16] 15
122.12-13	Though . . . Conantum.] Though *added and* not . . . Conantum. *interlined below;* not *followed by cancelled* ap.
122.14	also] *inserted*
122.17	Boat] boat
122.19	Some] some
122.26	white oak] *preceded by cancelled* swamp
122.27-28	red . . . & white] *interlined with a caret*
122.30	by sassafras] *inserted*
122.31-32	prob. . . . Fern] *interlined with a caret*
122.33	surmounted with green.] *interlined below*
122.34	rich crimson] *interlined with a caret*
122.35	yesterday] *preceded by cancelled* day before
122.36-123.1	scattered . . . vine] *interlined with a caret*
123.3-4	prob. . . . then] *interlined with a caret*
123.11	Golden . . . nest] *interlined (see Emendation* *123.11)*
123.14	just] *preceded by cancelled* in
123.15	highest] *interlined above cancelled* shallowest
123.16	generally] *interlined with a caret*
123.19	2 . . . diameter] *interlined with a caret and* inches *marked for transposition with* or more
123.24	filled] fitted

123.29-30	quite ... bridge] *interlined with a caret*
123.36	of] *interlined with a caret*
124.5	sandy] *interlined with a caret*
124.15	Hill] hill
124.18	at one nest] *interlined with a caret*
124.26	leaf] *interlined with a caret*
124.26	It] it
124.28	them] their
124.29	within] with *inserted*
124.31	dates] days
124.35	red or crimsoned] *interlined with a caret above cancelled* crimson *and preceded by cancelled* or
125.1	inclining] *preceded by cancelled* or
125.1	salmon-red (?)] *interlined with a caret*
125.3	in ... leaflets] *interlined with a caret and 5 preceded by cancelled* about
125.5	warm] *interlined with a caret*
125.12	of] a
125.18	& ... air] *interlined above*
125.20	Conantum] conantum
125.26	C.] *interlined with a caret*
125.26-27	var *Pumila*] *interlined with a caret*
125.27	now] *added in margin*
125.31	some starting] & starting
125.31-32	unclenching ... fists] *interlined with a caret*
126.15	small] *interlined with a caret*
126.31	2] 1
126.36	shells] *preceded by cancelled* hull
127.11	just] *interlined with a caret*
127.12	scolloped] *interlined with a caret*
127.13	reached] ed *inserted*
127.22	boat] *preceded by cancelled* boat
128.2-3	which ... depressed] *interlined with a caret*
128.5	rather triangular] *interlined with a caret*
128.8	of ... bluish grey] *interlined above*
128.10-12	& ... long] *interlined with a caret*
128.12	spiteful] *followed by cancelled* looking
128.13	eye–] ~)
128.14	& ample] *interlined with a caret*
128.16	& ... moss] *interlined with a caret*
128.21	flesh &] *interlined with a caret*
128.26	flippers] *interlined with a caret*

128.33	curved] *preceded by cancelled* curl
129.2	convulsively] *interlined with a caret*
129.3	&] Or
129.6	great blunt] *interlined with a caret*
129.8	spines] *preceded by cancelled* scales or
129.10	on] in
129.13	*toe* (?)] (?) *inserted*
129.14	fore] *preceded by cancelled* 4
129.19-20	before . . . meadows] *interlined with a caret*
129.27-29	Farrar . . . 29] *added*
129.35	flour] *interlined with a caret*
129.35	would not quite] *interlined with a caret*
130.6	some distance] *interlined with a caret*
130.17	ap.] *interlined with a caret*
130.23	of broad] *preceded by cancelled* large
130.24	luxuriant] *interlined with a caret*
130.24	leaves–] ~.
130.26	green–] ~.
131.13	head] *followed by cancelled* cut off
131.22-23	or palpitating] *interlined with a caret*
131.29	shore] *interlined above cancelled* side
131.30	fluttering] *followed by cancelled* & shining
131.31	seen] *preceded by cancelled* still
132.2	sometimes] *interlined with a caret*
132.7	where] &
132.7	lighter] *preceded by cancelled* feebler
132.24	It] Its
132.28	June-Berry] June-berry
133.20	oak–] ~.
133.21	catkins] *interlined above cancelled* blossoms
133.22	bear] *interlined above cancelled* wht
133.25	around . . . shoots] *interlined with a caret*
133.36	plants] *interlined with a caret*
134.13	some of] *interlined with a caret*
134.14	began] an *inserted*
134.18	4] *preceded by cancelled* 3 or
134.18-19	though . . . large] *interlined with a caret*
134.25	lobed] lobes
135.1	& cool] *interlined above*
135.31	late] *interlined above cancelled* dusk
136.4	The] Then
136.4	late] *followed by cancelled* though

136.11	All] *inserted*
136.12-13	the C. . . . late] *interlined with a caret (see Emendation 136.12-13)*
136.24	already] *preceded by cancelled* now
136.26	plum–] ~.
136.32	the wild red] *interlined with a caret*
137.6	Brick] brick
137.7	long] *added*
137.9-10	The . . . thorn.] *added; eng. interlined above* The *and* opens *interlined above cancelled* ap
137.12-13	saw . . . thunder] *interlined above*
137.26	& but] & *added in margin*
137.29	some] *interlined above cancelled* the
137.30	Sunday] *added*
137.33	these throats] *interlined with a caret*
138.1-2	spread . . . night] *interlined with a caret*
138.6	effete] *followed by cancelled* The
138.8	A] The
138.8	lightining] lighting
138.13	larger] *interlined with a caret*
138.14	here] *interlined with a caret*
138.27	reddish] *interlined with a caret*
138.31-32	a . . . spoons] *interlined with a caret*
138.34	a . . . more] *interlined with a caret*
139.2	flags] *interlined with a caret*
139.18	naked fl] *interlined with a caret*
139.23	The] the
139.25-26	NB . . . 26th.] *added*
139.27	bloom] *followed by cancelled* day bef
139.33	plowing] &
139.35	searching carefully] *interlined with a caret*
140.1	When I] *interlined with a caret*
140.1	returned] Returning
140.21	oak] *interlined with a caret*
140.28	& . . . any] *interlined with a caret*
140.31	these] this
140.34	away–] ~.
140.35	ground] *interlined above cancelled* lodge
141.2	in] on
141.3	islands] an island
141.5	edge] *preceded by cancelled* bank
141.6	sweeping] *interlined above cancelled* curving

141.7-8	in . . . flood] *interlined with a caret*
141.20	Canadensis] canadensis
141.20-21	at . . . sumachs] *interlined with a caret*
141.33	callow] *interlined with a caret*
142.2	particular] *interlined with a caret*
142.4	plant–] ~.
142.16	reminding . . . butter] *interlined with a caret*
142.22	landscape–] ~.
142.28	groves] *interlined with a caret*
142.28	great] *interlined with a caret*
142.29	curveing] curved
142.34	oppressive] *interlined with a caret*
143.4	young . . . reddish] *interlined with a caret*
143.12	It . . . hill-sides] *interlined with a caret*
143.13	Miles] miles
143.14	racemes] *interlined above cancelled* masses
143.18	Canadensis] canadensis
143.21	2??] *interlined above cancelled* several
143.25	comparatively] *interlined with a caret*
143.32	pursuits–] ~.
144.2	the] *preceded by cancelled* We
144.4	heaven] *preceded by cancelled* dwell
144.10	God] god
144.12	Truth] truth
144.21	all] *inserted*
144.24	hummingbird] bird *interlined with a caret*
144.31	Hill] hill
145.6	The . . . hen-hawk.] *interlined below*
145.13	now lies] *interlined above cancelled* lying
145.15	the deep] the *interlined above cancelled* its
145.18	as] *followed by cancelled* in a
145.19-20	But . . . wind] *interlined with a caret*
145.20	Moreover] *interlined with a caret and preceded by cancelled* Now &
145.24	perfect] perfectly
145.27-28	from . . . upward] *interlined with a caret*
145.29	one of] *interlined with a caret*
145.32	erect] *interlined with a caret*
146.3	quite] *interlined with a caret*
146.6-7	fit . . . parterre.] *interlined with a caret*
146.9	rather the 25] *interlined above cancelled* tomorrow
146.12	Nature] nature

146.16	Nature] nature
146.21-22	now . . . swamps] *interlined with a caret*
146.24	the last] *preceded by cancelled* but
146.24	God–] ~.
146.27	earth–] ~.
146.31	springs] *interlined above cancelled* years
146.33	Nature] nature
147.29	upright] *interlined with a caret*
147.34	the other] another
148.6-8	As . . . fog.] *interlined with a caret*
148.17	horizon–] ~.
148.21	on our sideboards] *interlined with a caret*
148.30	& peculiar] *interlined with a caret*
148.31	Cedar] *followed by cancelled* both
148.32	22nd] 21st
148.32	Stow's] stow's
149.3-4	The . . . thin.] *interlined below*
149.10	even . . . tips] *interlined with a caret*
149.22	nearly] *followed by cancelled* altogether
149.23	some] *interlined with a caret*
149.25-26	May . . . kind??] *added*
149.31-32	Their . . . leaf–] *added*
149.35-36	? –Elder . . . 5)] *interlined*
149.36	(May 5)] ((v May 5))
150.8	? 2nd Gooseberry] *interlined above cancelled* ? 2nd Gooseberry
150.10	?? Black . . . seen] *interlined*
150.11	(?)] *interlined with a caret*
150.13	?? Muhlenbergs (?)] *interlined*
150.21	Young] *added*
150.24	Sweet . . . advance] *interlined*
150.29	? –Late . . . seen] *interlined*
150.32	? Beaked . . . distinguished] *interlined*
151.3	?? –Clematis . . . 16] *interlined*
151.7	?? May . . . seen] *interlined*
151.9	?? Fever . . . 12] *interlined*
151.15	? Semper . . . seen] *interlined*
151.17	? Large White ″] *interlined below cancelled* ? Large White ″
151.19	?? Linnaea–not seen] *interlined*
151.21	Amlelanchier oblongifolia] *interlined*
151.23	?? Dwarf Cassandra–] *interlined*
151.25	Early] Large

151.26   ? –Late . . . seen] *interlined*

151.27   birch–] *followed by cancelled* large not seen

151.28   ? –Cockspur . . . seen] *interlined*

151.34   ?? Bear . . . seen] *interlined*

151.37   Young hornbeam] *interlined*

152.2   ? –Round . . . late] *interlined*

152.3   Panicled– –Cornel] *interlined*

152.4   Silky   ″] *interlined*

152.5   Sweetgale May 11] *cancelled* ?? Mt laurel *interlined above*

152.7   ?? Scarlet (?)   ″] *interlined*

152.13   ?? –Maple-leaved . . . late] *interlined*

152.20   ? Swamp . . . late] *interlined*

152.29   Great . . . 13] *cancelled* ? Huckleberry / ? Dangleberry not seen *interlined below*

152.30   clustered Andromeda 13] *cancelled* ? –Blue whortle berry / ? –Red   ″   ″   *interlined above*

153.1   Celtis] *preceded on separate line by cancelled* ?? Scarlet (?)   ″

153.4   Nemopanthes] *interlined*

153.7   ? Large . . . observed.] *preceded on separate line by cancelled* Prinos verticullatus

153.10   C. Florida] *interlined*

153.13   ? waxwork– . . . place] *interlined*

153.16   ?? Black walnut] *interlined*

153.17   15 slow]   15 *followed by*) *altered to* s

153.20   Huckleberries black] *interlined*

153.21   ? – – &c] *interlined*

153.25   ?? Cistus . . . least] *interlined*

153.27   ?? Carrion . . . May] *interlined*

153.30   Lambkill] *cancelled* ? Dwarf cassandra *interlined above*

153.31   ?? –Mt . . . early] *interlined*

154.13-25   Of . . . more?] *added*

154.13   deciduous] *interlined with a caret*

154.27-28   The . . . fields] *added*

155.1   probably onoclea] *interlined above cancelled* flowering ferns

155.4   5½ . . . ivy] *added*

155.5   Pipe]   pipe

155.18   (?)]   –

155.21   bountifulness–]   ~.

156.2	Nathan] nathan
156.3	black] *preceded by cancelled* wild
156.6	young] *added in margin*
156.8	ap] *interlined with a caret*
156.12	or scarlet?] *interlined with a caret*
156.13	*i.e.*] *interlined above cancelled* now
156.29	young] *interlined with a caret*
156.36	clouds–] ~.
157.1	strong] *interlined with a caret*
157.6	Close] close
157.18	They] they
157.30	a fork] a *interlined above cancelled* the
158.13-14	it . . . 29th] *interlined with a caret*
158.14	ago] *followed by cancelled* (the last perhaps 10 days ago?)
158.14	NB] *added in margin (see Emendation 158.14)*
158.14-15	also . . . finch] *interlined with a caret*
158.23	especially at night] *interlined with a caret*
158.30	or expect] *interlined with a caret*
159.5-6	Pads . . . appeared] *interlined with a caret*
159.11	high] *interlined with a caret*
159.18	about 6 rods] *interlined with a caret*
159.25-26	It . . . it] *interlined below*
159.31	water–] *cancelled* like *interlined with a caret*
160.3	have] *preceded by cancelled* appear to
160.3-4	& are occupied] *interlined with a caret*
160.10	black,] ~–
160.11	sides;] ~–
160.11	light] *interlined above cancelled* pale
160.13	bluish] blue
160.13	slate] *interlined with a caret*
160.26	paler but] *interlined with a caret*
160.29	Family–] family.
160.30	The] the
160.31	& figs] *interlined with a caret*
160.31-32	not . . . like.] *interlined with a caret*
160.32	is] *interlined above cancelled* are
161.11	on . . . hill-side] *interlined with a caret*
161.16	green?] *inserted*
161.16	finely] *interlined with a caret*
161.21-22	Yesterday . . . fire!!] *interlined with a caret*
161.25	X] *inserted*

161.29	Young] *interlined with a caret*
162.4	Fair Haven Cliffs] F. H. Cliffs *added (see Emendation 162.4)*
162.6	to be seen] *interlined with a caret*
162.7	evergreens–] ~.
162.7	The] the
162.14	the] there
162.14	How] how
162.17	The] the
162.36	& . . . water] *interlined with a caret*
163.10	one] *preceded by cancelled* up
163.10	Other] other
163.13	X] XXX
163.16	i.e. abundantly] *interlined with a caret*
163.20-21	prob. . . . red-house–] *interlined with a caret*
163.28	ap.] *inserted*
163.35	is as impertinent] *added*
163.36	paper.] ~?
164.1	packs] pack
164.3	unoffending] *interlined with a caret*
164.4	of] a
164.14	ever] *interlined with a caret*
164.32	that] –
164.32	& have been] *interlined with a caret*
164.36	Traveler] traveler
164.36	Post] post
165.2	any] *interlined with a caret*
165.2	of government are] *interlined with a caret*
165.4	secures] secured
165.6	who] *preceded by cancelled* serves the
165.9	one] *preceded by cancelled* a man
165.11	Protection] protection
165.21	while] *interlined above cancelled* though
165.23	inhumanities] *interlined with a caret above cancelled* injuries
165.30	peaceably] *interlined above cancelled* meekly
165.31	chosen] *interlined with a caret*
166.2-3	Dark Earth] dark earth
166.3	roll] *preceded by cancelled* go
166.17	about–] ~.
166.27-28	dark cellar-like] *interlined with a caret*
167.2-4	May . . . freshet–] *interlined below*

167.8	suddenly] *interlined with a caret*
167.11-12	Eriophorum . . . peduncles.] *interlined above*
167.16	at . . . distance] *interlined with a caret*
167.19	in sproutlands] *interlined with a caret*
167.28	or hemispheres] *interlined with a caret*
167.30-31	of . . . 8] *interlined above*
168.3	pincushion?] *interlined with a caret*
168.7	June 1st] *interlined above cancelled* tomorrow
168.7	1st X] 1st XX
168.11-12	Old . . . river–] *added*
168.21-22	It . . . flock] *interlined above*
168.24	Remarkable . . . birds] *added*
168.27	to leaf] *added in margin*
168.33	a smaller one] *added*
169.14	seringo,] ~–
169.18-19	sounding rather raspingly] *interlined with a caret*
169.22	it] if
169.32	or connivance] *interlined with a caret*
169.32	the] *interlined with a caret*
169.34	black] *interlined with a caret*
169.34	I . . . grown] *interlined with a caret*
170.2	see] *followed by cancelled* an
170.3	black] *interlined with a caret*
170.15	black] *preceded by cancelled* white half
170.17	Sea] sea
170.20	umbralla] *uncancelled* parasol *interlined above*
170.26	the country] this country
170.29-30	they . . . tender] *interlined with a caret*
170.35	on] in
171.20	shady] *interlined with a caret*
172.9	of the 1st] *interlined with a caret*
172.11	its] *preceded by cancelled* the
172.12	handsome] *interlined with a caret*
172.14	now commonly] now *added in margin and* commonly *interlined with a caret*
172.17	The] *preceded by cancelled* Is that *and added in margin*
172.25	*Great*] great
172.27	They . . . see] *interlined with a caret*

172.34	of] *inserted*
172.35	examined] *preceded by cancelled* saw
173.17	in] on
173.21	where we dined] *interlined with a caret*
173.27	the opposite] the *added in margin*
173.31	Farm] farm
174.1	Indians his] Indians *followed by cancelled apostrophe and* his *interlined with a caret*
174.18	as . . . water] *interlined with a caret*
174.23	or] *preceded by cancelled* of
174.36	brown paper] *interlined with a caret*
175.2	more] *preceded by cancelled* as th
175.12-14	The . . . of] *interlined with a caret*
175.29	energy] *interlined above cancelled* heroism
175.29	the] those *and followed by cancelled* who enjoyed
175.31	disinterestedly] *preceded by cancelled* truly
176.7	the] *interlined above cancelled* his
176.18	Nature] nature
176.19	serenity–] ~.
176.29	horizon] *followed by cancelled* were
177.25	ap.] to
177.28	see] *preceded by cancelled* on
178.2	yellowish] *interlined with a caret*
178.2	reddish] *interlined with a caret*
179.8	mikania] *followed by cancelled* vines–
179.9	fish lines] *interlined with a caret*
179.10	within–] *added in margin*
179.12	evening] *preceded by cancelled* night
179.21	or chaff (?)] *interlined above*
179.30	5] 3
*179.34	Joe] oe *inserted*
179.36	in] *inserted*
180.2	shad-bush] *interlined with a caret*
180.4	As] I
180.14	its shell about] *interlined with a caret*
180.15	its] *interlined above cancelled* his
180.17	especially] *interlined with a caret*
180.17	deeply] *preceded by cancelled* thickly
180.20	that–] ~.
180.20	& claws] *interlined with a caret*
180.28	Heartleaf] heartleaf
180.32	Were] Was

180.33	scarlet] *interlined above cancelled* red
180.34-35	yes . . . dying–] *interlined with a caret*
181.4	NB] *added in margin*
181.9	muggy] *interlined with a caret*
181.30	like] *preceded by cancelled* not
181.33	draws out] "draws out"
182.5	there] then
182.20	For] for
182.21	only?] ? *inserted*
182.31	Linnaea] linnaea
182.31	Call] *preceded by cancelled* or aparine?
182.31-34	Call . . . later?] *interlined with a caret*
183.11	Provincetown] provincetown
183.18	peculiarly] *interlined with a caret*
183.21	one of] *interlined with a caret*
183.26	man–] ~.
183.27	more delicate] *interlined with a caret*
183.28	swamp] *preceded by cancelled* woods
184.5-6	Ferns . . . there.] *added*
184.19	far as] far &c
184.30	who] *followed by cancelled* behaved
185.32	clear] *interlined with a caret*
186.2	i.e. . . . bay-wing] *interlined with a caret*
186.4	sparrows–?] ? *inserted*
186.11	them–] ~.
186.13	fairly] *preceded by cancelled* in its p
186.24	Farm] farm
186.26	–pursuing] *preceded by cancelled* meandering very much
187.9-10	pretty high] *interlined with a caret*
187.14	White-hall] white-hall
187.16	at Ashland] *interlined with a caret*
187.21	streams of] *interlined with a caret*
187.22	spotted] *interlined with a caret*
187.30-31	These . . . elms.] *added*
188.2	latifolium?] ? *added*
188.10	chlorantha] *interlined above cancelled* sassifolia
188.10-11	the 11th] *interlined with a caret*
188.11	Judging . . . 10] *interlined with a caret*
188.14-16	Perhaps . . . rare.] *interlined with a caret and* & v dentatum *interlined with a caret*
188.17	Walden] walden

188.25	Savannah?] ? *inserted*
189.8	W.S.W.] *first* W. *inserted*
189.31	it–] ~.
190.7	busily] busy
190.22	prob. . . . elsewhere] *interlined with a caret*
191.10	dead] *interlined with a caret*
191.12	just] *preceded by cancelled* at
191.13	small . . . basins] *interlined with a caret*
192.5	(?)] *inserted*
192.9	Simon] Simon's
192.31	canicularis] *interlined above cancelled* Cansheularse
192.33	Harris] *interlined with a caret*
192.34	July] july
192.35-36	Bacon . . . sure–] *added*
193.8	NB] *added in margin (see Emendation 193.8)*
193.32	white] *inserted*
193.36	merely–] ~,
194.1	tortoises] *inserted*
194.3-4	I . . . Assabet–] *added*
194.16	warmth] *preceded by cancelled* moist
194.23	5] 5½
194.24	round] *preceded by cancelled* in a
195.3	NB] *added in margin (see Emendation 195.3)*
195.4	NB] *added in margin (see Emendation 195.4)*
195.7	the 19th] *interlined above cancelled* tomorrow
195.29	Nature] *followed by cancelled* is part
197.5	(?)] *inserted*
197.26-27	Other . . . &c] *added*
197.33	ago–] ~.
197.36	–of . . . odoratus] *added*
198.4	The] *preceded by cancelled* We can a
198.16	last] *added in margin*
198.18	anthony Burns] *interlined with a caret*
198.18	slavery] *followed by cancelled* the other day
198.20	hell–] ~.
198.25	there is any] *interlined with a caret*
198.25	more] *preceded by cancelled* is
198.29	around] *interlined with a caret*
199.7	see] some *interlined with a caret and cancelled*
199.12	cows] *followed by cancelled* which is

199.15	less] *interlined above cancelled* but little
199.26	what] *preceded by cancelled* of
199.28	God] god
200.11	2] *interlined above cancelled* more
200.11	abundant] Abundant
200.17	Heywood] heywood
200.19	very] *interlined with a caret*
201.18	thickly] *interlined with a caret*
201.20	the earlier (?)] *interlined with a caret*
201.25	deeper colored &] *interlined with a caret*
201.29	perhaps more] *interlined with a caret*
201.34-35	also . . . glory &] *interlined with a caret*
202.4	one] *interlined above cancelled* It
202.11	The] That
202.15	& . . . now]] *interlined with a caret*
202.19	rare–] ~.
202.20	mead. sweet tomorrow] *added*
202.30	fine] *preceded by cancelled* a
202.35	dark] *interlined with a caret*
203.20	Fugitive] fugitive
203.35	any] *interlined with a caret*
204.6	obey] *preceded by cancelled* in such
204.10	via almshouse] *added*
204.12	on] &
204.12	Wht] *inserted*
204.12	Pine] pine
204.17	(often more notes)] (often *added in margin and* more notes) *interlined with a caret*
204.25	4] 3
204.27	are] *interlined with a caret*
204.33	as] –
205.5	in] on
205.16	bell] &
205.24	drought–] ~.
205.24	&] *inserted*
205.26	his] *preceded by cancelled* the
205.35	the Devil . . . God] the Devil *marked for transposition with* God *and* tr *written in margin*
205.35	God] god
206.6	by & by] *interlined with a caret*
206.9	thing] *interlined with a caret*
206.20	healthy] *interlined with a caret*

206.22	partial] *preceded by cancelled* our
206.25	at all] *interlined with a caret*
206.29	Garrison] garrison
206.31	at] *interlined with a caret*
206.31	this] then
207.11	Water?] ? *inserted*
207.16	in] on
207.24-25	but . . . men] *interlined with a caret above cancelled* but first
207.25	a] *preceded by cancelled* just
207.27	a] *interlined above cancelled* the
208.11	nearly] *interlined with a caret and preceded by cancelled* about
208.16	says he] *added in margin*
208.16	had] have
208.17-19	Daniel . . . Princeton.] *interlined below*
208.19	They] they
208.21	permanent] *interlined with a caret*
208.26-27	as soon as emptied] *interlined above*
208.35	somewhat] *interlined with a caret*
209.1-2	carrying . . . branches] *interlined with a caret*
209.10	small] *interlined with a caret*
209.24	fresh] *interlined with a caret*
209.28	on] *preceded by cancelled* while
209.30	green . . . &] *interlined with a caret*
209.34	red or red-purple] *interlined with a caret*
210.6	i.e.] *interlined above cancelled* or
210.18	respectable] *interlined with a caret*
210.18	precedent] precedence
210.31	Just] just
210.34	Suddenly] *interlined above cancelled* At length
211.2	near] *added in margin*
211.12	& then] & *interlined above cancelled* They *and followed by cancelled* will
211.13	duty for them] *interlined above cancelled* work
211.17	minute] *interlined above cancelled* little
211.22	Olivaceous?] ? *inserted*
211.27	flower] *added in margin*
212.4	dense] *preceded by cancelled* whole sha

212.10	where] *preceded by cancelled* concealing the birds &
212.18	countless] *interlined with a caret*
212.18	close . . . shore] *interlined with a caret*
212.18-19	The . . . colored] *interlined above*
212.26-27	is . . . out.] *interlined with a caret*
212.29-30	now on . . . pollywogs] *interlined with a caret*
212.33	At] at
212.34	One . . . ap.] *interlined with a caret (see Textual Note 212.34)*
213.4-5	in schools] *interlined with a caret*
213.10	2 or 3] *interlined above cancelled* on
213.23-24	& . . . it] *interlined with a caret*
214.2	least–] ~.
214.22	concealed] *interlined with a caret*
214.35	perhaps yesterday] *interlined with a caret*
215.2	From] *preceded by cancelled* Specularia
215.3	glossy & light-reflecting] *interlined with a caret*
215.11	by Heywood meadow] *interlined with a caret*
215.14	Well] *preceded by cancelled* Spring
215.24	*zskeow-xskeow*] *zskeow-zskeow*
215.28-29	the mucronate . . . what?] *interlined with a caret above cancelled* Cornuti
215.30	RR] rR
216.2	Purp.] purp.
216.10	silvery] *interlined with a caret*
216.24	near] *interlined with a caret*
216.26	Haven] haven
216.29	the weeds] *interlined with a caret*
216.29	of] *interlined with a caret*
217.12	in diam.] *interlined with a caret*
217.13	inner] *interlined with a caret*
217.24	6 to 10] *interlined with a caret*
217.27	Pm. to Cliffs] *added (see Emendation 217.27)*
217.33-34	fine grained] *interlined with a caret*
218.6-7	from this hill] *interlined with a caret*
218.12	The . . . springs] *added and* almost *interlined below*
218.18	spawn (?)] ~–

218.22	river] *interlined with a caret*
218.24	Purshiana] purshiana
218.35	E. side] e. side
219.1	blue] *interlined with a caret*
219.3	dry] *interlined with a caret*
219.4	from . . . high] *interlined with a caret*
219.5	dark shade of] *interlined with a caret*
219.8	like . . . heat.] *interlined below*
219.14-15	also . . . 8.] *interlined with a caret and* N *of interlined with a caret*
219.27	water-milkweed] *preceded by cancelled* smaller
219.32	condition–] ~.
219.34	seething] *interlined with a caret*
220.13	them] *interlined with a caret*
220.15	clams] *interlined with a caret*
220.22-23	However . . . purple] *interlined (see Emendation 220.22-23)*
220.23	(plucked June 25)] *interlined with a caret above cancelled* just Wednesday
220.27	H. Corymbosum] H. *inserted*
220.29	some] *interlined with a caret*
220.32	golden] *interlined with a caret*
220.33	from] *interlined with a caret*
220.36	reflected–] ~.
221.2	Hill] hill
221.8	8] 7
221.10	Some] *interlined with a caret*
221.15	Lysim.] ysim. *inserted*
221.26	I] *interlined above cancelled* you
221.28	&c &c] *interlined with a caret*
221.34	Stow's] stow's
222.5	On] *interlined above cancelled* In
222.5	hot] *interlined with a caret*
222.6-7	had . . . body] *interlined with a caret*
222.8	upper] *interlined with a caret*
222.14-15	the . . . &] *interlined with a caret*
222.22-23	yellowish–] ~.
222.31-32	back . . . Shore] *interlined with a caret and* flat *interlined with a caret*
222.34	ap. 3 or 4] *interlined above cancelled* several
223.3	half] *interlined with a caret*
223.6	3 4 or 5] *interlined with a caret*

223.22	2–? XXX A Lysimachia] ? *inserted on top of* *dash*
223.24	about June] *preceded by cancelled* lower
223.26	Bathing] bathing
223.30	Bend] bend
223.36	gutturally &] *interlined with a caret*
224.5	Carolina?] ? *inserted*
224.10-11	Is . . . like?] *interlined with a caret*
224.15	pressed] impressed
224.22	very] *interlined with a caret*
224.29	red–] ~.
225.2	Low] low
225.20	month methinks] *interlined below*
225.21	& in morning] *interlined with a caret*
225.21-23	heard . . . river] *interlined with a caret*
225.25	Crow . . . chatter–] *interlined*
225.28	Saw] saw *and preceded by cancelled* Think I
225.28	& July 11th] *added*
225.31	Cuckoo . . . time] *interlined*
225.34	I . . . birds] *interlined*
226.2-3	& tanager all] *interlined with a caret*
226.7	Sum] *added in margin*
226.12	*Rarely*] *uncancelled* Hardly *interlined above*
226.15	Think . . . 2] *interlined below*
226.24	Pm . . . Haven] *added*
226.27	& their young] & their *interlined with a caret* (*see Emendation 226.27*)
226.33	Fair] fair
226.33-34	The . . . shore] *interlined below*
227.3-4	Some . . . pan] *interlined above*
227.4	3 or 4] *interlined above cancelled* several
227.7	Fair] fair
227.8	shining] *interlined with a caret*
227.9-11	a day . . . done] *added*
227.12	large] *interlined with a caret*
227.12	leaves] *interlined with a caret*
227.14-16	I heard . . . begun.] *interlined below*
227.18	massy] *interlined with a caret*
227.20	fawn?] ? *inserted*
227.21	lightning up with] *interlined with a caret*
227.21-22	& shorne] *interlined with a caret*
227.32-33	& tortoises . . . it] *interlined with a caret*
227.34	darker] er *inserted*

228.10	resist] *preceded by cancelled* enable it to keep fore
228.11-12	direction–] ~.
228.13-14	See . . . aphides.] *added*
228.15	Dodge] dodge
228.20	2] *added in margin*
228.25-26	The . . . berries.] *interlined with a caret*
*228.30	Pyrus] yrus *inserted*
229.5	The] the
229.9	on . . . top] *interlined with a caret*
229.16-17	Scent . . . now] *added*
229.18-19	v. radical leaves] *interlined with a caret*
229.21	Friday] *followed by cancelled* Sat
229.35	2 or 3 days] *interlined above cancelled* a day or more
230.1	red] *interlined with a caret*
230.4	Sat. July 15] *added and followed by cancelled* A thick fog began last night lasting till late this morning.
230.5	Bridge] bridge
230.11	autumnal &] *interlined with a caret*
230.24	calamint] *interlined with a caret*
230.25	standing . . . wall] *interlined with a caret*
231.3	broad] *interlined with a caret*
231.17-18	& nut hatch] *interlined with a caret*
231.18	like] the
231.25	some] *preceded by cancelled* per
231.27	The] *preceded by cancelled* The *(see Textual Note 231.26-27)*
231.34-35	A thick . . . methinks] *added*
231.36	Pm] *interlined above*
231.36	&] to
232.3	yellow] yellowish
232.8	a day or two] *interlined with a caret*
232.12	leaves are] *interlined with a caret preceding cancelled* is
232.15	it . . . white] *interlined with a caret*
232.17	it] It
232.33	I] It
233.4	here & there] *interlined above*
233.6	4th] *preceded by cancelled* 12
233.13-14	I . . . numerous] *interlined with a caret*
233.14-15	I . . . half] *interlined below*

233.16	At] at *and preceded by cancelled* Again
233.22	about] *interlined with a caret*
233.22-23	& . . . off] *interlined with a caret and* petal *preceded by cancelled* white
233.25	though] (
233.25-27	I . . . lilies] *interlined with a caret*
233.34-35	where . . . surface] *interlined with a caret*
234.3-4	Why . . . beneath?] *interlined below*
234.5	under] *preceded by cancelled* between the
234.8	red-eye] *preceded by cancelled* the
234.22	it] *preceded by cancelled* of
234.32	decaying] decayed
*235.11-12	some . . . wind] *interlined*
235.16	flying] *preceded by cancelled* for
235.18	It . . . bold] *interlined with a caret*
235.22-23	Woodbine . . . there] *interlined with a caret*
235.23	green] *interlined with a caret*
236.1	highway–] ~.
236.1	some . . . yellowing] *interlined with a caret*
236.7	Barretts] barretts
236.8	House] house
236.9	A] *preceded by cancelled* In mid summer when
236.10-15	suddenly . . . morning.] *interlined with a caret and* The river . . . aside *interlined with a caret*
236.12	had] has
236.15	NB] *added in margin (see Emendation 236.15)*
236.17-18	This . . . distance–] *added vertically in margin (see Emendation 236.17-18)*
236.35	some of] *interlined with a caret*
237.1	Island] island
237.7	a faint] *interlined with a caret*
237.31	though] thought
237.32	dark.] say . . . later *interlined with a caret*
237.32	By] *preceded by cancelled* That wonderf
237.35	whorl] whorls
237.35-36	very showy] *interlined with a caret*
237.36-238.1	with . . . beneath] *interlined with a caret*
238.13	short stout recurved] *interlined with a caret*
238.16	many thick] *interlined with a caret*
238.20	only] *interlined with a caret*

238.23-24	in road] *interlined with a caret*
238.25-26	many flowered] *added*
239.3	which] *preceded by cancelled* with f
239.20	High] *inserted*
239.24	perhaps ... more] *interlined with a caret*
239.25	on right hand] *interlined above*
239.26	NB] *added in margin (see Emendation 239.26)*
239.28	Beck] beck
239.30	Hubbards] hubbards
239.35	surprised] *preceded by cancelled* to s
239.36	Walden a] Walden an
239.36	single] *interlined with a caret*
240.6	warm ... this] *added*
240.20-21	Skunk ... mowers] *added*
241.2	The ... much.] *interlined below*
241.15	prob.] *interlined above cancelled* may be
241.16-17	those ... brighter] *interlined with a caret*
241.17	Some] *interlined with a caret*
241.18-19	prob ... road] *interlined with a caret above cancelled* a day or so. XXX
241.26	up] *preceded by cancelled* near
241.28	puberula?] *? inserted*
242.5	& fences] &c
242.6	right side] *interlined with a caret*
242.8	Radula] radula
242.10	House] house
242.10-11	blue? bery] blue-bery
242.11-12	& narrow leaves] *interlined with a caret*
242.12	conspicuous calyx] *interlined with a caret*
242.13-14	some ... high.] *added*
242.18	day] *followed by cancelled* or s
242.26	At] at
242.34-35	which ... much–] *interlined with a caret*
243.3	20th] *interlined above cancelled* 24th
243.6	ever] *interlined with a caret and followed by cancelled* ?
243.23	longifolia] *interlined with a caret*
244.7	pale] *interlined above*
244.7-9	I ... weeds] *interlined above*
244.15	I] It
244.25	languid or stagnant] *interlined with a caret*
245.5	Beauty] beauty

245.10	yet] *interlined above cancelled* now
245.14	Almost] *added in margin*
245.15	clusters] *preceded by cancelled* of
245.16	sprinkled] spring
245.18	nearly] *interlined with a caret*
245.18	agreeable] *interlined with a caret above cancelled* rich
245.20	some dull . . . blue–] some dull *black– marked for transposition with* some blue–
245.23	in . . . kilns] *interlined below*
245.25	yesterday–] ~.
245.26-27	mingling . . . wind] *interlined with a caret*
245.28	day] *followed by cancelled* or 2
245.32	1st] *interlined with a caret*
246.7	(?)] *inserted*
246.19	Hill] hill
246.25	thistles–?] ? *inserted*
246.27	squirming] *interlined with a caret*
246.28	ap.] *interlined with a caret*
246.28	shell & all] *interlined with a caret*
246.35	clammy] *interlined with a caret*
246.35	cool] *interlined with a caret*
246.35	sub-acid] *hyphen inserted*
247.5	I . . . it] *interlined with a caret*
247.9	ap 4] ap *interlined with a caret*
247.10	Barn swallows still] *interlined below*
247.13	hirta] *interlined above cancelled* capitata
247.18	Pond.] *followed by cancelled* Sun
247.28-29	Chenopod. . . . open] *interlined above*
247.31-32	My . . . month.] *interlined*
248.5	Bath] bath
248.6	Wheelers–] ~.
248.10	20th] *preceded by cancelled* last
248.12-13	Though . . . lately] *interlined with a caret*
248.20	Quercifolia?] ? *inserted*
248.25	ap.] *interlined with a caret*
248.27	influence] influences
248.29	large] *interlined with a caret*
249.7	youth?] ~!
249.10	surrounsded . . . setting] surrounsded . . . shadow *marked for transposition with* while . . . setting

249.12-13	Save . . . blows] *interlined with a caret*
249.19	River] river
249.26-28	& . . . disappeared.] *interlined with a caret*
249.35-250.1	Day . . . ground] *interlined with a caret*
250.6	sun–] ~.
250.10	stand] *preceded by cancelled* appear
250.23	whether] to
250.35-36	Rain . . . objects] *interlined with a caret*
251.2-3	this . . . bloom] *interlined with a caret*
251.7	NB] *added in margin (see Emendation 251.7)*
251.11	Is . . . weather?] *added*
251.14	red–] ~.
251.22	patches of] *interlined with a caret*
252.9	Wheeler] wheeler
252.11	On] on
252.23	after . . . &] *interlined with a caret*
252.24	& the willows] *interlined with a caret*
253.4	Beckii] beckii
253.16	shade–] ~.
253.18	today–] ~.
253.31	trying to sleep] *interlined with a caret*
254.5	many] *interlined with a caret*
254.11	at noon] *interlined with a caret*
254.13-14	It . . . day] *interlined with a caret*
254.20	after dinner] *interlined with a caret*
254.24	raking] ~.
254.24-25	with . . . rows] *interlined with a caret*
254.26	placing . . . down] *interlined with a caret*
254.27	with rakes] *interlined with a caret*
255.10	maybe?] ? *inserted*
255.16	The rippled . . . &] *interlined with a caret*
255.20	&c] *interlined with a caret*
255.21	Flint's] flint's
255.21	Hill] hill
255.25	bounded] *preceded by cancelled* very evenly
255.36-256.1	a slight . . . them] *interlined with a caret*
256.13	cow] *preceded by cancelled* old
256.19-21	The . . . up.] *interlined with a caret*
256.22	green] Green
256.22-23	almost black] *interlined with a caret*
257.26	about] *interlined with a caret*
257.32	this imbricated slope] *interlined with a caret*

257.34	(less absorbed)] *interlined with a caret*
257.36-37	& . . . dust] *interlined with a caret*
258.2	prior] *inserted*
258.11	fording] *preceded by cancelled* crossing
258.14	bear oak] *interlined with a caret*
258.18	blackened] *interlined above cancelled* reddened
258.21	high blue berry] *interlined with a caret*
258.23-25	a . . . stung] *interlined with a caret*
258.26-27	so . . . finger] *interlined with a caret*
258.28	at] I
259.7	crisped &] *interlined with a caret*
259.8	Horn–] ~.
259.12	(feathers?)] *interlined with a caret*
259.23	Harp] harp
260.18	Nature's] nature's
260.23	continued] *interlined with a caret*
260.28	from] *interlined with a caret*
260.29-30	Poa . . . Hollow.] *interlined with a caret*
261.3	viewed] ed *inserted*
261.14	House] house
261.17	House] house
261.26	red] *interlined with a caret*
261.32	NB] *added in margin*
262.2	watermelon–X] *added*
262.16	early] *interlined with a caret*
262.22	on one . . . other] *interlined with a caret*
262.24-25	the . . . green] *interlined with a caret*
263.5	produce] *preceded by cancelled* make
263.14	a minute] *preceded by cancelled* nearly
263.16	Fawn-like] *interlined with a caret*
264.4	hairy–?] ? *added in margin*
264.8	russet] *preceded by cancelled* brown
264.9-11	For . . . today–] *added*
264.13	plaintively] *preceded by cancelled* as in sprin
264.21	No . . . time] *interlined*
264.30	hear . . . 14] *interlined with a caret*
264.33	hear one today] *interlined with a caret*
265.2-4	The . . . evening] *interlined*
265.6	Gold . . . partially] *interlined*
265.23	small] *interlined with a caret*
265.27-28	field (] ~–
266.2	Squirrels] squirrels

266.9	or checkered] *interlined with a caret*
266.17	fresh] flesh
266.22-23	& cool] *interlined with a caret*
266.24	Since] *preceded by cancelled* I not
266.27	this yesterday] *interlined with a caret*
266.30	on] &
266.33	to] &
267.4-5	paspalum ciliatifolium] *interlined with a caret*
267.9	&] –
267.10	Solely] *interlined with a caret*
267.11	both . . . night] *interlined with a caret*
267.21	I . . . meadow] *added*
267.23	I] The
267.36	strong–] ~.
268.9	Haden's] haden's
268.19	half strain] *interlined with a caret*
268.20	golden-robin] robin *inserted and followed by cancelled* golden–
268.20-21	Pig. woodpecker] *interlined with a caret*
268.26	nowadays] *preceded by cancelled* but
269.2	rivers] *preceded by cancelled* meadow
269.6	shorn] shorne
269.11	river] *interlined with a caret*
269.11	meadows] *followed by cancelled* have
269.14	Are] *followed by cancelled* not
269.14	(?)] *added*
269.31	Hill] hill
270.6-7	& nearer] *interlined with a caret*
270.10-11	half . . . off] *interlined with a caret*
270.14	most] *interlined above cancelled* many
270.21	white] *interlined with a caret*
270.25	Nagog] nagog
270.34	behind] *preceded by cancelled* of
270.35	finely] *interlined with a caret*
270.37	arranging] *preceded by cancelled* all
271.5	green] *interlined with a caret*
271.6-7	The . . . bell] *interlined with a caret*
271.10	off] *preceded by cancelled* or more
271.18	lemon?] ? *inserted*
271.22	3] *preceded by cancelled* i.e.
271.24	sweet] *interlined above cancelled* some cinnamon

271.25	browning &] *interlined with a caret*
271.27	through woods] *interlined with a caret*
271.32	8 or] *interlined with a caret*
271.32	rods] *preceded by cancelled* or a dozen
271.35	high blue-berry] high *interlined with a caret*
272.10	& a . . . pond] *interlined with a caret*
272.14	Westford] westford
272.17	rocky] *preceded by cancelled* hills
272.23	C–] ~.
272.31	a] *inserted*
272.34	that] *interlined above cancelled* a
272.35-36	with rusty patches] *interlined with a caret*
273.3	commonly . . . broad] *interlined with a caret*
273.4-5	Was . . . altissima?] *added*
273.10-11	& lichen do] *interlined with a caret*
273.11	last] *interlined with a caret*
273.15-16	the . . . &] *interlined with a caret*
273.25	X] XX
274.4	ball–] ~.
274.10	½′ wide] *interlined with a caret*
274.15	Road] road
274.15-18	Hypnum . . . characters] *interlined with a caret*
275.1	else] *interlined with a caret*
275.4	black] *interlined with a caret*
275.5	behind some weeds] *interlined with a caret*
275.6-7	Nuphar . . . remaining.] *added*
275.11	while] *followed by cancelled* from
275.12	June] june
275.15-16	various . . . land] *interlined with a caret*
275.20	season] *interlined above cancelled* time
275.28-29	No . . . now] *added*
276.10-11	That . . . grew.] *added*
276.10	Fern] fern
276.13-14	Best . . . July] *added*
276.21-24	Of . . . it.] *added and* hole *interlined with a caret*
277.13	Its] It
277.13	shell is] *interlined with a caret above cancelled* is
277.14	3 wide in front] *interlined with a caret*
277.15-16	with . . . not] *interlined with a caret*

277.18	concentrically . . . side–] *interlined with a caret and followed by cancelled* like the E insculpta
277.18-21	leaving . . . scale] *interlined with a caret*
277.24	above] *interlined with a caret*
277.24	Head] Heads
277.25	Head light] *interlined with a caret*
277.26	legs] *followed by cancelled* & tail
277.26	passing . . . white] *interlined with a caret*
277.29	keeping . . . out] *interlined with a caret*
277.34	a large] *interlined with a caret*
277.35	blotche] blotches
278.5	or shoves forward] *interlined with a caret*
278.12	semi] *interlined with a caret*
278.14-16	sometimes . . . leaves] *interlined with a caret*
278.18	Saw a snipe] *interlined above*
278.19	are covered . . . sun-dew] *interlined with a caret*
278.22	& larger] *interlined with a caret*
278.34	Holt] holt
279.1	NB] *added in margin*
279.8	& like a] *interlined with a caret*
279.16	early] *interlined with a caret*
279.24-25	– The . . . mud.] *interlined below*
279.25	Green Bittern] green bittern
279.33	from the R.R.] *interlined with a caret*
279.36	darker] –
280.15	red] *added in margin*
280.21	wilted–] ~.
280.27	at . . . cutting] *interlined with a caret*
280.30	and . . . dry] *interlined with a caret*
280.34	evenly] *interlined with a caret*
281.10	had . . . set] *interlined with a caret above cancelled* were
281.10	by the engine] by *preceded by cancelled* from
281.13	some] *interlined with a caret*
*281.13-15	A . . . swamp] *added*
281.16	Pond] pond
281.19-21	There . . . *mt*] *interlined above*
281.23	There] *preceded by cancelled* What
283.2	I . . . early.] *added*
283.4	red wing] *interlined with a caret*

283.16	generally] *interlined with a caret*
283.17	if] *inserted*
283.17	remember] *preceded by cancelled* think
283.24	Bath] bath
283.27	Island] island
283.29-30	for . . . lichen] *interlined with a caret*
283.31	slender pointed] pointed *interlined with a caret*
284.5	Rock] ~)
284.21	4] 3 *or* 2
284.22	nowa-d-ays] nowadays
284.29-30	lying . . . downward] *interlined with a caret*
284.35	for] *preceded by cancelled* was *and followed by cancelled* 2 or
284.36	lacerated] *interlined with a caret*
285.5	weighed] *preceded by cancelled* measured
285.8	darkest . . . head] *interlined with a caret*
285.13	a line of] *interlined with a caret*
285.17-18	those . . . skin] *interlined with a caret*
285.19-20	I . . . tail.] *added vertically in margin (see Emendation 285.19-20)*
285.22-24	It . . . part] *interlined with a caret*
286.6	all] *preceded by cancelled* them
286.7-9	Assabet . . . top] *added*
286.13-14	They . . . shore] *interlined*
286.15	sharp] *interlined with a caret*
286.19	bluish] *interlined with a caret*
286.20	½ mile off] *interlined with a caret*
286.27	Bath] bath
287.3	A.] *inserted*
287.16	Wood] wood
287.17	a flexuous] a *added*
287.17	small] *interlined with a caret*
287.34	Head] head
288.5-6	A . . . leaves] *added*
288.9	Beck-Stows] Beck-stows
288.20	Mill Brook] mill brook
288.23	5 or] 5 *preceded by cancelled* 4 or
288.23	4 or 5] *interlined above cancelled* 3 or 4
*288.28-29	Was . . . it] *interlined*
288.31	bet.] *preceded by cancelled* midway
289.1	formed] *interlined with a caret*
289.10	muddy] *interlined with a caret*

289.26-27	some . . . heron] *interlined with a caret*
289.28	heron] *interlined above cancelled* former
289.28	about] *interlined above cancelled* nearly
289.29	transfix] *preceded by cancelled* gobble
289.36-290.1	Here . . . feed.] *interlined with a caret*
290.2	small] *interlined with a caret*
290.5	small] *preceded by cancelled* the
290.6	more beautifully spotted] *interlined with a caret*
290.10	i.e.] *inserted*
290.21	arguta] *followed by cancelled* &
290.21	or] ?
290.21	& altissima] *interlined with a caret*
290.26	& bitterns] *interlined above*
290.35	a rod] *preceded by cancelled* of a pecu
291.4	in] In
291.5-6	where . . . through] *interlined with a caret*
291.6	through–] ~.
291.9	half . . . wide] *interlined with a caret*
291.10	A.] a.
291.16	now] ~,
291.16	high] *inserted*
292.3	NB] *added in margin*
292.6	cranberry . . . there] *interlined with a caret*
292.9	flat . . . sphagnum] *interlined with a caret*
292.11	strongly] *interlined with a caret*
292.16	–several] *preceded by cancelled* now
292.20	making . . . say.] *interlined with a caret*
292.20-21	The . . . cinder.] *interlined*
292.24-25	perfectly dry] *interlined with a caret*
292.25	beginning to] *interlined with a caret*
292.25	go] going
292.36-293.1	& I . . . off–] *interlined with a caret*
293.6	opens] *interlined with a caret*
293.8	of both kinds] *interlined with a caret*
293.9	beg. to] *interlined with a caret*
293.11	with . . . 303-304] *interlined with a caret (see Emendation 293.11)*
293.26	more or less] *interlined with a caret*
293.29-31	At . . . white-oak] *interlined with a caret*
293.31	suggests] suggest
*293.35	Cliffs–] *followed by cancelled* at Lee's
*294.2-3	The . . . there] *interlined below*

294.7 At] at
294.12-13 to some extent] *interlined with a caret*
294.17 Aug 25] *added*
294.18 11] *preceded by cancelled* 11
294.25 Tortoise] *cancelled* Aug 25th *interlined above*
295.1 not purple] *interlined with a caret*
295.13 Pm] *interlined with a caret*
295.21 woods-] ~.
296.4 too . . . grass] *interlined with a caret*
296.8 me] *followed by cancelled* of
296.14 –august] *preceded by cancelled* autumn
296.21-22 The . . . touch] *interlined with a caret*
296.23 shell & all] *interlined with a caret*
296.24-25 & . . . reduced.] *interlined below*
296.25 very deep] *interlined with a caret*
296.29 also its great] *interlined with a caret above cancelled* its
296.29 held in] *interlined with a caret above cancelled* covered *and* held *followed by cancelled* drawn
296.30 puts] *preceded by cancelled* stretch
296.31 though] *preceded by cancelled* almost
297.5 had] &
297.5 the] this
298.1 inches] *interlined with a caret*
298.3 & . . . also] *interlined with a caret*
298.9 soft] *interlined with a caret*
298.10 (?)] *interlined with a caret*
298.13 ago–] *followed by cancelled* when
298.26 green] *preceded by cancelled* large
298.32-33 Hear . . . York–] *added and* Hear *altered from* hear *and preceded by cancelled* I
299.8 red–] ~.
299.12 or pale tawny] *interlined with a caret*
299.13 & hard] *interlined with a caret*
299.16-17 & has . . . acid.] *interlined with a caret*
299.18 v. p 304] *interlined with a caret (see Emendation 299.18)*
299.33 Andromeda] *interlined with a caret*
300.12 They] they
300.27 how] *preceded by cancelled* what
301.17 relieved,] *interlined with a caret*

302.16-17	Improve ... meadows] *added*
302.31	Great] great
302.32	coarse] *interlined with a caret*
303.2-4	It ... ground] *interlined with a caret*
303.5	dark colored] *interlined with a caret*
303.18	hundreds of them] *interlined with a caret*
303.19	all ... die] *interlined with a caret*
303.19-20	Several ... water.] *interlined below*
303.26	perhaps] *interlined with a caret*
303.26-27	in ... meadow] *interlined above cancelled* at least
303.28	or tilted] *interlined with a caret*
303.29-30	& here ... it.] *interlined (see Emendation 303.29-30)*
303.31-32	with ... trenches] *interlined with a caret*
303.32	as well] *preceded by cancelled* This
304.7	high] *interlined with a caret*
304.14	cup] *preceded by cancelled* side
304.18	and] *preceded by cancelled* as
304.24	galls–] ~.
304.28	Moles ... meadows] *added*
305.5	yesterday] *preceded by cancelled* day before
305.5	what was] *interlined with a caret*
305.8-9	rooting ... bottom] *interlined with a caret*
305.21	but] *preceded by cancelled* then
305.30	& often pointed] *interlined with a caret*
306.5	cooler] cooled
306.5	a] an
306.5	steady] *interlined with a caret*
306.11	fire] *interlined with a caret*
306.12	the fire] *interlined with a caret*
306.17	The] *preceded by cancelled* Saw a po
306.31	black] *interlined with a caret*
306.31	Front] *interlined above cancelled* behind
306.33	directly] *interlined with a caret*
306.34	&] *interlined*
306.35	Nature] nature
307.1	is] *interlined with a caret*
307.4	genial] *preceded by cancelled* war
307.7	N.B] *added in margin (see Emendation 307.7)*
307.9	still ... pretty] *interlined above*

307.11	rest] *preceded by cancelled* sit
307.12-13	as . . . impulse] *interlined with a caret*
307.21	kernel from the] *interlined with a caret*
307.21	all] *preceded by cancelled* from
307.33	at] *preceded by cancelled* with
308.5	in flower] *interlined with a caret*
308.9	Kali] kali
308.16	on the elms.] *added*
308.27	Perhaps] perhaps
308.32	of them] *interlined with a caret*
308.33	they . . . open.] *added*
308.35	by] *interlined above cancelled* near
309.3	balls] *interlined with a caret*
309.8	young] *interlined with a caret*
309.15	ammannia] *preceded by cancelled* &c
309.15	walk] *followed by cancelled* quite
309.19-20	with red stems] *interlined with a caret*
309.21	small] *interlined with a caret*
309.21	scarlet] *preceded by cancelled* red
309.24	quite] *interlined above cancelled* very
309.25	or bog wood?] *interlined with a caret*
309.34	reddened] *interlined with a caret*
310.6	Some] *interlined above cancelled* The
310.9	a] *preceded by cancelled* the
310.23-24	near him] *interlined with a caret*
310.28-29	i.e. . . . reserve] *interlined with a caret*
310.32	dry] *preceded by cancelled* dry
310.33	loosened] loosed
310.35	Said] *interlined with a caret*
311.2	Pond] pond
311.5	It] *preceded by cancelled* as a
311.7-9	But . . . heard.] *written vertically in margin with an arrow for position*
311.10	& strongly] *interlined with a caret*
311.13-14	Is . . . earth?] *added*
311.22	&] *added in margin*
311.31	like . . . veil] *interlined with a caret*
311.33-34	lighter or darker] *interlined with a caret*
311.35	river] *preceded by cancelled* tow
312.12	mizzling] *preceded by cancelled* &
312.17	clear] *preceded by cancelled* at
312.20-21	Heard . . . trees] *added*

312.23	but . . . lively] *interlined with a caret*
312.24-25	and is considerably] *interlined with a caret and followed by interlined and cancelled* about
312.25	longer] *preceded by cancelled* as
312.25	than] *added in margin*
312.25	& slender] *interlined with a caret*
312.27-28	which . . . old.] *interlined with a caret (see Textual Note 312.28)*
312.28	V. p 313] *added (see Emendation 312.28)*
312.31	quite . . . scene] *interlined with a caret*
313.12	wht] *interlined with a caret*
313.16	eaten?] ? *inserted*
313.17	wood?] ? *inserted*
313.20	quacking] quack
313.26-27	thought . . . dying &] *interlined with a caret*
313.27	yesterday] *preceded by cancelled* last
313.31	holding . . . one.] *interlined above*
313.33	of a] *preceded by cancelled* every
314.7	cools . . . ponds] *interlined with a caret*
314.12	distinctly] *interlined with a caret*
314.23	loose] *added in margin*
314.24	not] *interlined with a caret*
314.32-33	Some . . . deep!] *interlined with a caret*
315.1	especially] *interlined with a caret*
315.1	Champlain] champlain
315.3	smart] *interlined above cancelled* ache

End-of-Line Hyphenation

THIS table lists all compound or possibly compound words that are hyphenated at end-line in manuscript and must therefore be resolved as hyphenated or closed. The table derives from a master list of all end-line hyphens in manuscript. The editor identifies as a "compound" any word containing two or more words of standard English: *keystone, highways, child-like*. Words formed with prefixes and suffixes, such as *unguarded* or *forward*, and words inadvertently resembling compounds, such as *seasons* or *handsome*, are excluded. For a discussion of the rationale affecting resolutions of compound words as hyphenated or closed, see Textual Introduction, pp. 419-420.

Numbers at the left margin key the entry to page and line. Because the Princeton Edition text is printed with a ragged right margin, it introduces no nonauthorial end-of-line hyphens. Subsequent reprintings or quotations of the text should therefore consider its hyphenation to be authorial.

MS Volume XVII

8.3	swamp-pink	43.12	watercourses
13.4	close-hugging	51.19	blackbirds
15.15	satin-like	53.30	red-wings
15.26	wind-hairs	54.32	marsh-hawks
19.36	apple-trees	55.5	meadowside
20.30	sandstone	55.29	well-meaning
21.4	midsummer	61.18	tree-sparrows
23.32	nuthatch	63.14	Pine-warbler
26.20	checkerberries	67.10	fox-col.
31.15	checkerberrying	67.22	steel-colored
31.16	Skunk-cabbage	69.30	fourpence
33.15	well-known	69.32	blackbird
38.32	song-sparrows	70.2	hedge-row
40.25	song-sparrow	71.8	blue-bird

73.30	black-striped	202.30	threadlike
73.35	honey-bees	202.36	lowgrounds
76.8	mouse-ears	207.20	archAngelica
79.6	skunk-cabbage	208.35	underwood
89.2	threadlike	209.16	upper-parts
93.28	amber-like	211.37	may-flower
101.15	barn-swallows	213.27	woodchuck
101.24	May-day	214.15	barn-swallows
103.9	leaf-buds	215.20	poke-logan
109.26	chip-bird	216.3	front-rank
113.7	tree-toad	217.9	woodcocks
114.30	shrub-oak	218.22	sunrising
115.10	thundershower	219.18	sproutland
115.15	wood-thrush	221.2	Clam-shell
118.24	yellow-bird	222.34	clam-shell
119.5	evergreen	224.10	blue-huckleberry
121.2	witch-hazel	225.8	huckleberry
121.8	Swamp-pink	226.18	Goldfinch
121.28	evergreens	226.20	chee-wink
124.1	worm-skins	227.13	Clam-shell
124.15	Clam-shell	231.27	golden-rods
133.24	shrub-oaks	236.9	midsummer
135.30	yellow-green	240.9	heart-leaf
136.21	chokeberry's	243.3	dark-blue
144.35	wood-pewee	244.7	lake-color
156.7	deep-sproutland	247.8	Bunchberries
157.3	broom-rape	248.17	blackberries
157.9	red-eye	249.2	Fair-Haven
161.10	blackberry	251.10	turnpike
162.35	mouse-ear	252.30	midsummer
170.7	sproutland	253.9	late-roses
175.10	sproutlands	255.19	swamp-white
176.7	Cliff-Hill	256.13	huckleberry
179.5	crow-blackbird's	257.31	golden-rods
180.3	choke-cherries	261.8	flower-like
180.34	shad-bush	263.16	wood-god
182.21	cherry-birds	263.36	blackberries
182.25	half-turned	264.1	huckleberries
183.6	yellow-throated	269.29	dog-day
183.9	flower-like	274.35	Hornwort
195.31	white-water	278.14	heart-leaf
197.17	Summer-yel	283.6	nuthatch
201.21	rose-pink	286.19	dog-days

287.10	woodchuck	299.6	turnpike
287.26	throughout	305.6	Turnpike
287.29	elsewhere	309.23	skunk-cabbage
288.9	Beck-Stows		

Later Revisions

Tʜɪs table is a complete list of Thoreau's substantive revisions and additions to his Journal. When a later revision has been further revised, only the final version is reported. The table does not include use marks drawn through passages, or reference marks occurring in the margins of the manuscript volume. Numbers at the left margin key the entry to page and line; if the number is marked with an asterisk, the later revision is discussed in a Textual Note. Revisions are in pencil unless otherwise noted.

MS Volume XVII

10.9   for . . . wit: *cancelled*

13.25   on wings–: were they goldfinches? *interlined above*

16.35   forms.: How will it look behind a tight fence? *interlined with a caret*

17.2   inward: looking *interlined with a caret*

22.9   running.: Sportsmen speak of the deer's "white flag" *interlined to the right of the drawing*

25.18-20   reminding . . . not: This as if you were approaching the vitals of the globe for this sandy overflow is something such a foliaceous mass as the *interlined*

25.32-33   The . . . labor-lapsus?): *revised in pencil and ink to read* The lobe principle a lobe of lung brain or ear (labor-lapsus Λειβω Λ [ ] λοβος labium?) lip lap flap globe lobus globus

26.8   with law: *revised to read* with this law

26.10-12   including . . . clay-color: *revised to read* including the different iron colors–brown–grey–yellowish reddish–also clay-color

26.36   now–:   v bottom *interlined with a caret*

34.24   Peter: ? *added in margin*

35.14   rain–rain: Misty *added in margin with a caret*

41.33   field: *cancelled and* tree *interlined above*

42.18   bottom: *followed by* ?

43.27   be summer ducks.: were they not the female of the others? *interlined above*

43.27   ducks.:   *revised to read* ducks??

43.29-30   Golden   ...   Whistlers: Probably   both   shell drakes– V. Ap 6 & 7 '55 *interlined above*

44.34   years?:   guess not *added*

46.3   shiners: minnows? *interlined above*

48.10   are.:   *revised to read* are!

48.25   Lily: *cancelled and* Willow? *interlined with a caret*

*48.31-32   either ... woodcock: *revised in ink and pencil to read* prob. a snipe

52.34   liverwort: marchantia? *interlined above*

57.11   march: ? *added in margin in ink*

60.18   week: v 16th *interlined in ink with a caret*

60.34   Division: v. 16th *interlined in ink with a caret*

64.8   18:   *followed by* v 23d *in ink*

64.11-12   low ... Heard: may it have been a young male harrier? *interlined above*

64.29   fungus: auricularia *interlined with a caret*

66.12   bay ... the: *revised to read* (bay ... the)

67.14   than native shrub: must be blossom buds. *interlined above*

69.5   crowned at: *revised in ink and pencil to read* crowned? v Ap 26   prob hermit T. at

69.15   warbler–:   v Ap. 26 *interlined above in ink*

69.20-21   b (?):   v Ap 26 *interlined above in ink*

72.3   crosswise: Veronica *interlined with a caret*

74.16-18   [they ... lilack: *revised to read* [they are blossom buds] most forward–except the spiraea–honeysuckle vine the earliest gooseberry in woods & garden thimbleberry & the lilack & Missouri currant

74.18-19   the chokeberry ... blossom?:   *cancelled*

75.4   bay-wing: *cancelled and* one of the seringos *interlined above*

76.3   Concord.:   Excepting the Spiraea & perhaps the honeysuckle vine the thimble berry in some places equally forward *interlined in pencil with a caret and written over in ink*

80.25   *bill* ... not: certainly Mergansers prob. sheldrakes *interlined above*

81.22   laevigata?:   v May 1st *interlined with a caret*

82.13   grackles?:   v May 9th *added in ink*

82.17   cones–Its little: v. May 1st *interlined above in ink*

82.35   plant: racemed andromeda *interlined with a caret*

83.35   *golden*:   *cancelled and* Ruby *interlined above*

84.1-2   or . . . flycatcher.:   *cancelled*

84.21   Golden: *cancelled and* Ruby *interlined above*

85.25   flowering: sensitive *interlined above*

89.12   se: v May 1st *interlined with a caret*

90.11-17   I . . . it.:   1 *and* 2 *written in margin to mark transposition of* It is remarkable . . . known it. *with* I . . . unsteadily.

90.12   &:   a *interlined with a caret*

90.15   requires: *revised to read* appears to require

90.16   it: *revised to read* the water

92.35   24th: rare yet *added*

93.8   Sweet Fern   29th: *cancelled and* Not yet at all *added*

94.20   earliest: wild & some willows *interlined with a caret and* wild *written in ink over pencil*

94.21   gooseberry: in garden & swamp *interlined with a caret*

97.7   Low blackberry–:   Quince? *interlined below*

97.23   goldfinch: yes & for several days after *interlined with a caret*

98.27   love: to sing *interlined with a caret*

105.19-28   Saw . . . black.:   Could mine have been the F. Fuscus & so small? *written vertically in margin*

105.22   hawk: no: for that is barred with white *interlined with a caret*

105.28   black . . . XXX.:   Could the Boston Pig. hawk have been barred with black– *interlined above*

113.35   young: *cancelled*

114.5   pitch . . . now: Canada plum I think here *interlined above*

114.6   Cornus: Norway? *interlined above*

116.2   leaves: heart shaped *interlined with a caret*

116.4-5   Stellaria . . . leaf–:   May 27th the green shoots are covered with bristly prickles but I can find no flowers. Is it the same with that by Maple swamp in Hub's Close with young fruit? *interlined and* shoots *interlined with a caret*

117.13   young in: V list p 220 *interlined above*

118.20   night.:   Fever Root up 4 or 5 inches *added*

120.15   troublesome.:   *Young* P. Grandidentatas just opening–(Panicled andromeda leaf to-morrow Not for 3 or 4 days generally) *added and* leaf *interlined with a caret*

121.3   and red azalea: *cancelled*

121.11   all: wild *interlined with a caret*

121.12   currant?:   they do not show so soon *added*

122.25   black–then: see forward *interlined below*

130.26   green: This to be said the 12 or 13 or 14 ult *interlined with a caret*

131.35   mistiness–:   unlike the dry blue haze of dog days *interlined with a caret and* dry *interlined with a caret*

133.23   tomorrow: V 22nd *interlined with a caret*

137.28   blowing: ing *cancelled*

143.14   of the: *preceded by drawing, possibly of a raceme*

143.18   triflorus?:   yes *interlined above*

145.35   sides.:   V scrapbook *interlined with a caret*

149.29   There . . . no: With Correction in pencil from 55– 6–7–& 8– *interlined above*

149.30   leaf: v p 172 *interlined above*

149.33-154.12   The . . . Potters.:   *revised in ink and pencil to read*

> The earliest Gooseberry in garden & swamp
> 17–55 Ap 20
>
> ? –Elder longest shoots of any *in some* places (May 5)
>   Ap 6–58½ inch before other shrub or tree at Lees
>   Raspberry in swamps
>   Some low blackberry on rocks 18–55
>   Thimble berry (perhaps in favorable places only–)
>   even in swamp by Ap 23d–59–at <u>Lees</u> Ap. 11–58
>   Wild red cherry in some places–some the 20th 55 not
>   generally till May 3d
>   Meadow sweet 25–59 2 or 3 days
>   Lilac with Common Currant on 23–55
>
> ? Red currant–but slow to advance–observed only ours
>   which is late?
>
> ? 2nd Gooseberry v top n.p.–This & Red currant 23–55
>   S. humilis (?) 25–55
>   Salix alba Ap. 27–24–55
>
> ?? Black currant not seen–Ap 21–55–or a little before
>   red.
>   Small dark native willow blossoming (?) & leafing
>   S petiolum? 25?–55
>
> ?? Early Willow 2 Colored? not seen v forward
> ?? Muhlenbergs (?)–v forward "
>   Young Black Cherry–25–55
>   Some birch sprouts as much as any shrub or tree
>   Ap 29–56
>   Choke cherry shoots
>   Viburnum lentago ⎫ not carefully distinguished
>   ⎪ between–Both 25–55
> ?   "   Nudum ⎭ ==(May 4–56

Diervilla–advances fast (25–55 or with Viburnum
Barberry in favorable places
Some young apples "   "
Young Alders–slow to advance–*both kinds*–
Sweet briar–with early rose–say Ap. 22 55
Early Rose–At <u>Lees</u> ap 11–56–26–55
? – –Moss Rose not seen
Sweet fern–slow to advance–May 4–55
Mt ash May 5 larger leaves than any tree & 1st to show
    green at a distance May 6–56
Cultivated cherry
Pyrus arbutifolia 25–55
?   –Late pyrus not seen say 27–55
Yew when?
Horse chestnut May 6–56–30–55
Privet–30–55
Hazel May 5
?   Beaked hazel–not distinguished
Early–large apples May 7–58 earliest beg. to leaf & show
    green veils–
Late goose berry in garden
?   Pears not seen–2d or *some* before May 2d–55
Wild red cherry generally–or let it go with the earliest.
    20th–55 but not generally till May 3d
?   Dwarf or Sand Cherry–May 3d–55 *generally*
Hard-hack–May 3d–*say* May 1st one place
??   –Clematis– – –shoots 5 or 6 inches long May 16
Low blackberry
??   R. Triflorus 8 inches high May 22nd–May 7–55 2 inch
    long say after raspberry or 23d
?   Quince–May 2–55
??   May flower not seen
Young red maples–May 4–55–hardly before 9th–55
    later than sugar young–
??   Fever root–4 or 5 inches high May 12
Creeping juniper comes forward like fir balsam
Larch–open slowly   makes a show May 12 say
    ap. 28–55
V. Pennsylvanicum–May 2d–55
All kinds of *young* maples & *some* large May 4–55
Amelanchier botryapium–fast (May 2d 55 *leafed*
A small native willow May 2d–55 (S. Pet.?) or 1st
High blackberry in some places May 4–55

?   Semper virens– –not seen

Young rock-maple.–Perhaps some May 3–55 earlier than large white May 6–55 more conspic– than any maples–

Flowering rasp berry when?

?   Large White   ″   May 11–56–May 6–56 at least
                                 4–56 not quite

Alders generally v forward

Ostrya–May 5–55

Amlelanchier oblongifolia–May 4–55

Early trembles suddenly–Young May 1st–55 q.v.
2d May 4–56–1 inch over big as ninepence May 9–57 May 5–58

Balm of Gilead–May 7–55

Sweet fern May 4–55

Early thorns–May 4–55

?   –Late   ″   not seen

Yel. birch– –Young say–8th–55

?   –Cockspur–thorn not seen–with early thorns on May 4 55

Peach May 5–55

Canoe-birch–shoots–¾ inch over May 11–55–but not trees

S. humilis say 6–55

White   –shoots some W. birch May 4–55

?   Black young (large not on 12)

Panicled andromeda May 7–55 & then slow

?   Canada Plum–May 10–55

Domestic ″ – ″ ″ ″

Pitch pine–May 28–55 2 to 5 inch long

??   Bear berry not seen

?   Norway pine ″   ″

White pine–May 28–2 to 5 inch long

Young hornbeam

Cornus alternifolia–May 9–55

?   –Round leaved seen late–May 11–55 XXX

Panicled– –Cornel– –May 9–55

Silky–cornel–May 13–55

Large red maple May 9–55–just begun *one*

C. Florida say just after sericea in 55

Sweetgale May 11–May 12–55

S. discolor (at bridge S side not N sides) May 7–55

Red oak May 11–55 (before black o & hickory near

Bass–sudden–May 8–55 (some shoots 7th)–large
  begins 13–1 inch 16th
Large Rock maple not yet May 11–55 later than large
  white & somewhat than large red
Young chestnuts & lower limbs–full leafing of large not
  seen
Old hornbeam
?? –Maple-leaved arrowwood not seen till late
Arrow-wood–May 7–55
Night-shade May 26–55 8 inches–say 12
Butter-nut–May 12–55
Late Rose May 25–55 2 inches say 11
High blueberry
Dwarf Cornel when?
Rhus toxicodendron–May 7 55 under rocks
?   var. radicans seen late–May 12–55 or say *11th*
Sweetbriar generally–earliest not seen
? Swamp rose seen late
?? Beech not seen–larger than hickory May 15–56– –some
  10th–55–more back than chestnut prob. about
  16 (?)–(buds the 4th 55)
White ash May 12–14–55
Large yel– birches *not yet* generally May 13–55
Fir balsam
? Fever-bush seen rather late <u>not</u> on May 12–55–(say just
  before black willow–
?? Wood-bine not seen
Slip elm before common say May 11–55
Black-shrub oak–May 14 55
Elm–young–*Some Young* May 11–55 & only young 12th
? Slippery not seen
Lombardy poplar ⎞
Silvery abele   ⎠ May 12–55
Great red maples May 13
clustered Andromeda 13
young P. grandidentatas (large 3 or 4 days later?)
Black oak–May 15–55
Scarlet O. May 15–55
Black willow–16–55
Black ash–*say* with late willow in 55
?? Sage   ″ seen late May 22 10 days or more say <u>12th</u> 55
? Chinquapin oak–May 14–55
vac. oxycoccus when?
?? Chestnut   ″ not seen

Cassandra–15–55

V. vacillans May 14–55–how long?

Celtis–1 inch on 18–55

?? Cranberry–¾ inch May 21–55

Clethra May 14–55

Waxwork May 14–55

Locust 14th–15–55

Nemopanthes–before tupelo

? Witch hazel in our garden

Swamp White oak–slow–prob 15–55

Arbutus May 14–55 (some new shoots)

White swamp pink–55 long before lambkill

Button wood–*some* 15–55

Panicled andromeda (15–55 in some places not generally, several days later.

Pignut hickory–make a show suddenly some May 10–55–14 opening leaves 55

? Mockernut ″

?? Black walnut

Young whit oak (old 15 slow

Buckthorn when?

Prinos verticillatus 15–May 14–55

? Single berry P. seen late

Huckleberries black some May 14–55

? – – &c

NB –Trees generally!! May 16th–55

Grape–16–55

Smilax say 14–55

?? Pinweeds seen late 6 or more inches high the large May 22nd

?? Cistus as early at least

Mulberry May 16

?? Carrion flower 4 or 5 feet long the 31st of May

Black Spruce white var.–slow 26–55

Sassafras–slow

Lambkill–say May 19–55

?? –Mt Laurel–not seen early–ap May 26–55

?? Andromeda polifolia seen late–3 or 4 inch June 13–58

Kalmia glauca say just after Lambkill

? Rhodora ″

Tupelo say 18th 55 (before Button bush)

Poison dogwood–(3 or 4 inches the 30th 55

??? Jersey tea

Vac. dumosum when?

Azalea nudiflora 17–

Button bush–but does not show being few buds. *some* May 21–55–26th generally begins

Fir balsam begins May 18–55 (or say with flower)

some mt sumac 1 inch May 27–55 prob. after button bush)

Beach Plum 19 *scarcely* makes any show the 24th no more than the button bush 24–55–several days in some places those which bloom at least

? Red cedar ⎞
  White " ⎟ growth not obvious–& difference in
  arbor vitae ⎠ trees–not sure of date

Smooth Sumac–when?

Partridge berry when

Deciduous trees beg. to invest evergreens May 22–55

Young hemlocks 20 old 21 (old *say* June 1st–55

oaks a little more than in gray–May 22–55

checkerberry 20 shoots just visible 26–55–1 inch high

Linnaea–growing June 1st (say 28)–(one inch the 4th)

?) *Mt* sumach 22 (The 31st May it is much more forward than the button bush at Cliffs–& perhaps started first)

? Black spruce 24 hardly yet at Potters. June 2nd 55

Ledum decidedly–30th–58 dark var– 3 or 4 inch June 13–58

? Bay-berry but slightly expanded May 30–55

Andromeda racemosa slightly <u>below</u> (dead top) June 8–56

*152.11 ?? Clethra seen late: *cancelled; followed by* v forward

*153.7 ? Large ... observed.: *cancelled; followed by* Greater part on common May 15–55

158.9 beginning: ? *added in margin in ink*

158.12-15 tree ... finch: *revised in pencil and ink to read* tree sparrows have all gone by–long ago NB also the purple finch

158.12-158.31 The ... that.: *marked for transposition with* Larch ... &c *at 158.33-159.1*

159.1 Pontederias: &c *added in margin*

159.15 long.: Prob sium *interlined with a caret*

160.1 radical heart: Nuphar Kalmiana *interlined above*

164.5 fool ... coat.: *revised to read* fool made conspicuous by a painted coat.

164.20   profession: Time somebody worked *interlined above*

164.21   governor–:   At last the Governor is heard from & what a governor was there? at a congratulatory dinner– *added and* & what a governor was there? *interlined with a caret*

164.22   I . . . speeches: We don't complain of what a coward does.–but of what he does not do *interlined above*

164.26   doubt.:   It takes all the legal heads & they they cannot settle it *interlined with a caret*

164.29   God.:   not Edward G. God–but simple God *interlined with a caret*

164.34   sin: is feeble *interlined with a caret*

165.6   who: when moral right is concerned *interlined in ink with a caret*

165.7   Devil.:   Witness the President of the U.S. *added in ink*

165.8   Massachusetts: Massa-chooses-it– *interlined in ink with a caret*

165.10-16   What . . . here.:   *vertical line drawn in margin from* What *to* here.

165.10   *She's*:   *Freedom* & *interlined in ink with a caret*

165.12   will: one day *interlined in ink with a caret*

165.12   offer: me *interlined in ink with a caret*

165.13   made . . . Court-House: *revised in ink and pencil to read* made of California gold which she has stolen in the form of a Court-House

165.16   Men are: *revised in ink to read* Men profess to be

165.17   The: majority of the *interlined in ink with a caret*

166.1   together: I will not accept life in America or on this planet on such terms *interlined with a caret*

166.4   me.:   –The US gv never performed an act of pure justice in its life– *added*

168.26-32   The . . . The: *vertical line drawn in margin from* The *to* The

173.22   locust.:   was it not a cricket? *interlined with a caret*

180.32   rust: the same on thimbleberry the 13th June *interlined in ink with a caret*

181.5   note?:   no *interlined with a caret*

181.19   tomorrow: V 14th *interlined in ink with a caret*

182.7   than: even *added in margin*

184.32-33   their . . . impertinence.:   And The one whom

truth requires at present to plead guilty is perchance the one who is preeminently innocent– *interlined*

185.16   slaveholder: this particular Gubernator now at the wheel whom I never saw *interlined with a caret*

185.17   slave: But the worst I shall say of the governor is that he was no better than the majority of his constituents–he was not equal to the occasion *interlined in ink with a caret*

185.17   not: *revised in ink to read* Not

185.20   past: Have they been trained merely to rob mex-ico & carry back fugitive slaves to their masters *interlined with a caret*

185.22-23   The . . . men: The citizens of Mass. not being men of principle–will it appears send back this fugitive slave– i.e. to call the same thing by another name will crucify christ just so long as the majority decide that it shall be done. V 17th *interlined in ink*

185.26   sits still: *marked for transposition in ink*

185.28   handle.:   He believes that all the music resides in the handle–& the crowd toss him their coppers just the same as before. *added in ink*

188.7   ter te,:   V *interlined with a caret*

188.9   Warbler?:   V June 17th *interlined with a caret*

192.21   mosquitoes: Russell makes them many other creatures also *interlined with a caret*

193.10   hard.:   These were stink pots & only a few feet from waters edge *added*

196.9   midst.:   It is the resurrection of virtue. *interlined with a caret*

198.12-32   vast . . . located: I had never respected this government–near *which* I lived but I had foolishly thought that I might manage to live here–minding my private affairs– & forget it. It is the discovery of what kind of men your coun-trymen are– *written vertically in margin in ink and pencil and* near *which* I lived *interlined with a caret*

198.12   loss.:   as last it occurs to him that what he has lost is a country   I did not know at first what aild me *interlined with a caret*

198.19   before: perchance *interlined with a caret*

198.24   imagined–:   in the Infernal regions *interlined with a caret*

198.26   our . . . it.:   *revised to read* we the people–it occurs to me to visit it out of mere curiosity.

198.27   that feed: *cancelled and* which minister to *interlined above*

198.32-33   is one . . . angels: *enclosed in parentheses and cancelled*

198.34-35   do . . . eyes.:   *cancelled*

198.35   eyes.:   Are you not suddenly disposed to sell at a great sacrifice *interlined in ink and pencil with a caret*

199.1   just & proper: *cancelled and* lawful *interlined above*

199.3-4   to some extent: *enclosed in parentheses*

199.6   behind: What business had it to remind me of Court Street? *interlined with a caret*

199.7   which: even *interlined with a caret*

199.10   news–:   I am surprised *interlined with a caret*

199.18-19   under these circumstances: *enclosed in parentheses and* now *interlined above*

199.22-23   It . . . ancestors–:   *cancelled*

199.25   If: It is not an era of repose. *interlined in ink with a caret and marked for transposition with* We . . . egg– *at 199.23-25*

199.35   it–:   I would have such a man wear his bishops hat & his clerical bib & tucker that we may know him– *added*

200.16   Gronovii–:   think not v. forward July 1st *interlined with a caret*

200.17   Peak: ? *added in margin in ink*

200.30   state–:   I am calculating how many miscreants each honest man can dispose of *interlined with a caret*

201.4   sagittatum: yes *interlined in ink with a caret*

201.5   (or *arifolium*:   *cancelled in ink and* v Aug 19. *interlined in ink with a caret*

203.17   peculiarly: rippled *interlined with a caret*

204.7   law.:   who discovers it to be according to their constitution to interfere–   They at least cut off the ears of the police   the others pocket the 30 pieces of silver *added at bottom of MS page and vertically in margin*

204.8   could: better *interlined with a caret*

206.16   men.:   The fate of The country does not depend on how you vote at the polls but on how you vote every where though you should be removed to solitary confinement on what manner of man you are *added*

206.27-28   Are . . . governors: The slave holders know–& I know *interlined above in ink*

206.30   Co?:   The politicians do now & always will in-
stinctively stand aloof from such *added*

207.36   precedents.:   office is indeed another President.
interlined above

209.18   warbler?:   Probably is   v July 7 '55 *added*

213.23   reason: maybe frosts & *interlined with a caret*

216.18   Smooth sumach: Smooth *cancelled and* Prob
staghorn smooth not for a week probably *interlined with a
caret*

217.6   cherries a week: *cancelled*

217.28-29   but . . . &:   one all out of bloom July 13 *interlined above in ink*

218.31   Thimbleberries: X *added in margin in ink*

225.12   few hawks about: *horizontal line added below in
ink*

225.13   heard owls: *horizontal line added below in ink*

225.14   more: *horizontal line added below in ink*

225.17   Partridge young: *horizontal line added below in
ink*

225.18   Lark not: *horizontal line added below in ink*

225.21   Robin still sings: *horizontal line added below in
ink*

225.21   morning–&:   *horizontal line added below in ink*

225.22   conqueree July 11th: *horizontal line added below
in ink*

226.18   song-sparrow: seringos *interlined with a caret*

228.29   eaten: June is the time to collect perfect ones
interlined with a caret

229.19   perhaps: prob. *interlined above*

232.1   yarrow: ? *added in margin in ink*

232.10   palustris: ? *inserted and* box kind *interlined
above*

237.23   Are: not *interlined with a caret*

237.23   mountains: hills *interlined above*

237.32   later: & ate some black Aug 8th *interlined in ink*

238.22   smooth?:   (The pods have soft spinous projections–& it must be A Cornuti of Gray– –July 30th) The 1st kind
ap. the Monarda–has no spinous projections. *added in ink*

244.3   Am.:   Methinks I have heard toads within a
week A white mildew on ground in woods this morning
added

246.9   warbler: see forward *interlined below*

246.17   Sunday July 30:   To Lygodium *added*

252.10   now: v aug 15 *interlined in ink with a caret*

256.2   wind: v Aug 20 *interlined in ink with a caret*

261.32   humilis: ? *added*

265.24   maples about: pond? *added*

270.10   Merriams: It is the Brooks Meadows–on fire   V aug 23 *interlined with a caret*

275.33   B. connata: because 4 armed *interlined with a caret*

275.33-34   or cernua?:   *cancelled*

284.16   head: *period added and* could it have been the female rose-breasted Gross beak? *interlined with a caret*

284.32-33   king fisher?:   *cancelled and* fish hawk? *interlined above*

285.25   frog near: mole cricket *interlined above*

285.33   palustris: mole cricket *interlined above*

287.3   with longer: V Jul 26 '56 *interlined above*

293.24   trees: except the white ash   v. p 448 *interlined in ink with a caret*

296.9   done: leaving off though I see some pretty handsome Sep 4th– *interlined with a caret*

299.19   The great: were they not cast down? *interlined above*

307.19-20   Let ... heard: *revised in ink to read* If so, the sound of my flail will be heard

307.25-26   that ... flour: grain may be reduced to *enclosed in parentheses in ink and* may be ready *interlined in ink with a caret*

307.31   with some thing: *cancelled in ink and* resolution *interlined below in ink*

307.33   with: by lamplight. *interlined in ink with a caret*

307.33   shut–:   & only the pile of husks behind him for warmth *interlined in ink with a caret*

310.33   wagons.:   *revised to read* wagons".

310.34   word: prob. "tires" *interlined with a caret*

311.29   *beginning*:   v. sep 14th *interlined in ink with a caret*

Cross-References to Published Versions

THIS table provides cross-references between literary drafts in *Journal 8* and their published versions. The first two columns furnish page, line, and keyword references for the Journal version; the third column provides abbreviated page references to the corresponding published versions. The following abbreviations refer to works printed in the Princeton Edition of *The Writings of Henry D. Thoreau* that are used in this table:

RP (LwP) "Life without Principle" in *Reform Papers* (1973)

RP (SM) "Slavery in Massachusetts" in *Reform Papers* (1973)

Wa   *Walden* (1971)

The following abbreviation refers to an essay included in *Excursions* (Boston: Houghton Mifflin, 1906).

Ex (AT) "Autumnal Tints"

"H" refers to "Huckleberries," a lecture draft first edited for publication by Leo Stoller in 1970. References to "Huckleberries" in this table are keyed to the printing of this text in Henry D. Thoreau, *The Natural History Essays*, ed. Robert Sattelmeyer (Layton, Utah: Peregrine Smith, 1980), pp. 211-262.

"D" and "WF" refer, respectively, to "The Dispersion of Seeds" and "Wild Fruits," two natural history projects that Thoreau left incomplete. Bradley P. Dean has edited the surviving manuscripts of these projects, and references to them in this table are keyed to the published texts. "The Dispersion of Seeds" is in Henry D. Thoreau, *Faith in a Seed* (Washington, D.C.: Island Press/Shearwater Books, 1993), pp. 23-173; "Wild Fruits" is in Henry D. Thoreau, *Wild Fruits* (New York: W. W. Norton and Company, 2000), pp. 3-239.

MS Volume XVII

4.18-20	I . . . blue–	Wa, 297
5.28-6.2	That . . . relievo.	Wa, 179-180
15.17-21	The . . . antennae	WF, 226
17.1-4	Not . . . garnishing.	Wa, 47
25.18-19	The . . . body–	Wa, 306
25.23	How . . . itself	Wa, 307
25.32-33	The . . . (labor-lapsus?)	Wa, 306
25.36-26.1	you find in . . . leaf–	Wa, 306
26.2-3	The . . . law	Wa, 306
26.4-8	No . . . law–	Wa, 306
26.9-12	The . . . clay-color.	Wa, 305
26.20-21	The . . . them.	WF, 221
30.2-10	In . . . man.	WF, 199
30.20-21	Thus . . . leaves–	Wa, 307
30.21-22	& birds . . . leaves	Wa, 306
30.22-23	& trees . . . leaves	Wa, 307
57.25-31	At . . . lecture.	RP (LwP), 155
75.11-21	How . . . will?	RP (LwP), 162
90.9-17	It . . . it.	Wa, 181
98.13-15	If . . . planet–	RP (LwP), 170
143.13-15	the dense . . . puff–	WF, 73
158.1	as big . . . peas.	WF, 62
160.27-30	These . . . berries	H, 240
160.30-33	The . . . these–	H, 239
160.33-35	The . . . ambrosia	H, 240
161.1	Vine . . . Ida	H, 238
161.1-9	yet . . . Mahometans?	H, 240
162.36-163.2	These . . . fall.	WF, 6
163.32-34	Does . . . decision?	RP (SM), 92
163.34-164.1	Such . . . packs.	RP (SM), 92
164.7-21	I . . . governor–	RP (SM), 92-93
164.23-25	I . . . *Slave.*	RP (SM), 92